# Draco's Herbal Grimoire

**Copyright**

Copyright © 2001, 2008, 2017 by Robert Haigh

All rights reserved. This book or any portion thereof may not be reproduced without the express written permission of the publisher except for the use of brief quotations in a book review or scholarly journal.

First Printed: 2001

**Edition 1** was collected, edited and first printed in 2001.

**Edition 2** has been updated to include Herb descriptions and growing information. Much of this data has been collected from Northern Hemisphere resources and the seasons transposed, so care should be taken to confirm the details within your local area.

**Edition 3** includes expanded growing notes and correspondences.

**I cannot stress highly enough, the medicinal and poisonous (or non-poisonous) properties of herbs as listed should NOT be taken as definitive.**

This document really should be used as a primer for your detailed and specific investigation.

The magickal properties are as detailed in other publicly available resources and no assertion as to the validity of these properties is made and should not be assumed.

(A compilation from Herbal Magick resources)

| | |
|---|---|
| Section 1 – Magickal purpose table | Page 4 |
| Section 2 – Medicinal purposes table | Page 11 |
| Section 3 – Growing your own herbs | Page 20 |
| Section 4 - Preparation of Herbs | Page 24 |
| Section 5 – Correspondences | Page 30 |
| Section 6 - Alphabetic list of Herbs | Page 38 |
| Section 7 – Index | Page 226 |
| Section 8 – Acknowledgements | Page 233 |

# Section 1 - Magickal Purpose Table

| Uses | Herb |
|---|---|
| Accept Change | Marjoram |
| Ambition | Aries |
| Anti-Hunger | Norfolk Island Pine |
| Anti-Lightening | Hazel, Holly, Mahogany |
| Anti-Theft | Aspen, Caraway, Garlic, Juniper, Larch, Vetivert |
| Aphrodisiac | Althea, Fennel |
| Astral Projection | Belladonna (Caution Poison), Mugwort |
| Attract Faeries | Foxglove (Caution Poison), Straw |
| Attract Spirits | Sweetgrass |
| Banishing | Lemon Verbena, Elecampane, Onion, Pennyroyal, Rue, Sloe |
| Beauty | Avocado, Catnip, Flax, Ginseng, Maidenhair, Yerba Santa |
| Binding | Knotweed |
| Breaking Love Spells | Lily, Pistachio |
| Calming | Masterwort |
| Chastity | Cactus, Camphor, Coconut, Cucumber, Blessed Thistle, Camphor, Fleabane, Hawthorn, Lavender, Lettuce, Pineapple, Sweet Pea, Vervain, Witch Hazel |
| Clairvoyance | Eyebright, Nutmeg |
| Clears Negativity | Arabic Gum |
| Comfort | Cypress |
| Concentration | Benzoin, Henbane |
| Courage | Aries, Borage, Cohosh – Black, Columbine, Mullein, Poke, Ragweed, Rose, Sweet Pea, Tea, Thyme, Yarrow. |
| Crocodiles | Papyrus |
| Depression | Witch Grass |
| Destroys Sex Drive | Hemlock (Caution, Poison!) |
| Diplomacy | Aquarius |

| | |
|---|---|
| Disgrace (Brings) | Oleander |
| Divination | Black Willow, Broom, Camphor, Cherry, Clove, Corn, Dandelion, Fig, Goldenrod, Ground Ivy, Hibiscus, Ivy, Lettuce, Meadow Rue, Meadowsweet, Mullein, Orange, Orris, Pansy, Pomegranate, Roots, Rose, St John's Wort, Sloe, Willow |
| Dream Magick | Anise, Cinnamon, Holly, Huckleberry, Lemon Verbena, Marigold, Morning Glory, Mugwort, Valerian, Yarrow |
| Eloquence | Aspen |
| Employment | Devil's Shoestring, Lucky Hand, Pecan |
| Ending Relationships | Turnip, Oregano |
| Energy | Lovage |
| Escape | Celandine |
| Exorcism | Angelica, Arbutus, Asafoetida, Avens, Basil, Bean, Birch, Boneset, Buckthorn, Clove, Clover, Cumin, Dragon's Blood, Elder, Fern, Fleabane, Frankincense, Heliotrope, Horehound, Horseradish, Lilac, Leek, Mallow, Mint, Mistletoe, Mullein, Myrrh, Nettle, Onion, Peach, Peony, Pepper, Pine, Rosemary, Rue, Sagebrush, Sandalwood, Solomon's Seal, Tamarisk, Yarrow |
| Favours | Chickweed |
| Femininity | Mallow |
| Fertility | Agaric, Banana, Bistort, Bodhi, Carrot, Chickweed, Cucumber, Cyclamen, Daffodil, Dock, Drape, Fig, Geranium, Ginseng, Grape, Hawthorn, Hazel, Horsetail, Ivy, Mandrake (Poison), Mistletoe, Mugwort, Mustard, Myrtle, Nuts, Oak, Olive, Palm - Date, Patchouly, Peach, Pomegranate, Poppy, Pine, Rye, Rice, Sunflower, Walnut, Wheat |
| Fidelity | Chilli Pepper, Clover, Cumin. Licorice, Magnolia, Rice, Scullcap, Vetch – Giant, Yerba Mate |
| Fishing Magick | Hawthorne |
| Flying | Basil, Belladonna (poison), Cinquefoil, Poplar |
| Friendship | Apple blossom, Aquarius, Lemon, Love Seed, Sweet Pea, Love Seed, Passion Flower |
| Frugality | Chickweed |
| Gambling | Devil's Shoestring |
| Garden Magick | Apple, Grape |
| Happiness | Apple Blossom, Catnip, Celandine, Cyclamen, Hawthorn, High John the Conqueror, Hyacinth, Lavender, Lily of the Valley, Mallow, Marjoram, |

| | |
|---|---|
| | Meadowsweet, Saffron, Witch Grass, Purslane, Quince, St John's Wort |
| Harmony | Dulse |
| Healing | Adders Tongue, Allspice, Amaranth, Anemone, Angelica, Apple, Balm of Gilead, Barley, Bay, Bittersweet, Blackberry, Bracken Fern, Burdock, Calamus, Carnation, Camomile, Camphor, Cedar, Cinnamon, Citron, Comfrey, Coriander, Cotton, Cowslip, Cucumber, Cypress, Dock, Elder, Eucalyptus, Fennel, Flax, Gardenia, Garlic, Ginseng, Goats Rue, Goldenseal, Groundsel, Heliotrope, Hemp, Henna, Hops, Horehound, Horse Chestnut, Hyssop, Ivy, Jobs Tear's, Lemon Balm, Life Everlasting, Lime, Melilot, Mesquite, Mint, Mugwort, Myrrh, Nettle, Oak, Olive, Onion, Parsley, Peppermint, Pepper Tree, Persimmon, Pine, Plantain, Plum, Potato, Rose, Rosemary, Rowan, Rue, Saffron, Sage, Sandalwood, Sorrel Wood, Spearmint, Tobacco, Thistle, Thyme, Vervain, Violet, Willow, Yerba Santa |
| Health | Anemone, Ash, Camphor, Carob, Carroway, Coriander, Dock, Fern, Figwort, Geranium, Ginseng, Goats Rue, Groundsel, Juniper, Knotweed, Larkspur, Life Everlasting, Mandrake, Marjoram, Mistletoe, Mullein, Nutmeg, Oak, Rose, Rue, Thyme, St John's Wort, Sassafras, Sorrel Wood, Sumbul, Sunflower, Tansy, Walnut |
| Hex-Breaking | Bamboo, Bergamot, Chilli Pepper, Cinquefoil, Datura, Dragon's Blood, Galangal, Huckleberry, Hydrangea, Mimosa, Poke, Thistle, Squill, Thistle – Holy, Toadflax, Vetivert, Witch Grass |
| Hunting | Mistletoe, Yellow Evening Primrose |
| Image Magick | Straw, Bryony, Potato |
| Immortality | Apple, Linden, Sage |
| Invisibility | Aconite, Amaranth, Chicory, Edelweiss, Heliotrope, Hellebore – Black, Poppy |
| Invoking Good Spirits | Mints, Sweetgrass, Wormwood |
| Knot Magick | Dodder |
| Legal Matters | Buckthorn, Cascara Sagrada, Celandine, Hickory, Marigold, Skunk Cabbage |
| Lift Spirits | Borage |
| Lock Opening | Lotus |
| Longevity | Angelica, Cypress, Lavender, Lemon, Life Everlasting, Maple, Peach, Sage, Tansy |
| Love | Aloe's - Wood, Almond, Apple, Apricot, Aster, Avens, Avocado, Balm of Gilead, Barley, Bachelor Buttons, Barley, Basil, Bean, Bed Straw, Beet, Betony Wood, Bleeding Heart, Bloodroot, Brazil Nut, Cardamon, Catnip, Chamomile, Cherry, Chestnut, Chickweed, Chilli Pepper, Cinnamon, Cinquefoil, Clove, Clover, Cohosh – Black, Coltsfoot, Columbine, Copal, Coriander, Crocus, Daffodil, Damiana, Dogbane, Dragon's Blood, Elecampane, Elm, Endive, Fig, Gardenia, Geranium, Ginger, Ginseng, Grains of Paradise, Hemp, Henbane, Henna, Hibiscus, High John the Conqueror, Houseleek, Hyacinth, Indian Paint Brush, Ivy, Jasmine, Joe Pye |

|  | |
|---|---|
|  | Weed, Juniper, Lady's Mantle, Lavender, Leek, Lemon Balm, Lemon Verbena, Lettuce, Licorice, Lime, Linden, Liverwort, Lobelia, Lovage, Love Seed, Maidenhair, Male Fern, Mallow, Mandrake, Maple, Marjoram, Meadow Rue, Meadowsweet, Mimosa, Mint. Mistletoe, Moonwort, Mullein, Myrtle, Orange, Orchid, Orris, Pansy, Parsley, Pea, Peach, Pear, Peppermint, Periwinkle, Pimento, Poppy. Prickly Ash, Primrose, Purslane, Quassia, Quince, Raspberry, Rose, Rosemary, Rue, Rye, Saffron, St John's Wort, Sarsaparilla, Scullcap, Senna, Southernwood, Spearmint, Spiderwort, Spikenard, Strawberry, Sugar Cane, Sumbul, Tomato, Tonka Beans, Trillium, Tulip, Valerian, Vanilla, Venus Fly Trap, Vetivert, Violet, Willow, Witch Grass, Wormwood, Yarrow, Yerba Mate, Yohimbe |
| Luck | Allspice, Aloe, Bayberry, Bamboo, Banyan, Be-Still, Bluebell, Buckeye Leaf, Cabbage, Calamus, China Berry, Clover, Corn, Cotton, Daffodil, Daisy, Devil's Shoestring, Dill, Fern, Galangal, Goldenrod, Grains of Paradise, Hazel, Heather, Houseleek, Huckleberry, Holly, Honeysuckle, Irish Moss, Jobs Tears, Kava-Kava, Linden, Lucky Hand, Male Fern, Moss, Nuts, Oak, Orange, Peony, Pineapple, Pomegranate, Poppy, Purslane, Rose, Snakeroot – Black, Star Anise, Straw, Strawberry, Sumbul, Tulip, Vetivert, Violet, Wintergreen, Wood Rose |
| Lust | Avocado, Caraway, Cardamon, Carrot, Cattail, Celery, Cinnamon, Cyclamen, Daisy, Damiana, Deerstongue, Dill, Dulse, Endive, Galangal, Garlic, Ginseng, Grains of Paradise, Hibiscus, Lemongrass, Licorice, Maguey, Mastic, Mint, Nettle, Olive, Onion, Patchouly, Pear, Periwinkle, Persimmon, Radish, Rosemary, Saffron, Sesame, Southernwood, Sugar Cane, Vanilla, Violet, Yerba Mate, Yohimbe |
| Manifestations | Masterwort, Mastic |
| Mental Health | Chrysanthemum |
| Mental Powers | Caraway, Celery, Eyebright, Fern, Grape, Horehound, Lily of the Valley, Mace, Mustard, Orange, Rosemary, Walnut, Periwinkle, Rue, Savory – Summer, Spearmint, Vanilla, Walnut |
| Meditation | Anise, Bodhi, Eyebright, Gotu Kola, Hemp, |
| Memory | Melilot |
| Moderating Anger | Alyssum |
| Moon Magic | Willow |
| Money | Alfalfa, Allspice, Almond, Bayberry, Bergamot – Orange, Bladderwrack Blackberry, Blue Flag, Buckwheat, Bryony, Bromeliaed, Calamus, Cascara Sagrada, Cashew, Chamomile, Cedar, Clove, Clover, Comfrey, Dill, Dock, Fenugreek, Flax, Ginger, Galangal, Goldenrod, Goldenseal, Gorse, Grains of Paradise, Grape, High John the Conqueror, Honesty, Honeysuckle, Horse Chestnut, Irish Moss, Jasmine, Lucky Hand, Mandrake, Maple, Marjoram, May Apple, Moonwort, Moss, Myrtle, Oak, Oats, Onion, Orange, Oregon Grape, Patchouly, Pea, Pecan, Periwinkle, Pine, Pineapple, Poplar, Poppy, Rattlesnake Root, Sarsaparilla, Sassafras, Sesame, Snakeroot – Black, Squill, Trillium, Tulip, Vervain, Vetivert, Wheat, Woodruff |

| | |
|---|---|
| Peace | Amber, Bayberry, Elder, Gardenia, Lavender, Loosestrife, Mallow, Meadowsweet, Olive, Pennyroyal, Violet, Morning Glory, Myrtle, Passion Flower, Scullcap, Vervain, Violet |
| Power | Cinnamon, Club Moss, Devil's Shoestring, Ebony, Elecampane, Gardenia, Ginger, Roots, St John's Wort, Wax Plant |
| Potency | Banana, Bean, Cohosh – Black, Dragon's Blood, Oak, Olive, Palm - Date |
| Prevent Deception | Pimpernell |
| Prevent Seasickness | Pennyroyal |
| Prophetic Dreams | Bracken Fern, Buchu, Heliotrope, Jasmine, Marigold, Mimosa, Mugwort, Onion |
| Prosperity | Alfalfa, Alkanet, Almond, Ash, Banana, Benzoin, Camomile, Elder, Nuts, Oak, Tulip |
| Protection | Acacia, Acacia, Aconite, African Violet, Agrimony, Ague Root, Aloe, Althea, Alyssum, Amaranth, Anemone, Angelica, Anise, Arbutus, Asafoetida, Ash, Balm of Gilead, Bamboo, Barley, Basil, Bay, Bean, Birch, Betony Wood, Bittersweet, Blackberry, Bloodroot, Blueberry, Bodhi, Broom, Bryony, Bromeliaed, Buckthorn, Buckwheat, Burdock, Calamus, Cactus, Caraway, Carnation, Carob, Cascara Sagrada, Castor, Cedar, Celandine, Chrysanthemum, Cinnamon, Cinquefoil, Cloves, Clover, Club Moss, Coconut, Cohosh – Black, Corn, Cotton, Cumin, Curry, Cyclamen, Cypress, Dill, Dogwood, Dragon's Blood, Ebony, Elder, Elecampane, Eucalyptus, Fennel, Fern, Feverfew, Figwort, Flax, Fleabane, Foxglove, Frankincense, Garlic, Geranium, Ginseng, Gorse, Gourd, Grain, Grass, Hawthorne, Hazel, Hellebore – Black, Heather, Holly, Honeysuckle, Horehound, Houseleek, Huckleberry, Hyacinth, Hyssop, Irish Moss, Ivy, Juniper, Kava-Kava, Lady's Slipper, Larch, Larkspur, Lavender, Leek, Lettuce, Lilac, Lime, Linden, Liquidambar, Liverwort, Loosestrife, Lotus, Lucky Hand, Mallow, Mandrake, Marigold, Marjoram, Meadow Rue, Mimosa, Mint, Mistletoe, Mugwort, Mulberry, Mullein, Mustard, Myrrh, Nettle, Norfolk Island Pine, Oak, Olive, Onion, Parsley, Pennyroyal, Peony, Pepper, Pepper Tree, Periwinkle, Pimpernel, Pine, Primrose, Purslane, Quince, Radish, Ragwort, Raspberry, Rattlesnake Root, Rice, Roots, Rose, Rosemary, Rowan, Sage, Sandalwood, St John's Wort, Sloe, Snapdragon, Solomon's Seal, Southernwood, Spanish Moss, Squill, Thistle, Toadflax, Tomato, Tormentil, Tulip, Turnip, Valerian, Venus Fly Trap, Vervain, Violet, Wax Plant, Willow, Wintergreen, Witch Hazel, Woodruff, Wormwood, Yerba Santa, Yucca |
| Psychic Powers | Acacia, Althea, Anise, Bay, Bistort, Bladderwrack, Borage, Buchu, Celery, Cinnamon, Citron, Deerstongue, Elecampane, Eyebright, Flax, Galangal, Grass, Honeysuckle, Lemongrass, Lovage, Mace, Marigold, Mastic, Peppermint, Rose, Mugwort, Rowan, Saffron, Start Anise, Stillengia, Sumbull, Thyme, Uva Ursa, Wormwood, Yarrow, Yerba Santa |
| Purification | Alkanet, Anise, Asafoetida, Avens, Bay, Benzoin, Birch, Betony Wood, Bloodroot, Broom, Cedar, Chamomile, Coconut, Copal, Fennel, Gum Arabic, Hawthorne, Hemlock (Caution, Poison!), Horseradish, Hyssop, Iris, Lemon, Lemon Verbena, Lavender, Lovage, Mimosa, Neem, Peppermint, Pepper Tree, Sage, Sagebrush, Shallot, Thistle- Holy, Thyme, Tobacco, Tumeric, Valerian, Vervain, Woodruff, Yucca |

| | |
|---|---|
| Rain Making | Heather, Pansy, Rice, Toadstool |
| Raise Dead Spirits | Yew |
| Reconciliation | Bean, Eucalyptus |
| Repel Evil | Tomato, Tormentil |
| Repel Monsters | Honesty |
| Repel Snakes | Lemongrass |
| Respect | Joe Pye Weed, Oregon Grape |
| Riches | Camellia, Fern, Tea |
| Rune Magick | Bracken Fern |
| Science | Aquarius |
| Sea Spells | Ash, Bladderwrack |
| Sickness (Brings) | Oleander |
| Sleep | Agrimony, Anise, Chamomile, Dandelion, Datura, Elder, Eucalyptus, Hops, Lavender, Lettuce, Linden, Passion Flower, , Peppermint Poppy, Purslane, Rosemary, Thyme, Valerian, Vervain |
| Snake Charming | Horsetail, Tamarisk, Thistle- Milk, Yellow Evening Primrose |
| Sobriety | Chrysanthemum |
| Spirit Calling | Dandelion |
| Spirituality | African Violet, Aloe's Wood, Cinnamon, Frankincense, Gardenia, Heather, Myrrh, Sandalwood |
| Stop Dogs Barking | Houndstongue |
| Stop Gossip | Slippery Elm |
| Strength | Bay, Carnation, Masterwort, Mugwort, Mulberry, Pennyroyal, Saffron, St John's Wort, Sweet Pea, Tea, Thistle |
| Strengthening Spells | Echinacea |
| Success | Clover, Ginger, Hawthorn, High John the Conqueror, Rowan |
| Transmutation | Yucca |
| Tranquillity | Coltsfoot, Morning Glory |
| Travel | Lucky Hand, Mint |

| | |
|---|---|
| Treasure Finding | Cowslip |
| Truth | Bluebell |
| Virility | Henna |
| Visions | Angelica, Coltsfoot, Crocus, Damiana, Hemp, Kava-Kava |
| Vitality | Parsley |
| Ward off Colds | Eucalyptus |
| Ward off Evil | Celandine, Five Finger Grass, Pennyroyal, Solomon's Seal, Sulphur Powder |
| Wealth | Basil, Heliotrope, Pomegranate |
| Weather | Lobelia, Ti |
| Wind | Bladderwrack, Broom, Saffron |
| Wisdom | Almond, Bodhi, Hazel, Iris, Sage, Sunflower |
| Wishes | Bamboo, Beech, Buckthorn, Dandelion, Dogwood, Ginseng, Hazel, Job's Tears, Peach, Pomegranate, Sage, Sandalwood, Sunflower, Violet, Walnut |
| Youth | Anise, Cowslip, Myrtle, Rosemary, Vervain |

# Section 2 – Medicinal Purposes Table

Medicinal use of herbs **MUST** only be undertaken with the guidance of a properly trained and qualified expert. This information is provided for interest only and **MUST** not be used as a prescribing guide.

| Ailment | Herb |
| --- | --- |
| Acne | Bouncing Bet, Elm, Garlic, Horsetail, Soapwort |
| Alcohol Withdrawal | Alfalfa, Angelica, Kudzu, Skulcap, Valerian |
| Alcohol tremors | Cayenne |
| Allergies | Echinacea, Jujube, Kombucha, Nettle, Parsley |
| Alzheimers | Ginko, Marigold. |
| Amenorrhea (Irregular Menstruation) | Arbor vitae, Chaste berry, Chaste tree, Ephendra, Fennel, Fenugreek, gentian, Horehound, Juniper, Lovage, Mint, Pulsatilla, Rosemary, Rue, Tansy, Vanilla |
| Anemia | Amaranth, Blue Cohosh, Dong Quai, Nettle, Onion, Watercress |
| Angina | Willow |
| Anxiety and stress | Chamomile, Black cohosh, Black walnut, Catnip, kava kava, Lady's slipper, Lemongrass, Linden, Mistletoe, Passionflower, Pulsatilla, St Johns wort, Skullcap, Valerian |
| Appetite Control | Artichoke, Chickweed, Dandelion, Vervain |
| Appetite Stimulation | Beech, Devils Claw, fennel, Feverbush, Gentian, Ginger, Ginko, Ginseng, Hops, Mugwort, Papaya, Saw Palmetto, tarragon, Yellow Root |
| Arthritis and Rheumatism | Aloe vera, Angelica, Barley, Birch, Bladderwrack, Bloodroot, Boneset, Cayenne, Devil's claw, Dogwood, Dyer's weed, Echinacea, Evening Primrose, Feverfew, Gentian, Goldenseal, Hyssop, Joe-Pye weed, Juniper, Kalmia, Luffa, Mustard, Nettle, Pokeweed, Rosemary, Sarsparilla, Suma, Tarragon, Turmeric, Vervain, Violet, Wild yam, Willow, Wintergreen. |
| Asthma | Bamboo, Chamomile, Devil's Dung, Echinacea, Eucalyptus, Feverfew, Garlic, Ginko, Kola nut, Marigold, Mullein, Sage, Yerba Santa. |
| Athlete's Foot | Black Walnut |
| Back Pain | Gentian, hydrangea, Luffa, Willow |
| Bed wetting | Mullein, St John's Wort |
| Bladder and Kidney Infection | Cornsilk, Cranberry, Doddler, Horsetail, Irish moss, Kinnikinnik, Mallow, Pumpkin |
| Bleeding gums | Amaranth, Bayberry, Bilberry, Echinacea, Watercress |

| | |
|---|---|
| Bleeding, External | Horsetail, Puffball, Yarrow, Yellow bedstraw |
| Bleeding, Internal | Dead nettle, Nettle, Witch hazel |
| Bloating | Celery Seed, Dandelion, marigold, Mate, Sarsaparilla, Watercress |
| Boils and Abscesses | Burdock, Echinacea, Elm, Evening Primrose, fenugreek, Fig, Goldenseal, Horsetail, Indigo, Joe Pye Weed, Marijuana, Olive, Onion, Soapwort |
| Broken Bones | Comfrey |
| Bronchitis | Cacao, Coltsfoot, Elecampane, Ephedra, Eucalyptus, Garlic, horehound, Hyssop, Irish moss, Juniper, Luffa, Marijuana, Mint, Mullein, Mustard, onion, Oregano, Pine, Watercress, Yerba Santa |
| Bruises | Arnica, Hyssop, Jewelweed, St. John's Wort |
| Burns | Aloe vera, Borage, Balsam fir, Bamboo, beech, Comfrey, Flax, Garlic, jewelweed, Joe Pye Weed, Jojoba, Mallow, marigold, Oak, oats, onion, Pineapple, Prickly Pear, Pumpkin, St. John's Wort |
| Caffeine Withdrawal | Beech, Cacao, Cleavers, Dandelion, Kola nut, Sage |
| Calluses | Marigold |
| Cancer Prevention | Acerola, Alum Root, Blessed thistle, Bloodroot, Broccoli, Devil's Dung, Echinacea, Evening Primrose, Garlic, Indigo (Wild), Licorice, marijuana, Mayapple, Pokeweed, Pumpkin, Red Clover, Turmeric |
| Canker Sores | Acacia Gum, Balsam Fir, Blackberry, Sage, Toadflax, Yellow Root |
| Cardiac arrhythmia | Ginko, Night-blooming cereus |
| Cellulite | Konbucha |
| Chapped lips | Jojoba |
| Chilblains | Garlic, Ginko, Jew's Ear |
| Cholesterol | Artichoke, Dong Quai, Ginger, Onion, Turmeric |
| Circulation Problems | Cayenne, Dong Quai, Ginger, Horseradish, Luffa, Marigold, Mugwort, Rosemary |
| Cirrhosis of the Liver | Licorice |
| Colds and Flue | Acacia Gum, Acerola, Alder, Boneset, Cacao, Catnip, Echinacea, Epehedra, Garlic, Ginger, Goldenrod, Marigold, Mustard, Oregano, Oswego Tea, Red Clover |
| Cold Sores | Ash, Balm, Camphor, Cayenne, Comfrey, Lavender, Luffa |
| Colic | Angelica, Catnip, Chamomile, Fennel, lovage, Wild Yam |
| Congestion, Chest | Devil's Dung, Eucalyptus, Ginger, Ground ivy, horehound, Hyssop, Ipecac, |

| | |
|---|---|
| | Jewelweed, Juniper, Licorice, Luffa, Mint, Mustard, Oregano, pine, Red Clover, Saw Palmetto, Slippery Elm, Sweet gum, Thyme, Violet |
| Congestion, Head or Sinus | Ephedra, Ginger, Luffa, Magnolia, Mint, Oswego tea, Red Clover, Sage |
| Conjunctivitis | Barberry |
| Constipation (Adults) | Aloe Vera, Apples, Ash, Asparagas, Boneset, Broom, Cascara Sagrada, Castor Oil, Cayenne, Culver's Root, Cumin, Dodder, Dogwood, Dyer's Weed, Elder, Feverfew, Flax, Ginseng, Kola Nut, Lavender, Marsh Marigold, Olive, Parsley, Pitcher Plant, Plantain Herb, Rhubarb, Rose Hips, Sage, Senna, Sheep Sorrel, Walnut |
| Constipation (Child) | Elder |
| Corns | Fig |
| Coughing | Acacia, Alder, Anise, Bamboo, Bayberry, Cayenne, Coltsfoot, Elecampane, Fig, garlic, Ginger, Goldenrod, Gum, Horehound, Hyssop, Ipecac, Irish moss, Luffa, Marigold, Marijuana, Marshmallow, Marsh Marigold, Onion, Pine, Slippery Elm, Thyme, Violet |
| Cuts, scrapes and sores | Basam Fir, Bayberry, Bladderwrack, Borage, Bouncing bet, Burdock, Chickweed, Comfrey, Coriander, Garlic, Hyssop, Indigo, Mallow, Onion, Papaya, Parsley, Pineapple, Prickly Pear, Sage, St. Johns Wort, Thyme, Turmeric, virgins bower, Walnut, Yellow Flag |
| Dandruff | Eucalyptus, Garlic, Soapwort |
| Dehydration | Kaolin |
| Depression | Balmony, Basil, Borage, Cloves, Oats, St. John's Wort |
| Diabetes | Alfalfa, Celery Seed, Devils Club, Fenugreek, Ginseng, Jerusalem Artichoke, Watercress |
| Diarrhoea | Acacia Gum, Agrimony, Alum Root, Amaranth, Anise, Apples, Ash, Bael, balsam fir, Barberry, Beech, Blackberry, Black Walnut, Dead Nettle, Elecampane, Garlic, Indigo, Kaolin, Knotweed, marigold, Mesquite, Nutmeg, Oak, oregano, Pomegranate, Potato, Raspberry, Rhubarb, Sage, Sarsaparilla, Strawberry, thyme, Water Lily, Wintergreen |
| Drug Overdose | Birch, Boneset, Garlic, Ipecac, Kelp, Milk Thistle, Pineapple |
| Drug Withdrawal | Skullcap |
| Dry, Chapped Skin | Bladderwrack, Eucalyptus, Fenugreek, Flax, Jojoba, Oats, Olive, Potato, Violet, Yellow Flag |
| Ear Ache | Garlic, Licorice, Mullein |
| Eczema | Burdock, Chickweed, Evening Primrose, Nettle, Red Clover, Walnut |
| Electrolyte Imbalance | Barley, Kelp, Plantain Herb, Banana |

| | |
|---|---|
| Epilepsy | Lady's Slipper, Valerian, Yellow bedstraw |
| Exhaustion | Bayberry, Dong Quai, Ginger, Ginseng, Guarana, Kola Nut, Mate, Onion |
| Eye Irritation | Flax, Goldenseal, Horseradish, Mesquite |
| Eye Problems | Bilberry, Goldenseal |
| Eye Puffiness | Maple, Potato |
| Eye strain | Barley, Bilberry, Mesquite |
| Fainting | Basil, Horseradish |
| Fever | Alder, Ash. Balm, Blackberry, Blessed Thistle, Boneset, Borage, Dogwood, Echinacea, Fever Bush, Feverfew, Horhound, Joe-Pye Weed, Lemongrass, Luffa, Senna, Vervain, Willow, Yarrow |
| Flatulence | Anise, Calamus, Fennel, Fenugreek, Ginger, Goldenrod, Lovage |
| Fluid Retention | Artichoke, Asparagus, Celery Seed, Cornsilk, Dandelion, Dyer's Weed, Echinacea, Elder, Elm, Fennel, Goldenseal, Juniper, Knapweed, Kola Nut, Lovage, Marjoram, Nettle, Papaya, Pineapple, Pitcher plant, Potato, Rose Hips. Sarsaparilla, Sassafras, Saw Palmetto, Sheep Sorrel, Strawberry, Tarragon, Vervain |
| Food Poisoning | Rosemary |
| Fungal Skin Infections | Adder's Tongue, Aloe Vera, Black Walnut, Chickweed, Coriander, Echinacea, Evening Primrose, Fenugreek, Goldenseal, Marigold, Sarsaparilla, Soapwort, Sweet gum, Virgin's Bower, Walnut |
| Gall Bladder Disorder | Turmeric |
| Gastritis | Angelica, Balm, Balmony, Caraway, Cinnamon, Cumin, Fenugreek, Garlic, Gentian, Goldenrod, Lemongrass, Licorice, Mallow, Marigold, Mint, Onion, Parsley, Slippery Elm |
| Gingivitis | Sage |
| Glaucoma | Marijuana |
| Goiter | Kelp |
| Gout | Devil's Claw, Dyer's Weed, Nettle, Violet, Willow |
| Hair loss | Horsetail, Jojoba, Vervain |
| Halitosis | Angelica, Dill, Fennel, Lovage, Parsley |
| Hay Fever | Echinacea, Ground Ivy, Nettle |
| Headaches | Asprin, Cayenne, Fennel, Feverfew, Guarana, Kola nut, Lavender, Magnolia, Potato, Pumpkin, Rosemary, Sage, Skulcap, Thyme, Vervain, Willow |

| | |
|---|---|
| Head Injury | Ginko |
| Heart Disease | Blessed Thistle, Dandelion. Ephedra, Garlic, Ginko, Hawthorn, Magnolia, Nettle, Turmeric |
| Heat Rash | Marigold |
| Haemorrhoids | Alder, Aloe vera, Butcher's broom, Elder, Ground ivy, Indigo, Luffa, Mallow, Mullein, Nettle, Oak, Plantain herb, Sweet Gum, Witch Hazel |
| Hepatitis | Garlic, Licorice, Turmeric |
| Herpes | Cayenne, Comfrey, Luffa, Walnut |
| Hives | Evening Primrose, Fenugreek, Jewelweed |
| Hyperactivity in Children | Evening Primrose, Valerian |
| Hypertension (High Blood pressure) | Motherwort, Rosemary |
| Hypoxia | Ginko |
| Immune System (to strengthen) | Astragalus, Barberry, Boneset, Devil's Claw, Echinacea, ginseng, St. John's Wort, Tragacanth |
| Impotence | Cayenne, Ginko, Saw Palmetto, Yohimbe |
| Incontinence | Cranberry Juice, Kinnikinnik, Pumpkin |
| Indigestion and Heartburn | Artichoke, Cacao, Calamus, Caraway, Cayenne, Coriander, Culver's Root, Dandelion, Devil's Claw, Dill, Fennel, Feverfew, Gentian, Goldenrod, Hops, Horehound, Indigo, Lemongrass, Mint, Nutmeg, Oregano, Papaya, Rosemary, Skullcap, Vanilla |
| Insect Bites and Stings | Aloe Vera, Comfrey, Garlic, Indigo, Mallow, Oak, Oats, Onion, Papaya, Parsley, Potato, Witch Hazel |
| Insect Repellant | Arbor Vitae, Black cohosh, Chamomile, Garlic, Mint, Tansy |
| Insomnia (Adults) | Chamomile, Chaste Berry, Chaste Tree, ginseng, Hops, Kava Kava, Lavender, Linden, Mint, Passionflower, St. John's Wort, Thyme, Turmeric, Valerian |
| Insomnia (Children) | Chamomile, Lavender |
| Intestinal Parasites | Black Walnut, Kamala, Neem, Oregano, Pomegranate, Pumpkin, Tansy |
| Iodine Deficiency | Bladderwrack |
| Irritable Bowel Syndrome and Colitis | Barly, Chamomile, Hops, Mesquite, Slipery Elm, Wild yam |
| Ischemia | Ginko |

© Copyright 2001 Robert Haigh

| | |
|---|---|
| Itchy Skin | Kalmia, Oak, Oats, Parsley, Pine |
| Kidney Stones | Hydrangea, Knotweed, Pipsissewa, Sassafras |
| Labour Pain | Black Cohosh, Blue Cohosh, Life Root, Mugwort, Raspberry |
| Leprosy | Sarsaparilla |
| Lethargy | Bayberry, Dong Quai, Ginger, ginseng, Guarana, Kola Nut, Mate |
| Lice | Delphinium, Indigo, Walnut |
| Liver Disorders | Artichoke, Balmony, Blessed Thistle, Cascara Sagrada, Dandelion, Devil's Claw, Kombucha, Licorice, Milk Thistle, Toadflax, Turmeric |
| Malaria | Neem |
| Memory Loss | Ginko, Marigold, Rosemary |
| Menopause | Chaste Berry, Chaste tree, Dong Quai, Fennel, Motherwort, Mugwort |
| Menstrual Cycle Irregularity | Blue Cohosh, Chaste Berry, Chaste Tree, Fennel, Fenugreek, Gentian, horehound, Juniper, Lovage, Mint, Motherwort, Oregano, Pulsatilla, Rosemary, Rue, Tansy |
| Menstrual Flow Excessive | Agrimony, Blackberry, Marigold, Nettle, Witch Hazel |
| Menstrual Pain | Angelica, Black Cohosh, Blue Cohosh, Butcher's Broom, Caraway, Chaste Berry, Chaste Tree, Dong Quai, Feverfew, Lavender, Milk Thistle, Mugwort, Oregano, Parsley, Pulsatilla, Willow |
| Morning Sickness | Chamomile, Ginger, Mint, Raspberry |
| Motion Sickness | Ginger, Mint, Passionflower |
| Muscle Cramps | Alder, Chamomile, Wild Yam |
| Muscles Sore or Stiff | Arnica, Birch, Camphor, Ginger, Mint, Willow |
| Nappy Rash | Burdock, Comfrey, Marigold, Plantain herb |
| Nausea and Vomiting | Alum Root, Amaranth, Anise, Bael, Caraway, Cardamom, Cloves, Elecampane, Fennel, Gentian, Ginger, Lavender, Marigold, Marjoram, Mint, Nutmeg, Oregano |
| Neuralgia | Cayenne, Lady's Slipper, Lavender, Lemongrass, Passionflower, St. John's Wort |
| Nicotine Withdrawal | Cardinal Flower, Marigold, oats |
| Nosebleed | Garlic, Knotweed, Nettle, Parsley, Yarrow |
| Obesity | Kelp, Pitcher Plant, Turmeric |

| | |
|---|---|
| Oedema | Butcher's Broom, Devil's Claw, Elm |
| Panic Attack | Black Cohosh, Black Walnut, Lady's Slipper |
| Phlebitis | Bilberry |
| Pneumonia | Garlic, Mint |
| Poison (Ingested) | Birch, Boneset, Garlic, Ipecac, Kelp, Milk Thistle, Sarsaparilla, Violet |
| Poison Ivy/Poison Oak | Beech, Bouncing Bet, Jewelweed, oak, Oats, Plantain Herb, Witch Hazel |
| Pleurisy | Pleurisy Root |
| Premenstrual Syndrome (PMS) | Black Cohosh, Chaste berry, Chaste tree, Dandelion, Dong Quai, Evening Primrose, Guarana, Mate, Oregano, Sarsaparilla, Skullcap, Valerian |
| Prostate problems | Cornsilk, Horsetail, Mallow, Nettle, Pyegum, Saw Palmetto |
| Psoriasis | Bouncing Bet, Cleavers, Fig, Oats, Red Clover, Sarsaparilla, Walnut, Yellow Flag |
| Rabies | Skullcap |
| Respiratory problems | Ground Ivy, Hyssop, Mint, Pleurisy Root, St. John's Wort |
| Ringworm | Black Walnut, Sweet gum, Walnut |
| Runny nose | Thyme |
| Scabies | Kalmia |
| Skin Rashes | Fenugreek, Horsetail, Jewelweed, Joe-Pye Weed, Kalmia, Luffa, Marigold, Oak, Oats, Pine, Sweet Gum |
| Sleep Disorders | Feverfew, Guarana, Kava Kava, Lavender, Linden, Marijuana, Mint, Passionflower, Valerian |
| Smokers Cough | Pleurisy Root |
| Snakebite | Echinacea, Plantain Herb |
| Sore Throat | Alum Root, Barberry, Barley, Bay Berry, Bladderwrack, Bloodroot, Borage, Echinacea, Elecampane, Elm, Fenugreek, Fig, Horehound, Horseradish, Jerusalem Artichoke, Jew's Ear, Linden, Mallow, Marjoram, Marshmallow, Oak, Onion, Oswego tea, Pine, Prickly Pear, St. John's Wort, Slippery Elm, Strawberry, Tarragon, Yarrow |
| Splinters | Marijuana, Plantain Herb |
| Sprains and Strains | Alder, Amaranth, Arnica, Birch, Camphor, Comfrey, Kalmia, Plantain Herb, Wintergreen, Witch Hazel |
| Staph infections | Licorice |

| | |
|---|---|
| Stomach Cramps | Jalap, Lavender, Lovage, Marjoram, Motherwort, Passionflower, Pulsatilla, Rue, Thyme, Vanilla |
| Stomach upsets (Adult) | Beech, Black Cohosh, Caraway, Cardamom, Cascara Sagrada, Cinnamon, Feverfew, Licorice, Luffa, Marjoram, Mint, Oregano, Papaya, Pitcher Plant, potato, Slippery Elm, Vervain, Yellow Root. |
| Stomach upsets (Children) | Chamomile |
| Strep throat | Licorice, Mallow, tarragon |
| Stress and Nervous Tension | Balm, Catnip, Chamomile, Ginseng, Hops, Kava Kava, Kola nut, Lavender, Lemongrass, Passionflower, Skullcap, Suma, Turmeric, Valerian |
| Sunburn | Aloe Vera, Jewelweed, Jojoba, Mallow, Marigold, oats, pine, Plantain Herb, Potato, Prickly Pear, Witch Hazel |
| Swollen glands/tonsils | Mallow, Marjoram, Prickly Pear |
| Syphilis | Sarsaparilla |
| Tapeworm | Black Walnut, Kamala, Male Fern, Neem, Olive, Papaya, Pomegranate, Pumpkin, Tansy |
| Teething Pain | Chamomile, Mallow, Marshmallow |
| Testicles Swollen | Luffa |
| Thyroid Problems | Saw Palmetto |
| Toothache (Adults) | Alder, Amaranth, Catnip, Cinnamon, Cloves, Garlic, Mallow, Marjoram, Prickly Ash, Rosemary, Tarragon, Vervain, Willow. |
| Tonsillitis | Echinacea, Indigo, Jew's Ear, Mallow, Prickly Pear |
| Tuberculosis | Echinacea, Lady's Slipper, Licorice, St. John's Wort |
| Tumour | Barberry |
| Ulcer (Stomach) | Alder, Angelica, Barberry, Garlic, Ginseng, Goldenseal, Horsetail, Jujube, Licorice, marigold, Nettle, Papaya, Prickly Pear, Slippery Elm, Yarrow |
| Urinary Tract Infection and Cystitis | Cornsilk, Cranberry, Horsetail, Hydrangea, Irish moss, Kinnikinnik, Licorice, St. John's Wort, Saw Palmetto, Sheep Sorrel, Vervain, Willow |
| Urination Difficulty | Arbor Vitae, Artichoke, Asparagus, Burdock, Cornsilk, Horseradish, Horsetail, Hydrangea, Kola Nut, Lovage, Marjoram, Nettle, Papaya, Pitcher Plant, Pyegum, Sarsaparilla, Sassafras, Saw Palmetto, Sheep Sorrel, Tarragon, Yellow Bedstraw |
| Vaginal Infections | Comfrey |

| | |
|---|---|
| Vaginal Itching | Alder |
| Varicose Veins | Bilberry, Butcher's Broom, Milk Thistle |
| Vitamin A Deficiency | Broccoli, Strawberry |
| Vitamin C Deficiency | Acerola, Amaranth, Broccoli, Cleavers, Cranberry, Garlic, Ground Ivy, Mate, Onion, Pine, Prickly Pear, Rose Hips, Sheep Sorrel, Watercress |
| Warts | Bloodroot, Fig, Marsh Marigold, Plantain Herb |
| Whooping Cough | Coltsfoot, Garlic, Thyme |
| Yeast Infection | Dandelion, Echinacea, Licorice, Oak |

# Section 3 – Growing your own Herbs

Growing your own herbs has its own magick. The time spent in preparing the garden beds, planting, watering, weeding and harvesting your own herbs brings with it not only financial savings, and freshness which cannot be matched by dried herbs, but also personal satisfaction, and the spiritual wealth that comes from meditation and reflection whilst undertaking these tasks.

Biodynamic Gardening sees a relationship between the elements of earth, air, fire, or water that corresponded to specific parts of the plants and are based on the heliocentric, or astronomical, position of the moon.

Earth corresponds to root, water to leaf growth, fire to seed production, and air corresponds to flowers. Hence, when planting crops for their fleshy roots, you would plant them in an earth sign, and so forth.

Herbs as a group are relatively easy to grow. Begin your herb garden with the herbs you enjoy using the most. For example, choose basil, oregano, and fennel for Italian cooking; lavender and lemon verbena for making potpourri; or chamomile, peppermint, and blue balsam mint if you plan to make your own teas.

The optimum growing conditions vary with each individual herb species. Some of the herbs familiar to us, such as lavender, rosemary, thyme, bay laurel, marjoram, dill, and oregano are native to the Mediterranean region. These herbs grow best in soils with excellent drainage, bright sun, and moderate temperatures.

When growing herbs follow these basic guidelines:

- Plant herbs in average garden soil with organic matter added to improve texture and drainage.

- Choose a site that receives at least 6 hours of direct sun each day.

- Avoid ground where water stands or runs during heavy rains.

- Compensate for poor drainage with raised beds amended with compost.

- Plant early in the morning or late in the afternoon to prevent the transplants from wilting in the midday sun.

- Dig each planting hole to about twice the width of the root ball of the new plant.

- Space herbs about 40 cm apart to give them room to spread out and grow.

- Place taller herbs, like sage, rosemary and marjoram, towards the back of the garden. Parsley and cilantro are good for the front.

- Plant perennials on one side and annuals on the other for easier replanting next year.

- Give the new transplants plenty of water. Once established, make sure your herbs get 3 cm of water each week throughout the growing season.

- Begin harvesting from the herbs as soon as they are mature, but take only a little bit each time you harvest. If you remove more than a third of the plant at one time, it takes longer to recover and produce new foliage.

- To promote branching, keep the tops of the plants pinched back in early summer. With judicious picking, most herbs can be harvested for several months.

- Fresh herbs taste best when harvested in the morning. Also, herbs are most flavourful if harvested before they bloom.

Plan your herb garden by grouping herbs according to light, irrigation, and soil requirements. Most herbs enjoy full sun, but a few tolerate shade. Herbs can be classified as either annual, biennial, or perennial.

Be aware of the growth habits of the plants before you purchase them. Some herbs, such as borage, anise, caraway, chervil, coriander, cumin, dill, and fennel, should be direct-seeded, because they grow easily from seed or do not transplant well. Other herbs, such as mints, oregano, rosemary, thyme, and tarragon, should be purchased as plants and transplanted or propagated by cuttings to ensure production of the desired plant (do not come true from seeds).

Specific information for each herb can be found in the alphabetic list of herbs that follows in section five.

To prepare your area for planting, loosen the soil. If the soil is compacted or consists of heavy clay, improve drainage by adding some compost, peat moss or coarse sand. Work the material into the top 30 cm of soil before you plant.

Apply balanced fertilizers sparingly to leafy, fast-growing herbs. Heavy applications of fertilizer, especially those containing large amounts of nitrogen, will decrease the concentration of essential oils in the lush green growth.

To conserve moisture and prevent splashing mud, mulch your garden after planting. Use 3 – 5 cm of organic material. The use of a landscape fabric covered with mulch has proven to provide excellent weed control and slows down the spread of invasive herbs, such as mints. For Mediterranean herbs, mulch with white "concrete" sand or gravel to provide drainage and light reflection.

When grown outdoors and given ample air circulation, sunlight, and water drainage, herbs rarely suffer severe disease or insect damage. Natural predators and parasites usually keep mite and aphid populations below damaging levels. This is especially true in gardens with a wide diversity of plants.

Traditional synthetic pesticides are not necessarily considered safe or appropriate for use on culinary or magickal herbs, so it is advisable to rely on cultural, biological, and physical control techniques. Insecticidal soap or horticultural oil are useful against severe outbreaks of aphids, mites, and whiteflies. Hand-pick larger pests such as beetles and caterpillars.

Growing a diverse group of herbs can be attractive; they can provide colour, fragrance, and interest throughout the season, and they can help keep pest problems to a minimum. You often will find populations of predators and pests co-existing in a balanced situation.

Many plants defend themselves against insects by being poisonous to them or developing a strong scent that frightens them away, and it is possible that a plant growing close by might benefit from being in this bug-free zone. Similarly some plants benefit from this effect, being planted within close proximity. It should also be noted that the reverse is also true, some plants suffer for being planted within this proximity. Where known, companion plants are listed for the herbs in section five.

## Solar and Lunar Cycle

We all understand planting by the Solar Cycle, broadly following new growth in spring, followed by fruiting in summer producing seeds in the cooler autumn or fall followed by dormancy in winter, with some variation depending on the plants in question.

It follows therefore that there would be a cycle following other heavenly bodies such as the moon, and so it is no surpeise that planting by the moon is an idea as old as agriculture, with principals based in folklore and Magick.

The Earth is in a large gravitational field which is influenced by both the sun and moon. The tides are highest at the time of the new and the full moon, when sun and moon are lined up with earth.

Just as the moon pulls the tides in the oceans, it also pulls upon the subtle bodies of water, causing moisture to rise in the earth, which encourages growth. The greatest amount of soil moisture occurs at this time, and tests have proven that seeds will absorb the most water at the time of the full moon.

At the new moon, with the waxing moon the lunar gravity pulls water up, and causes the seeds to swell and burst. This factor, coupled with the increasing moonlight creates balanced root and leaf growth. This is the best time for planting above ground annual crops that produce their seeds outside the fruit. Examples are lettuce, spinach, celery, broccoli, cabbage, cauliflower, and grain crops. Cucumbers like this phase also, even though they are an exception to that rule.

In the second quarter around the full moon the gravitational pull is less, but the moonlight is strong, creating strong leaf growth. It is generally a good time for planting, especially two days before the full moon. The types of crops that prefer the second quarter are annuals that produce above ground, but their seeds form inside the fruit, such as beans, melons, peas, peppers, squash, and tomatoes. Mow lawns in the first or second quarter to increase growth

After the full moon, as the moon wanes, the energy is drawing down. The gravitation pull is high, creating more moisture in the soil, but the moonlight is decreasing, putting energy into the roots. This is a favorable time for planting root crops, including beets, carrots, onions, potatoes, and peanuts. It is also good for perennials, biennials, bulbs and transplanting because of the active root growth. Pruning is best done in the third quarter, in the sign of Scorpio

In the fourth quarter around the dark moon there is decreased gravitational pull and moonlight, and it is considered a resting period. This is also the best time to cultivate, harvest, transplant and prune. Mow lawns in the third or fourth quarter to retard growth.

## The Organic Garden

When working with the powers of nature and Magickit seems obvious that we should encourage the balance of nature at all times, and imitate or apply the laws of nature to our benefit.

When gardening by the moon, all normal rules for gardening apply, especially the health of your soil and lunar planting has been proven to be more effective in organic, non-chemically treated soil.

There is no substitute for creating a wonderfully rich microclimate by continually adding organic matter to your growing beds. This creates a living system that includes microbes to break down the soil, and adds nutrients and nitrogen content. This is the backbone of healthy, disease resistant plants.

Think of your garden as a complete ecosystem that includes life and decay in the soil, the needs of the plants, and insect life cycle as well. Work in harmony with nature to duplicate and replenish the essential elements at the base of the food chain.

Taking this care will produce herbs (and vegetables) with the greatest nutrirional and Magickal potency.

There is too much written about organic gardening and biodiversity to attempt to include it here, but it is worth further research.

# Section 4 - Preparation of Herbs

**CAUTION: Before consuming any herb or herbal preparations, be sure you <u>know</u> what medicinal, edible, cleansing, or poisonous properties the herbs may have and use them `accordingly. "It's better to be safe than sorry"**

The information contained in this work is in no way meant to be an alternative to seeking medical attention for an ailment or condition. It is provided for informational purposes only and should be used and considered as such.

## Obtaining Herbs

Herbs are beautiful additions to any garden. Beginning with the most common herbs if actually planting them for the first time, is preferable. They're more easily found and hardy enough to practice on. As you learn specific properties of individual herbs, you can slowly integrate your knowledge and experience into an herbal lifestyle. Of course dried herbs can also be used, and is probably the only practical way to get many of the less common varieties. An advantage with dried herbs is that they can be purchased in a pre-prepared state, to suit your needs.

## Harvesting

Plants located above ground should be harvested in the morning, some say with dew still on the plants from the night before and some say after the dew has evaporated. I'd say it's safe to "dew" it both ways and choose what's right for you. Harvest leaves before the buds and blooms appear and harvest flowers before the fruits and seeds appear.

If you're harvesting bark or roots, do it in the spring or in the fall. Strip tree bark from small patches or from limbs, instead of around the trunk of trees. Stripping the trunk may cause the tree's demise and you want to preserve the life of the tree.

If you're using an entire plant, hang it upside down in a dry area free from pests and allow to dry thoroughly before storing. Carefully scrape, wash and chop roots. Allow them to dry uniformly before storing. String bulbs together and hang to dry.

The best storage containers for herbs are made of coloured glass. Plastic is not recommended. Store in a cool, dry and dark area. Light can break down the healing properties of your herbs, thus shortening their shelf life. Stored properly, your herbs can have a shelf life of one year or longer.

## Tools

### Mortar and Pestle

This is used to grind, mix, crush and compose herbs.

### Brewing Pot

Preferably glass or enamel, a brewing pot is used to boil decoctions or infusions, among other uses.

### Cutting Board

Everyone has a cutting board, but if possible you should have a cutting board set aside specifically for herb preparation.

### Bolline

A sharp cutting knife used when harvesting herbs and in the kitchen, preparing herbs for cooking or other uses.

### Glass Containers

Coloured glass is best for keeping your herbs and preparations fresh and/or dry. Of course, you need to start with a **clean** jar and tight lid.

### Labels

Always Label your herb preparations to include the date (so that you know it's shelf life and when to replenish the jar) on containers of dried herbs and spices, tinctures, infusions, decoctions, compresses, poultices, etc.

### Cheesecloth

Always good for straining herb preparations when needed.

### Measuring Spoons, Eyedroppers, Funnels, Tea Balls, and Stirring Spoons

A good selection of these tools is important when working with herbs. Maintain your tools by keeping them cleaned and stored for easy access when you need them.

## Preparations

### Infusion:

An infusion is best described as a tea made by pouring boiled water over fresh or dried herbs. Allow the tea to steep for 15 to 20 Minutes to allow therapeutic properties of the herb to pass into the water.

Herbs for infusions and teas are generally cut and sifted, or crumbled dry leaves and flowers. Steep the herbs in a non-metallic container. Adding pure honey or stevia to sweeten herbal teas is recommended in the place of sugar.

### Decoction:

A decoction is best described as a tea made from roots and twigs. It is more difficult to extract medicinal properties from roots and twigs. Decoction requires at least one or two teaspoons of root(s) or twig(s) per cup of water - boiled for a half an hour to an hour - depending upon strength desired.

### Tincture:

A Tincture is made using alcohol, usually vodka, everclear, or Rum and has a longer shelf life than infusions or decoctions - of up to two years. Put your herbs into a jar, adding enough alcohol to cover the herbs. Allow the mixture to sit for two to six weeks in a cool spot, shaking the mixture occasionally. Finally, strain the mixture and discard the herb material.

Store the tincture in a bottle. Add glycerine to help preserve the tincture (optional). Using a dropper bottle is ideal for storage.

Make sure you label and date the tincture so you do not exceed its shelf life. Begin your tinctures on the night of the new moon; strain it on the full moon. This way, the waxing powers of the moon extract the maximum amount of healing properties from the herbs.

### Oils:

Aromatic oils and rectified alcohol can be combined. The oils seep into the alcohol to produce and essence.

Oils may be captured by evaporation from flower petals. Vegetable, nut, or fruit oils can be used as a medium for steeping aromatic plants to extract volatile oils. Aromatic oils can also be steeped in alcohol to extract essence.

To make oil, pick your own fresh herbs or purchase dried herbs form a reputable source. Pack a large jar with the chosen herb and pour in any favourite mono unsaturated or polyunsaturated oil. Use enough to cover the herb. Close tightly.

Label the jar and place aside for several weeks. Strain out the herb by pouring through cheesecloth into a fresh jar. Hold the cheesecloth over the opening of the jar containing the herbs and secure with a rubber band. Invert the jar and pour the infused oil through the cheesecloth.

Before discarding the herbs, squeeze all the oil out of them. Repeat the entire procedure. Repack a clean jar with more of the same herb. Add the infused oil, plus enough additional oil to cover the herbs. Strain again through cheesecloth. Pour the oil into a labelled jar and store until needed.

Store the oil in dark coloured glass containers. Adding one capsule of vitamin E to each bottle will help to preserve the oil. Best done on the new moon.

### Syrups:

Medicinal syrups are formed when sugar is incorporated with vegetable infusions, decoctions, expressed juices, fermented liquors, or simple water solutions.

Sometimes tinctures are added to a simple syrup, and the alcohol is evaporated. The tincture is sometimes combined with sugar and gently heated, or exposed to the sun until the alcohol is evaporated.

The syrup is then prepared with the impregnated sugar and water. Refined sugar makes a clearer and better-flavoured syrup. Any simple syrup can be preserved, simply by substituting glycerine for a portion of the syrup. Always make syrups in small quantities.

To make an herbal syrup, add 2 ounces of dried herb with 1 quart water in a large pot. Boil down and reduce to 1 pint, then add 1-2 tablespoons of honey. If you want to use fresh fruit, leaves, or roots in syrups, you should double the amount of herbs. Store in refrigerator for up to a month. Honey-based syrups are simple and effective way to preserve healing qualities of herbs. Syrups can soothe sore throats and provide some relief from coughs.

### Teas:

Homemade herbal teas are much more potent than the store bought teas. Their flavour can be quite strong and sometimes unpleasant. To make a tea, boil 1 pint of water. Add 1 ounce of dried herb tops (leaves flowers, stems) steep 3 -5 minutes.

### Ointments:

An ointment is a soothing, healing, slightly oily or fatty substance into which the essence of a healing plant has been dissolved.

This is done by heating the fat or oil with the plant, until it loses its normal colour and the oil or fat has absorbed the healing chemical principles.

The plant is then strained out, and beeswax is added to harden the ointment. Preservatives such as drops of tincture of benzoin, poplar bud tincture, or glycerine are optional additions. If you make ointments in small batches and keep them tightly closed with paraffin wax, they don't decompose.

The traditional folk, herbal, and pharmaceutical base for ointments is pork lard. Purify it by simmering and straining. It has healing abilities even without the addition of herbs, but so do a lot of fats and oils. It is said to have great drawing power.

Purified, liquefied anhydrous lanolin is also used as a base for ointments. Lanolin is the substance washed from the wool of sheep. It comes in many levels of purity, so the results vary depending on the product. This oil is the closest to skin oil. Almond oil, cocoa butter, wheat germ, and vitamin E are neutral bases for ointments. If no other product is available, Vaseline may be used, but is listed here in case nothing else is available.

All ointments must contain one substance that will thicken the final product. Lanolin is a thickener, as is cocoa butter. Both are non-sticky and mix well with most other oils.

Other useful but sticky thickeners are glycerine, honey, or liquid lecithin. Also, various powdered resins and gum swell up and thicken when first soaked in cold water, then simmered in gently boiling water, and added to preparations. Agar-agar and Irish moss are seaweed thickeners. Green apples provide and excellent acid fruit pectin that is a good addition to creams and ointments.

While any of the above sticky and non-sticky thickeners will help swell a product and keep it emulsified, you will still need some wax to harden a cold cream or ointment. Beeswax is perfect, although expensive. It may be combined with paraffin wax.

**Poultices:**

A poultice is a raw or mashed herb applied directly to the body, or applied wet directly to the body, or encased in a clean cloth and then applied. Poultices are used to heal bruises, putrid sores, soothe abrasions, or withdraw toxins from an area.

They may be applied hot or cold, depending on the health need. Cold poultices (and compresses) are used to withdraw the heat from an inflamed or congested area. Use a hot poultice or compress to relax spasms and for some pains.

To make a poultice, use fresh or dried herbs that have been soaked in boiling water until soft. Mix with enough slippery elm powder to make poultice stick together. Place on affected part then wrap body part and poultice with clean cloth.

**Vinegars:**

Herbs that are soluble in alcohol are usually soluble in vinegar, and are useful for salad vinegars, cosmetic vinegars, some liniments and preventive sickroom "washes".

Fill any size jar with fresh-cut aromatic herbs. For best results and highest mineral content, be sure the jar is very well filled with your chosen herb, not just a few springs, and be sure to cut the herbs or roots up into small pieces.

Pour room-temperature apple cider vinegar into the jar until it is full. Cover jar with a plastic screw-on lid, several layers of plastic or wax paper held on with a rubber band, or a cork. Vinegar disintegrates metal lids. Label the jar with the name of the herb and the date. Put it some place away from direct sunlight, though it doesn't have to be in the dark, and some place that isn't too hot, but not too cold either. A kitchen cupboard is fine, but choose one that you open a lot so you remember to use your vinegar, which will be ready in six weeks.

Among the many powers of vinegar, it lowers cholesterol, improves skin tone, moderates high blood pressure, prevents/counters osteoporosis, and improves metabolic functioning. Herbal vinegars are an unstoppable combination, the healing and nutritional properties of vinegar married to the aromatic and health-protective effects of herbs.

### Waters:

Steeped herbs, water, and alcohol and steeped herbs plus honey and other fruits are often called waters. Sometimes extracts or spirits of various herbs, such as lavender, are also called waters.

### Incense:

Once you have gathered all the tools and materials together grind each dry item - except the charcoal - unless it is already powdered. Use a mortar and pestle or a coffee grinder for this purpose. You may need to use a knife to chop bits of stem and root. Once powdered, keep everything tightly sealed in plastic bags or glass jars.

Gum Arabic is used to mould your mixture into sticks, cones, or blocks. Place a tablespoon of the powdered gum into a medium-sized bowl and fill is with 8 oz of warm water. Whisk it until the gum is totally dissolved. Skim off any foam that develops. Let the dissolved gum absorb the water until you have a thick, gelatine-like paste. Cover the bowl with a wet cloth and set it aside while it thickens. This will take at least two hours. You can adjust the consistency by adding more gum or water.

Now, assemble the powdered ingredients you have chosen for your recipe.

***It is important to make sure that the herbs or flowers you use are not toxic.***

Measure them with the kitchen scale. If one part equals one tablespoon, you'll end up with enough incense mixture to make approx. 60-80 small cones. Determine what ten percent of the weight is, and add exactly that much saltpetre. This must be exact if your incense is to burn properly. Mix in the saltpetre completely.

Add the paste, one teaspoon or so at a time, until you are satisfied with the consistency. It should be dough-like - very similar to that of piecrust - and easily moulded with your hands.

When your mixture has reached the desired consistency, it's ready to be moulded into shapes. Cone and blocks are the easiest to mould. Sticks are much more difficult - so try the cones and blocks first.

### Cones:

Roll the incense mixture into small marble sized balls with your hands, and then shape them into 3 cm long cones. Arrange them upright on a sheet of waxed paper and place them somewhere to dry. During this drying time, (three to seven days) turn them regularly so that they dry evenly and don't crack.

**Blocks**:

Shape incense into long strips approx. 1 cm in both height and width, and then cut the strips into 3 cm long rectangles. Use the same drying process as you would for cones - except to lay the blocks flat.

**Sticks**:

Add more paste to the mixture until it's wet but still thick. Pat the dough on waxed paper until it's very thin. Place one stick at a time onto the dough and roll a thin coat around the stick. Leave about 5 cm on one end uncoated! The incense coating should be no more than twice the thickness of the stick. Squeeze or press the dough onto the stick so it will stay put. Place the uncoated end into some clay or sand that will allow it to stand upright while drying.

# Section 5 – Correspondences

Many people feel that spells are more powerful when they are cast during certain moon phases and moon signs and even during specific days of the week. This is because various planetary energies are believed to be more available for use during this time and those energies can add a bit of strength to your own.

Similarly Planetary Hours are believed to enhance a certain spells effectiveness, as does the selection of other correspondences.

There are many, many options for spell timing and you should not feel that you need to time your spell to coincide with *all* of these options.

Layering the day, planetary hour and moon phase may be benificial, that is for you to decide.

## GENDER

**Masculine** elements are strong and active.

Use for protection, purification, hex breaking, exorcism, lust, sexual potency, health, strength, courage, and financial success.

**Feminine** elements are subtler and softer.

Use to attract love, increase beauty, youth, healing, psychic abilities, increase fertility, draw wealth, promote happiness and peace, aid sleep and cause visions.

## ELEMENTAL

**Earth** - A Feminine element.

Direction - North.

Color - green.

Elemental beings - gnomes.

Earth Animals - the wolf, owl, dragon, stag, and wild cats.

Stones - onyx, jade, amethyst, and fluorite.

Rules spells dealing with fertility, jobs, money, business, health, ecology and nature, and stability.

**Air** - A Masculine element.

Direction - East.

Color - yellow.

Elemental beings - sylphs.

Air animals - doves, the wolf, fox, deer, and turtle.

Stones - moonstone, turquoise, and rhodochrosite.

Rules spells dealing with memory, intellect, test taking, divination and psychic ability, travel, and overcoming addictions.

**Fire** - A Masculine element.

> Direction - South.
>
> Color - red.
>
> Elemental beings - salamanders.
>
> Fire animals - the porcupine, coyote, fox, squirrel, hawk, mouse, deer, bear, and snakes.
>
> Stones - amber, citrine, smoky crystals, gold, and copper.
>
> Fire rules spells dealing with success, sex, illness, protection, legal matters, competitions, strength, and energy.

**Water** - A Feminine element.

> Direction - West.
>
> Color - blue.
>
> Elemental beings - undines.
>
> Animals - sea mammals and sea birds, fish, night creatures, and the raven.
>
> Stones - silver, river rocks, amethyst, coral, seashells, and rainbow colored crystals.
>
> Water rules spells dealing with love, friendship, meditation, healing, dreams, childbirth, clairvoyance and purification.

## PLANETARY

### Moon

Goddess mysteries, women's health, the home, children, prophetic dreams, reincarnation, sleep, emotional healing.

### Sun

God mysteries, physical health, employment, leadership, prosperity, money, the performing arts and celebrity, self confidence, and new ventures.

### Mercury

The intellect, communications written or spoken, teaching and learning, travel, diplomacy, influencing others.

### Venus

Inner and outer beauty, love, romance, family, the creative arts, friendship, gardening, peace, happiness, fertility and sexuality.

### Mars

Passion, force, power, lust, courage, strength of will, the military, physical exertion, machinery, and competition.

### Jupiter

Money, prosperity, success, legal judgments, luck, friendship, investments, social gatherings, ambition, the seeking and granting of favors.

### Saturn

Land and real estate, past lives, overcoming self-sabotage, lies, and losses, learning life's lessons and protection from psychic attack.

### Uranus

Unexpected changes, higher consciousness, metaphysics, new inventions, regathering scattered energies, clairvoyance, freedom, and independence.

### Neptune

Inner vision and perception, intuition, dreams, divination, chaos, confusion and revolution.

### Pluto

Death, transformations, astral travel, the otherworld, materializations, transfigurations, and metamorphosis.

## PLANETARY HOURS

The **planetary hours** are an ancient system in which one of the seven classical planets is given rulership over each day as well as various parts of every day.

The classical planets are Saturn, Jupiter, Mars, the Sun, Venus, Mercury and the Moon.

The first planetary hour of the day begins at sunrise.and corresponds to the planetary day. This means that Monday's first planetary hour after sunrise corresponds to the moon, Tuesday's to Mars, Wednesday's to Mercury, Thursday's to Jupiter, Friday's to Venus, Saturday's to Saturn and Sunday's to the Sun.

The planets take rulership over the hours in this sequence, known as the "Chaldean order" as follows,  Saturn, Jupiter, Mars, Sun, Venus, Mercury, Moon

As each day is divided into 24 hours, the first hour of a day is ruled by the planet three places down in the Chaldean order from the planet ruling the first hour of the preceding day.

You may wish to schedule your ceremony during a corresponding planetary hour on the day you have chosen in order to bring as much planetary energy into your working as possible.

Unlike hours on the clock, which are 60 minutes, planetary hours are calculated from the time of sunrise one day to the time of sunrise the next and thus vay in length as the daylight hours vary.  There are 12 daylight hours and 12 night hours.

In order to calculate the planetary hours you need the following information for your location:

> The time of sunrise on a given day,
>
> The time of sunset on that day, and
>
> The time of sunrise the next day.

To calculate the length of the daylight hours you must calculate how many minutes there are from the time of sunrise to the time of sunset and divide that by twelve. Next, calculate how many minutes there are between sunset and sunrise the following morning and divide that by twelve. This is the length of your night hours.

**DAYS**

**Sunday** - Is associated with the Sun and the colours of - Yellow, Gold and Orange.

Sunday is the best time to deal with such matters as: Health, Success, Careers Goals, Ambition, Personnel Finances, Advancement, Drama, Fun, Authority, Figures, Law, Fairs, Crops, Totem Animals, Volunteer and Civic Services, Promotion, Men's Mysteries, Children, Buying, Selling and Speculation. Also used for Physical Strength, Achievement, Healing Energy and Divination.

**Monday** - Is associated with the Moon and the colours of - White, Silver, Grey and Pearl.

Monday is the best time to deal with such matters as: Psychic Pursuits, Psychology, Dreams, Astral Travel, Imagination, Women's Mysteries, Reincarnation, Short Trips, Women, Children, Public, Domestic Concerns, Emotions, Fluids, Magick, Spirituality, Nursing, Full moon magic, Purity, Protection, Truth, Meditation, Peace, Sincerity, Justice, Warding off Doubts and Fears, Anything to do with Water and Bodies of Water, Antiques, Trip Planning, Household Activities, Initiation, Astrology, New-Age Pursuits, Archetypes, Totem Animals, Shape-shifting and Religious Experiences.

**Tuesday** - Is associated with Mars and the colours of - Red, Pink and Orange.

Tuesday is the best time to deal with such matters as: Passion, Partnerships, Courage, Swift Movement, Action, Energy, Strife, Aggression, Sex, Physical Energy, Sports, Muscular Activity, Guns, Tools, Metals, Cutting, Surgery, Police, Soldiers, Combat, Confrontation, Business, Buying and Selling Animals, Mechanical Things, Repairs, Gardening, Woodworking, Hunting and New Beginnings.

**Wednesday** - Is associated with Mercury and the colours of Purple, Magenta and Silver.

Wednesday is the best time to deal with such matters as: Wisdom, Healing, Communication, Intelligence, Memory, Education, Correspondence, Phone Calls, Computers, Messages, Students, Merchants, Editing, Writing, Advertising, Signing Contracts, Siblings, Neighbours, Kin, Accounting, Clarks, Critics, Music, Editors, Journalists, Visual Arts, Hiring Employees, Learning Languages, Placing Ads, Visiting Friends, Legal Appointments and Astrology.

**Thursday** - Is associated with Jupiter and the colours of - Blue and Metallic Colours.

Thursday is the best time to deal with such matters as: Business, Gambling, Logic, Social Matters, Political Power, Material Wealth, Publishing, Collage Education, Long Distance Travel, Foreign Interests, Religion, Philosophy, Forecasting, Broadcasting, Publicity, Expansion, Luck, Growth, Sports, Horses, The Law, Doctors, Guardians, Merchants, Psychologists, Charity, Correspondence Courses, Self-improvement, Researching, Reading and Studying.

**Friday** - Is associated with Venus and the colours of - Green, Pink and White.

Friday is the best time to deal with such matters as: Romantic Love, Friendship, Beauty, Soul-mates, Artistic Ability, Affection, Partners, Alliances, Grace, Luxury, Social Activity, Marriage, Decorating, Cosmetics, Gifts, Income, Gardening, Architects, Artists, Beauticians, Chiropractors, Dancers, Designers, Engineers, Entertainers, Fashion, Music, Painting, Poetry, Courtship, Dating, Household

Improvements, Planning Parties, Shopping, Herbal Magick, Luck, Fertility, Physical Healing, Balance, Prosperity, Courage, Change, Material Things, Peace, Harmony, Relationships and Success.

**Saturday** - Is associated with Saturn and the colours of - Black, Grey, Red and White.

Saturday is the best time to deal with such matters as: Binding, Patience, Stability, Neutralization, Material Gain, Protection, Karma, Death, Manifestation, Structure's, Reality, Laws of society, Limits, Obstacles, Tests, Handwork, Real Estate, Dentists, Bones, Teeth, Farm Workers, Sacrifice, Separation, Stalkers, Murderers, Criminals, Civil Servants, Justice, Math's, Plumbing, Joint Money Matters, Wills, Debts, Financing, Real Estate, Discoveries, Transformation and Relations with Older People.

## COLORS

**Black** - Is used to invoke the power of Saturn. Contrary to popular belief, black does not indicate evil. Far from it, black is the absence of colour. It is protective and symbolises the night, the universe and the lack of falsehood. Black is symbolic of the blackness of outer space and considered the ultimate source of divine energy.

**Blue** - Is used to induce the power of Jupiter. Blue is a Goddess colour and the colour most associated with the elements of water.

**Brown** - Is the element of Earth and is symbolic of endurance and animal health. Brown is a good colour for Grounding, Solidifying and Strengthening.

**Green** - Induces the power of Venus and is symbolic of the Earth's elements.

**Gold** - Induces the power of the Sun and is used to attune with the God. Gold brings Self-realization and Inner-strength.

**Pink** - Induces the power of Venus but can be used to influence Mars. Pink represents: Love, Friendship and Harmony

**Purple** - Induces the power of Mercury and influences Occult Forces, Hidden Aspects and Secret Dealings. Purple is used by those who work with pure divine power (Magicians, Priests and Priestesses) and those who wish to deepen their spiritual awareness of the God and Goddess.

**Red** - Induces the power of Mars and can be used to influence Saturn. Is used when attuning with the God in his fiery aspect. Red is the colour of Vitality, Power, Strength and Courage and is Invigorating, Motivating and Passionate.

**Silver** - Induces the power of the Moon and can be used with Mercury influences. It is used to attune to the Goddess while bringing the ability to respond to life's energies.

**Yellow** - Induces the power of the Sun and can be used to attune with the God. Yellow is also representative of the Elements of Air.

**White** - Induces the power of the Moon and is used to attune with the Goddess. Can also be used with Venus and Saturn. Pure dazzling white light can be called upon to bring about: Realisation, Intention, Insight and power itself.

**Orange** - Induces the power of Mercury and is sometimes used for solar energy. Representative of the God, it can be used and combined with other candles to simulate their actions.

**Violet** - Induces the power of Jupiter.

**Indigo** - Induces the power of Saturn. Indigo is the colour of inertia and is used to stop situations or people. Use in rituals that require a deep meditational state.

**Lavender** - Induces the power of Mercury to influence Occult Forces, Spiritual Development, Psychic Growth and Divination.

## SPELL CASTING AND THE MOON

Witches are intimately connected to the moon, and this is not just by coincidence.

The moon is considered one of the most powerful forces to affect Magickal energy. The way the ebb and flow of the moon can affect the tides, menstrual cycles, moods, growing cycles of our magickal herbs as well as vegetables. It can also affect magick.

**The effects of the Moon on growing cycles are discussed separately in the section on growing your herbs.**

The moon has essentially 4 main phases, Dark Moon where there is little or no moonlight, Waning Half Moon (or First Quarter moon) where half the moon is illuminated and visible and increasing in size, the Full Moon and the Waning Half Moon (or Third Quarter Moon) where the moon is half illuminated and diminishing in size.

The waxing and waning stages are broken down further into Crescent, and Gibbous stages. The Crescent moon is where the moon is where less than half of the moon visible whilst the Gibbous Moon stages and is where the moon is more than half visible. Crescent moons happen either side of the Dark moon stage whilst the Gibbous moons occur either side of the Full moon stage

So a Waxing Crescent Moon is a moon with less than half visible, but more becoming visible each night as it approaches the Full Moon, whilst a Waning Gibbous moon is more than half visible, but getting less each night as it is after the full moon, and heading towards the Dark Moon, or moonless nights.

### Dark Moon Magic

Magickal workings conducive to the dark moon include destroying or very powerful banishings. Do not use this time lightly—it's got a little too much drive behind it to just get rid of minor irritations and is better used for something that poses a serious threat.
The Dark Moon is also a good time to go within for soul-searching and to perform divination.

### Waxing Cresent Moon Magic

When the moon is "waxing" it appears to be growing, the period from the dark to full moon phases. It's magnetic energy assists with bringing things to out. This entire waxing period is the best time to work with *constructive magic,* or Magickthat builds things/brings things to us.

The waxing crescent is the best time for Magickon yourself (or on the subject) pertaining to new beginnings, such as starting a new project or making plans for the future

When you want to cast spells for self improvement this is the time to do it. Artists or anyone artistic/creative will find this the best time to cast spells or perform meditations that will bring inspiration and passion into your work.

**Waxing Half Moon Magic**

The Waxing Half Moon, or First Quarter Moon is the time when energies are most conducive to attraction. This is the best time for Magick to draw things outside of yourself *to* you.

It's also an ideal time for attracting people into your life, such as friends, lovers and clients.

If you're looking for an animal companion or have one that you want to bond with, this is a good time to perform the workings.

If you're looking for a lost object, or house hunting, etc., this is a good time to perform spells for success in that area to help you bring that which you most desire into manifestation.

**Waxing Gibbous Moon Magic**

The Waxing Gibbous is still a time for constructive magic, best used to assist with finalising that which you've been working for already.

This phase is a great energy for renewing your strength, will and determination to see your efforts through.

If you are giving in to temptation on your diet, working hard toward something and feeling burnt out or are at the point where you're getting lazy and distracted from completing your tasks, give yourself a power boost during the Waxing Gibbous.

**Full Moon Moon Magic**

The Full Moon is often seen as 'all purpose'—it's energies it flow into all areas and needs, be it constructive or destructive.

Even more so than the Dark Moon, the Full Moon is a time you would utilize for extra power when you're facing very difficult challenges.

**Waning Gibbous Moon Magic**

After the Full Moon peaks, we enter the *waning* half of the lunar cycle. Waning energies repel rather than attract, so it's a good time to begin working on spells to get rid of things.

Minor banishings can begin with the Waning Gibbous.

This is a good time for general cleansings to upkeep your home, office, garden or any of your personal spaces, etc., to keep things from mounting up, it's a good time for introspection and closure, or bringing things to their fruition.

**Third Quarter Moon Magic**

The Waning Half-Moon, or Third Quarter Moon, is the perfect timing for dealing with obstacles or road blocks in your path.

A good use of this moon phase's energy is in aiding with transitions, whether these are transitions that you have to make or simply want to make in your life. It can help smooth out any wrinkles that might cause snags as you go on your way.

**Waning Half Moon Magic**

The Waning Crescent moon or waxing half moon, as it approaches the Dark Moon phase, it suitable for stronger banishing than at any other time of the waning moon phases. Get rid of whatever you need to clear your life of negativity, stress, chaos, etc

If you need things that no longer serve you to end this moon phase is a good time to do it.

This is a good time to cast a spell for anything for which you wish to bring about a swift and benign ending. Dropping a hopeless project, relationship, friendship, etc. is best done at this time.

# Section 6 - Alphabetic List of Herbs

**Acacia** (*Acacia Nilotica*) Also called gum arabic.

**Description:** Acacias are legumes and are able to take-up ("fix") their nutrient requirements for nitrogen directly from the atmosphere with the aid of soil bacteria. They are spiny shrubs or small trees, preferring sandy or sterile regions, with the climate dry during the greater part of the year.

**Gender:** Masculine, **Planet:** Sun, **Element:** Air, **Deities:** Osiris, Astarte, Diana, Ra

**Influence:** Protection, Psychic Powers.

Burn with sandalwood to open psychic centres. Parts used: dried gum, leaves, wood

**Cultivation**: In Australia prickly acacia is a Weed of National Significance. It is regarded as one of the worst weeds in Australia because of its invasiveness, potential for spread, and economic and environmental impacts. Although capable of regenerating from cut stumps, prickly acacia only reproduces by seeds. A medium-sized tree in a well watered environment can produce as many as 175, 000 seeds per year. Other Acacia species also provide gum and may be substituted.

**Aconite** (*Aconitum Napellus*)  **POISONOUS**

**Description:** It is a small plant, about 30 cm high with pale, divided green leaves and yellow flowers. The stem is firm, angular and hairy. The flowers, large and hooded, grow on top of the branches in spikes. The root is tuberous.

**Gender:** Feminine, **Planet:** Saturn, **Sign:** Capricorn, **Element:** Water, **Deities:** Hecate, Medea

**Influence:** Protection, Invisibility.

Use this herb with great caution to consecrate the athame or ritual knife. Make an infusion with the leaves or root to banish prior energy from magickal blades and to infuse it with protection. The root or leaves may be burned as incense for the same purpose. Gather the fresh flowers to make a tincture to refresh the power of the knives. Use an infusion as a magickal wash for ritual tools or sacred space. Brings protection and magickal watchfulness against negative energies in ritual. Wash a new cauldron in the infusion or burn aconite in its first fire. Used to invoke Hecate. Wrap the seed in a lizard skin and carry to become invisible at will. Used to poison arrow tips in early times. Also as protection from and a cure for werewolves.

**Cultivation:** Aconite prefers a soil slightly retentive of moisture, such as a moist loam, and flourishes best in shade. It would probably grow luxuriantly in a moist, open wood, and would yield returns with little further trouble than weeding, digging up and drying. In preparing beds for growing Aconite, the soil should be well dug and pulverized by early winter frosts - the digging in of rotten leaves or stable manure is advantageous. It can be raised from seed, sown 1 cm deep in a cold frame in March, or in a warm position outside in April, but great care must be exercised that the right kind is obtained, as there are many varieties of Aconite as do not all have the same active medicinal properties. It takes two or three years to flower from seed. Propagation is usually by division of roots in the autumn.

**African Violet** (*Saintpaulia ionantha*)

**Description:** Tropical African plant cultivated as a houseplant for its violet or white or pink flowers

**Gender:** Feminine, **Planet:** Venus, **Element:** Water

**Influence:** Spirituality, Protection.

Promotes spirituality when grown in the home.

**Cultivation:** African Violet is easy to propagate African violets, especially as there are several methods to increase successfully the number of plants from one. These methods are from a leaf, by a sucker or offset, by division and by seed.

**Agaric** (Amanita muscaria)  **POISONOUS**

**Description:** With its bright red, sometimes dinner plate-sized caps, *Amanita muscaria* is one of the most striking of all mushrooms. The white warts that adorn the cap, white gills, well developed ring and distinctive volva of concentric rings separate the Fly Agaric from all other red mushrooms.

**Gender:** Masculine, **Planet:** Mercury, **Element:** Air, **Deity:** Dionysus

**Influence:** Fertility.

Place on the altar or in the bedroom to increase fertility.

**Cultivation:** Grows wild on the ground, under pine, spruce, fir, birch, live oak and madrone. They grow solitary, scattered, densely, or in large rings in forests and at their edges. Often found in coastal pine forests and along freeways where pines have been planted.

**Agrimony** (*Agrimonia eupatoria*) Also called Church steeples, cocklebur, stickwort, sticklewort

**Description:** Perennial growing to 0.6m by 0.45m . It is not frost tender. The scented flowers are hermaphrodite (have both male and female organs) and are pollinated by Bees and flies. The plant is self-fertile.

**Gender:** Masculine, **Planet:** Jupiter, **Element:** Air

**Influence:** Protection, Sleep.

Agrimony is best known for its sleep-inducing qualities, therefore it is excellent in dream pillows, especially mixed with mugwort. Enhances magickal healing. A wash or oil increases effectiveness of all forms of ritual healing, psychic healing, or distance healing. Anoint hands with oil to cleanse auras. Creates a barrier against negative energies. Use if you feel to be under psychic attack. A counter-magick herb, it not only breaks hexes, but sends them back to the hexer.

**Cultivation:** Agrimony grows in most types of soil. It is naturally adapted to alkaline soils, but also tolerates somewhat acidic soil. While easy to cultivate in dry soil, the plants do need water during dry periods or they may not flower. Prefers full sun, but keep the soil moderately moist. Also tolerates partial shade. Sow seeds outdoors in the early spring. (You can improve germination considerably by storing the seeds in damp soil in the refrigerator for 6 weeks prior to planting.) Plant seeds 1 cm deep. Once established, agrimony tends to self-seed. May also be propagated by root division. Divide the plants in spring to provide time for the winter buds to form. When dividing the crown, be sure to include a live stem. Space plants 25 cm apart. Usually pest- and disease-free.

**Alfalfa** (*Medicavo Sativa*)

**Description:** Alfalfa is an herb belonging to the legume family, closely related to beans and peas.

**Gender**: Feminine, **Planet**: Venus, **Element**: Earth

**Influence:** Prosperity, Anti-hunger, Money.

Brings in money and protects against financial misfortune. Harvest a small quantity at the full moon. Dry and burn in the cauldron. Place ashes in a magickal amulet.

**Cultivation:** Most commonly grown as sprouts for consumption with salads. AlfAlfa is also grown commercially as Lucerne, and can grow to an average 60 cm in height with a root system as deep as 6m depending on the soil type. The best soils are deep, fertile and well draining loam that are kept free of pests and weeds. This will give 5-6 years of productive growth. Lucerne grows from a central clump that puts up multiple stalks, each with many nodes along its length. The leaves grow from the nodes in sets of three, with a new branch. Each branch is capable of ending in flower stems and branching several times. The flowers grow in clusters and are each about 9mm in length. They are normally purple or white in colour and have 5 petals like all Legumes. Flowering takes place approx 4-6 weeks after it was last cut depending on the amount of water it has had and the temperature.

**Allspice** (*Pimenta officinalis* or *P. dioica*)

**Description:** Tropical American tree having small white flowers and aromatic berries

**Gender**: Masculine, **Planet**: Mars, **Element**: Fire

**Influence:** Money, Luck, Healing.

Burn the crushed dried berries for attracting money and luck. Add to mixtures for healing. Can use in a healing herbal bath.

**Cultivation:** Prefers hilly areas on limestone soils. In temperate northern zones the tree can be grown under glass but will not flower.

**Almond** (*Prunus dulcis*)

**Description:** The Almond is a small deciduous tree belonging to the Subfamily Prunoideae of the Family Rosaceae. An *almond* is also the fruit of this tree. The fruit lacks the sweet fleshy outer covering of other members of *Prunus* (such as the plum and cherry), this being replaced by a leathery coat containing the edible kernel which is often called a "nut" in common and culinary usage, but which is a drupe and not a nut in botanical parlance.

**Gender**: Masculine, **Planet**: Mercury. **Element**: Air. **Deities**: Attis, Mercury, Thoth, Hermes

**Influence:** Money, Prosperity, Wisdom.

Use oil, wash, or incense to anoint magickal wands or ritual candlesticks. (Almond wood makes excellent wands, especially for use in love magick). Excellent herbs for handfastings or other rituals of union. Also good for overcoming alcohol dependency. Almonds, leaves, and wood may be used in money magick. Placing almonds in your pocket will lead you to treasures.

**Cultivation**: Almonds produce best on deep, loamy, well-drained soils, but will tolerate poor soils, and even drought during the latter portion of fruit development better than most tree crops. Almonds are budded onto seedling rootstocks so that the integrity of the cultivar is kept intact. Propagation of trees by seed is possible, and practiced in some regions of the Mediterranean. However, tree uniformity is poor in seedling orchards since almonds are self-incompatible and heterozygous as a species. Almonds root poorly from cuttings,

## Aloe (*Aloe vera*)

**Description:** Aloe is a succulent that's native to tropical Africa, but it's incredibly easy to grow. Grows to 2 metres.

**Gender**: Feminine. **Planet**: Moon. **Element**: Water.

**Influence:** Protection, Luck.

Guards against evil influences and prevents household accidents. Plant aloe on the graves of loved ones to promote a peaceful existence until the deceased is reborn. Use for success in the world. Prevents feelings of loneliness.

**Cultivation**: Aloe Vera is easily propagated from offsets from an established plant. It is possible to raise plants from seed which is sown in spring. The plant requires a well-drained position, protected from hot late afternoon sun and needs more water than many succulents. However it cannot cope with being water-logged, so plant in a raised bed or in a freely-draining pot.

## Aloes, Wood (*Aquilaria agallocha*)

**Description:** An endangered tropical forest tree of South and Southeast Asia.

**Gender**: Feminine. **Planet**: Venus. **Element**: Water.

**Influence:** Love, Spirituality.

It is almost impossible to get this plant today; however, wood aloes have been used for many centuries. It was used in ancient Egypt to attract good fortune, and burned as incense in magickal evocatory rites during the Renaissance. It possesses high spiritual vibrations and will bring love if carried or worn. Modern magickal herbalists use wood aloes as a strengthening herb, by adding a small amount to other mixtures to intensify their powers. It is usually used in incenses of protection, consecration, success and prosperity. The scent is similar to a combination of sandalwood and ambergris and if the wood is unobtainable add a few drops of synthetic ambergris or an equal combination of cypress and patchouli to sandalwood as an adequate substitute.

**Cultivation:** Currently under scientific investigation and not domestically available. Developing a sustainable production system for this resource will require a clear understanding of how these various natural elements function, separately and synergistically. Although limited management of wild trees has failed to bring the resin-producing species under cultivation, it has been recognized that the complex ecology of resin formation involves two, or maybe three, living organisms—the tree, one or more fungi, and possibly an insect intermediary.

**Althea** (Althea officinalis)

**Description:** Althea or English Mallow grows to about 1 metre in height. It has small but attractive pink flowers carried without stems. As the flowers fade, round, flat seed capsules called "cheeses" form. The root yields a mucilage used in confectionary and medicines. A tea can be made from the dried roots to alleviate coughs and colds. As a vegetable the leaves can be lightly boiled then fried with onion and served with bacon.

**Gender**: Feminine. **Planet**: Venus. **Element**: Water.

**Influence:** Protection, Psychic Powers, Aphrodisiac

Burn as incense or carry as a sachet for a good psychic power stimulator. A good "spirit puller." It draws good spirits into workings and rituals when placed on the altar. An aphrodisiac, make an oil from seeds gathered under the full moon to use on the genitals. An amulet made of the leaf or root worn near the genitals will accomplish the same ends.

**Cultivation:** Althea prefers marshy fields and tidal zones, and is cultivated for medicinal use. Propogation is from seed, sown thinly in nursery rows then thinned to 30cm (12 inces) between plants. Division of the plants also can be done in late winter or early spring. The aerial parts are gathered in summer as the plant begins to flower, and the root is unearthed in autumn

**Alyssum** (*Alyssum* spp.)

**Description:** Alyssum is a low spreading plant that likes full sun & well-drained soils.

**Influence:** Protection, Moderating Anger

Has the power to expel charms. Has also the power to calm down one who is angry. Alyssum is recommended as an amulet because it as the power to expel charms. Hung up in the house, it protects against fascination (also known as glamour). It also has the power to calm an angry person if placed in the hand, or on the body. It was even claimed to have been able to cure rabies

**Gender:** Male, **Element:** Air, **Planet:** Mercury

**Cultivation:** A hardy, fast growing plant for borders, mass displays and rockeries that flowers within 8 weeks of sowing seed. Alyssum withstands coastal conditions and likes a position in full sun. Moist soil is preferred however the plant will stand drought conditions. Lightly clip Alyssum after the first flush of flowers to encourage a continuous display. Older plants can be removed as new self-sown plants appear.

**Amaranth** (*Amaranthus hypochondriacus*)

**Description:** Amaranth is a green tropical spinach. The leaves, stems and seeds are edible, delicious and very nutritious.

**Influence:** Healing, Protection, Invisibility

**Gender**; Feminine, **Planet**: Saturn, **Element**: Fire

Amaranth is used to repair a broken heart. It is also associated with immortality, and is used to decorate images of gods and goddesses. It is sacred to the god Artemis. Woven into a wreath, it is said to render the wearer invisible. Also used in pagan burial ceremonies Applied externally, it can reduce tissue swelling from sprains and tick bites. **Not to be used by pregnant or lactating women.**

**Cultivation:** Sow seeds in the soil - they don't like to be transplanted. Take a mature flower stalk and rub it between your hands, letting the seed and husks fall over the prepared bed. If you don't want to collect seed, pick the flower shoots as they emerge to keep the plant growing and producing leaves. Amaranth is not as greedy as other greens but will be much tastier if well fed. It will grow in semi-shade or full sun. Amaranth can become pretty rampant in the garden but if you want to get rid of it, just cover it with newspaper and it won't persist.

**Anemone** (*Anemone pulsatilla*)

**Description:** This is an evergreen perennial with shiny spotted leaves. It has a clump forming growth habit and is rhizomatous. Bears funnel-shaped flowers from late winter to late spring. Nice with spring flowering bulbs, rhododendron, azaleas and ferns.

**Influence:** Health, Protection, Healing

**Gender**: Masculine, **Planet**: Mars, **Element**: Fire

Gather a perfect bloom when the first are seen in spring, tie up in a red cloth and carry as a guard against disease. Red anemones grow in the yard to protect the home. Use it in healing rituals.

**Cultivation:** Sow from late winter to early summer, transplant when large enough to handle into 8cm (3in) pots. Plant out 30cm (12in) apart into well drained soil in a sunny spot in the autumn. Prone to powdery mildew, in dry conditions.

**American Mandrake** see May Apple

**American Nightshade** see Poke

**Angelica** (*Angelica Archangelica*)

**Description:** A perennial plant growing 1.5 or 1.8 metres high with large leaves and flat heads of greenish-white flowers.

**Influence:** Exorcism, Protection, Healing, Visions

**Gender:** Masculine, **Element:** Fire, **Planet:** Sun

Burn sun-dried herbs while you announce your desire and retain it in your mind. Candle Magick is also very useful with this herb. Grown for protection. Use in protection, healing, and exorcism incenses. Sprinkle in the four corners of the house to ward off evil.

**Cultivation:** Angelica requires a sheltered, shaded position and rich, moist soil. Sow fresh seed in autumn, or in spring. Sown in nursery rows or on site. Moist fertile soil is required, enriched with organic matter. Angelica prefers light shade but will tolerate full sun provided the soil remains moist. The tall flower stems may require staking.

**Anise** (*Pimpinella anisum*)

**Description:** It is a member of the parsley family and is related botanically to caraway, cumin, dill and fennel. Anise is well known as a digestive and breath sweetener. It is the ingredient which gives Pernod and Sambuco its distinctive flavour.

**Influence:** Protection, Psychic enhancement, Sleep,

**Gender**: Feminine, **Element**: Air, **Planet**: Jupiter

Wear on your person in sachet. Used often in Aromatherapy. Used too in dream pillows for a good night sleep. Burn while meditating. Used in purification baths, to call spirits to aid magickal operations, and to drive off evil.

**Cultivation**: Plant seeds directly where they are to grow in spring and again in autumn in mild areas. Soil should be light and well-drained. Add lime if the soil is acid. Choose a sunny, protected spot. Water well in dry weather. Anise and coriander are good companion plants.

## Apple (*Pyrus* spp.)

**Description:** The Crab-tree or Wild Apple Tree (*Pyrus malus*), is key to the history of apples. It is a native to Britain and is the ancestor of all the cultivated varieties of apple trees we grow today. It was the rootstock on which new varieties were grafted when brought from Europe.

The Apple tree is from the temperate zones and flourishes best in their cooler regions such as the UK. It is a tree which has been cultivated from before the Norman Conquest.

**Influence:** Love, Healing, Garden Magick, Immortality

**Gender**: Feminine, **Element**: Water, **Planet**: Venus

Add apple blossoms to love and healing incenses. Cut an apple in three pieces, rub each on a sick person's body, and then bury them. The decaying apple will cure the illness. The same ritual is done with warts. Pour cider to give life to a newly-dug field. Give an apple to a lover as a present, cut it in half and eat one half while your lover eats their half. Eat apples on Samhain

**Cultivation**: Apple trees prefer full sun, although they will tolerate some shade. Pick a position that will not become water-logged, and that is not in a low-lying area where frost settles. Apple trees are tolerant of most soil conditions - extremes of acid or alkaline soil will need to be corrected before planting. Perfect conditions are a crumbly soil with medium fertility and slightly on the acid side.

## Apricot (*Prunus Armeniaca*)

**Description:** Small to medium deciduous tree with spreading shape, typically fast growing to 3.6 metres tall and wide, but able to get much larger, size varies with the variety and rootstock; cordate leaves, about 7.5 cm wide.

**Influence:** Love

**Gender**: Feminine, **Element**: Water, **Planet**: Venus

Eat the fruit to obtain a sweet disposition, or use the juice in love potions. The leaves and flowers are added to love sachets, and the pits are carried to attract love

**Cultivation:** Grows best with full sun, this stone fruit tree originates from North Eastern china. Moderate to regular water, needs good drainage, tolerates some alkalinity and salinity. It is propagated by grafting on seedling rootstock

**Arabic Gum** See Gum Arabic

**Aromatic Wintergreen**, see Wintergreen

**Arbutus** (*Arbutus unede*)

> **Description:** The strawberry tree, a genus of evergreen shrubs, of the Heath family. It has a berry externally resembling the strawberry.
>
> **Influence:** Exorcism, Protection
>
> **Gender:** Masculine, **Element:** Fire, **Planet:** Mars
>
> The ancient Romans used this plant to chase away evil and to protect young children. It has been used in exorcisms since ancient Greek times.
>
> **Cultivation**: Although a native of South Europe the Arbutus will thrive almost anywhere in warm and coastal regions, where it will grow 7 metres high, making huge, globular masses of green, though ordinarily its height is only from 2.5 to 3.5 metres. It grows quickly in sheltered places but dislikes shade, and seems to be most at home in a deep, light soil, flourishing best in a sandy loam.

**Artemis Herb see** Mugwort

**Artemisia see** Mugwort

**Asafoetida** (*Ferula foetida*)

> **Description:** Perennial growing to 1m. It is in flower from Early spring to mid summer. The scented flowers are hermaphrodite (have both male and female organs) and are pollinated by Insects.
>
> **Influence:** Exorcism, Purification, Protection CAUTION: TERRIBLE SMELL!
>
> **Gender**: Masculine, **Element**: Fire, **Planet**: Mars
>
> Burn the crushed roots and leaves for incense. This is a powerful banishing herb. You will banish yourself out of the room with this stuff!
>
> **Cultivation:** The plant is self-fertile. It is happy in most soil types but requires well-drained soil and full sun. Propogation is from seed - best sown as soon as the seed is ripe. Prick out the seedlings into individual pots as soon as they are large enough to handle. Plant them out into their permanent positions whilst still small because the plants dislike root disturbance. Give the plants a protective mulch for at least their first winter outdoors.

**Ash** (*Fraxinus excelsior* or *F. americana*)

> **Description:** A decidious tree growing to 30m by 20m at a fast rate It is in leaf from mid spring to mid autumn, in flower during autumn. The flowers are dioecious (individual flowers are either male or female, but only one sex is to be found on any one plant so both male and female plants must be grown if seed is required) and are pollinated by Wind.
>
> **Influence:** Protection, Prosperity, Sea Rituals, Health
>
> **Gender**: Masculine, **Element**: Fire, **Planet**: Sun
>
> Carve some of the wood into an equal-armed cross as a protection against drowning. Place ash leaves beneath the pillow to induce prophetic dreaming. Use in sea-rituals of all

kinds. Snakes are afraid of the ash tree. If you want your newborn to be a good singer, bury its first nail clippings under an ash tree.

**Cultivation**: Sow seed directly into an outdoor seedbed, preferably in the autumn. Grow the seedlings on in the seedbed for 2 years before transplanting either to their permanent positions or to nursery beds. Cuttings of mature wood, placed in a sheltered outdoor bed in the winter, sometimes strike. The tree prefers a deep loamy soil, even if it is on the heavy side and is a gross feeder requiring rich soil. It requires good sunlight preferring full sun and cannot grow in the shade. It requires moist or wet soil. The plant can tolerate maritime exposure and tolerate atmospheric pollution.

## Aspen (*Populus* spp.)

**Description:** European aspen is one of the most widely distributed trees in the world, the bark is grey, or sometimes greenish-grey, and is either smooth or in some cases is pitted with diamond-shaped lenticels. On old, mature trees the bark is often covered with a dark-coloured lichen, which gives the trunk a black appearance. Aspen has a distinctive branching pattern, which is most visible in winter when the tree is leafless, and in mature trees the topmost branches are often bent over horizontally. Aspen has an extensive root system, and suckers have been recorded growing up to 40 metres from a parent tree.

**Influence:** Eloquence, Anti-Theft

**Gender**: Masculine, **Element**: Air, **Planet**: Mercury

Plant on your property to prevent theft, and use in anti-theft spells. Place an aspen leaf under your tongue if you wish to become eloquent.

**Cultivation**: Aspen is dioecious, so individual trees are either male or female. Trees flower in spring, before the leaves appear, with both the male and female trees producing catkins. Pollinated female catkins ripen in early summer and release tiny seeds. It grows on many soil types, especially sandy and gravelly slopes, and it is quick to pioneer disturbed sites where there is bare soil. This fast-growing tree is short lived and pure stands are gradually replaced by slower-growing species.

## Aster (*Callistephus chinensis*)

**Description:** Though not the easiest to grow, asters are among the most beloved of flowers. The large blooms can take a variety of forms, and daisy- and chrysanthemum-like forms are common. You'll also find a wide variety of colors including white, creamy yellow, pink, red, blue, lavender or purple, often with yellow centers. Varieties range in height from 15 cm up.

**Influence:** Love

**Gender:** Feminine, **Element**: Water, **Planet**: Venus

Use in love sachets or carry the flower to attract love.

**Cultivation:** Grown from seed these plants do well in beds and borders or plant seedlings to the same level in the pot and 50-60cm apart. For best results, keep well watered whilst actively growing. Flowers from Mid Summer to Autumn - these are great for adding late colour to the garden. Prefers soil that is well drained and full sun is ideal but they will tolerate a very light shade. Ideally prefers cool to temperate climates. Since they are prone to disease, avoid planting in the same location year after year. In dry weather, water by soaking the soil; don't sprinkle the plant. Keep faded flowers and yellowing foliage pinched off to encourage new blooms.

**Avens** (*Geum urbanum*)

**Description:** Perennial growing to 0.5m by 0.5m that is frost tolerant. It is in flower from during summer. The scented flowers are hermaphrodite (have both male and female organs) and are pollinated by Bees. The plant is self-fertile.

**Influence:** Exorcism, Purification, Love

**Gender:** Feminine, **Element**: Water, **Planet**: Venus

Carry as an amulet to guard against wild animals. Burn during exorcism and cleansing rituals or sprinkle around the area for that purpose. Use also in purification rites. It was also use by male Native Americans to gain the love of the opposite sex.. Add to protective sachets, amulets and incenses.

**Cultivation**: The plant requires well-drained soil and tolerates sandy, loamy and heavy clay soil. It can grow in semi-shade or no shade. It requires moist soil and will not tolerate long spells of dry soil

**Avocado** (*Persea americana*)

**Description:** A great shade tree growing to 12 m or more, the avocado fits well into the residential garden. Happy to be pruned the tree can be kept to an open shape in the garden. Flowers late in winter.

**Influence:** Love, Beauty, Lust

**Gender:** Feminine, **Element**: Water, **Planet**: Venus

Eat the fruit to become lustful. Carry the pit to promote beauty. Make a wand from avocado wood

**Cultivation**: Cultivated for its fruit in tropical and subtropical areas, Avocado is propagated from seed. grow quickly in full sun through light shade and prefer well drained soils. Regular watering until established is required. Thick mulching will assist the retention of water and growth of the tree and grass should be kept from under the tree using this method. Avocado flowers late in winter, with fruit ripening in late summer through to spring, depending on variety.

**Bachelor's Buttons** (*Centaurea cyanus*)

**Description:** Centaurea cyanus is a hardy annual formerly familiar as a cornfield weed before the advent of modern farming methods and weedkillers. It is an annual, growing to a height of 30 cm – 60 cm, with strong stems and greyish slightly furry leaves, with small clusters of bright blue flowers. Garden hybrids are now available in all shades of blues, pinks and white, in heights ranging from just a few centimetres to around 60cm. It is a good plant for a wild garden, a border or rockery, and is a useful cut flower.

**Influence:** Love

**Gender:** Feminine, **Element**: Water, **Planet**: Venus

Women wear the flower on their breast to attract the love of a man or, put the flower in your pocket. If it wilts, you will not have success in love: the opposite is true if the flower remains fresh.

**Cultivation:** May be started early inside, but they grow and bloom very fast from direct seeding outside. Sow seed about 2 weeks before last frost. Just cover and they usually germinate in 7 days. Successive sowings will provide blooms all season. Space 30 cm apart in full sun.

**Balm, Lemon** (*Melissa officinalis*)

**Description:** Lemon balm is an attractive herb with yellow or variegated leaves smelling strongly of lemons. It is a great addition to any garden since it is very attractive to bees. This vigorous plant will readily spread throughout the border. It reaches a height of 60 cm with a spread of 60 cm. The flowers, which bloom from mid- to late summer are small, white, and insignificant.

**Influence:** Love, Success, Healing

**Gender:** Feminine, **Element**: Water, **Planet**: Moon

Carry the herb to find love. Used in healing incenses and sachets

**Cultivation:** Lemon Balm is a perennial herb that is grown mostly for culinary purposes. Seeds are slow to germinate and are so fine that they hardly need covering at all. An alternative method of propagation is to take cuttings in late spring and root them in water. Plant in warm, moist soil in a sunny location. Good sun and moisture are necessary for the production of essential oil and good fragrance. Cut back to soil level in the fall to encourage strong growth. The plant will not tolerate high humidity. Lemon Balm performs well in containers.

**Balm of Gilead** *(Populus balsamifera L)*

**Description:** Large deciduous tree with winter buds that are large resinous and aromatic; yellowish, gummy, strongly fragrant, end buds more than 1 cm long.

**Influence:** Love, Manifestations, Protection, Healing, Soothes love pains, de-stressing

**Gender:** Feminine, **Element**: Water, **Planet**: Venus

Throw the fresh herbs in a bath, as you soak visualize your wish coming true, place in red wine for attracting a new love

**Cultivation**: Sow seeds in spring (note that seedlings resemble nettles). Take stem cuttings in early autumn. Thin or transplant to 45 cm apart. Balm of Gilead (balsamifera) makes an excellent conservatory plant, but a 23-25 cm pot is needed for it to reach a reasonable size. Requires full sun and well-drained, medium loamy soil. Tree can grow up to 20 metres.

**Bamboo** (*Bambusa Vulgaris*)

**Description:** Bamboos are giant, fast-growing grasses that have woody stems. The woody, hollow stems of bamboo grow in branching clusters from a thick underground stem or rhizome. These stems often form a dense undergrowth that excludes other plants and can reach heights ranging from 10 cm to more than 40 m in the largest. The stems have hollow walls with internodes and thick hard nodes joining them. Mature bamboos sprout horizontal branches that bear sword-shaped leaves on stalked blades. The leaves on young culms arise directly from the stem. Most bamboo flower, but only once in 60-120 years, with large heads much like those of sugar cane. After blooming, all of the bamboo plants of the same species die back. This happens worldwide at the same time!

**Influence:** Protection, Luck, Hex-Breaking, Wishes

**Gender:** Masculine. **Element:** _____ **Planet:** _____

**Deity:** Hina

Excellent for magick wands, representing all four elements. "Growing up from the earth through water, it passes through the sky as it reaches toward the fire of the Sun." Crush the wood to a powder and burn for protection or grow by the house for good fortune.

**Cultivation:** Propagation is by division as most bamboo flower only once in 60-120 years. Plant cuttings in well structured moist soil. Water regularly. Grows well in pots.

## Banana (*Musa sapientum*)

**Description:** Banana is a tropical herbaceous plant consisting of an underground corm and a trunk comprised of concentric layers of leaf sheaths. At 10 to 15 months after the emergence of a new plant, its true stem rapidly grows up through the centre and emerges as a terminal inflorescence, which bears fruit. The flowers appear in groups (hands) along the stem and are covered by purplish bracts, which roll back and shed as the fruit stem develops. The first hands to appear contain female flowers which will develop into bananas. The number of hands of female flowers varies from a few to more than 10, after which numerous hands of sterile flowers appear and shed in succession, followed by numerous hands of male flowers which also shed. Generally, a bract rolls up and sheds to expose a new hand of flowers almost daily.

**Influence:** Fertility, Potency, Prosperity

**Gender:** Feminine, **Element:** Water, **Planet:** Venus

Increases fertility and cures impotence. The leaves, flowers and fruit are used in money and prosperity spells.

**Cultivation:** Grown from Rhizomes, banana's are cloned rather than grown from seed. As trees they vary in size and with the myriad of varieties available, select one best suited to your environment. Banana plants need a rich, humus soil, and heavy feeding when they are actively growing. Banana plants like it hot and humid so it is helpful to mist the leaves often, and sponge them off when they get dusty. Give them a lot of root space, and the plant will grow proportionately.

## Banewort see Belladonna

## Banyan (*Ficus benghalensis*)

**Description:** Banyan starts out life as an epiphyte growing on another tree where some fig-eating bird deposited a seed. As it grows, banyan produces aerial roots that hang down from horizontal branches and take root where they touch the ground. These vertical "prop roots" can create a forest on their own. Banyan can get 100' tall and, with its massive limbs supported by prop roots, spread over an area of several acres.

**Influence:** Luck

**Gender:** Masculine, **Element:** Air, **Planet:** Jupiter

Sit beneath or look at this tree for good luck, and being married under one ensures the couple's happiness.

**Cultivation**: Banyans like a light position away from direct sunlight, so a north-facing windowsill is ideal. As the plant grows move it into a bigger flowerpot, but you may have to grow it in a pot on the floor when it gets very large! Use a good brand of ordinary potting compost to repot it with. Feed the plant occasionally with a soluble fertilizer during the summer. Banyans like to be lightly misted with a fine spray of water every day during the growing season - if you can, use rainwater for this, as tap water sometimes leaves greyish marks on the leaves.

## Barley (*Hordeum* spp.)

**Description:** Barley plants are annual grasses which may be either winter annuals or spring annuals.

**Influence:** Love, Healing, Protection

**Gender**: Feminine, **Element**: Earth, **Planet**: Venus

Use the grain in love spells. Can be scattered on the ground to keep evil and negativity away.

**Cultivation:** Grown from seed, barley thrives well on well-drained fertile deep loam soils. Barley requires cool weather during early growth and warm and dry weather at maturity. The crop needs less water and is more tolerant of salinity and alkali conditions than other winter cereals. As it has low water requirement, barley is grown as a rainfed crop. To give good yields, barley requires 2-3 irrigations with its efficiency increased by a proper timing of application at the critical stages of growth of the crop.

## Basil (*Ocimum Basilicum*)

**Description:** Sweet basil, with it's wonderful aroma and flavour, is one of the most popular and widely grown herbs in the world. It is a tender low-growing annual herb, originally native to tropical Asia. It grows to between twenty and sixty centimetres tall, with opposite, light green, silky leaves one and a half to five centimetres long and one to three centimetres broad. It tastes somewhat like cloves, with a strong, pungent, sweet smell. Basil is very sensitive to cold, with best growth in hot, dry conditions.

**Influence:** Love, Exorcism, Wealth, Flying, Protection

**Gender**: Masculine, **Element**: Fire, **Planet**: Mars or Jupiter

Burn crushed powdered Basil while you announce your desire. You can also sprinkle a little on your person. Can be mixed with other herbs for protection and love. Added to love incenses and sachets. Brings wealth to those who carry it in their pockets, and attracts customers to a place of business by placing some in the cash register. No evil can live where it is placed. Place a sprig of fresh basil in someone's hand to find out if they are promiscuous: it will immediately wither in this case. If secretly placed under someone's plate, he or she will not be able to eat from it

**Cultivation**: Sow seeds in late spring or purchase seedlings. Choose the sunniest part of the garden. Soil should be light and well-drained. Add a little lime when the bed is being prepared. As seedlings grow, pinch out regularly to create a compact plant. Harvesting the leaves regularly for culinary use will also keep the plants nice and bushy. If drying, harvest before the plants flower in autumn.

**Bay** (*Laurus nobilis*)

**Description:** The Bay Laurel is an evergreen tree or large shrub reaching 10–18 m tall, native to the Mediterranean region.

The leaves are 6–12 cm long and 2–4 cm broad, with a characteristic serrated and wrinkled margin. It is dioecious, with male and female flowers on separate plants; each flower is pale yellow-green, about 1 cm diameter, borne in pairs together beside a leaf. The fruit is a small black berry about 1 cm long, containing a single seed.

**Influence:** Protection, Psychic Powers, Healing, Purification, Strength

**Gender**: Masculine, **Element**: Fire, **Planet** Jupiter

Burn the fresh leaves for divination, hang up at the highest point in the home for protection or burn and let the smoke hit the four corners of a room for purifying and cleansing of negative energies. Place in a dream pillow for safe sound sleep or with other herbs for psychic dreams.

**Cultivation**: The Bay Tree is known for its hardiness and adaptability. It prefers a well-drained position in full sun, though it will also grow in semi-shade. The plants are tolerant of drought, wind and salt-spray. They will self-sow very readily. Bay Trees respond well to pot culture and they are often used as topiary specimens. Heeled cuttings can be taken in spring.

**Bayberry Tree see** Myrtle

**Bean** (*Phaseolus* spp.)

**Description:** *Bean* originally meant the seed of the broad bean, but was later broadened to include members of the genus *Phaseolus* such as the common bean or haricot and the runner bean and the related genus *Vigna*.

**Influence:** Protection, Exorcism, Wart Charming, Reconciliations, Potency, Love

**Gender:** Masculine, **Element**: Air, **Planet**: Mercury

Dried beans are worn as an amulet against evil and negativity. Beans help cure impotency when eaten or carried.

**Cultivation**: Beans are sensitive to cold temperatures and frost. They should be planted after all danger of frost is past in the spring. Plant seeds of all varieties around 3 cm deep. Plant seeds of bush beans 5cm to 10 cm apart in rows at least 45 cm to 60 cm apart. Plant seeds of pole beans 10cm to 15 cm apart in rows 1 metre apart; or in hills (four to six seeds per hill) 1 metre apart, with 1 metre between rows.

**Bedstraw** (*Galium triflorum*)

**Description:** *Galium* is a large genus of annual and perennial herbaceous plants in the family Rubiaceae, with about 400 species occurring in both temperate zones.. The species are variously known as bedstraw, goosegrass, cleavers and woodruff.

**Influence:** Love

**Gender:** Feminine, **Element**: Water, **Planet**: Venus

Carry or wear to attract love.

**Cultivation**: Perennial growing to 0.6m by 1m. It is hardy and is not frost tender. It is in flower during summer, and the seeds ripen in Autumn. The flowers are hermaphrodite (have both male and female organs) and are pollinated by Insects. The plant is self-fertile. It is noted for attracting wildlife. The plant tolerates all soils providing they are well-drained. It can grow in semi-shade to full sun.

## Beech (*Fagus sylvatica*)

**Description:** Beech (*Fagus*) is a genus of ten species of deciduous trees in the family Fagaceae. The leaves are entire or sparsely toothed, from 5-15 cm long and 4-10 cm broad. The flowers are small single-sex, wind-pollinated catkins, produced in spring shortly after the new leaves appear. The fruit is a small, sharply 3-angled nut 10-15 mm long, borne in pairs in soft-spined husks 1.5-2.5 cm long, known as cupules. The nuts are edible, though bitter with a high tannin content. The beech most commonly grown as an ornamental tree is the European Beech (*Fagus sylvatica*), widely cultivated in North America as well as its native Europe. The European species yields a widely used timber, an easy-to-work utility wood.

**Influence:** Wishes

**Gender**: Feminine, **Planet**: Saturn

Take a stick of beech, carve your wishes onto it and bury it in the ground. You wishes will come true if they were meant to. Carry the wood or leaves to increase creative powers.

**Cultivation**: The species is fairly easy to grow from seed. Sown outside when first ripe and picked in early fall, it should germinate the following spring. Indoors, mix the seed with an equal quantity of just-moist peat moss, enclose in a plastic bag and store in the refrigerator at 5°C or lower for 60 to 90 days to improve the germination rate. It is able to grow in both slightly acidic and alkaline soils though their main drawback is a high sensitivity to salt.

## Beet (*Beta vulgaris*)

**Description**: The beet is a plant with a rounded fleshy taproot. Cultivars of the beet include beetroot, table beet or in the 19th century blood turnip used as a root vegetable, Fodder beet, wurzel or mangold used as animal fodder, sugar beet grown for sugar, Chard, a beet which has been bred for the leaves instead of the roots and is used as a leaf vegetable. These are all related to the original Sea Beet, a maritime salt-tolerant plant of North West Europe.

**Influence:** Love

**Gender:** Feminine, **Element**: Earth, **Planet**: Saturn

If a man and a woman eat of the same beet, they will fall in love. Beet juice is used as an ink in love spells and is also used as a blood substitute.

**Cultivation**: Beet and chard seeds are contained in a dry and corky cube-shaped calyx. The entire aggregate (containing 2-5 seeds) is planted, and later the seedlings are thinned to 10 -20 cm. Care must be taken when thinning since the tiny roots are often intertwined. The seed clusters can be broken apart before planting by gently crushing with a rolling pin, but this can damage some of the seeds. Beets produce best in full sun, but can tolerate partial shade, especially in the summer and at midday. Beets are a little less sensitive to drought, but should be watered before the soil is completely dried. Excessive fluctuation in soil moisture will cause beet roots to crack.

**Belladonna** (*Atropa belladonna*)  **POISONOUS**

**Description:** A perennial branching herb growing to 1.5 metres tall, with 20 cm long ovate leaves. The leaves in first-year plants are larger than those of older plants. The flowers are bell-shaped, blue-purple or dull red, followed by a shiny, black or purple 1 cm berry. Native of Europe and Asia

**Influence:** Encourages astral projection and produces visions, A primary ingredient in flying ointments. Used in funeral rituals to aspurge the circle, helping the deceased to let go and move forward. Used to invoke Circe.

**Gender**: Feminine. **Planet**: Saturn. **Element**: Water. **Deities**: Hecate, Bellona, Circe

**Highly toxic. All parts of the plant are extremely poisonous and so is best avoided.**

Gather berries when they are ripe (around Samhain.) Store with onyx. Medicinally, it has been used as a sedative.

**Cultivation**: Belladonna prefers a well-drained, well-limed soil in full sun or part shade. The soil should be kept moist at all times. Plants exposed to too much sun will be stunted. It is most frequently propagated by seed, sown in flats in early spring. Because the seeds take 4-6 weeks to germinate, they should be started early. When the seedlings are 2 cm or so high they may be set out 45 cm apart. Belladonna may also be propagated by cuttings of the green branch tips.

**Benzoin** (*Styrax benzoin*)

**Description:** A tree native to Sumatra and Java

**Influence:** Purification, Prosperity. Provides focus. Enhances concentration

**Gender**: Masculine. **Planet**: Sun. **Element**: Air. **Deities**: Venus, Aphrodite, Mut.

Useful in astral travel (protects spirit while travelling). Promotes generosity. Brings increased success to any magickal working or to attain magickal goals. Used as a base for incense. Make an incense of benzoin, cinnamon, and basil to attract customers to your place of business.

**Cultivation**: Whilst normally harvested in the wild it can be propagated from seed planted in autumn, or by striking semi ripe cuttings in summer. Requires moist to wet soils and full sun through partial shade. Flowers during spring and summer.

**Bergamot** (*Monarda fistulosa*)

**Description:** Not to be confused with the small evergreen tree *(Citrus bergamia)* that belongs to the Rutaceae family, a citrus that is well-known for its strong and pleasant scent used in the perfume industry, and is part of the bergamot flavoured teas. Bergamot is a clump forming perennial growing to 90cm and is best grown in flower beds and as a border.

**Influence:** Money

**Gender**: Masculine, **Element**: Earth, **Planet**: Jupiter

Use the oil of this herb or place herb in wallets and purses to attract money. Fresh leaves are rubbed on money to ensure its return. Use in success rituals and spells.

**Cultivation**: Sunny or partly shaded areas are well suited to bergamot. The plant likes moist, but well-drained soil with plenty of organic matter added. Propagate by division or by seed sown in seed trays in spring. It will also grow from cuttings. Cut back to the ground after flowering. The plant will regenerate in spring. Water well in dry periods.

## Be-Still (*Thevetia nereifolia*)  **POISONOUS**

**Description:** *Thevetia nereifolia*, widely known as Yellow Oleander, but also bearing the names Lucky Nut and Exile Tree. It belongs to the Dogbane family, and comes from South America and the West Indies. A clambering shrub with thick, fleshy, narrow leaves, and showy fragrant yellow or orange funnel shaped flowers, it bears large seeds which are often carried as talismans.

**Influence:** Luck

**Gender:** Masculine, **Element:** Fire, **Planet:** Sun

In Sri Lanka, the seeds are known as "lucky beads" and are worn as talismans to attract luck.

**Cultivation:** It is cold tolerant to 25 degrees and is drought and soil tolerant and probably only limited by its tenderness. Propagation is effected by using well-ripened wood for cuttings, placed in a close frame; or the slips may be rooted in a bottle or can of water, care being taken to supply water as evaporation takes place. After being rooted, they may be potted, using soil with a large proportion of sand. Well-established plants may be repotted in good loam and well-rotted manure. They should bloom the second year. Available as a Greenhouse shrub in the UK.

Beth Root, See Trillium

## Betony, Wood (*Betonica officinalis*)

**Description:** Perennial growing to 0.6m by 0.45m and is frost tolerant. The flowers are hermaphrodite (have both male and female organs) and are pollinated by Bees. It is noted for attracting wildlife.

**Influence:** Protection, Purification, Love

**Gender**: Masculine, **Element:** Fire, **Planet**: Jupiter

Carry a sachet for protection and/or scatter at the four corners of a room in the house. Burn and let the smoke cover you for purification. Carry with you in an amulet for love advances. Burn for banishing disharmony in a relationship. A protective and purifying herb. Grown in gardens to protect the home. Is a good plant to wear when making love advances, and is said to reunite fighting couples if added to food. Strengthens the body when worn.

**Cultivation**: The plant prefers light to medium well-drained soil though it can grow in heavy clay soil. It can grow in full sun to semi-shade. It requires moist soil. Grows well from seed sown spring. Prick out the seedlings into individual pots once they are large enough to handle and plant them out in the summer. Also by division in spring. Very easy, the plant can be successfully divided at almost any time of the year. Larger divisions can be planted out direct into their permanent positions.

**Birch** (*Betula alba*)

**Description:** White birch is a tree found growing to a height of 20 metres in the northern US, Canada, and northern Europe. It has white bark which can be peeled off in horizontal strips. Its leaves are cordate, with bright green above and lighter beneath, serrated, and minutely hairy. The flowers are borne in male and female catkins, with the female developing into seed cones.

**Influence:** Protection, Exorcism, Purification

**Gender**: Feminine, **Element**: Air, **Planet**: Saturn

Sacred tree of the Celts. Use the wood for making wands and other magick tools. Also can be mixed with other herbs for a peaceful sleep. A purifying and cleansing herb. You can tie a red ribbon around the stem of a birch to protect yourself from the evil eye.

**Cultivation**: The Birch will grow in moist situations, but requires good drainage, and so seems to flourish best on light soils. It has an enormous production of seeds, which are scattered far and wide by the wind, owing to the little wing attached to them. It spreads rapidly, springing up spontaneously wherever the soil is dry and fertile.

**Biscuits,** See Tormentil

**Bison grass,** See Sweetgrass

**Bistort** (*Betula alba*)

**Description:** This vigorous, semi-evergreen perennial is excellent groundcover for moist areas of the garden. Flourishing in sun or shade, the poker-like flower-heads are an important late summer source of nectar for bees.

**Influence:** Psychic Powers, Fertility

**Gender**: Feminine, **Element**: Earth, **Planet**: Saturn

Carry as a sachet for fertility and conception. Added as a booster with other herbs for divination. Burn with frankincense to improve psychic powers or when divining. Is added to money and wealth sachets and incenses.

**Cultivation:** Divisions or seedlings can be planted into their final positions in spring or autumn. Grows well in any kind of moist soil, preferring full sun through partial shade. This hardy fast growing plant eventually grows to 90cm high and wide. Contact with all parts of the plant may cause skin irritation; the sap may cause a mild stomach upset if ingested; highly attractive to bees and other pollinating insects

**Bittersweet** (*Celastrus scandens; Solanum dulcamara*)  **POISONOUS**

**Description:** These woody vines are inconspicuous throughout the spring and summer, indistinguishable from many green-leafed twining plants in natural settings. In the autumn their brilliant orange berries punctuate drab landscapes, adding a burst of colour to the browns of falling leaves.

**Influence:** Protection, Healing

**Gender**: Masculine, **Element**: Air, **Planet**: Mercury

Place some bittersweet beneath your pillow to help forget a past love. Also used to remove and protect against evil from both humans and animals. Tie the herb somewhere on the body for this purpose. Also tie to the neck to cure vertigo or dizziness.

**Cultivation**: Grown from seed, plants average 60% female to 40% male. Transplant them in early spring, before they leaf out and then expect more in the same spot. It freely propagates from any root over 3 mm that is severed or severely damaged, and will send up a shoot that will develop into the same sex as the parent plant. Bittersweet in nature grows both in full sun, such as on fences and in partial shade. In deep shade, it will get very leggy with wide spaces between leaf nodes and there will be little if any fruit production. Bittersweet will, if not attended to, climb on just about anything that it can grab on to. It has male and female flowers, produced on separate plants. Both must be present, and within range, for pollination to take place. Female plants produce the berries

**Blackberry** (*Rubus villosus*)

**Description:** This perennial herb is also known as bramble, dewberry and goutberry. The berries can be made into jam, gelatin, jelly and vinegar. Blackberries are high in fiber and vitamin C.

**Influence:** Healing, Money, Protection

**Gender**: Feminine, **Element**: Water, **Planet**: Venus

A syrup made from the root is used to treat diarrhea and upset stomach (good for treating children). An infusion of the leaves is good for treating diarrhea and sore throat. Blackberry leaves are used in money spells, as are the berries. Sacred to the Goddess Brid.

**Cultivation**: Plant Blackberry in loose, moist soil in a sunny location. Harvest the leaves and roots any time and the berries as they ripen.

**Black Nightshade** see Henbane


**Bladderwrack** (*Fucus vesiculosus*)

**Description:** Also known as Brown Kelp. Bladerwrack is a sea weed.

**Influence:** Protection, Sea Spells, Wind Spells, Money, Psychic Powers

**Gender**: Feminine, **Element**: Water, **Planet**: Moon

Also known as seaweed. Make an infusion of the plant and scrub the floors and doors of your place of business to attract customers. To ensure a steady flow of money into the household, fill a small jar with whiskey, put some kelp in it, cap it tightly, and place in the kitchen window

**Cultivation**: As a seaweed bladderwrack is harvested from the wild.

**Bleeding Heart** (*Dicentra spectabilis* or *D. formosa*)

**Description:** Bleeding heart (Dicentra) has attractive mounded foliage with arching stems of delicate, heart-shaped flowers in spring. It thrives in moist woodland gardens along with ferns and other shade-lovers. Flower colors include yellow, pink, red, and white. It blooms in spring and may rebloom sporadically throughout the summer in cool areas. Height ranges from 15 cm to 50 cm, depending on variety.

**Influence:** Love.

**Gender**: Feminine. **Planet**: Venus. **Element**: Water

When grown, the plant brings love. If growing indoors, plant a penny in the soil to offset negative vibrations. (For some reason, this plant emits negativity when grown indoors maybe because love needs freedom to grow?) Lore: crush the flower. If the juice is red, your love has a heart full of love for you. If it is white, he or she does not.

**Cultivation**: Plant in spring or autumn, spacing plants 15 cm to 60 cm apart, depending on the variety. Prepare the garden bed to a depth of 30cm to 45cm, adding a good layer of compost. Dig a hole twice the diameter of the plant's container. Carefully remove the plant from its pot and place it in the hole so the top of the root ball is level with the soil surface. If planting a bare-root plant, set the eye, or growing point, about 2 cm below the soil surface. Carefully fill in around the root ball, firm the soil with your fingers, and water thoroughly. Maintain even soil moisture throughout the plant's first growing season. Bleeding heart grows best in cool, moist conditions.

**Blessed Thistle,** See Holy Thistle

**Bloodroot** (*Sanguinaria canadensis*)  **POISONOUS**

**Description:** Perennial woodland native of North America having a red root and red sap and bearing a solitary lobed leave and white flower in early spring and having acrid emetic properties

**Influence:** Love, Protection, Purification

**Gender**: Masculine, **Element**: Fire, **Planet**: Mars

The root is carried to draw love, and to avert evil spells and negativity. Place near doorways and windowsills to be protected. The darkest red roots are considered the best, and are called King Roots.

**Cultivation**: Propagation is typically done through seed or root division. Bloodroot is more easily propagated by dividing the rhizomes in spring or in autumn. Seed can be directly sown into the ground, but the rhizome divisions allow for a faster harvestable plant. To plant rhizomes, cut the roots into vertical sections, 5 cm in length, making sure there is at least one bud attached. There can be up to twelve buds on a rhizome of one bloodroot plant. In a well-prepared 1 metre wide bed, plant rhizome pieces deep enough to cover the top of the rhizome with one to 5 cm of soil. Any fibrous roots connected to the rhizome pieces can remain attached. Stagger plantings 15 cm apart, making sure the bud is pointed upright when placing the rhizome pieces in the ground. While bloodroot does not like a soggy soil, irrigation should be provided during dry periods. Plants should be ready to harvest four to five years after planting.

**Blue Buttons see** Periwinkle

**Bluebell** (*Campanula rotundifolia*)

**Description:** The Bluebell is very prolific with leaves that are strap shaped, shiny and mid-green. They grow basally, and are 20 cm to 30 cm long. Small, blue bell-shaped flowers grow pendently along a flower stalk to 45 cm tall. This common and vigorous plant easily spreads.

**Influence:** Luck, Truth

**Gender**_____, **Element**_____, **Planet:** _____

If you can turn a bluebell inside out without damaging it, you will eventually have the one you love. The next time you see a bluebell, pick it and say "Bluebell, bluebell, bring me some luck before tomorrow night." Then, slip it into your shoe. Anyone who wears a bluebell must tell the truth.

**Cultivation**: Autumn is usually the best time to plant spring bulbs. As a general rule of thumb they should be planted in a hole at least 2 to 3 times deeper than the height of the bulb. Don't tie the stalks of daffodils in a knot once they have finished flowering, nor should you cut them off. The leaves will replenish the bulb enabling it to flower the following year. Let the foliage of bulbs die down naturally. If you don't like the sight of it once the flowers have gone, plant them amongst summer flowering plants so that, when they come through, they hide the foliage of the spring bulbs from sight.

## Blueberry (*Vaccinum frondosum*)

**Description:** Fresh blueberries are one of summer's best-tasting treats. Blueberries don't have to be relegated to the backyard garden as they are also attractive ornamental shrubs. Plants produce white to pink, urn-shaped flowers in the spring

**Influence:** Protection

Place some blueberries under your doormat to keep undesirables away from your property and out of your house, and to protect against evil. Make and eat blueberry pies or tarts while under psychic attack to get the herb's protection inside you: this will increase its effectiveness.

**Gender**_____, **Element**_____, **Planet:** _____

**Cultivation**: Blueberries can be propagated by both hardwood and softwood cuttings. Most propagation is done with hardwood cuttings, as they are easier to handle and are less perishable than softwood cuttings. However, softwood cuttings allow more rapid multiplication of plants. Cuttings are whips or shoots that are cut into several pieces, each 10 cm to 15 cm long. There are 3 types of cuttings: leaf buds only, 1 to 2 fruit buds in addition to at least 2 good leaf buds, and a cutting taken from the middle of the previous year's growth with one or more fruit buds removed. Propagation beds should be located in full sun with a suitable well-drained medium. Place beds either on the ground or raised above the ground. Water the cuttings thoroughly about once a week to keep the medium moist but not water logged. Water more frequently when the leaves have developed. Full sun is best for growing quality plants.

## Blue Flag (*Iris versicolor*)  **POISONOUS**

**Description:** *Iris versicolor* is a perennial flower also known as blue flag, flag-lily, fleur-de-lis, flower-de-luce, iris, liver lily, poison flag, snake lily, water flag, and wild iris. This plant ranges from 60 to 90 cm in height The stem stands upright and it contains sword-shaped leaves, which are shorter than the stem. The flowers are large and each stem has from two to six or more

**Influence:** Money

**Gender:** Feminine, **Element:** Water, **Planet:** Venus

Carry the root for financial gain. Place in cash registers to increase business.

**Cultivation:** *Iris versicolor* needs full sun to partial shade with a heavy, rich moist soil. Use a soil mix consisting of 2 parts clay to 1 part loam to 1 part sand. The plants need to be kept moist at all times, which makes it a great plant for water features. The plant should be fertilized in the spring before flowering and again after the blooms have faded. They grow quickly and should be re-potted on a yearly basis. The plant grows best in nutrient rich soils with plenty of organic matter.

**Bodhi** (*Ficus religiosa*)

**Description:** Fig tree of India noted for great size and longevity. It lacks the support roots of the Banyan. It is a sacred tree to the Buddhists.

**Influence:** Fertility, Protection, Wisdom, Meditation

**Gender:** Masculine, **Element:** Air, **Planet:** Jupiter

Both Buddha and Vishnu are said to have been born under a bodhi tree: sacred fires are made with its wood. To cause evil to flee, circle the tree several times. Barren women walk naked under a bodhi tree to become fertile. Use the leaves in meditation incenses and all mixtures designed to give wisdom.

**Cultivation:** This fast growing tree usually begins as an epiphyte (air plant, grows on trees) but develops roots to support its height of 30 plus metres..

**Boneset** (*Eupatorium perfoliatum*)

**Description:** Perennial growing to 1.2m. It is in flower during late summer. The flowers are hermaphrodite (have both male and female organs) and are pollinated by Insects. The plant is self-fertile. The plant requires well-drained soil and can grow in semi-shade through to full sun. It requires moist soil.

**Influence:** Protection, Exorcism

**Gender:** Feminine, **Element:** Water, **Planet:** Saturn

Used for treating severe fevers, as well as flu and catarrh conditions. One to two tablespoons of the tincture in hot water is used for sweat therapy to break fevers. An infusion sprinked around the house will drive away evil spirits and negativity. Wards off evil spirits.

**Cultivation:** Seed, sown in spring with soil only just covering the seed. Prick out the seedlings into individual pots when they are large enough to handle and plant them out into their permanent positions in the summer. Division in spring or autumn is very easy and the clumps can be replanted direct into their permanent positions.

**Borage** (*Borago officinalis*)

**Description:** Borage (Borago officinalis) is a lovely garden plant, with small bright blue flowers and an informal growth habit, reaching a height of 60cm. It is waterwise, easily growing in poor soil in a sunny spot. Although an annual it seeds itself, coming up year after year.

**Influence:** Courage, Psychic Powers

**Gender**: Masculine, **Element**: Air, **Planet**: Jupiter

Carrying the fresh blossoms brings courage. The tea will induce your psychic powers.

**Cultivation**: Borage is one of the few herbs that prefer a semi-shaded spot, though it will grow in full sun. It needs shelter from strong winds as it is easily blown over. Soil should be moist, loose and friable. Seeds germinate in all seasons except very cold winters. The plant is an annual but self-seeds easily.

**Boxberry,** see Wintergreen

**Bracken** (*Pteridium aquilinum*)

**Description:** Brackenfern is a large, coarse, perennial fern that has almost horizontal leaves and can grow 40 cm to 2 metres tall. Unlike our more typical broadleaf perennials, this primitive perennial lacks true stems. Each leaf arises directly from a rhizome (horizontal underground stem), and is supported on a rigid leaf stalk. In addition, brackenfern does not produce flowers or seeds. Instead, it reproduces by spores and creeping rhizomes. This species often forms large colonies.

**Influence:** Healing, Rune Magick, Prophetic Dreams

**Gender**: Masculine, **Element**: Air, **Planet**: Jupiter

If you burn bracken outside, rain will fall. Bracken is used for protection, healing, and fertility. If the root is placed beneath the pillow it causes the solutions to problems to appear in your dreams.

**Cultivation**: Reproduces by spores and vegetatively by rhizomes. Most regeneration is vegetative. Many have searched for young plants growing from spores, but few have found them. However, spores do germinate and grow readily in culture. Young plants produce spores by the end of the second growing season in cultivation but normally do not produce spores until the third or fourth growing season. A single, fertile frond can produce 300, 000, 000 spores annually.

**Brazil Nut** (*Bertholletia excellsa*)

**Description:** Slow growing native tree from Brazil.

**Influence:** Love

**Gender**: masculine, **Element**: Air, **Planet**: Mercury

Brings good luck in love affairs if carried as a talisman.

**Cultivation**: Harvested exclusively from the wild, the Brazil nut has difficulty growing domestically because it's a particularly hardy organism only conquered by a specific insect for pollination and a specific rodent for random germination.

**Bryony** (*Bryony* spp.)  **POISONOUS**

**Description:** White bryony, a fast-growing perennial with a thick root and angular, branching stems, has yellow-white flowers with green veins. White bryony bears one or two seeded, thin-skinned black berries.

**Influence:** Image Magick, Money, Protection

**Gender**: Masculine, **Element**: Fire, **Planet**: Mars

The briony root is often used as a substitute for the mandrake root. Place money near a briony root to increase it, as long as it is left there. The root is also hung in houses and gardens to protect against bad weather.

**Cultivation**: A rapid grower, it is of easy cultivation succeeding in most soils that are well drained, avoiding acid soils in the wild it prefers a sunny position. A very deep-rooted climbing plant, attaching itself to other plants by means of tendrils. Plants can be easily encouraged by scattering ripe seed along the base of hedgerows. Dioecious, male and female plants must be grown if seed is required.

## Bromeliad (*Crypanthus* spp.)

**Description:** Bromeliads are members of a plant family known as Bromeliaceae. The family contains over 3000 described species in approximately 56 genera. The most well known bromeliad is the pineapple. The family contains a wide range of plants including some very un-pineapple like members such as Spanish Moss. Other members resemble aloes or yuccas while still others look like green, leafy grasses.

In general they are inexpensive, easy to grow, require very little care, and reward the grower with brilliant, long lasting blooms and ornamental foliage. They come in a wide range of sizes from tiny miniatures to giants.

**Influence:** Protection, Money

**Gender**: Masculine, **Element**: Air, **Planet**: Sun

Grow this plant in the home for money and luxuries. It is also protective, which makes it a good house plant.

**Cultivation**: For epiphytic (non-terrestrial) varieties, we grow bromeliads in small pine bark as a soil base. This provides excellent aeration and circulation for the roots that form, and provides sufficient support for the plant. For terrestrials, use a loose and light organic soil mixture. After the plant flowers, it will produce "pups" or young plants then die. The young pups will take over the next generation. Pups should not be removed until visible root structures can be seen at their base or they are at least 1/3 to 1/2 the size of the mother plant. Make sure the pups are cut off with a solid base. Some bromeliads reproduce so abundantly, you'll be sharing them with friends.

## Broom (*Cytisus scoparius*)

**Description:** English broom is an upright evergreen shrub up to 4 m, but more commonly 1 to 2 m high. It reproduces by seed which germinates mainly in spring and autumn. Young plants usually do not flower until their third year. Plants live for up to 27 years, although 10-15 years is more usual. After about 20 years they collapse and grow prostrate for the remainder of their life. English broom is native to most of Europe. ***It is an important weed*** in the Pacific coast states of the USA, Hawaii, New Zealand, Australia and in parts of Asia and its native range.

**Influence:** Purification, Protection, Wind Spells, Divination

**Gender**: Masculine, **Element**: Air, **Planet**: Mars

Use the plant to sweep the surrounding area when working Magick outside. Use in purification incenses and hang a little in your magick room as a protection. Use to raise calm winds. Raise them by throwing the herb into the air, preferably off a mountain top, and calm them by burning the herb. Use in purification and protection spells, and hang in the home to keep evil out. An infusion of broom sprinkled about the home exorcises poltergeists. Carry to increase psychic powers.

**Cultivation**: English broom is a legume and has root nodules that fix nitrogen. It is found mainly in cool temperate areas and grows most successfully on moist, fertile soils. It is common at altitudes of 300 to 800 metres and is a problem weed at higher altitudes in the Alpine National Park. Seedlings establish readily on sites where the soil has been disturbed or after fire, and can survive in shade. Successful establishment does not occur in existing dense broom stands. Seedlings require protection from drought and grazing. It Is a **Noxious Weed** in many areas.

**Bruisewort,** See Comfrey

**Buchu** (*Agathosma betulina; Barosma betulina*)

**Description**: This woody shrub produces slender stems of small, dark green, shiny, oval or round leaves. The aroma and taste are bitter and astringent. The small, star shaped flowers are white or pink.

**Influence:** Psychic Powers, Prophetic Dreams

**Gender**: Feminine, **Element**: Water, **Planet**: Moon

Drink an infusion of this plant to be able to tell the future. Mix with frankincense and burn right before bed to induce prophetic dreams. Burn only a small amount, and it must be in the bedroom.

**Cultivation**: This perennial herb is not readily available. Propagate either from seeds or cuttings. Grow established plants in a well drained, sunny, hot position. Minimum care is needed. Water on very hot days, or during dry spells. Buchu benefits from compost, but the use of fertilizer is not recommended.

**Buckeye,** See Horse Chestnut

**Buckthorn** (*Rhamnus* spp.)

**Description:** Buckthorn (Rhamnus alaternus) is a large, dense, evergreen shrub that grows to 4m. It is often found growing at the base of trees in which birds have perched and defecated the seeds. The leaves are a dark, glossy green while the underside is paler. The flowers which appear in early spring are small, pale green and rather inconspicuous. The berries (smooth, round and smaller than a pea) form clusters that ripen from green to red to black. It is native to the Mediterranean region.

**Influence:** Protection, Exorcism, Wishes, Legal Matters

**Gender:** Feminine, **Element:** Water, **Planet:** Saturn

Place the branches near doors and windows to drive away black magick. A legend states that if you sprinkle buckthorn in a circle and dance inside it under a Full Moon, an elf will appear. Before it runs away, say "Halt and grant my boon!" and it will grant you a wish.

Also carry or wear buckthorn for use in legal matters and for good luck.

**Cultivation**: The best growing area is in sun or partial shade. The shrub has no particular soil preference, transplants well and has a moderate growth rate. The mature height is 2 metres to 4 metrest, with a spread of 2 metres to 3 metres. The fruits are red, then black but not especially ornamental.

**Buckwheat** (*Fagopyrum* spp.)

**Description:** Buckwheat, is a quick growing summer crop traditionally grown across the northern hemisphere in Northern Europe, China, Mongolia and Japan. It produces black triangular starch-rich seeds, which are mainly used to produce products such as noodles and pancakes for human consumption. Although used for products such as noodles, it is not a true cereal but a broad - leafed crop related to docks and bindweeds.

**Influence:** Money, Protection

**Gender**: Feminine, **Element**: Earth, **Planet**: Venus

Make flour from the seeds and sprinkle around your house in a circle to keep evil from it. Add some grains of buckwheat to money incenses, and keep some in the kitchen to guard against poverty.

**Cultivation**: Buckwheat is sown in late spring and harvested late in summer. Buckwheat needs a temperate climate but is sensitive to frost. It needs irrigation, so regular water access is a priority. The soil type is not an issue - although better soils produce better crops.

**Buffalo grass,** See Sweetgrass

**Buglos**, See Borage

**Burdock** (*Arctium lappa*)

**Description:** Burdock, refers to any of a group of biennial thistles in the genus *Arctium*, family Asteraceae. Common Burdock (*A. minus*) grows wild throughout most of North America, Europe and Asia. Plants of the genus *Arctium* have dark green leaves that can grow up to 45 cm long. They are generally large, coarse and ovate, with the lower ones being heart-shaped. They are woolly underneath. Plants are cultivated for their slender roots, which can grow up to 1 meter long and 2 cm across. Burdock root is very crisp and has a sweet, mild, and pungent flavor. Immature flower stalks may also be harvested in late spring, before flowers appear; the taste resembles that of artichoke, to which the burdock is related.

**Influence:** Protection, Healing

**Gender**: Feminine, **Element**: Water, **Planet**: Venus

Carry as a protection sachet or burn for purification of the room, Rinse with a root decoction for ridding oneself of a gloomy feeling about yourself or others and to ward off all sorts of negativity, making it invaluable for protective amulets and sachets. Add to potpourri in the house. Burdock Root is used to treat skin diseases, boils, fevers, inflammations, hepatitis, swollen glands, and fluid retention. It is an excellent blood purifier. A tea made of the leaves of Burdock is also used for indigestion. Helps clear persistent teenage acne if taken for three to four weeks. Used with dandelion root for a very effective liver cleanser and stimulator.

**Cultivation**: Sow seed in spring; harvest autumn to the next spring when they go to seed. Burdock are INCREDIBLY hardy - actively growing with massive tops and roots and no watering whatsoever. As a root vegetable with a length of up to 1 metre sandy friable soils is preferred. They are heat and cold tolerant, and will even grow in poor shallow soil, though of course the roots won't be as long. Burdock runs to seed in their second spring, and the seeds are in big round cases.

**Burn Plant see** Aloe

**Buttons,** See Tansy

**Cabbage** (*Brassica oleracea*)

**Description:** Cabbage is a hardy vegetable that grows especially well in fertile soils. There are various shades of green available, as well as red or purple types. Head shape varies from the standard round to flattened or pointed. Most varieties have smooth leaves, but the Savoy types have crinkly textured leaves. Cabbage is easy to grow if you select suitable varieties and practice proper culture and insect management. Always regarded as a good source of vitamins, cabbage recently has been shown to have disease-preventive properties as well.

**Influence:** Luck

**Gender**: Feminine, **Element**: Water, **Planet**: Moon

Should be planted in the garden soon after a couple has been married if they wish to have good luck in their marriage and in the garden.

**Cultivation**: Cabbage is easily transplanted from either bare-root or cell-pack-grown plants. Late cabbage must be started during the heat of mid-summer, but it develops its main head during the cooling weather of fall. It may be transplanted or seeded directly in the garden. In summer, if possible, place seed flats or seedbeds where some protection from the sun is available, either natural or artificial. Try especially hard during this season to transplant on cloudy, overcast or rainy days for minimizing shock from the direct sun of summer. Space plants 30 cm to 60 cm apart in the row, depending upon the variety and the size of head desired. The closer the spacing, the smaller the heads

**Cactus**

**Description:** Cacti are a group of plants that are not only easy to grow, but offer a variety of shapes, color and form. They can be grown in any sunny, well-drained area. They require little maintenance. They make excellent houseplants and many hardy varieties may be grown outside.

**Influence:** Protection, Chastity

**Gender**: Male, **Element**: Water, **Planet**: Mercury

All cacti are protective because of their spines. Grow indoors to protect against burglaries, intrusions, and to absorb negativity. Outside, one cactus should be placed facing each direction to further protect the house. Cactus spines are sometimes used in Witch bottles and to mark symbols on candles and roots. Then, they are carried or buried to release their power (if you're going to carry a cactus thorn in your pocket, make sure you have thick pants!).

**Cultivation**: Cacti can be propagated from branches or offshoots. The offshoot should be removed from the plant and allowed to dry for 2 weeks. After the broken or cut edge has healed, plant it shallowly in dry medium. When taking a cutting from a stem section, use a clean, sharp knife. If you are taking several sections from one long stem, you must remember which was the top and the bottom of each piece, because a stem piece that is planted upside down will not grow. Cacti can also be grown from seed, and many seed companies offer packets of mixed varieties. These can be fun to grow if you can stand the suspense. Some cacti seed take a year to germinate, and it may take a few years to see what your young cacti will look like. Despite their slow germination, cacti are no more difficult to raise from seed than many half-hardy plants. Many can be flowered within 2 years or even earlier after sowing the seed. It's possible to get a fine collection within in a few years.

**Calamus** (*Acorus calamus*)

**Description:** Sweet flag is a grass-like, rhizome forming, perennial that can grow to 2 meters high, resembling an iris. This species inhabits perpetually wet areas like the edges of streams and around ponds and lakes, in ditches and seeps. The plants have long creeping roots that spread out just below the surface of the soil. These roots spread horizontally and can grow to almost 2 meters in length for old, well established specimens. The thick, erect leaves are very similar in appearance to those of an iris, but with edges that are crimped. Plants very rarely flower or set fruit, but when they do, the flowers are 3-8 cm long, cylindrical in shape, greenish brown and covered in a multitude of rounded spikes. The fruits are small and berry-like, containing few seeds. Flowers from early to late summer.

**Influence:** Luck, Healing, Money, Protection

**Gender**: Feminine, **Element**: Water, **Planet**: Moon

String the seeds as beads to use for healing, or put the powdered root in healing incenses and sachets. Small pieces of the root placed in all corners of the kitchen protect against hunger and poverty. Grow the plant to bring good luck, and use also to strengthen and bind spells.

**Cultivation**: It thrives best in a rich soil, but can be grown in shallow water on dry land. It is propagated by division of the rootstock in spring or fall. Pieces of the rhizome should be planted horizontally, and 3 -5 cm deep, 30 cm apart in each direction, with the leaf-shoots upward. They can be planted in marshes and at the edges of ponds and streams. They will do well in the garden if the soil is rich and is kept moist by frequent watering.

**Calendula see** Marigold

**Camellia** (*Camellia japonica*)

**Description:** An evergreen, large shrub or small tree, growing to around 5m tall and 4m wide in cultivation, but larger in its native habitat. The leaves are dark, glossy green with a paler reverse. The flowers, which range in colour from pure white to deep red, are produced from winter to spring. There are thousands of named cultivars and they vary in foliage and habit, as well as in flower size and form.

**Influence:** Riches

**Gender**: Feminine, **Element**: Water, **Planet**: Moon

Brings riches and luxuries, and is used in spells with these goals. Place fresh blossoms in vessels of water on the altar during money and prosperity rituals.

**Cultivation**: Camellias will grow in most areas apart from the hot tropics and inland. In areas with alkaline soils, they may need to be grown in containers with potting mix for acid loving plants. They prefer a slightly acid (pH 5.5-6.0), humus-rich soil with good drainage, and protection from direct sun and strong winds. Fertilise in spring with camellia and azalea food, and mulch with compost (such as composted autumn leaves) or milled cow manure. Keep well watered, particularly when it is hot and dry.

**Camphor** (*Cinnamomum Camphora*)

**Description:** Camphor Laurel (Cinnamomum camphora) is an attractive, fast growing tree. It originated in China and Japan, where its timber and oil are used in a variety of ways, including embalming and soap scent. The moth repellent properties of camphor have made it a popular wood for storage chests and natural history cabinets. Its spread as a weed has been facilitated by the popularity of its berries with birds. Unfortunately, many birds are feeding on camphor laurel berries in preference to the fruit of native Australian laurels which grow in rainforests. Camphor laurels suppress the growth of neighbouring plants, and have become monocultural forests in paddocks that were once dairy farms. They are also a big problem in creek beds and along river banks. They can clog up waterways, where their seeds germinate readily.

**Influence:** Chastity, Health, Divination

**Gender**: Feminine, **Element**: Water, **Planet**: Moon

Place beside the bed to lessen sexual desire. A bag of camphor, or the bark, hung around the neck prevents colds and flu. Sometimes used in divination incenses.

**Cultivation**: Some people still plant this tree, not realising its weed potential. If you need a large, fast-growing shade tree, seek advice from your local nursery, but don't plant camphor laurel in Australia.

**Cancer Jalap** see Poke

**Candleberry**, See Myrtle

**Caraway** (*Carum carvi*)

**Description:** Caraway is a biennial and grows to a height of up to 60 cm with a spread of 30 cm. It has a thick, tapering root like that of a parsnip. The leaves resemble those of carrots but tend to droop more. The flowers, in umbellifer clusters, are white tinged with pink and appear in mid summer. The oval seeds are pointed at each end and are very dark brown. It takes two years for caraway to mature and bear flowers. The stems of the delicate flowers produce seed cases, each containing two seeds.

**Influence:** Protection, Lust, Health, Anti-Theft, Mental Powers

**Gender**: Masculine, **Element**: Air, **Planet**: Mercury

Protects against evil spirits and negativity. an object which holds caraway seeds is theft proof. Used to encourage fidelity and to attract a mate. Strengthens the memory, and a small bag of the seeds placed in a child's bed protects him/her from illness. Carry in a sachet for protection, add with other appropriate herbs for love, and use in sleep pillows to help remember your dreams.

**Cultivation**: Seedlings do not transplant well, so sow in the garden in spring or autumn. Work the soil deeply, as caraway is deep-rooted. Germination is slow. It thrives in all but the most humid warm regions and does best from fall-sown seeds. The plants should be thinned so that they are about 15 cm apart. It needs well-drained soil and plenty of sun for the best flavour.

**Cardamom** (*Elettario Cardamomum*)

**Description**: This slow growing perennial is grown widely in warm-temperate to tropical gardens. Relatively drought resistant tree, which is indigenous to India and Ceylon bears violet-striped white flowers and aromatic green fruits on erect or trailing racemes.

**Influence:** Lust, Love

**Gender**: Feminine, **Element**: Water, **Planet**: Venus

Grind the seeds and add to warmed wine for a quick lust potion. Also baked into apple pies for the same purpose. The seeds are also added to love sachets and incenses.

**Cultivation**: Planted from seed, Cardamom likes it shady and moist and is frost tender. It grows well in the house with adequate light.

**Carnation** (*Dianthus carophyllus*)

**Description**: Carnations are a useful ornamental plant for the garden as well as being a favourite cut flower which makes it a valuable addition to commercial horticulture. Carnations are in the Caprifoliaceae family.

**Influence:** Protection, Strength, Healing Creativity, enhance magickal powers, achieve balance, Energy.

**Gender**: Masculine, **Element**: Fire, **Planet**: Sun

Light a scented candle, use in bath, place with other herbs for added energy, Burn flower tops for creativity. Used in healing spells. Add the dried blossoms to sachets and incenses for healing.

**Cultivation**: Plant cuttings with the 'crown' level with the soil surface. Plant 30cm apart in rich soil with excellent drainage however, keep soil moist. It prefers full sun and flowers in early to mid summer. It is frost hardy. Feed with well rotted manure or a slow release fertiliser.

**Carob** (*Jacaranda procera; Prosopis dulcis*)

**Description**: The carob tree is a slow growing, medium sized evergreen tree originating in the eastern Mediterranean. It is a member of the Legume (Pea) family and is the only member of the genus Ceratonia. It is a xerophilous scleophphyllous species well suited to dry infertile environments. The species is trioecious with male, female and hermaphrodite inflorescences and is often multi stemmed growing up to 15 meters in height. The production of fruit begins around the age of 15 and continues for the life of the plant. The leaves are broad, dark green and offering substantial shade. The pods are long and leathery often growing up to 300mm long.

**Influence:** Protection, Health

**Gender**: Masculine, **Element**: Fire, **Planet**: Mars

Carry or wear to maintain good health and to guard against evil.

**Cultivation**: Prior to planting Carob, pre-soak the seed in warm water for approximately 24hrs. This species prefers sandy loams, medium loam and clay loam soils but can tolerate poorer soil conditions including rocky areas. Good drainage and full to semi-sun is also prefered if the species is to grow well. Carob will tolerate pH in the range 6.2 to 8.6. This species is extremely drought resistant and irrigation is not required. It is also free of many pests and diseases, however it is susceptible to Texas Root Rot. After the plant has established itself it requires little maintenance except form pruning to encourage a single stem if required.

**Carragheen**, See Irish Moss

**Carrot** (*Dancus carota*)

**Description:** Carrots need no description for most of us, being a common root vegetable. Carrot - annual (cultivated varieties) or biennial (wild). Carrot has erect stem growing to 3 ft (1 m), feathery leaves, small white flowers, and flat green seeds. Cultivated subspecies have fleshy orange taproots. They grow three to four crops a year in temperate climates, and are best planted following a leafy crop such as cabbages.

**Influence:** Fertility, Lust

**Gender**: Masculine, **Element**: Fire, **Planet**: Mars

When eaten, the seeds help a woman become pregnant. Eat them to promote lust and to cure impotency.

**Cultivation**: They like a good friable soil at least 300mm deep, sow seeds after an above the ground crop such as tomatoes or cabbages. Sow seeds directly in the soil in rows twice the depth of the seed. Keep moist; don't let them dry out, especially in the summer. When the carrots starts to form, around four to six weeks they will need to be thinned out.

**Cascara Sagrada** (*Rhamnus Purshiana*)

**Description:** An evergreen tree growing to 10 M tall, Cascara has a wide, open crown with many stout branches. Its gray to dark brown bark is often reddish and scaly. Egg-shaped to oblong with a washboardy surface, the alternate deciduous leaves are a dark glossy green. Flowers are small and greenish-yellow, in umbrella shaped clusters of 8-50 buds.

**Influence:** Legal Matters, Money, Protection

**Gender**_____, **Element**_____, **Planet:** _____

Used in treating chronic constipation, and is a stimulant to the whole digestive system. It is a safe laxative, and is useful for treating intestinal gas, liver and gall bladder complaints, and enlarged liver. Sprinkled around the home before going to court, it will help you to win your case. It is used in money spells and in repelling evil and hexes.

**Cultivation**: Happy in dry to wet sites this tree is shade tolerant. It is often found growing with alder.

**Cashew** (*Anacardium occidentale*)

**Description:** Anacardium occidentale is a medium-sized tree, spreading, evergreen, much branched; grows to a height of 12 m. The root system of a mature A. occidentale, when grown from the seed, consists of a very prominent taproot and a well-developed and extensive network of lateral and sinker roots. Leaves simple, alternate, coriaceus, glabrous, obovate, rounded at ends, 10-18 x 8-15 cm, with short petiole, pale green or reddish when young and dark green when mature. The flower is a terminal panicle-like cluster commonly bearing male and hermaphroditic flowers. The male flowers are the most numerous and usually bear 1 exserted stamen and 9 small inserted ones. A. occidentale normally comes into flowering in 3 to 5 years. The nut, which is the true fruit, dries and does not split open. Inside the poisonous shell is a large curved seed, nearly 2.5 cm long, the edible cashew nut.

**Influence:** Money

**Gender:** Masculine, **Element:** Fire, **Planet:** Sun

Used in prosperity and money spells. The bark is utilised in South America as a contraceptive and the gum makes an insecticide. Tribal paints and indelible ink can be made from the juice of the fruit and the leaves give a yellow dye.

**Cultivation:** Cashew germinates slowly and poorly; several nuts are usually planted to the hole and thinned later. Propagation is generally by seeds, but may be vegetative from grafting, air-layering or inarching. Planting should be done in situ as cashew seedlings do not transplant easily. Recommended spacing is 10 x 10 m, thinned to 20 x 20 m after about 10 years, with maximum planting of 250 trees/ha. Once established, field needs little care. Intercropping may be done the first few years, with cotton, peanut, or yams. Fruits are produced after three years, during which lower branches and suckers are removed. Full production is attained by 10th year and continues to bear until about 30 years old.

**Castor** (*Ricinus communis*)  **POISONOUS**

**Description:** In frost-free areas, castor bean is an evergreen herbaceous or semiwoody large shrub or small tree that gets up to 40 ft (12 m) tall and 15ft (4.6 m) wide. In the tropics, it can have a trunk that is woody near the base and up to 30 cm in diameter. Elsewhere, castor bean plant grows as an annual that can get 2.4 - 4.6 m tall in a single growing season. This is a fast growing, suckering, colony forming plant with decidedly tropical looking foliage. They tend to grow straight up at first, developing branches only later in the season. The flower is not particularly showy; small, 1 cm wide greenish yellow flowers are borne in fat spikes 20 – 40 cm tall near the tops of the stems. Female flowers are on the top half of the spike and have conspicuous red stigmas whilst the male flowers on the lower half of the spike have conspicuous yellow anthers. The female flowers are followed by reddish brown egg-shaped capsules, about an 2.5 cm long, thickly covered with soft flexible spines. Each capsule contains three seeds that look like fat swollen dog ticks and are **deadly poisonous**.

**Influence:** Protection

**Gender:** Masculine, **Element:** Fire, **Planet:** Sun

Castor beans are good protection against the evil eye and all negativity because they absorb evil.

**Cultivation**: Castor is propagated entirely by seed treated to resist disease. Seeds retain their viability 2–3 years. After seedbed has been deeply cultivated, seeds of dwarf cultivars are planted 3.7–7.5 cm deep in rows 1 m apart; seeds about 25 cm apart in the rows or for larger cultivars, seeds are planted 60 by 90 cm apart, 2–4 seeds per hole, and then thinned to one plant. Cultivate shallowly until 0.6–0.9 m high. Castor exhausts the soil quickly. Leaves, stalks and seed hulls are disked into the field following harvest. Normally irrigation commences after plants have 6–8 leaves

**Catchweed**, See Bedstraw

**Catmint, See Catnip**

**Catnip** (*Nepeta cataria*)

**Description:** Catnip is a perennial herb of the mint family. Its erect, square, branching stem is hairy and grows from 1.2 – 2 metres high. The oblong or cordate, pointed leaves have scalloped edges and grey or whitish hairs on the lower side. The flowers are white with purple spots and grow in spikes.

**Influence:** Cat Magick, Love, Beauty, Happiness

**Gender**: Feminine, **Element**: Water, **Planet**: Mars

Happiness, Animal Magick, Psychic Enhancement, Healing Pets. Use as a tea for happiness and increasing the pet healing. Can also be used as a relaxant during meditation, burn dried leaves for love wishes. If you feed your cat some catnip, it will build a psychic bond between you and your cat! You can also make a pink sachet and fill it with Catnip to wear or carry to draw love to you. Grow some in your home, aside from pleasing your cat, it will draw positive vibrations and good luck to you and to your house. Hung over the door, it attracts good spirits and great luck. Used in spells designed to enhance beauty and happiness.

**Cultivation**: It is easily cultivated in any garden soil, with little care, as the plant does not require the moisture that most mint plants need. Plants should be grown from seed sown where they are going to stand. Bruised or recently transplanted plants are likely to be eaten by cats unless protected. The seed should be sown very thinly in rows 50 cm apart and the seedlings thinned out to 50 cm apart in the rows. It requires almost no care except occasional weeding. A bed will last several years. It can also be propagated by division of the roots in spring.

**Catsfoot**, See Ground Ivy

**Cattail** *(Typha Spp.)*

**Description:** The cattail genus (Typha spp.) is an erect, perennial freshwater aquatic herb, which can grow 3 or more meters in height. The linear cattail leaves are thick, ribbon-like structures, which have a spongy cross-section exhibiting air channels. The subterranean stem arises from thick creeping rhizomes.

**Influence:** Lust

**Gender**: Masculine, **Element**: Fire, **Planet**: Mars

If a woman carries some Cattail with her at all times it will cure her frigidity.

**Cultivation:** Cattail can be propagated by either seed or vegetative met hods. Best growth over spring and summer months whilst the plant dies off during autumn and winter.

## Cedar (*Cedrus libani* or *C.* spp.)

**Description:** This is a large stately evergreen, with a massive trunk when mature, and wide-sweeping, sometimes upright branches (more often horizontal) which originate on the lower trunk. Allow plenty of space for proper development. Dark green needles and cones, which are held upright above the foliage, add to the impressive appearance. Young specimens retain a pyramidal shape but the tree takes on a more open form with age. Like most true cedars, it does not like to be transplanted, and prefers a pollution-free, sunny environment.

**Influence:** Healing, Purification, Money, Protection

**Gender**: Masculine, **Element**: Fire, **Planet**: Sun

Made into a purifying incense. Hanging cedar in the home prevents against lightning strikes. Keeping a piece of cedar in your wallet or purse draws money, and it is also used in money incenses. Can be burned to induce psychic powers or to purify an area.

**Cultivation**: Seeds should be sown in light, sandy soil in a propagating house or frame. When they are large enough to handle, the seedlings are planted in a nursery border outside about 7 - 8 cm apart in rows 4 metres apart. They are transplanted every two years while they are young. Varieties that won't come true from seed should be grafted in the spring on stocks of their respective types. The stocks must be established in pots and the grafted plants placed in a closed propagating frame until the union is complete. They will thrive in almost any good, well-drained soil from acid sand to clay and limestone. The best soil is one that is light, well-drained, loam and peat.

## Celandine (*Chelidonium majus*)  **POISONOUS**

**Description:** Perennial herb, growing to 0.5m by 0.4m and developing a thick, fleshy, bright-orange taproot. Rosette of basal, attractively lobed, dark green imparipinnate leaves to 40cm long. Thin, leafy, hairy stems, bear a terminal cluster of bright-yellow, four-petalled flowers 2cm in diameter, followed by fine seed capsules to 5cm long, bearing 12-20 brown, pin-head size seeds. As soon as the capsules are dry, the seeds are released and self-seed readily, around the parent plant. To collect seed, the capsules need to be picked, as they mature to a yellow/brown colour, so that the seeds do not drop. **The whole plant is poisonous**

**Influence:** Protection, Escape, Happiness, Legal Matters

**Gender**: Masculine, **Element**: Fire, **Planet**: Sun

Use when feeling trapped in a undue negative situation, wear as an amulet for protection and happiness. This plant helps in escaping wrongful imprisonment and entrapments of every kind: Wear next to the skin and replace every three days. Celandine also creates joy and happiness when worn, and it cures depression. Also wear to court to win the favour of judge or jury, or as a protective herb.

**Cultivation**: It is in flower from mid autumn to mid winter, and the seeds ripen through to early spring. The flowers are hermaphrodite and are pollinated by Bees, flies and beetles. The plant is self-fertile. The plant can grow in full shade through to full sun. It requires moist soil.

**Celery** (*Apium graveolens*)

**Description:** Celery, Apium graveolens L., is an annual or biennial member of the family Apiaceae native to Eurasia, occurring in wild habitats in saline soils near coastal regions. Celery is one of the oldest vegetables ever used in recorded history. The ancient Egyptians were known to gather wild celery from marshy seaside areas for food. Celery is a plant of many uses and little waste; the leaves and dried seeds make good seasoning; the outer ribs are best cooked and the inner ribs may be consumed raw because they are good for the heart.

**Influence:** Mental Powers, Lust, Psychic Powers

**Gender**: Masculine, **Element**: Fire, **Planet**: Mercury

Induces sleep when put in pillows, and chew the seeds to aid in concentration. Eating the stalk induces lust.

**Cultivation**: Native to Britain and other European countries, celery is often found growing wild along the English and Welsh coasts, and in marshlands. Widely grown as a vegetable, cultivated celery is less fragrant than the wild variety. Celery is propagated from seed in spring and harvested from midsummer to autumn. Stalks should be protected from the light to promote tall growth.

**Centaury** (*Centaurium* spp.)

**Description:** Centaury - annual with erect, square stem from 15-30cm(6-12in) that branches near the top. The leaves at the base of the stem form a rosette; the stem leaves are smaller, pale green, lance-shaped and arranged in pairs at intervals. From late summer to mid-autumn the stem is crowned with clusters of attractive rosy pink, star-like flowers with yellow stamens.

**Influence:** Snake Removing

**Gender**: Masculine, **Element**: Fire, **Planet**: Sun

The smoke from this burning herb drives away snakes.

**Cultivation**: Typical growing conditions are full sun and a moist soil that contains loam, clay-loam, or gravelly material. A limy soil and occasional flooding are tolerated. The blooming period occurs during the summer and early autumn and lasts about 2-3 months. As older flowers begin to fade away, ovoid seed capsules are formed. Each seed capsule is open at the top and has 5 recurved teeth along its upper rim. Each of these capsules contains several tiny seeds that can be blown about by the wind or float on water. The root system consists of shallow fibrous roots. This plant spreads by reseeding itself.

**Chamomile** (*Anthemis nobilis* or *chamaemelum noblis*)

**Description:** *Anthemis nobilis* is a perenial of creeping habit - the herb growing to a height of 30cm with flower spikes during the flowering season (July, August) to 45cm. Both the flower and upper parts of the green herb contain an essential oil which gives the plant its characteristic odour. The foliage is of a dark green sometimes almost greyish colour with a much branched 'feathery' appearence. The flowers are characterised by their flattened corolla which is easily disinguished from the dome shaped corrolla of *Matricaria recutica*

**Influence:** Money, Sleep, Love, Purification

**Gender**: Masculine, **Element**: Water, **Planet**: Sun

Used to attract money, and in sleep and meditation incenses. It is a purifying and protective herb. Drink Chamomile tea whenever you need to get a good night's sleep. Chamomile is useful in spells for luck and gambling as well. Make a green amulet and fill with Chamomile Flowers to carry as a good-luck amulet.

**Cultivation**: Sow seed in trays, pots, etc of good seed compost in a propagator or warm place to maintain an optimum temperature of 18-20C. Surface sow and do not exclude light. Germination usually takes 14-30 days. Transplant seedlings when large enough to handle into 7.5 cm pots. Acclimatise young plants to outdoor conditions before planting out 30 cm apart in full sun. Prefers well drained soil.

**Checkerberry,** see Wintergreen

**Cherry** (*Prunus avium*)

**Description:** There are many cultivars and imported relatives, some with very large, showy blossoms and others producing very good cherries for eating. Wild cherry, also known as bird cherry, is very attractive when in bloom and its autumn fruits - when you are able to gather them before the birds do - are good to eat. Growing to a maximum height of around 25 metres, and with a preference for lime-rich soil, *Prunus avium* grows with a neat rounded crown and a straight trunk.

**Influence:** Love, Divination

**Gender**: Feminine, **Element**: Water, **Planet**: Venus

Used to stimulate or attract love. To find love, tie a single strand of your hair to a blossoming cherry tree. Cherry juice can substitute for blood in old recipes.

**Cultivation**: Cherry trees are very particular about their climate. They don't like long hot summers and need a chilling out period during the winter; however, they don't like late frosts! Cherries are best planted as immature trees, though growing from seed is possible, if slow. Soil Ph should be between 6.2 and 6.8. Check and adjust accordingly. Land must be well-drained. Cherry trees can't tolerate wet feet. As a rule sour cherries - the wilder varieties - are self-pollinating. Sweet cherries generally need cross-pollination and should be planted near a compatible variety.

**Chestnut** (*Castanea* spp.)

**Description:** Chestnut (Castanea sp.) contains about 7 to 12 species distributed in: North America, Europe and Asia. European Chestnut (Castanea sativa) was introduced into England by the Romans probably as food for domestic animals. Chestnuts grow to heights of 40 metres. Its ability to sprout from the cut or dead stump has kept this species in existence.

**Influence:** Love

**Gender**: Masculine, **Element**: Fire, **Planet**: Jupiter

Used to remove obstacles in your life. If you anoint your body with chicory juice, you will obtain favors from great persons. Carry it to promote frugality.

**Cultivation**: In the past, chestnuts have been grown from seedlings. This has resulted in a lot of trees which produce poor quality nuts. This problem can be overcome by planting only grafted trees. Grafting of chestnuts is relatively simple and good results can be obtained with a little practice. Softwood and hardwood cuttings have also been used to produce chestnut trees. Collect seed at harvest time and keep it moist until germination takes place. Place the seed between layers of sand or a similar medium and water it regularly. Keep the medium moist but not wet. Plant the germinated seeds 50mm to 80mm deep and 200mm to 250mm apart in nursery rows which are between 0.75m and 1m apart. A seedling normally takes two years to grow big enough for budding or grafting (at least 10mm in diameter, or pencil thickness).

## Chickweed (*Stellaria media*)

**Description:** Chickweed is an annual, but is somewhat unusual in that it often germinates in autumn (though it also germinates year-round), and hangs on through the winter, flowering and setting seed in the early spring, and dying off by summer. It's at its best in the spring and autumn, as it greatly prefers cool and damp conditions, and will not survive where it's dry and hot.

**Influence:** Fertility, Love

**Gender**: Feminine, **Element**: Water, **Planet**: Moon

Chickweed is an excellent source of many B vitamins and various minerals. It is used to treat bronchitis, pleurisy, coughs, colds, and as a blood builder. Externally it is good for skin diseases, and the tea added to the bath is good for soothing skin irritations and rashes. Chickweed is carried and/or used in spells to attract love and to maintain a relationship

**Cultivation**: Chickweed is a prolific seed producer and quickly becomes a problem for most gardeners. Seeds remain viable for several seasons.

## Chicory (*Cichorium intybus*)

**Description:** Chicory (*Cichorium intybus*) is a perennial herb with flowers that are usually blue. It grows to between 90 cm and 120 cm in height. It is originally from the Old World and was naturalized in North America, where it is seen as a rank, roadside weed. Its roots may be used as a substitute for coffee. It is also used as a flavoring in coffee.

**Influence:** Removing Obstacles, Invisibility, Favours, Frugality

**Gender**: Masculine, **Element**: Air, **Planet**: Sun

Used to remove obstacles in your life. If you anoint your body with chicory juice, you will obtain favors from great persons. Carry it to promote frugality.

**Cultivation**: Seed is the only means of increase. Choose a sunny, well-drained location to which organic material and a complete fertiliser have been added. Sow seeds in spring where they are to grow and thin out later. To make the leaves more palatable, the roots of established plants (foliage removed) are dug up and replanted into deep boxes of moist medium. As the "witloof" grows up through the sand the leaves are blanched and the flavour becomes much milder.

## Chilli Pepper (*Capsicum* spp.)

**Description:** All peppers grow on 45 cm to 60 cm tall handsome, bushy plants. Use plants as temporary low informal hedge, or grow and display them in containers. The two basic kinds of peppers are sweet and hot. Sweet peppers always remain mild, even when flesh ripens to red. Hot peppers range from tiny (pea-size) types to narrow, 15 cmt to 20 cm long forms, but all are pungent, their flavour ranging from the mild heat of Italian peperoncini to the near-incandescence of the 'Habanero'. 'Anaheim' is a mild but spicy pepper used for making canned green chillies.

**Influence:** Fidelity, Hex Breaking, Love

**Gender**: Masculine, **Element**: Fire, **Planet**: Mars

To keep your mate faithful, buy two large dried chilli peppers. Cross them and tie them together with a red or pink ribbon and place them beneath your pillow. Scatter red pepper around the house to break curses. Also used in love spells.

**Cultivation**: Seeds can be collected from chilli's that you favour. You can either cut the chilli open and carefully separate the seeds from the fruit pods or dry the entire chilli pod. Plant seeds 5 to 6 weeks before the last frost of the season. Use peat pots to plant in. These are small 5 cm – 8 cm deep pots that are made out of compressed peat moss. When your seedlings are a 5 cm tall and have developed secondary leaves and all danger of frost is past then it is time to plant in the sunniest part of your garden, you can't over do sunshine. Chilli plants like a long thorough drink of water and then do best if they are allowed to dry out and get thirsty before getting watered again.

## China Berry (*Melia azederach*)  **<u>POISONOUS</u>**

**Description:** The Chinaberry or Bead Tree (*Melia azedarach*), is a deciduous tree in the mahogany family Meliaceae, native to India and southern China. It is also occasionally known as Persian Lilac, White Cedar and other names. The genus *Melia* includes four other species, occurring from southeast Asia to northern Australia. They are all deciduous or semi-evergreen small trees. The adult tree has a rounded to upright top, and measures between 7 and 12 metres in height. The flowers are small and fragrant, with five pale purple or lilac petals, growing in clusters. The fruit is a drupe, marble-sized, light yellow at maturity, hanging on the tree all winter, and gradually becoming almost white. The leaves are up to 50 cm long, alternate, long-petioled, 2 or 3 times compound (odd-pinnate); the leaflets are dark green above and lighter green below, with serrate margins. The flowers are unattractive to bees and butterflies. The hard, spherical seeds were widely used for making rosaries and other products requiring beads, before their replacement by modern plastics.

**Influence:** Luck

**Gender**_____. **Planet:** _____. **Element**_____.

The seeds of this plant are used as good luck charms and are carried to bring a change into your life

**Cultivation**: Today it is considered an invasive species there, but nurseries continue to sell the trees, and seeds are also widely available. It is planted in temperate and subtemperate areas around the world.

**Chinese Parsley see** Coriander

## Chrysanthemum (*Anacylus pyrethrum*)

**Description:** The chrysanthemum, also known as the mum, is a flowering perennial plant of the genus *Chrysanthemum* in the daisy family (Asteraceae). The flowers occur in various forms, and can be daisy-like, decorative, pompons or buttons. This genus contains many hybrids developed for horticultural purposes. In addition to the traditional yellow, other colours are available, such as white, purple, and red.

**Influence:** Protection. Promotes mental health, Sobriety

**Gender**: Masculine. **Planet**: Sun. **Element**: Fire.

Use in rituals of death and dying. Drink an infusion of this herb to cure drunkenness. Wearing the flowers protects against the wrath of the Gods, and grown in the garden, it protects from evil spirits.

**Cultivation**: Chrysanthemums prefer fertile, highly organic, well-drained soil in full sun. Mature plants set in a shady area will give nice colour the first year but do very poorly the following year. The right amount of water is vital to success with chrysanthemums. Too little water will slow their growth or stop it completely. Mums especially need plenty of water when they bloom. Give plenty of water to field-grown mums to prevent wilting until they re-establish a good root system. Mums are heavy feeders. A weekly application of soluble fertilizer is a good practice. Mulch will help retain soil moisture, control weeds and improve appearance. Chrysanthemums can be planted in the autumn or in early spring. Spring planted mums will give a more robust, full plant for the fall landscape. Pinch the tip growth of spring-planted mums regularly to cause them to branch and bloom well.

**Church Steeples,** See Burdock

**Cilantro,** See Coriander

**Cinnamon** (*Cinnamonum zeylanicum*)

**Description:** Native to Sri Lanka, and southern India, cinnamon is a beautiful evergreen tree growing to 10 metres or more, with a bushy canopy of glossy, ovate-lanceolate 7cm long leaves. Tiny, cream coloured flowers form in clusters on the end of stems, followed by small, brown seed capsules with one brown, oval seed. All new growth on the tree is a vivid, vibrant red, which makes the tree quite stunning in appearance several times a year. The red leaves, called a flush, mature into bright green leaves, which are fragrant when crushed.

**Influence:** Spirituality, Success, Healing, Power, Psychic Powers, Lust, Protection, Love, Empower with tourmaline.

**Gender**: Masculine. **Planet**: Sun. **Element**: Fire. **Deities**: Venus, Aphrodite

Cinnamon is a wonderful herb to either burn as an incense or make into a sachet. When burned as an incense, it raises high spiritual vibrations, enhancing skills of prophecy through channelling, working through an oracle, or through divination. Fill a green or gold sachet with Cinnamon to draw money and success or to use as a healing charm. A purple sachet can be used to increase your magickal and/or psychic powers. A pink or red sachet of Cinnamon can be worn, carried with you, or placed under your bed to draw love or to promote lust. Use a white sachet filled with Cinnamon to increase your spirituality and to confer protection.

**Cultivation**: Propagation of cinnamon is by cuttings as well as layers. For raising cinnamon from cuttings; semi hardwood cuttings of about 10 cm length with 2 leaves are taken and dipped in a rooting hormone and planted either in polythene bags filled with sand or a in sand beds raised in a shaded place. The cuttings in polythene bags must also be kept in a shaded place or in a nursery. The cuttings are to be watered regularly 2-3 times a day in order to maintain adequate moisture and prevent wilting. Rooting takes place in 45-60 days. The well rooted cuttings can be transplanted to polythene bags filled with potting mixture and maintained in a shaded place and watered regularly.

Cinnamon can also be propagated through seeds. In such cases variability is observed among the seedlings. The fully ripened fruits are either picked up from the tree or the fallen ones are collected from the ground. The seeds are removed from the fruits, washed free of pulp, and sown without much delay as the seeds have a low viability. The seeds are sown in sand beds or polythene bags containing a mixture of sand, well rotten cattle manure and soil (3: 3: 1). The seeds start to germinate within 15-20 days. Frequent irrigation is required for maintaining adequate moisture. The seedlings require artificial shading till they are about 6 months old.

## Cinquefoil (*Potentilla canadensis* or *P. reptans*)

**Description:** The Shrubby Cinquefoil, *Potentilla fruticosa,* is a small, low maintenance, deciduous shrub which is an excellent addition to a butterfly garden.
The yellow or pink buttercup-like flowers first appear on this 30 cm – 1.2 metre tall shrub in summer and will continue to brighten your landscape until the first frosts of autumn.

**Influence:** Love, Healing, Flying, Protection, Break Hexes

**Gender**: Masculine. **Planet**: Jupiter. **Element**: Fire.

The five points of the leaves represent love, money, health, power, and wisdom. If carried when asking favours, all these will be granted. Good for love magick and to promote an abundant harvest. Contains the energy to manifest one's ideas. An ingredient in mediaeval flying ointments. Hang at the door or place on the bed for protection. If you make an infusion of the leaves and bathe your forehead and hands in it nine times, it will wash away hexes. Placing a cinquefoil sprig with seven leaflets under your pillow will allow you to dream of a future lover. A bag of cinquefoil suspended from the bed ensures restful sleep. This plant is also added to purificatory bath sachets.

**Cultivation**: Potentillas prefer well-drained, reasonably rich soil, but will tolerate clay, rocky, or slightly alkaline soils as well. They are a quite durable plant, tolerating drought, flooding, extreme cold, and will easily survive transplanting. Potentillas should be planted in a sunny area, which receives light shade in the hottest part of the day to prevent the flower colour from fading. They are hardy in areas as cold, however they will not perform very well in warmer climates. Propagation can be accomplished by division in the Spring, softwood cuttings in the Summer, or from seeds sown in the Autumn. Prune out the oldest stems in late winter to prevent the plant from becoming leggy.

## Citron (*Citrus medica*)

**Description:** The citrois is a small evergreen tree or shrub growing to a height of about 3 metres; it has irregular straggling spiny branches, large pale-green broadly oblong, slightly serrate leaves and generally unisexual flowers purplish without and white within, the large fruit ovate or oblong, protuberant at the tip, and from 5 to 6 in. long, with a rough, furrowed, adherent rind, the inner portion of which is thick, white and fleshy, the outer, thin, greenish-yellow and very fragrant. The pulp is sub-acid and edible, and the seeds are bitter. There are many varieties of the fruit, some of them of great weight and size.

**Influence:** Psychic Powers, Healing

**Gender:** Masculine, **Element:** Air, **Planet:** Sun

Eat a citron to increase psychic powers. Use in healing spells and incenses.

**Cultivation:** Citron trees are grown readily from cuttings taken from branches 2 to 4 years old and quickly buried deeply in soil without defoliation. For quicker growth, the citron may be budded onto rough lemon, grapefruit, sour orange or sweet orange but the fruits do not attain the size of those produced from cuttings, and the citron tends to overgrow the rootstock.

**Cleavers,** See Bedstraw

**Clover** (*Trifolium* spp.)

**Description:** Clover (*Trifolium*) is a genus of about 300 species of plants in the pea family Fabaceae. They are found chiefly in northern temperate regions, but also, like many other north temperate genera, on the mountains in the tropics. The plants are small annual or perennial herbs with trifoliate (rarely 5- or 7-foliate) leaves, with stipules adnate to the leaf-stalk, and heads or dense spikes of small red, purple, white, or rarely yellow flowers; the small, few-seeded pods are enclosed in the calyx. Most *Trifolium* spp. have simple taproots; some also have stolons or rhizomes that extend the life of the plant. The heavy root systems of clovers improve soil tilth and life, increase water-holding capacity, and deepen the soil to enhance drainage

**Influence:** Protection, Love, Money, Fidelity, Exorcism, Success

**Gender:** Masculine, **Element:** Earth, **Planet:** Mercury

If two leaved, you will soon find a lover. The three-leafed type is used for protection, carry as a sachet or amulet. The four-leafed type is used as an amulet or sachet for luck and for keeping your head about you it also helps men avoid military service, protects against madness, strengthens psychic powers, and helps in detecting the presence of spirits. Five leaves attracts money. White clover works against hexes, while red is used in lust potions and is sprinkles around to remove evil. All keep snakes away from your property when grown.

**Cultivation:** Seed clovers using an alfalfa drill or disk to prepare seedbed, broadcast seed. Clover seed should be placed no more that 1/2 in deep because seeds are small and seedlings will be unable to reach the soil surface for development if buried too deeply. Smooth, firm seedbeds, with few large clods, can assist in maintaining uniformly shallow seeding

**Cloves** (*Syzygium aromaticum* or *Caryophyllus aromaticus*)

**Description:** The clove tree is an evergreen, which grows to a height ranging from 10-20 metres, having large oval leaves and crimson flowers in numerous groups of terminal clusters. The flower buds are at first of a pale color and gradually become green, after which they develop into a bright red, when they are ready for collecting. Cloves are harvested when 1.5-2 cm long, and consist of a long calyx, terminating in four spreading sepals, and four unopened petals which form a small ball in the centre.

**Influence:** Protection, Exorcism, Love, Money. Clearing your head

**Gender:** Masculine, **Element:** Fire, **Planet:** Sun

Burn cloves as an incense to draw wealth and prosperity, drive away hostile and negative forces, produce positive spiritual vibrations, and purify the area in which they are burned. Wear or carry cloves to draw members of the opposite sex to you. Using cloves in your magickal spells is said to ensure that your magickal intention is realized. Also, said to protect babies in their cribs if hung over them strung together.

**Cultivation**: Cloves tree thrives best with insular maritime climates in the tropics at low altitudes. Continuously humid climates are not so suitable. In the original habitat, where the trees are semi-wild, annual rainfall is 218 – 355 cm and temperatures 24 – 33°C. Drier weather is desirable for harvesting and drying the crop. The best soils for cloves are deep, sandy, red and acid-loams. Good deep drainage is essential and water logging is fatal. Seedlings are raised immediately after harvesting because the seed may lose its viability within few weeks. Hulled washed seeds produce better seedlings than un-hulled seeds. Propagation is usually carried out in shaded nurseries and then transplanted into the field . Clove plants are notoriously difficult to propagate vegetatively. The young plants grow slowly and juvenile phase lasts about 4 years. Clove yields increase until the tree is about 20 years and it will be productive until 80 years.

**Club Moss** (*Lycopodium clavatum*)

**Description:** Club Moss, is a mosslike plant, an evergreen fern growing to 10 cm by 1 metre that is in leaf all year. It exists already for ages on this planet in an almost unaltered form; Lycopodium clavatum has proven to survive many changes in climate and environment.

**Influence:** Protection, Power

**Gender**: Feminine, **Element**: Water, **Planet**: Moon

When gathered correctly, this herb gives protection, power, and blessings from the Gods. The correct way to gather club moss: take a purification bath in a running stream, offer bread and wine to the plant, then uproot it with your pinky or a silver blade.

**Cultivation**: Thrives in a rough spongy peat in a shady position. Requires a humid atmosphere. Terrestrial members of this genus are hard to establish. The roots are delicate and liable to rot, most water being absorbed through the foliage. This species is said to be a native of Britain and possibly a tropical plant It is reported to be hardy to at least -15°c.

**Coakum** see Poke

**Cocklebur,** See Burdock

**Cockup Hat,** See Stillengia

**Coconut** (*Cocos nucifera*)

**Description:** The coconut palm is a long-lived plant that may live as long as 100 years; it has a single trunk, 20-30 m tall, its bark is smooth and grey, marked by ringed scars left by fallen leaf bases.The leaves, from 4 to 6 m long, are pinnate; they consist of linear-lanceolate, more or less recurved, rigid, bright green leaflets. The inflorescences, arising at leaf axils and enveloped by a carinate spathe, are unbranched spadices; female flowers are borne basally, male flowers at apex. Flowers bear lanceolate petals, 6 stamens and an ovary consisting of 3 connate carpels. Its fruit can be carried long distances by water while keeping its germinability for a long time. Inside it contains one seed, rich in reserve substances located in the endosperm which is partly liquid (**coconut milk**), partly solid (**flesh**). When its embryo germinates, its radicle breaks through one of the three germinating pores, visible from the outside as well.

**Influence:** Purification, Protection, Chastity

**Gender**: Feminine, **Element**: Water, **Planet**: Moon

Used in chastity spells and protection rituals. To protect your property, halve a coconut, drain it of its juice, fill with protective herbs, seal shut, and bury it. Hang a whole coconut in your home for the same purpose.

**Cultivation**: To start a coconut from the seed, it is best to have the outer fibrous husk intact. Get a 20-litre pot. Use high quality nursery soil mixed with 40% coarse sand. Add drainage rocks to the bottom of the pot. Lay your coconut husk on the ground and see what way it wants to rest. Plant your coconut husk 1/2 way into the soil in the same position. You can leave the pot in the sun or the shade. Water lightly to keep very lightly moist. Partial shade will likely be more successful. Be patient, it is common for many palms to take many months to sprout. Don't over water as you'll rot them out. Your coconut will first split its husk at the bottom and send down some roots. It may take several months before your coconut also splits the top of the husk pushing up its first fronds. In other words, your coconut will be growing and you won't even know it until it splits the top. After your coconut spouts it can live in your 20-litre pot, for about 3-6 months. After that, plant it out or in another larger pot or directly into the soil. Incorporate lots of manure. Fertilize properly starting after sprouting 3 fronds.

**Cohosh, Black** (*Cimicifuga racemosa*)

**Description:** A member of the *Ranunculaceae* family, Black Cohosh spans up to one metre and can reach a height of 2.5 metres when it flowers, in late spring to early summer. Its leaves have toothed margins and are divided into three lobed leaflets. Its foliage is lush, and its attractive flowers are cream-colored and fragrant. Roots and rhizomes are thick, knotty and very dark. Black Cohosh is native to the eastern woodlands of North America and ranges from southern Canada south to Georgia, across to Arkansas and up to Wisconsin. It's more abundant in its southern range. Black Cohosh is one of 15 species of *Cimicifuga* found worldwide.

**Influence:** Love, Courage, Protection, Potency

Black Cohosh leaves laid around a room is said to drive away bugs, and to drive away negativity. Use in love sachets and add an infusion to the bath to cure impotency. Carry black cohosh to strengthen courage. Make an infusion of this herb and sprinkle around a room or add to the bath to drive away the presence of evil.

**Gender:** Masculine, **Element**_____, **Planet:** _____

**Cultivation**: Black Cohosh is easiest to grow from root divisions, which are done best in the spring or autumn. It can be planted immediately after dividing or, if purchased, immediately after receiving the roots. Roots purchased in autumn can be healed for a spring planting. Growing Black Cohosh from seed is harder, and seeds are not readily available. Black Cohosh grows best in rich, fertile soil. It does not like prolonged drought and should be irrigated under dry conditions. Composting the planting area is recommended.

**Coltsfoot** (*Tussilago Farfara*)

**Description:** Perennial growing to 0.22m by 1m at a fast rate. Coltsfoot is one of the earliest of the spring wildflowers, growing 10 cm to 45 cm high. The flower heads, which bloom from early late winter through early summer, are yellow and remind one of dandelions. The stalks of the flower have brown-tipped scales, and the large leaves are broadly heart-shaped and toothed. The underside of the leaves have downy white hairs, and become aromatic after the flowers are in bloom. It is a perennial plant found growing wild in wet areas of the United States, Europe, and in the East Indies

**Influence:** Love, Tranquility, Visions

**Gender**: Feminine, **Element**: Water, **Planet**: Venus

Add to love sachets, and use in spells of peace and tranquility. When smoked, the leaves can cause visions (although it is not advisable!).

**Cultivation**: Coltsfoot spreads by underground rhizomes, which develop mainly in the plow layer. It is not a prolific seed producer compared to many annual weeds. Each flower head produces only a few hundred seeds. Coltsfoot is a perennial that prefers damp, clay soils. It grows 12 cm to 45 cm high, and likes full to partial sun.

## Columbine (*Aquilegia canadensis*)

**Description:** The Columbine is a delicate but hardy perennial which typically grows to heights of 30 cm – 60 cm tall from a slender and highly branched stem. The stem is frequented with both basal and alternate type leaves that are compound and grow in divisions of three. The classic appeal of the Columbine is largely attributed to its showy arrangement of spurred flowers which appear in shades of bright red and yellow. The flowers have regular parts up to 5 cm long that alternate with five reddish sepals. The flower petals are red with yellow lips and project backwards into long hollow spurs, sweetened with nectar for hungry pollinators. The fruit of the Columbine occurs in five erect follicles and contains shiny black seeds .

**Influence:** Love, Courage

Carry the herb to strengthen courage. Pulverize the seeds and anoint yourself with the resulting oil to attract love.

**Gender:** Feminine, **Element:** Water, **Planet:** Venus

**Cultivation**: Easily grown in average, medium wet, well-drained soil in full sun to part shade. Wide range of soil tolerance as long as drainage is good. Prefers rich, moist soils in light to moderate shade. Freely self-seeds and will naturalize to form large colonies in optimum growing conditions.

## Comfrey (*Symphytum officinale*)

**Description:** Plant origin, Asia and Europe; a perennial growing from a thick, fleshy, brown-skinned root system, that can delve deeply into the sub-soil in search of moisture and minerals. Oblonglanceolate, dark green leaves, 50-120cm long, with long, round-grooved, petiole stems. The whole plant is covered with short hairs that give a rough feel when touched. Flowers form as coiling, terminal racemes in colours of mauve, blue or pink.

**Influence:** Magickal healing, Safety, Money

**Gender**: Feminine. **Planet**: Saturn. **Element**: Water.

Worn or carried, it ensures safety during travel. The root is used in money spells.

**Cultivation**: As comfrey rarely sets seed, it is generally propagated by division of roots; in fact, each piece of broken root has potential to shoot. Plant in a permanent position, as comfrey can have a very long life. Comfrey prefers humus-enriched soil (abounding in aerobic bacteria, fungi and micro-elements) to artificial fertilisers. It likes a slightly alkaline soil at pH 7.2 but will also grow well in acid soil. It is only when comfrey roots get down to the subsoil, that the plant is able to draw up minerals from deep down; the plant then reaches its maximum in food value, in vigour of growth and palatability for stock feed. Plants will produce copiously with a plentiful supply of water, but dislike being waterlogged.

**Compas Weed,** See Rosemary

**Copal** (*Bursera odorata*)

**Description:** Copal incense is the dried resin of the copal tree. It is Sacred to the Mayans and Aztecs of South and Central America. Deciduous shrub or small tree, up to 3.6 metres, related to frankincense and myrrh. Their wood is also very odoriferous. Species from this genus are excellent candidates for succulent bonsais. Most of the species have thickened trunks, often with decorative barks. Most species cannot take heavy frost, but they resist intense sun, provided they get enough water. They are often deciduous in winter or in time of drought.

**Influence:** Love, Purification.

**Gender**: Masculine. **Planet**: Sun. **Element**: Fire.

Added to love and purification incenses. A piece of copal can represent the heart in spell dolls.

**Cultivation**: Propagation is by seeds or cuttings.

**Coriander** (*Coriandrum sativum*)

**Description:** Coriander is an annual, with erect stems, 30 cm to 90 cm high, slender and branched. The lowest leaves are stalked and pinnate, the leaflets roundish or oval, slightly lobed. The segments of the uppermost leaves are linear and more divided. The flowers are in shortly-stalked umbels, five to ten rays, pale mauve, almost white, delicately pretty. The seed clusters are very symmetrical and the seeds fall as soon as ripe. The plant is bright green, shining, glabrous and intensely foetid.

**Influence:** Love, Health, Healing.

**Gender**: Masculine. **Planet**: Mars. **Element**: Fire.

Used in love sachets and spells. Add the powdered seeds to warm wine to make a lust potion. Protects gardeners and all in their households. Gather at harvest and hang in the home for protection. The seeds promote peace between people who are unable to get along. Use it in drinks or crushed in incense. Helps one find romance and is an excellent herb to add to an elixir when the Great Rite is celebrated. Throw instead of rice at handfastings or add to the hand fasting cake.

**Cultivation**: Choose a position where there is morning sun and dappled afternoon shade for best results. Plant seeds in spring and again in autumn in temperate areas. Small stakes will prevent the bushes from being blown over. Water well and fertilise during the growing season. The plant quickly runs to seed in warm weather so try for autumn planting in a protected area if possible.

**Corn** (*Zea Mays*)

**Description: Maize** (*Zea mays* ssp. *mays*) is a cereal grain that was domesticated in Mesoamerica. It is called **corn** in the United States, Canada, and Australia but there are further regional differences in terminology. While some maize varieties grow 7 metres tall at certain locations, commercial maize has been bred for a high-end height of 2.5 m (9 ft). Sweet corn is usually shorter than field corn varieties.

**Influence:** Protection, Luck, Divination

**Gender**: Feminine, **Element**: Earth, **Planet**: Venus

An ear of corn placed in a baby's cradle protects it against negative forces. A bunch of cornstalks hung over a mirror brings good luck to the household.

**Cultivation**: Maize was planted by the Native Americans in hills, in a complex system where beans used the corn plant for support, and squashes provided ground cover to stop weeds. This method was replaced by single species hill planting where each hill 60–120 cm apart was planted with 3 or 4 seeds, a method still used by the home gardener. In more arid seed may be planted in the bottom of 10–12 cm deep furrows to collect water. Modern technique plants maize in rows which allows for cultivation while the plant is young.

**Coughwort,** See Ginger

**Cotton** (*Gossypium barbadense*)

**Description:** The cotton plant (*Gossypium*) is a genus of about 40 species of shrubs in the family Malvaceae, native to the tropical and subtropical regions of both the Old World and the New World. In the wild cotton shrubs can grow up to 3 m high. The leaves are broad and have three to five (or even seven) lobes. The seeds are contained in a capsule called a boll, each seed surrounded by a downy fibre called lint. Commercial species of cotton plant are *G. hirsutum, G. arboreum* and *G. herbaceum*, and *G. barbadense*. While the lint naturally occurs in colors of white, brown, and green, fears of contaminating the genetics of white cotton has led many cotton-growing locations to ban growing of colored cotton varieties.

**Influence:** Luck, Healing, Protection, Rain, Fishing Magick

**Gender**: Feminine, **Element**: Earth, **Planet**: Moon

When placed in a sugar bowl or thrown over the right shoulder at dawn, cotton will bring good luck. Cotton is placed in an aching tooth to stop the pain. Planted or scattered in the yard, cotton keeps ghosts away, and vinegar-soaked cotton balls placed on the windowsills keep evil away. Place a pepper in a piece of cotton, sew it into a sachet, and wear it to bring back a lost love. Cotton cloth is the best kind of cloth to use in all magickal workings where it is called for. When going fishing on a windy day, lay twenty cotton seeds at the edge of the water to ensure a catch. Burn cotton for rain.

**Cultivation**: The cotton seeds are planted in Spring. Then 4 to 14 days later, the seedlings appear. Seed capsules called "bolls" grow as big as an egg. After a further 35 to 55 days, the bolls burst open and expose the cotton. When most of the bolls are open, the crop is ready to pick. Cotton needs long, hot summers and clear skies. It is watered by irrigation. Cotton must be protected from disease and insects.

**Cowslip** (*Primula veris*)

**Description:** *Primula veris*, commonly known as the Cowslip, is a low growing perennial herbaceous flowering plant with yellow flowers, in the genus *Primula*. It is found throughout most of temperate Europe and Asia although absent from the more northerly. It flowers in the spring; the flowers are in clusters of several together on a single stem. It is often included in wild-flower seed mixes used to landscape motorway banks and similar civil engineering earth-works where it may be seen in dense stands.

**Influence:** Healing, Youth, Treasure Finding

**Gender**: Feminine, **Element**: Water, **Planet**: Venus

If you don't want to have company, put some cowslip under your front porch. Hold a bunch of the flower in your hand to find hidden treasure.

**Cultivation**: Sow late winter onwards in good seed compost. Sow seed on surface of compost and gently firm. Seal in a polythene bag or cover with a piece of glass and place in a shady spot but do not exclude light which is beneficial for germination. Keep the soil damp but not wet. Germination usually takes 10-15 days at 15-18°C, higher temperatures can prevent germination. Transplant when large enough to handle in 7.5cm pots. Grow cool and fairly moist and later plant out 23cm (9in) apart in good soil, sun or part shade.

**Crampweed see** Cinquefoil

**Crocus** (*Crocus vernus*)

**Description:** Crocus is a genus of perennial flowering plants that grows from a corm, growing naturally from the Aegean, across Central Asia. As one of the first flowers to bloom in the spring, the large hybridized and selected "Dutch crocus" are popular with gardeners. However, in areas in which snow and frost occasionally occur in the early spring one has to plant them carefully as it is not uncommon in these regions for the crocuses to bloom early, only to suddenly wither and die from a unseasonable "post-winter" frost or snowfall. The spice saffron is obtained from the stamens of *Crocus sativus*, a fall-blooming species.

**Influence:** Love, Visions

**Gender**: Feminine, **Element**: Water, **Planet**: Venus

Grow the plant to attract love. If someone has robbed you, burn crocus along with alum and you may have a vision of the thief.

**Cultivation**: Crocus enjoy well drained soil, deep planting (10-15cm) with a South facing aspect, plus a layer of mulch to keep them cool in summer. They do need to be dry over summer as with many other bulbs. They may be left undisturbed and are relatively disease free. Crocus Chrysanthus feature multiple smaller flowers per bulbs. The bulbs are also generally much smaller than the Crocus Vernus cultivars.

**Cucumber** (*Cucumis sativus*)

**Description:** The cucumber is the edible fruit of the cucumber plant *Cucumis sativus*, which belongs to the gourd family Cucurbitaceae, as do melons and squash. The cucumber plant has large leaves that form a canopy over the fruit. The fruit is commonly harvested while still green, and eaten as a vegetable, whether raw, cooked, or made into pickled cucumbers. Although less nutritious than most fruit, the fresh cucumber is still a very good source of vitamin C, vitamin K, and potassium, and also provides some dietary fiber, vitamin A, vitamin B6, thiamin, folate, pantothenic acid, magnesium, phosphorus, potassium, copper, and manganese.

**Influence:** Chastity, Healing, Fertility

**Gender**: Feminine, **Element**: Water, **Planet**: Moon

Bind peel around head to cure headache. Add seeds to lunar incenses. The cucumber aids fertility if kept in the bedroom or eat the seeds. Eat the fruit of the cucumber to hinder lust.

**Cultivation**: Cucumbers are usually started by planting seeds directly in the garden after the danger of frost has passed, and the soil has warmed in the spring. Warm soil is necessary for germination of seeds and proper growth of plants. With ample soil moisture, cucumbers thrive in warm summer weather. Plant seeds 1 cm to 2 cm deep and thin the seedlings to one plant every 30 cm in the row or to three plants every metre in the hill system. If you use transplants, plant them carefully in warm soil 30 cm apart in the row. Cucumber plants have shallow roots and require ample soil moisture at all stages of growth. When fruit begins setting and maturing, adequate moisture becomes especially critical. For best yields, incorporate compost or well-rotted manure before planting.

**Cumin** (*Cumimum Cyminum*)

**Description:** Cumin is the seed of a small umbelliferous plant growing to about 25cm. The seeds come as paired or separate carpels, and are 3-6mm long. They have a striped pattern of nine ridges and oil canals, and are hairy, brownish in colour, boat-shaped, tapering at each extremity, with tiny stalks attached. They resemble caraway seeds, but are lighter in colour and unlike caraway, have minute bristles hardly visible to the naked eye. They are available dried, or ground to a brownish-green powder. Cumin is freely available in the West, although it is not a traditional European spice.

**Influence:** Protection, Fidelity, Exorcism

**Gender:** Masculine, **Element**: Fire, **Planet**: Mars

Burn with frankincense for protection. Mix with salt and scattered on the floor to dispel evil spirits. Used in love spells and promotes fidelity if given to a lover. Steep seeds in wine to promote lust.

**Cultivation**: Select an open, well-drained and very sunny position. Sow seed in spring or early summer when all danger of frost is over and the soil has warmed up. Sow seed where it is to grow and keep moist until germination. Plants take at least 4 months of warm weather to flower and produce seed. If seedlings are to be raised under glass, sow into individual pots and transplant with as little disturbance as possible.

**Curry** (*Murraya Koenigii*)

**Description:** Curry leaf has fern-like leaves that only need to be brushed against or gently touched to share their spicy aroma, with overtones of citrus and anise. An attractive, upright, branching tree growing 2-5 metres. Clusters of small, white fragrant flowers form in summer, followed by 1cm edible, shiny black berries. **Influence:** Protection

**Gender**: Masculine, **Element**: Fire, **Planet**: Mars

Burn the curry plant (not the mixture of spices used in cooking) at night to keep evil away.

**Cultivation**: The curry leaf tree requires rich, well-drained soil in a warm, sheltered position, as it is a tropical to sub-tropical tree. With regular watering during dry times, the tree will flourish. The tree will adapt to warm temperate areas, and if wishing to grow it in colder climates, keep it in a large pot and move it to a warm veranda in winter. In cold areas the tree may go dormant in winter.

**Cyclamen** (*Cyclamen* spp.)

**Description:** Cyclamens are perennial herbaceous plants, with a surface or underground corm 4-12 cm diameter, which produces leaves in late winter, and flowers in the autumn; the leaves die down duting the hottest part of the summer to conserve water. The leaves are rounded to triangular, 2-10 cm long and 2-7 cm broad, and usually variegated with a pale silvery horseshoe-shaped mark round the middle of the leaf. The flowers are produced in whorls of 3-10, each flower on a slender stem 3-12 cm tall, with five united petals; the petals are usually reflexed back 90° to 180° erect above the flower, and vary from white through pink to red-purple, most commonly pale pink. The fruit is a five-chambered capsule 1-2 cm diameter, containing numerous sticky seeds about 2 mm diameter.

**Influence:** Fertility, Protection, Happiness, Lust

**Gender**: Feminine, **Element**: Water, **Planet**: Venus

Grow in the bedroom as protection while sleeping. Carry the blossoms to remove the grief of an ended love affair. Grow outside to protect the garden and the house. Carry the flower to aid in fertility matters.

**Cultivation**: Best grown from established corms. If grown from seeds the seeds are best sown as fresh as possible. After collection, put the seeds in water overnight to soften the outer shell. The seeds, which are around 3mm in size, will eventually separate from the shell. A drop of washing up liquid will help speed the process up but is not absolutely necessary. Once the seeds have been soaked and have separated from their shells, plant the seeds in a well-drained pot with an equal mix of compost and grit. Seeds germinate more effectively in the dark, so cover the compost and the seeds with a layer of grit to exclude the light. Label the plant clearly and water well then store the pot somewhere cool and shaded, and water once a fortnight. It will take between one to two years for the seeds to germinate and grow, so be patient.

**Cypress** (*Cupressus sempervirens*)

**Description:** It is a medium-sized evergreen tree to 35 m tall, with a conic crown with level branches and variably pendulous branchlets. It is very long-lived, with some trees reported to be over 1, 000 years old. The foliage grows in dense sprays, dark green in colour. The leaves are scale-like, 2-5 mm long, and produced on rounded (not flattened) shoots. The seed cones are ovoid or oblong, 25-40 mm long, with 10-14 scales, green at first, maturing brown about 20-24 months after pollination. The male cones are 3-5 mm long, and release pollen in mid to late summer.

**Influence:** Longevity, Healing, Comfort, Protection

**Gender**: Feminine, **Element**: Earth, **Planet**: Saturn

Cypress is used at times of crisis (i.e., the death of a loved one). When carried to a funeral, cypress eases the mind and rids the wearer of grief. The tree is very protective, and its boughs are used for protection and blessings. The wood is also carried to promote longevity. Healing wands are made of cypress: a branch is cut from the tree over a three month period. To use, pass it over the sick person, touch the affected area, and put the tip of the wand into a fire to cleanse it. Use also in invocations to the gods. Use the roots and cones of this tree in healing rituals, and burn the greenery as incense for this purpose. Throw a sprig of cypress into a grave to give the deceased luck and love in the afterlife.

**Cultivation**: Cypress originally from Southern Europe and western Asia is grown from seed, preferring full sun to part sun. It is an evergreen tree growing to 12-18 m tall, spread varies depending on cultivar, but up to 3 m. It benefits from regular water when first planted, and then needs very little to no water when established. Being sensitive to root rot it needs well drained soil.

## Daffodil (*Narcissus* spp.)

**Description:** Daffodils form a group of large-flowered members of the genus Narcissus. Most daffodils look yellow, but yellow-and-white, yellow-and-orange, white-and-orange, pink, and lime-green cultivars also exist. Daffodils grow perennially from bulbs. In temperate climates they flower among the earliest blooms in spring. They often grow in large clusters, covering lawns and even entire hillsides with yellow. All daffodils have a central trumpet-shaped corona surrounded by a ring of petals. The traditional daffodil has a golden yellow color all over, but the corona may often feature a contrasting color. Breeders have developed some daffodils with a double or triple row of petals, making them resemble a small golden ball. Other cultivars have frilled petals, or an elongated or compressed central corona. All daffodils belong to the genus Narcissus. Daffodil is the common English name for them all, and Narcissus is the Latin, botanical name for them all.

**Influence:** Love, Fertility, Luck

**Gender**: Feminine, **Element**: Water, **Planet**: Venus

Place on the altar during love spells. Put fresh flowers in the bedroom to increase fertility.

**Cultivation**: Choose a well-drained, sunny place. Hillsides and raised beds are best. DRAINAGE is the key. Spade at least 30 cm deep. Improve your clay with well-rotted compost, soil amendment, or planting mix and raise the bed. Slightly acidic soil is best, so you might add soil sulphur if you have alkaline soil. Plant your daffodils so that their top (pointed end) is at least two times as deep as the bulb is high. Exactness isn't crucial; they'll adjust. Plant the bulbs deeper in sandy soil than in clay. High-nitrogen fertilizer should be avoided. Daffodils need lots of water while they are growing. Water immediately after planting and keep them moist until the rains come. Continue watering for three weeks or so after blooming time; then stop watering. The bulbs make their next year's bloom after flowering. You may leave daffodils down in the ground for between 3 to 5 years. If blooming does not happen one season, it would be best to move them to a new location. After blooming, never cut the foliage until it begins to yellow. Then is the time to dig them. Wash the bulbs thoroughly and let them dry completely (at least a week). Put them in onion sacks (or panty hose) and hang them in the coolest place you can find until ready to plant. Good air circulation will keep storage rot at a minimum.

## Daisy (*Chyrsanthemum leucanthemum, Bellis perenis*)

**Description:** Bellis perennis is a common European species of daisy, often considered the archetypal species of that name, though many other related plants share the name; to distinguish it from other daisies, it is sometimes qualified as Common Daisy, or occasionally English daisy. It is native to western, central and northern Europe.

It is a herbaceous plant with short creeping rhizomes and small rounded or spoon shaped evergreen leaves 2-5 cm long. The flowerheads are 2-3 cm diameter, with white ray florets (often tipped red) and yellow disc florets; they are produced on leafless stems 2-10 cm (rarely 15 cm) tall.

**Influence:** Lust, Luck

**Gender**: Feminine, **Element**: Water, **Planet**: Venus

It is said that whoever picks the first daisy of the season will be possessed by an uncontrollable "spirit of coquetry", or flirtatious attitude. Place a daisy root beneath your pillow to bring back an absent lover. Wear a daisy to bring love.

**Cultivation**: Start them from seed and they will bloom the second and each following year. You can also divide and separate them as a planting gets too dense and thick. Do this every three or four years and they will reward you with bigger blooms .If you do not do this, the plants will begin to crowd each other out, competing for nutrients and the blooms will be smaller. Daisies like rich, well drained soil and full sunshine. But they are a hardy and forgiving plant and will readily tolerate poorer soils and partial shade. They need little attention during the year. A little general purpose fertilizer in the early growth stage will help the plants to develop big and strong stalks and leaves. Just before blooming, provide a fertilizer high in Phosphorous to help promote big, bright blooms.

## Damiana (*Turnera diffusa* or *T. aphrodisiaca*)

**Description:** Damiana is a small bushy plant with yellow flowers. Damiana grows abundantly in dry, rocky soils and is generally found in Mexico, South America, Texas and West Indies.

**Influence:** Lust, Love, Visions

**Gender**: Masculine, **Element**: Fire, **Planet**: Mars

Used in lust infusions and spells. Burn to produce visions.

**Cultivation**: Damiana may be planted outdoors in the warm areas, or in the greenhouse in those colder areas. It thrives in any good soil if given a sunny location. It should be watered freely from spring through summer, but sparingly in winter. In the greenhouse the temperature should stand around 55 degrees Fahrenheit at night. Damiana is propagated by seeds and cuttings.

## Dandelion (*Taraxacum officianle*)

**Description:** Perennial with rosette of leaves to 30cm long. Smooth leaves are bright green with uneven, jagged margins of backward pointing teeth, and for this reason the plant has been given the name dandelion which comes from the French 'dent de lion', meaning lion's tooth. Hollow flower-stem to 30cm with one terminal yellow daisy, which sets into a puffball-looking seedhead, with fluffy parachutes to carry each seed away in the wind, nature's way of plant preservation.

**Influence:** Divination, Wishes, Calling Spirits, Sleep Protection, Healing

**Gender**: Masculine, **Element**: Fire, **Planet**: Sun

The roots are used for sachets in dream pillows and sachets, the leaves and flowers are used in a tea for healing. Bury this plant in the northwest corner of your house to bring favorable winds. To send a message to a loved one, blow at the seeds in his/her direction and visualize the message. Dandelion plants are said to breathe out ethylene gas. Although this can have an inhibiting effect on the growth of some plants nearby, this same gas is utilized by some farmers to accelerate the ripening process of crops. By scattering dandelion seeds under fruit trees, the ethylene gas given off can aid in the early ripening of the crop, which can bring a higher price for fruit early in the season.

**Cultivation**: Propagation is by seed, and dandelion will grow under almost all conditions, thriving in dry areas, just as well as it handles the wet conditions. Dandelion will also grow in shade, although this plant family, the daisy, is always considered a sun lover. True dandelion should not be confused with Hawkbit (Leontodon Taraxocoides) or several Cats' Ears species (Hypochoeris glabra and radicata) which is easily mistaken and is often found in lawns.

**Deadly Nightshade,** See Belladonna

**Deadmen's Bells see** Foxglove

**Death Angel see** Agaric

**Death Cap see** Agaric

**Death's Herb see** Belladonna

**Deerberry**, see Wintergreen

**Deerstongue** (*Frasera speciosa; Liatris odoratissima*)  **POISONOUS**

**Description:** *Frasera speciosa* is a tall, elongated cone-shaped plant with flowers clustered around its stem. The plants may live for several years; they bloom only once, however, and then die. Flowering is unpredictable; some years none are seen. The monument plant's flowers are small—up to 2 cm in diameter—but striking when examined closely. Long sepals appear in the clefts between four petals. The petals are greenish-white with small purple spots along their margins. Each petal has two tiny depressions, or pits, at its base. Four stamens appear at the base of the petals surrounding an ovary that bears only one seed.

**Influence:** Lust, Psychic Powers

**Gender**: Masculine, **Element**: Fire, **Planet**: Mars

Wear or carry to attract men, or sprinkle on the bed for the same purpose. It also aids psychic powers when worn.

**Cultivation**: Can be grown from seed supplied by specialist seed suppliers.

**Devil's Cherries see** Belladonna

**Devil's Eye see** Henbane

**Dill** (*Anethum graveolens*)

**Description:** Dill is a short-lived annual herb, native to southwest and central Asia. It is the sole species of the genus *Anethum*. It grows to 40-60 cm tall, with slender stems and alternate, finely divided, softly delicate leaves 10-20 cm long. The ultimate leaf divisions are 1-2 mm broad, slightly broader than the similar leaves of Fennel, which are thread-like, less than 1 mm broad, but harder in texture. The flowers are white to yellow, in small umbels 2-9 cm diameter. The seeds are 4-5 mm long and 1 mm thick, and straight to slightly curved with a longitudinally ridged surface.

**Influence:** Protection, Money, Lust, Luck

**Gender**: Masculine, **Element**: Fire, **Planet**: Mercury

Carry in sachets (the tops) for protection or place over the crib for the baby, place seeds in muslin and hang in shower for attracting women, also used with other herbs for ridding negative energies. If you place it over the door, no disagreeable people can enter your house. Smell it to cure hiccups or to stimulate lust.

**Cultivation**: Seed is the only means of propagation and should be sown in spring, and summer in the milder areas. Thin seedlings with care to around 25cm. Water well during dry weather and keep the bed well weeded. Choose a sunny position sheltered from strong winds. Enrich soil with organic material and add a little lime. They self-seed prolifically.

**Dock** (*Rumex* spp.)

**Description:** The docks, are a genus of about 200 species of annual, biennial and perennial herbs in the buckwheat family. Members of this family are very common perennial herbs growing in acidic, sour soils mainly in the northern hemisphere, but have been introduced almost everywhere. Many are nuisance weeds, but some have edible leaves, used in salads. These are erect plants with long tap roots. The fleshy to leathery leaves form a basal rosette at the root. The basal leaves may be different from those near the inflorescence with minor leaf veins. The inconspicuous flowers are carried above the leaves in whorl-like clusters. The fertile flowers are mostly hermaphrodite, or they can be functionally male or female. The flowers and seeds grow on long clusters at the top of a stalk emerging from the basal rosette. Each seed is a 3-sided achene

**Influence:** Healing, Fertility, Money

**Gender**: Masculine, **Element**: Air, **Planet**: Jupiter

The seeds are used in money spells and incenses. Make into an infusion and sprinkle around a place of business to attract customers.

**Cultivation**: Little detail is available about growing Dock, most is about eradication of the weed.

**Dogbane** (*Apocynum adrosaemifolium*)  **POISONOUS**

**Description:** Dogbane is a perennial herbaceous plant that grows throughout much of North America, in the southern half of Canada and throughout the United States. It grows up to 2 meters tall. It prefers moist places. It is a poisonous plant; the name means "poisonous to dogs". All parts of the plant are poisonous and can cause cardiac arrest if ingested. The stems are reddish and contain a milky latex capable of causing skin blisters. The leaves are opposite, simple broad lanceolate, 7-15 cm long and 3-5 cm broad, entire, and smooth on top with white hairs on the underside. The flowers are produced in mid summer, with large sepals, and a five-lobed white corolla. It grows in open wooded areas, ditches, and hillsides; in gardens it can be invasive, growing from spreading roots.

**Influence:** Love

Use the flowers in magickal love mixtures.

**Gender**_____, **Element**_____, **Planet:** _____

**Cultivation**: Dog Bane grows easily in a sunny, well-drained position in a frost-free location. It is tolerant of dry conditions. Plants can easily be propagated from cuttings. Dog Bane is marketed in Australia under the name Dog Gone. Trim back after flowering to maintain a bushy habit.

**Dog's Finger see** Foxglove

**Dogwood** (*Pyiscidia erythrina, Cornus florida*)

**Description:** A tree growing to 10m tall it's bark has square fissures. The twigs are deep green to red, with malpighian hairs, opposite. Flowers appearing with or just before the leaves as single pedunculate flower cluster from between leaves of new seasons growth.

**Influence:** Wishes, Protection.

Keeps writings and meetings secret, therefore is an excellent herb for the Book of Shadows. An oil of the flowers is priceless in sealing letters and keeping unintended eyes from secret writings. Powdered flowers and dried bark may be used as incense. Place the sap of the dogwood onto a handkerchief on Midsummer Eve. This will grant any wish you have as long as you carry it faithfully. Dogwood leaves or wood can be placed in protective amulets.

**Gender**_____, **Element**_____, **Planet:** Moon, Pluto

**Cultivation**: Dogwood Family, performs best in evenly moist, well-drained, acidic soils in full sun to full shade but prefers partial sun; soil pH is extremely important for this species to survive and thrive, as it is intolerant of alkaline pH soils and struggles in neutral pH soils; it also does not do well in dry soils, poor soils, compacted soils, wet soils, or during periods of prolonged heat and drought, but performs well under high humidity conditions.

Vigorous flowering occurs in full sun to partial sun, while sparse flowering occurs in partial shade to full shade.

It is propagated by rooted stem cuttings, cuttings grafted onto seedling rootstock, or seeds and iscommercially available with many cultivars, in ball and hessian or container form

Flowering Dogwood is somewhat sensitive to being transplanted in Autumn, and care should be taken to amend the soil, fertilize, water thoroughly, mulch adequately, and avoid Winter salt spray, to enhance survival chances during the first Winter

**Donkey's Ear,** See Mullein

**Dragon's Blood** (*Daemomorops Draco*)

**Description:** Dragon's Blood, has several origins, the substance so named being contributed by widely differing species. Probably the best known is that from Sumatra. *Daemomorops Draco.* The long, slender stems of the genus are flexible, and the older trees develop climbing propensities. The leaves have prickly stalks which; often grow into long tails and the bark is provided with many hundreds of flattened spines. It flowers along the branches instead of them being gathered into catkins and produces berries which; are about the size of a cherry, and pointed. When ripe they are covered with a reddish, resinous substance which; is separated in several ways, the most satisfactory being by steaming, or by shaking or rubbing in coarse, canvas bags. An inferior kind is obtained by boiling the fruits to obtain a decoction after they have undergone the second process.

**Influence:** Love, Protection, Exorcism, Potency.

**Gender**: Masculine. **Planet**: Mars. **Element**: Fire.

Dragon's Blood is a resin which comes from a palm tree. Mix a little bit of it in with oils, sachets, charms, poppets (Spell Dolls), and incense to increase the powers of the other herbs. Place some on the altar to increase the power of spells. Other uses for Dragon's Blood include love, protection, and exorcism. Used in homemade magickal inks. Burn the resin to entice errant lovers to return. A stick placed under the pillow will cure impotency. A powerful protectant when sprinkled around the house or burned as incense. A pinch added to other incenses will increase their potency. Dragon's Blood is not acted upon by water, but most of it is soluble in alcohol.

**Cultivation**: Not much is known about the growing of Dragons Blood. It is not something that could be grown in most gardens. The resin is obtained from wild growing plants.

**Drunkard see** Marigold

**Duck's Foot see** May Apple

**Dulse** (*Rhodymenia palmata*)

**Description:** This is a common red seaweed found between the tides on rocky shores and named for its resemblance to the palm of the human hand. In Ireland, Scotland and England, it is known as Dillisk or Dulse. Dulse is good to eat, but only after being dried. In a fresh state it is leathery and unpalatable. After sun-drying and proper storage, it is a very pleasant plant to chew. It has very little fat and only a small amount of proteins and cellulose, but is very rich in trace elements and vitamins, particularly vitamin A. Dulse contains large amount of several unusual carbohydrates including an unusual short-chained one, floridoside, and this can form up to 30% of the dry weight. This may account for its palatability. Scotland, Norway, Iceland and eastern Canada all produce small amounts of dulse for human consumption. In Ireland about 20 dry tonnes are sold each year, mainly in the west and north-east.

**Influence:** Lust, Harmony

**Gender**: Feminine, **Element**: Water, **Planet**: Moon

Add to beverages to induce lust. Sprinkle around the home to encourage harmony. Use Dulse in sea rituals; it is usually thrown into the waves to appease the spirits of the sea. Toss Dulse from a high place to contact wind spirits.

**Cultivation**: At present natural dulse is in short supply and the Martin Ryan Institute and the Irish Seaweed Industry Organisation in collaboration with Queen's University, Belfast, are looking at ways of growing dulse artificially in the sea. Exploratory studies on ropes look good for cultivation.

**Dutchman's Britches** (*Dicentra cucullaria*)

**Description:** This small, herbaceous woodland plant is one of the most popular of the early bloomers, to those who visit the woods or mountains in early spring. Belonging to the same genus as Bleeding Hearts, the plants usually disappears by early summer. They are native to the rich moist woods of Eastern and central North America, ranging from North Dakota to Quebec and as far south as Georgia. These easily recognized native wildflowers typically occur on forest floors, rocky woods, north facing slopes, ledges, valleys, ravines and along streams. Dutchman's Breeches are a spring ephemeral: they make the most of the early spring sunshine by blooming and setting seed before the trees have leafed out, but when the tree canopy closes, even the leaves disappear.

**Influence:** Love

Wear the root of this plant to attract love.

**Gender**_____, **Element**_____, **Planet:** _____

**Cultivation**: Dutchman's Britches requires moist, humus rich well drained soil. It prefers shaded areas and grows to between 10 and 30 cm high spreading to the same width. Propagation is by shallow planting the bulbs, whilst seed may be dispersed by insects.

**Dwale,** See Belladonna

**Ebony** (*Diospyros lotus*)

**Description:** A decidious tree growing to 9m by 6m at a medium rate. It is frost tender and is in flower in summer. The seeds ripen late in autumn. The flowers are dioecious (individual flowers are either male or female, but only one sex is to be found on any one plant so both male and female plants must be grown if seed is required). The plant not is self-fertile.

**Influence:** Protection, Power

The wood of this tree is protective and is used in making amulets. Ebony wands give magicians pure power. Don't stand under an Ebony tree in a thunderstorm

**Gender**_____, **Element**_____, **Planet:** _____

**Cultivation**: Seed is best sown as soon as it is ripe as stored seed requires a period of cold-stratification. It usually germinates in 1 - 6 months at 15°c. Pot up the young seedlings as soon as they are large enough to handle into fairly deep pots and plant them out into their permanent positions in early summer. Give them some protection from excessive winter cold for their first year or two outdoors. Planting cuttings of half-ripe wood during late winter or layering in spring can also be successful methods of propagation. It requires a good deep loamy soil in sun or light shade. When being grown for its fruit, the tree should be given a warm, sheltered, sunny position. It dislikes very acid or wet and poorly drained soils. Dormant plants are very cold-hardy, but the young growth in spring, even on mature plants, is frost-tender and so it is best to grow the plants in a position sheltered from the early morning sun. The tree is Dioecious, but the female tree can produce seedless fruits in the absence of a pollinator. It is likely that unfertilized fruits are more astringent than fertilized fruits as this is the case with other. It has a long tap root and therefore is difficult to transplant, it is best to plant them out in their permanent position as soon as possible and to give protection over winter for the first year or two. This species is sometimes cultivated for its edible fruit in Italy and E. Asia, there are some named varieties.

**Echinacea** (*Echinacea augustifolia*)

**Description:** Echinecea is a short lived perennial plant widely used as a medicinal plant of the plains Indians commonly called the purple cone flower. Its name originated from the Greek "echinos" (hedgehog). It can be easily identified because of the raised cone in the middle of the flower with the petals hanging down. The colour of the flower can vary between species from white to a deep purpley pink. It is grown for both its flower garden and medicinal properties. Its height can range from 30 cm to 90 cm.

**Influence:** Strengthening Spells

Echinacea, also known as Purple Coneflower, is a natural antibiotic and immune system stimulator, helping to build resistance to colds, flus, and infections. It increases the production of white blood cells, and improves the lymph glands. The tea from this herb should be used in all infections, and has been used in treating skin cancers and other cancers. Please note that if you suffer from any auto-immune disorder, you should use Echinacea, or any other immune stimulant herb, only under the guidance of a professional, such as a naturopathic doctor. Echinacea is used as an offering to the spirits or gods and goddesses to strengthen a spell or ritual.

**Gender**_____, **Element**_____, **Planet:** _____

**Cultivation**: Preferably choose a sunny position though the plant can cope with semi-shade. It does best in low-nutrient soils that are well-drained. The plants can be grown from seed sown in spring but the seeds require stratification in freezing conditions and also light to germinate well.

**Edelwiess** (*Leontopodium alpinum*)

**Description:** This perennial plant with solver-white flowers made famous by the musical "The Sound of Music", is ideal for rock gardens and drying. The plant has been avidly collected from the wild in the past for its ornamental use as a dried flower - this has caused it to become rare in the wild and it is now a protected species

**Influence:** Invisibility, Bullet-Proofing

Make this plant into a wreath and wear it to gain invisibility. Pull up a whole edelweiss during the day on a Friday of the Full Moon. Worn wrapped in white linen, it protects from daggers and bullets. Grow and care for this plant to grant your heart's desire.

**Gender**_____, **Element**_____, **Planet:** _____

**Cultivation**: Requires a position in full sun in any gritty perfectly drained not too fertile neutral or slightly alkaline soil. Given a well-drained soil and protection from winter wet, this is one of the easier alpine plants to grow. Propagation is either by division or by seed - best sown as soon as it is ripe in the cold greenhouse. When they are large enough to handle, prick the seedlings out into individual pots and grow them on in the greenhouse for their first winter. Plant them out into their permanent positions in late spring or early summer, after the last expected frosts.

**Egyptian White Water-lily** See Lotus

**Elder** (*Sambucus canadensis*)

**Description:** The American Elderberry, Sambucus canadensis, is a deciduous, upright shrub. It produces black or purple berries that are great for wildlife or jams and jellies. It has light grey or brown bark and is arching in form. Produces attractive flowers and berries all season long. Flattened panicles of small white flowers are produced in midsummer. This plant is a showy ornamental ideal for the garden. The American Elderberry has a fast growth rate. It grows up to 4 metres in height and 3 metres in spread. Prefers moist soil and full sun. Native to North America.

**Influence:** Exorcism, Protection, Healing, Prosperity, Peace

**Gender**: Feminine, **Element**: Air, **Planet**: Venus

Sacred to the Goddess ("Elder be the Lady's tree, burn it not or cursed you'll be"). Wear this to ward off attackers. Hang over doorways and windows to protect the house against evil. Has the power to make an evil magician release any spells they may have cast on you. Grow elder to protect the house from sorcery and lightning. Scatter the leaves and berries of the Elder to the four winds in the name of a person, place, or thing, and then scatter more elder over the person or thing to bless it. Pregnant women kiss the tree for good luck for the coming baby. Carry to prevent the temptation to commit adultery. Grow in the garden to protect from sorcery and lightning. Place elderberries under your pillow to help you sleep. Make a flute from its branches to call spirits.

**Cultivation**: Plant in a sunny or semi-shaded position in moist, compost-enriched soil. Hardwood cuttings can be taken in August or tip cuttings in November. Suckers can also be dug up and transplanted. Water well.

**Elecampane** (*Inula Helenium*)

**Description:** Inula helenium is coarsely magnificent in flower but declines quickly after flowering, particularly if the soil in which it is growing is allowed to dry out. Most perennial species of this genus, grown in gardens are clump-forming plants, with erect stems bearing large leaves, and daisy-like flower-heads with numerous, very slender, yellow ray-florets. The basal leaves are 30 to 40 cm long and are held on petioles up to 30 cm long. Leaves become much reduced in size, and sessile or devoid of a petiole as they ascend the brownish, furrowed stem. Leaves are quite velvety on their undersides but rough hairy above. The 7.5 to 10 cm wide flowers are usually solitary but occasionally occur in groups of two to three.

**Influence:** Love, Protection, Psychic Powers, Banishing, Purification , dispels violent, angry vibrations .

**Gender**: Masculine, **Element**: Air, **Planet**: Mercury

Hide a sachet of the herb in a room, or sprinkle powdered herb along the doorways and hallways. Wear to attract love, or sew the leaves or flowers into a pink cloth for a love sachet. Carry for protection. Smoulder this herb on charcoal to sharpen psychic powers when scrying.

**Cultivation**: Division of mature plants in autumn or spring as well as seed planted in spring. These plants are easily grown providing they are in full sun, and planted in a moist, well-drained soil, although most will tolerate somewhat wetter, even boggy conditions. The basal leaves are large so give these plants room to spread, and look their best. Plant about 90 cm from other plants.

**Elf Leaf,** See Rosemary

**ElkWeed,** See Deerstongue

**Elm** (*Ulmus campestris*)

**Description:** When seen at its best the Elm is a very large tree, even exceeding 40 metres in height, and 12 or 16 metres in girth, though seldom over 30 metres high or 10 metres round; often sending out one or two huge horizontal limbs to a distance of 10 to 15 metres from the trunk, and generally forking above into ascending branches, whose multitudinous branchlets and twigs form a rounded top, towering over the green billowy masses that spring from the limbs. Its bark is corky, grey in colour, and scored by those grand vertical furrows of age that mark the expanding rings of wood within, and have earned for the tree the epithet of "rugged.

**Influence:** Love

**Gender**: Feminine, **Element**: Water, **Planet**: Saturn

Carry to protect against lightning strikes as well as to attract love. Once known as "Elven" because of its popularity among elves.

**Cultivation**: Elm is best grown from seed and should be sown in a cold frame (in colder regions) or outdoor seedbed as soon as ripe it usually germinates in a few days. A high proportion of the seed is not viable but seed is normally freely produced and can be sown thickly to take into account the poor viability. Stored seed does not germinate so well and should be sown in early spring. When they are large enough to handle, prick the seedlings out into individual pots and grow them on in the greenhouse for their first winter. Plant them out into their permanent positions in late spring or early summer, after the last expected frosts. Plants should not be allowed to grow for more than two years in a nursery bed since they form a tap root and will then move badly. It prefers a fertile soil in full sun, but is easily grown in any soil of at least moderate quality so long as it is well drained. The English elm is susceptible to 'Dutch elm disease', a disease that has destroyed the greater part of all the elm trees growing in Britain. Mature trees killed back by the disease will often regrow from suckers, but these too will succumb when they get larger. There is no effective cure (1992) for the problem, but most E. Asian, though not Himalayan, species are resistant to the disease so the potential exists to develop new resistant hybrids with the native species.

**Endive** (*Cichorium endivia*)

**Description:** Endive is a low growing, ruffled little plant, most cultivars just 15cm to 25 cm tall, whereas escarole has a central "head" of smooth fleshy leaves and is larger and more upright, some cultivars to 60 cm in height. The leaves of both endive and escarole are a little more thick and chewy than those of lettuce, which is also closely related. Endives and escaroles produce attractive pale blue flowers on stems that stand way above the leafy foliage. Most endives and escaroles are bright green, but there are some cultivars that are bronzy brown, and some with red midribs.

**Influence:** Love, Lust

When using Endive for magick, it is best to gather it in the following manner: dig it up on

June 27 or July 25 with a piece of gold or a stag's horn. Wear as a talisman to attract love. Replace ever three days. Serve in salads to induce lust.

**Gender**: Male, **Element**: Air, **Planet**: Jupiter

**Cultivation**: Endive are grown like lettuce, in rows, wide rows or patches with full sun to partial shade. Like other greens, endive taste best when grown quickly and require regular watering. Be sure to add nitrogen fertilizer to the soil. Spring planted endive do well only where summers are cool. Hot weather makes them too tough and too bitter. They tend to bolt and go to flower under a combination of short days and cool weather. Endive are grown from seed. In colder climates, plant in early spring, 2-4 weeks before the last expected frost, or in late summer, 12-15 weeks before the first expected frost for a fall crop. In the warmer areas, plant in autumn or even in winter. Endive and should be ready for blanching 2-3 months after sowing the seed.

English Sarsaparilla, See Tormentil

Eucalyptus (*Eucalyptus* spp.)

**Description:** The eucalyptus or Gum tree; as it is known in Australia is an evergreen trees with alternate or opposite, simple, smooth-margined leaves; flowers in small clusters, top- or bell-shaped, 4-petaled with many stamens; fruit a many-seeded capsule. Varieties vary in size from smallish shrubs to large trees up to around 100 m in height. In most Australian climatic zones, whether alpine snow field or near-desert, the principal tree will be a gum tree...the few exceptions being rainforest pockets on the eastern coast. Despite the great variety of forms, gum trees are easily recognized. All gum trees bear gum nuts, little woody capsules with a pointy lid which open in flowering and which contain the tree's microscopic seeds. It is the little gumnuts which gave the name 'eucalyptus' which comes from latin roots meaning 'well-lidded'. The soils of Australia are, generally speaking, thin and deficient, and to survive on them, gumtrees have evolved hardiness and aggressiveness. For a hardwood they are very fast in growth, both above and below the ground. Many types are adapted to not only survive bushfires, but actually exploit the post-fire conditions with the mature trees bursting with new growth and seeds germinating within days of a fire. Eucalpytus oil is very volatile and flammable, and so are best avoided close to dwellings.

**Influence:** Healing, Protection, Sleep and Reconciliations

**Gender**: Feminine, **Element**: Air, **Planet**: Moon

Used in sleep and dream sachets, place with other healing herbs for bringing healing especially chest area, hang in the home to ward off sicknesses, carry in an amulet or sachet to help in the reconciliation of relationship. String immature pods on green thread and wear to help heal sore throats.

**Cultivation**: As an Australian native, it grows in poor soils, and once established does not require much care or watering. Propagation from seed may be very difficult with species adapted to require fire for the seed to germinate. Selection of the correct plant for your climatic area is important. Best purchased as an established small tree from a native plant nursery.

Eyebright (*Euphrasia officianlis*)

**Description:** A meadow plant growing in a range of soils, eyebright produces small white or purple flowers. The plant is collected when in full flower, and cut off just above the root. It is used to improve sight and to aid in curing other eye diseases. An annual, eyebright is partially parasitic on grasses. It likes extra nitrogen, which may cause it to favour pasture land. The plant is chiefly collected from the wild. The impact of collection on wild populations is unknown, although concern for the sustainability of this plant is growing. If collected carefully, cutting the tops and leaving a few leaves, eyebright can send out side shoots, flower, and still produce seed during the growing season.

**Influence:** Mental Powers, Psychic Powers, Clairvoyance, Meditation

**Gender**: Masculine, **Element**: Air, **Planet**: Sun

Used in a tea form and anoint the eyes for aid in clairvoyance. Helps too with other appropriate herbs to open the third eye and aid in meditation.

**Cultivation**: Generally collected from the wild however it succeeds in most soils, preferring chalk or limestone. Eyebright is a semi-parasitic plant, growing on the roots of various species of grass and also on Trifolium pratense and Plantago species. The grass does not seem to suffer unduly from this parasitism since eyebright is an annual and its cells do not penetrate very deeply into the grass. It hybridizes freely with other members of this genus.

**Eye of the Star,** See Horehound

**Fairy Clock,** See Dandelion

**Fairy Cup,** See Cowslip

**Fairy Fingers,** See Foxglove

**Fairy Thimbles** See Foxglove

**Featherfew,** See Feverfew

**Febrifuge,** See Feverfew

**Felon Plant,** See Mugwort

**Felonwort,** See Bittersweet

**Fever Twig,** See Bittersweet

**Fennel** (*Foeniculum vulgare*)

**Description:** It is a highly aromatic perennial herb, erect, glaucous green, and grows to 2 m tall. The leaves grow up to 40 cm long; they are finely dissected, with the ultimate segments filiform, about 0.5 mm wide. The flowers are produced in terminal compound umbels 5-15 cm wide, each umbel section with 20-50 tiny yellow flowers on short pedicels. The fruit is a dry seed from 4-9 mm long, half as wide or less, and grooved.

**Influence:** Protection, Healing, Purification

**Gender**: Masculine, **Element**: Fire, **Planet**: Mercury

Protects the home when grown in the garden. Hung in windows and doors to ward off evil, and the seeds are carried for this purpose also. Used in purification and healing mixtures. Placing some in your left shoe prevents wood ticks from biting your legs. Use for scenting soaps and perfumes to ward off negativity and evil. Grow near the home for the same purpose.

**Cultivation**: Fennel is grown as an annual or biennial in cold-winter areas, usually from seed though division of mature plants in spring is an option.. Grow in a light, well-drained soil in full sun. The seed should be sown in early spring where the plants are to stand, and the seedlings thinned to 30 cm apart.

## Fenugreek (*Trigonella foenum-graecum*)

**Description:** An annual bush to 60cm, grown from seed, germinating in 2-7 days. Plant in spring/ summer, to early autumn, in full sun, in well limed soil. The soft leaves are three-lobed, triangular in appearance, which is indicated by the generic name 'trigonella', which in Greek means three-angled.

**Influence:** Money

**Gender**: Masculine, **Element**: Air, **Planet**: Mercury

Adding a few fenugreek seeds to the mop water used to clean your household floors will bring money into the household.

**Cultivation**: Prepare soil by adding plenty of composted organic material. Add a ration of lime if the soil is acid. A sunny, well-drained position and adequate water is required. Seed is sown in situ in spring.

## Fern

**Description:** Ferns are an ancient type of plant. They do not flower, but instead reproduce by means of spore. There are over 10, 000 species of ferns world.

Ferns may be huge and woody such as the tree ferns, medium sized, fleshy and clumping or fine and delicate. In the majority of ferns, the above ground part of the plant is nearly always leaves (fronds). The stem (rhizome) may be underground and very small, as in most ground ferns, or it may be large, woody and above ground as in tree ferns. New fronds are tightly coiled and gradually uncoil as they grow. The coiled frond is called a crozier or fiddlehead.

On the under-surface of the fertile fronds are brown or yellow patches which may sometimes be mistaken for disease. These patches may be lines, dots or markings in a specific pattern or they may be found as a continuous line around the margin of the frond. The patches are groups of spore sacs which contain spore. It is these shapes and patterns that may be used to identify different families of ferns.

**Influence:** Rain Making, Protection, Luck, Riches, Health, Exorcism, Mental Clarity

**Gender**: Masculine, **Element**: Air, **Planet**: Mercury

Hang an Air Fern in the study room to help concentration, burn a sprig before an exam. In the Earth element, hang for powerful protection, use sprigs in sachets and amulets for a powerful auric protection. Throw dried fern upon hot coals to exorcise evil spirits. Fern is burned outside to cause rain to fall. The smoke from the burning plant drives away snakes. Carry or wear to discover treasure, and break the first fern frond of spring to have good luck; if this frond is bitten, you will be guarded from toothache. Fern sap is said to confer youth when drunk. If you find yourself in a soundless spot covered with ferns, exactly at midnight, Puck will appear and give you a purse of gold. Carry the seed for invisibility.

**Cultivation**: Some ferns are readily propagated by means such as division of the rhizomes (under ground stems) or crowns, layering and plantlets. Division is best carried out just prior to the active growth period in spring. The rhizomes can be cut into lengths and those with a growing tip can be potted up. Fronds attached to the divisions may die but new fronds will grow. Ferns generally grow best in slightly acid soils which contain plenty of organic matter. Good soil conditions can be created by digging to spade depth and incorporating liberal quantities of coarse peat moss, well-rotted leaf-mould or compost. The structure of heavy soil may be improved by the addition of gypsum and coarse sand. Apart from the removal of dead fronds, ferns do not require a great deal of maintenance and, once established, the soil surface should be disturbed as little as possible. Daily watering is necessary while plants are young, even during winter. This should consist of deep soaking about once a week followed by a light daily watering. During the summer, watering needs to be consistent. Automatic sprinkler and drip irrigation systems are ideal for this purpose

**Feverfew** (*Chrysanthemum parthenium*)

**Description: Feverfew** (*Tanacetum parthenium*) is a traditional daisy like medicinal herb which is found in many old gardens, and is also occasionally grown for ornament. It is also commonly seen in the literature by its synonyms, *Chrysanthemum parthenium* (L.) Bernh. and *Pyrethrum parthenium* (L.) Sm. It is a short lived perennial, growing to about 60 cm.

**Influence:** Protection

**Gender**: Masculine, **Element**: Water, **Planet**: Venus

Feverfew is carried for protection against illnesses involving fever, as well as for preventing accidents.

**Cultivation**: Choose a semi-shaded location that is well-drained. While the plant is a perennial, it is often grown as an annual because it self-seeds so readily. This characteristic also makes it a candidate for weed status, so avoid planting it in sensitive areas. Dead-heading as soon as the flowers fade will help avoid self-seeding. Plant seed in autumn or in spring. Cut established plants down in autumn and they will reshoot in spring. Almost all soil types are suitable providing they are well drained, and a sunny site is preferred, producing the greatest proliferation of flowers, though it can tolerate up to half a day shade.

**Fig** (*Ficus carica*)

**Description:** The fig is a picturesque tropical looking tree or shrub with a dramatic spreading habit. The breadth is often wider than the height of 4 to9 m. The bark is a smooth, silvery gray and the 10 cm long deciduous leaves have 3 or 5 lobes. There are many cultivars available for the home landscape. Figs usually begin bearing fruit within two years. Drought tolerant, once established.

Originally from the eastern Mediterranean region, figs have been cultivated by humans for over 5000 years.
**Influence:** Divination, Fertility, Love

**Gender**: Masculine, **Element**: Fire, **Planet**: Jupiter

Small phallic images are carved from fig wood and carried by women who wish to conceive. Eat to overcome impotence or frigidity. Write a question on a fig leaf. If the leaf dries slowly, the answer is yes; the opposite is true if it dries quickly. Grow in the home for protection and good luck. Grow in the bedroom to ensure restful sleep, or grow in the kitchen to prevent hunger. To charm people, give them a fig and they will be spellbound by your presence (if they like figs). Place a fig branch in front of your door before you leave on a journey to ensure a safe return.

**Cultivation**: Take dormant hardwood cuttings during the winter, dust with rooting hormone powder and plant in sterile potting soil. Fig trees are very easy to propagate by transplanting root suckers at almost any time of year. Mulch heavily with organic materials in order to conserve moisture and improve soil structure. Responds well to pruning and can be espaliered or pruned heavily in the dormant season for size control and to increase the main crop. Prefers part sun to full sun with average, well-drained soils.

## Figwort (*Scrophularia nodosa*)

**Description:** Scrophularia is a coarse erect perennial with thick, sharply square, fleshy stems. Growing up to 150cm tall, it arises from a knotted horizontal rootstock. The leaves are opposite, short-stemmed ovate at base, lanceolate near the top, with toothed margins. The flowers are in loose cymes in pyramidal or oblong panicles; each flower is globular, five green sepals encircling a green or purple flower, giving way to an egg-shaped seed capsule. It grows in moist and cultivated waste ground, in woodlands and copses throughout the northern hemisphere except western North America.

**Influence:** Health, Protection

**Gender**: Feminine, **Element**: Water, **Planet**: Venus

Wear around the neck to retain health and to guard against the evil eye. Smoke this plant over Midsummer fires and hang in the home for protection.

**Cultivation**: It grows in moist and cultivated waste ground, in woodlands and copses throughout the northern hemisphere, Grow this figwort in a moist, semi-shade to full sun situation. This plant is at it best in moist growing conditions but will grow with average moisture. It will survive drought stress but the leaves will burn severely. It will also tolerate wet growing conditions. Sow seeds in spring or autumn. Larger divisions can be planted out direct into their permanent positions.

**Five Finger Blossom see** Cinquefoil

**Five Finger Grass,** See Cinquefoil

**Flanel Leaf, See Mullein**

## Flax (*Linum usitatissimum*)

**Description**: Flax, also known as linseed is an erect annual plant growing to 120 cm tall, with slender stems. The leaves are glaucous green, slender lanceolate, 2-4 cm long and 3 mm broad. The flowers are pure pale blue, 1.5-2.5 cm diameter, with five petals. The fruit is a round, dry capsule 5-9 mm diameter, containing several glossy brown seeds shaped like an apple pip, 4-7 mm long.

**Influence:** Money, Protection, Beauty, Psychic Powers, Healing

**Gender**: Masculine, **Element**: Fire, **Planet**: Mercury

The seeds are used in money spells. Put some flax in your shoe to ward off poverty. To protect yourself while asleep, mix equal parts flax seed and mustard seed and place the mixture by your bed. On the other side of the bed, place a pan of cold water. To be sure your child grows up to be good-looking, let him/her dance among growing flax at age seven.

**Cultivation**: Flax is grown from seed planted as soon as the danger of heavy frosts is over in well drained to dry soil with a sunny position. They take about two weeks to germinate. Fibre flax takes 80 days to mature.

**Fleabane** (*Inula dysenterica*)

**Description:** This creeping perennial sends up woolly stems from it's rootstock to a height of 30 cm – 60cm. The stems are branched and very leafy, the leaves also being woolly. Produces an early abundance of daisy-like flowers with purple rays and yellow centres used to make an insect repellent.. Cut back flowers as they die and it will continue to bloom until it freezes.

**Influence:** Exorcism, Protection, Chastity

**Gender**: Feminine, **Element**: Water, **Planet**: Venus

Used to exorcise evil spirits and prevent their entry into the home. To do this, tie some fleabane, along with some leaves of St. John's Wort, wheat, and some capers, into a satchet and hang over the lintel of the door. Place the seed on the sheets to cause chastity.

Cultivation: Seed - sow spring or autumn in a cold frame and only just cover the seed. When they are large enough to handle, prick the seedlings out into individual pots and plant them out in the summer. If you have plenty of seed then it can be sown in situ in the spring. Division in spring. Very easy, larger divisions can be planted out direct into their permanent positions. It is probably better in cooler climates to pot up the smaller divisions and grow them on in light shade in a cold frame until they are well established before planting them out in late spring or early summer. It also spreads by runners to form patches. Succeeds in an ordinary garden soil in a sunny position. Plants can be invasive, spreading freely at the roots.

**Florentine Iris see** Orris

**Fox Bells see** Foxglove

**Foxglove** (*Digitalis purpurea*) **POISONOUS**

**Description:** This bi-ennial plant is a wonderful plant for early summer, it produces tall stems covered in bell shaped drooping flowers in its second year from its rosette of leaves which are a favourite of bees.

**Gender**: Feminine. **Planet**: Venus. **Element**: Water.

**Influence:** Brings true magick to your garden by attracting faeries and plant devas. Assists in communion with the Underworld. Collect the juice of the herb under a favorable moon sign. Mark the very center of your circle with the juice and wait there to see the realm of faery.

**Cultivation**: Foxglove prefers acid soils, and grows well with rhododendrons or heathers. Grown from seed, it produces a rosette of leaves in its first year, before throwing stems of flowers in early summer, growing up to 90cm to 120 cm.

## Frankincense (*Boswellia spp.*)

**Description:** Frankincense is the gum portion of the deciduous boswellia genus, gathered in a similar way to rubber harvesting.

**Influence:** Protection, Exorcism, Spirituality

**Gender**: Masculine, **Element**: Fire, **Planet**: Sun

Magickal properties similar to Myrrh. Use the beads to drive out negativity and enhance positive vibrations. You can crush them and use them as an incense on a charcoal disc. Burn to raise vibrations, to purify, consecrate, protect and exorcise. Frankincense incense induces visions and is useful as an aid to meditation. You can also make a little white or purple sachet of Frankincense and carry it with you to aid in your spiritual growth. A sachet of Frankincense Tears can also be used as a protective amulet. Burn during sunrise rituals of all kinds. Mix with cumin and burn as a powerful protective incense useful for general working.

**Cultivation**: Harvested from the wild.

**Frogge stoles,** See Toadstool

**Frogstooles,** See Toadstool

**Furze,** See Broom

## Galangal (*Alpina officinalis* or *A. galanga*)

**Description:** A hardy, perennial root spice to 1-2 metres tall with long stems and leaves (6cm wide) which shoot directly from the roots called rhizomes. The roots are similar in appearance to ginger, but not as thick and tend to be more branching, twisting in different directions, with a shiny beige skin, and pink highlights. When cut, the root reveals a creamy/white flesh. Creamy-white, waxy, orchid like flowers form in clusters of 3-4 on thick spikes 20cm long. Each flower spike can have over 300 flowers.

**Influence:** Luck, Money, Break Spells/Curses, Psychic Development, Lust

**Gender**: Masculine, **Element**: Fire, **Planet**: Mars

Worn or carried, galangal is protective and brings good luck. Place in a leather satchet with silver to bring money. Burn powedered galangal to break spells and curses. Carry or sprinkle around the home to promote lust. Wear to aid psychic development and to guard the health. Use ginger as a substitute if galangal is unavailable.

**Cultivation**: Cultivation is easiest by division. Thick stems shoot directly from large, round, yellow rhizomes that can grow larger than a clenched fist. Smaller rhizomes form around the main root. Large 10cm wide leaves stand upright, taking the plant to 1.5 metres high. A red strip runs up the centre of the leaf. Maroon/red flowers form on thick 15cm spikes. The plant dies down over winter and shoots again in spring. Early spring, is a good time to divide the plant for propagation, however, they may be dug at any time for use. It will grow in sun or shade, and requires well-drained, rich soil and sufficient water during dry periods for good growth. Rhizomes are aromatic and pungent with a ginger-sour-lemon flavour.

## Gardenia (*Gardenia* spp.)

**Description:** Gardenias are mostly evergreen shrubs or small trees. They have luxuriant, opposite or whorled, often glossy, deep green leaves. The fragrant, large, tubular to funnel-shaped flowers can be white or yellow and are produced singly or in semi-double and double forms along or at the ends of branches. Cultivated forms often have double rose-like flowers, which open from large buds with a distinctive whorl of petals. Fleshy or leathery berries then follow.

**Influence:** Love, Peace, Healing, Spirituality

**Gender**: Feminine, **Element**: Water, **Planet**: Moon

Carry or wear the pure fragrance or the crushed flowers to attract a new easy love or friendship, Burn with other healing herbs for added peace and comfort for the person who is ailing.

**Cultivation**: Gardenias like semi shade - dappled light, or morning sun, with some warmth. Although sometimes they can be seen growing in a full sun position, their foliage will burn off and flowers damaged in the hot sun. They prefer an acidic soil enriched with composted organic matter. Gardenias grow quite well in containers, and for a spectacular specimen plant, a standard gardenia is excellent.

**Garget** see Poke

**Garlic** (*Allium sativum*)

**Description:** Garlic is a perennial herb that likes moderate soil and lots of sun and warmth. The plant grows to 60 cm tall. The bulb is the most common used portion, although the greens are often used in salads.

**Influence:** Protection, Healing, Exorcism, Lust, Anti-Theft

**Gender**: Masculine, **Element**: Fire, **Planet**: Sun, **Diety**: Hecate

Hang in kitchen, patio, windowsill, to help keep you strong in your will and/or to bring togetherness in the family. Burn while you make your wish. Add to banishing wishes for added punch, carry as a sachet for trips over water. Also said to ward off bad weather when you are participating in outside events. Rub fresh, peeled garlic onto an afflicted part of the body and then throw it into running water. Extremely protective. When evil spirits are around, bite into garlic to send them away. Place beneath children's pillows to protect them while asleep. Also acts as a lust inducer. Used as a sacrifice to Hecate by leaving it at a crossroads.

**Cultivation**: Garlic is grown as a winter crop. Prepare beds by digging over and adding compost. Good drainage is important, so plant into raised beds if the soil is heavy clay. Individual cloves of garlic are planted just below the soil surface from late autumn to the beginning of spring, spaced around 23cm apart. The strappy leaves grow throughout the summer and brown off in late summer/autumn. The clustered bulbs are then dug up with a fork and hung up to dry in an airy place.

**Gentian** (*Gentiana lutea*)

**Description:** The root is long, up to 30 cm or more and over 2.5 cm in diameter. The plant grows to over 120 cm with a pair of yellowish green leaves opposing at each joint. Lower leaves may grow supporting stems. It produces whirling clusters of yellow-orange flowers at the axial of the uppermost leaves. As an ornamental plant alone gentian is a worth addition to the herb garden.

**Influence:** Love, Power

**Gender:** Masculine, **Element:** Fire, **Planet:** Sun

Add to love baths and satchets. When used in an incense or satchet, adds a great deal of extra power. Used to break hexes and curses.

**Cultivation:** Readily grown from seed, Gentian requires deep, strong loamy soil which drains freely. It requires plenty of water and shelter from winds and extreme cold. Taking about 3 years to flowering size, the root is at it's best before this.

**Geranium** (*Pelargonium* spp.)

**Description:** This soft shrub grows to a height of around 90 cm. It has deeply five lobed leaves and grey green stems. The flowers form atop stalked clusters vary in colour from pink to purple and are around 2.5 cm across.

**Influence:** Fertility, Love, Health, Protection

**Gender:** Feminine, **Element:** Water, **Planet:** Venus

Geraniums of all types are protective when grown in the garden or placed freshly-cut into water inside the home. Protects against snakes. Red geraniums told of coming visitors, because they were magickally charged to point to the direction of approaching strangers. They're also very protective and strengthen health. Pink geraniums are used in love spells, and white ones increase fertility. The rose geranium (*Pelargonium graveolens*) is used in protection satchets, and the leaves are rubbed onto doorknobs and windows for protection. Scented geraniums possess powers which are deduced from the scent. For example, nutmeg-scented geraniums have the powers of nutmeg, etc. Use the oil for communication, mending spats between lovers and protecting against further disharmony.

**Cultivation:** Cuttings are the easiest way of propagation, taken in late spring. Welld rained soil is essential with moderately fertile soil in a position with full sun. Over rich soil causes leafy plants and sappy growth.

**Gill-Over-the-Ground,** See Ground Ivy

**Ginger** (*Zingiber officinalis*)

**Description:** Ginger is a perennial reaching to 15 cm in height and is grown for its root. The flowering stalk grows directly from the root and produces a yellow or white bloom.

**Influence:** Love, Money, Success, Power

**Gender:** Masculine, **Element:** Fire, **Planet:** Mars

Burn the crushed dried root for attracting money and success in a business endeavor, carry for power in a given situation (CAUTION: please be sure you have thought out the situation and your stand on it before trying this one, it could backfire on you!) Used in love wishes too as an added boost of power. Eat ginger before spells to make them more powerful. The powdered roots in sprinkled onto money to attract wealth.

**Cultivation:** Plant in spring, when the soil has warmed up, 5-10 cm deep. Ginger is often planted on ridges, usually about 30 cm apart and with 15-23 cm between plants. The crop is planted by setts (small rhizomes) with one or two buds. It thrives best on loamy or alluvial fertile soils and likes the addition of well-rotted manure or compost. It cannot stand water logging. Light shade is required, this is provided by pigeon pea in India. In a perm culture system it is a useful understorey plant.

**Ginseng** (*Panax quinquefolius*)

**Description:** A perennial plant with a large, fleshy slow-growing root with a stem growing to around 30cm high, with 3 leaves, consisting of smaller leaflets, and a single stem with small yellowish flowers, which ripen into a cluster of bright red berries.

**Influence:** Love, Wishes, Healing, Beauty, Protection, Lust

**Gender**: Masculine, **Element**: Fire, **Planet**: Sun

Ginseng stimulates the body to overcome all forms of illness, physical and mental, and is a sexual stimulant. The dried root is used for healing purposes. Ginseng is carried to guard your health and to attract love. It will also ensure sexual potency. Ginseng is an effective substitute for mandrake in all spells.

**Cultivation**: Ginseng can be very difficult to grow. Germination of disinfected seeds (to kill mould, which plagues ginseng at all stages of growth) can take up to a year or more. Plant in early autumn in raised beds of very humus-rich soil. Plants must be shaded at all times. Roots are not harvested until the plants are at least 6 years old. Take care during harvesting and drying not to break off any of the "arms" of the root. Dry for one month before use.

**Goats Leaves,** See Honeysuckle

**Goats Rue** (*Galega officinalis*)

**Description:** Goats Rue is a leguminous plant with stems which rise from the several headed root to about 90 cm. The stems have six to eight pairs of lance shaped bright green smooth leaves on short stalks. It produces small lilac, purplish or white flowers which develop into cylindrical pods. The plant has no scent unless bruised when it emits a disagreeable odour.

**Influence:** Healing, Health

**Gender**: Masculine, **Element**: Air, **Planet**: Mercury

Use in healing rituals. Place the leaves of this plant into the shoe to cure and prevent rheumatism

**Cultivation**: Propagation is from seed but can prove difficult. Once started Goats rue will grow in sandy or rocky soil, or even dry clay amidst the roots of trees. Best in a sunny spot, though will adapt to shade, with reduced growth. Best started as container plants or sow directly and leave to grow, as they do not stand division or replanting once established. Ideal in rock gardens.

**Goldenrod** (*Solidago odora*)

**Description:** Goldenrods are strong-stemmed plants, often growing to 2 metres tall, with either smooth or lightly toothed alternate leaves arising from a root crown or rhizome. They bloom in late summer or fall with sprays of small, usually golden-yellow flowers. Both leaves and flowers produce yellow dye.

**Influence:** Money, Divination

**Gender**: Feminine, **Element**: Air, **Planet**: Venus

Wear a piece of goldenrod to see your future love. When held in the hand, goldenrod nods in the direction of lost things or where buried treasure lies. Used in money spells. If goldenrod springs up suddenly near the front door, unexpected good fortune will come to the family living there.

**Cultivation**: Goldenrods are happy in full sun or partial shade with good, well-drained garden soil. They will also do well in moist conditions.

**Propagating goldenrod:** By division in spring or by seed

## Goldenseal (*Hydrastis canadensis*)

**Description:** Goldenseal prefers rich soils in partial shade. It is a perennial herb that grows 15 cm to 45 cm high. The dried ground root is the part most often used, although the dried leaves are used in teas. It is difficult to grow successfully, and the plants need to be at least 6 years old before harvesting.

**Influence:** Healing, Money

**Gender**: Masculine, **Element**: Fire, **Planet**: Sun

Goldenseal is another natural, powerful antibiotic. It should not be used by pregnant women. The herb goes straight to the bloodstream and eliminates infection in the body. It enables the liver to recover. When used in combination with other herbs, it will boost the properties for the accompanying herbs. Goldenseal is used in property spells, as well as healing spells and rituals.

**Cultivation**: Goldenseal prefers rich soils in partial shade. It is a perennial herb that grows 15 cm – 45 cm high. The dried ground root is the part most often used, although the dried leaves are used in teas. It is difficult to grow successfully, and the plants need to be at least 6 years old before harvesting.

## Golden Bough see Mistletoe

## Goosegrass, See Bedstraw

## Gorse (*Ulex europaeus*)

**Description:** Gorse is commonly seen is waste spaces and as a weed on pasture. It is a dense, multi branched shrub with spiny branches and bright yellow flowers situated on these spines. It seldom grows to over 180 cm in height though clumps to cover large areas. The spines are immature leaves which die and fall easily. In Australia it is a pasture weed.

**Influence:** Protection, Attracts Money

**Gender**: Masculine, **Element**: Fire, **Planet**: Mars

A good protectant against evil. In Wales, hedges of this prickly plant are used to protect the home against fairies, who cannot penetrate it. Use in money spells, for it attracts gold.

**Cultivation**: Sown from seed it grows easily in most soil types.

## Gotu Kola (*Ulex europaeus*)

**Description:** Perennial, creeping, ground cover, which roots at the nodes, as it spreads over the ground. Leaves, from 2-4cm wide, and kidney-shaped, with a v-shaped slot, where the leaf joins the stem: often with serrated margins, which gives them the appearance of miniature fans. Size of leaves can depend on climate, season, soil structure, fertility and growing position: whether in sun or shade. Small-sized leaves usually hug the ground and have a short petiole stem; however, large leaves can have a petiole up to 20cm long. When plants are grown in the shade, they tend to have large leaves and very long petioles. This petiole stem can have a pink/purple tinge. Pink flowers 5mm across, usually set 2 to 4, side by side, as an umbel, developing from the stem nodes. Flowers are so small (and often hidden underneath leaves) that, generally, the flower is not noticed at all. Although gotu kola belongs to the umbel family of plants, now classified as Apiaceae, there is very little resemblance to other umbel plants: like parsley, dill, fennel and coriander. Seeds, of gotu kola, form in flat, oval capsules, usually containing two tiny, brown, kidneyshaped seeds.

**Influence:** Meditation

Gotu Kola is and excellent mental stimulant. It is often used after mental breakdowns, and used regularly, can prevent nervous breakdown, as it is a brain cell stimulant. It relieves mental fatigue and senility, and aids the body in defending itself against toxins. Gotu Kola is used in meditation incenses. Burn a small amount prior to (but not during) meditation.

**Gender**_____, **Element**_____, **Planet:** _____

**Cultivation:** Growing gotu kola: Gotu kola is propagated from seed, which is sown in Spring. It prefers a tropical climate – very hot and wet – and it flourishes in areas such as rice paddies. Either the whole plant or just the leaves can be harvested at any time once mature.

**Gourd** (*Curcurbita* spp.)

**Description:** Ornamental gourds are the gaily coloured, oddly shaped, squash-like, hard-skinned fruits of plants closely related to the edible squashes and pumpkins. Most of the fancy gourds have long, climbing, or creeping stems. They can be grown on trellises, arbours, and fences, thus making attractive display plantings. However, usually the fruit rather than the growing plant is considered ornamental. These fruit are generally most useful and attractive as ornaments when the pulp dries and the shell becomes hard. There are many shapes and colours of these fancy gourds. Some are warty, some are smooth, some long, some round, some striped, and some banded. Most of them are not grown as vegetables, although some are edible if eaten at an immature stage, such as the luffa gourd (sometimes called running okra).

**Influence:** Protection

**Gender**: Feminine, **Element**: Water, **Planet**: Moon

Hang gourds at the front door to protect against fascination. Pieces of gourd carried in the pocket or purse ward off evil. Gourds filled with dried beans are used to make rattles which scare evil spirits away. Use a gourd with its top cut off as a scrying bowl.

**Cultivation**: Gourds do best if grown on a trellis because of their vining nature and for prevention of fruit rots. Hills (1-2 seeds each) may be spaced 30 cm to 60 cm apart at the base of the trellis. If planted in an open garden, allow 1.2 metres between vines in the row and 1.2 metres between rows. Plant as soon as the danger of killing frost is past.

**Grain**

**Description:** Grains are mostly grasses cultivated for their edible grains or seeds. Cereal grains are grown in greater quantities and provide more energy worldwide than any other type of crop. They are also a rich source of carbohydrate

**Influence:** Protection

Scatter grain around your bedroom to protect yourself against evil. To protect children while they are away from you, throw a handful of grain after them as they leave, but be sure they don't see you do this.

**Gender**_____, **Element**_____, **Planet:** _____

**Cultivation:** Grown from Seed. See specific grain for further details.

## Grains of Paradise (*Aframomum melegueta*)

**Description:** *Aframomum melegueta* is a species in the ginger family, Zingiberaceae. It is commonly known as Grains of Paradise, and is a herbaceous perennial plant native to swampy habitats along the West African coast. Its trumpet-shaped, purple flowers develop into 5 to 7 cm long pods containing numerous small, reddish-brown seeds. The seeds have a pungent, peppery taste. Essential oils, which are the dominating flavor components in the closely related cardamom, occur only in traces. The seeds can be ground in a mill like peppercorns or may be used in the same way as cardamom, either by frying whole or pounding with other spices. Store in an airtight container.

**Influence:** Love, Lust, Luck, attract money.

**Gender:** Masculine, **Element:** Fire, **Planet:** Mars

Used in love, lust, luck, and money spells and satchets. It is also an herb used for wishing; hold some in your hands, make a wish, then throw a little of the herb in each direction, beginning in the North and ending the the West.

**Cultivation:** Growing from a rhizome, it reaches 1m (3ft). The methods used are similar to those for cardamom and ginger.

## Grape (*Vitis vinifera*)

**Description:** Grape is a frost hardy deciduous vine best known for wine made from it's fruit. Grows to around 1.5 metres and is grown in rows.

**Influence:** Fertility, Garden Magick, Mental Powers, Money

**Gender:** Feminine, **Element:** Water, **Planet:** Moon

Paint pictures of grapes onto garden walls to ensure fertility. Eat grapes or raisins for increased fertility, as well as to strengthen mental powers. Place grapes on the altar during money spells.

**Cultivation:** This frost hardy deciduous vine prefers a sunny position with deep fertile, moist soil with an alkaline to neutral Ph. Seeds can be sown in autumn or semi ripe cuttings will sprout easily in summer, however commercial stock is often grafted onto disease resistant rootstock. Many fruit and wine varieties are available through nurseries.

## Grass

**Description:** Probably the most important group of plants can be classified under this herb name, including most grains such as wheat, barley, oats etc and the coarser kinds providing stock feed. Not to mention the humble backyard lawn.

**Influence:** Psychic Powers, Protection

Tie knots in grass around the home to drive out evil and protect it. Carry blades of grass to help psychic powers.

**Gender**_____, **Element**_____, **Planet:**_____

**Cultivation**: Sewn from seed, turf can also be purchased in rolls, where rootstock and leaf have been harvested with a layer of soil. Varieties are available for all soil types and conditions.

**Gravel Root,** See Meadowsweet

**Green Ginger,** See Wormwood

**Ground Ivy** (*Nepeta glechoma*)

**Description:** Although similar leaves to ivy, the plant is entirely different. Producing purplish-blue flowers over summer this hardy perennial grows to around 15 cm.

**Influence:** Divination

Use ground ivy to discover who is working negative magick against you. Place the herb around the base of a yellow candle and burn on a Tuesday; you will known the person.

**Gender**_____, **Element**_____, **Planet:**_____

**Cultivation**: Ground ivy will grow in either sunny or shaded positions, preferring moist well drained soil. Grown from seed sown in spring or by division in spring or autumn.

**Groundsel** (*Senecio* spp.)

**Description:** Groundsel gets it's name from Anglo Saxon where it literally means Ground Swallower. It is a world wide weed, growing anywhere ground has been tilled. It is an annual growing to 15 cm – 30 cm frequently purplish in colour with jagged oblong leaves. It produces yellow cylindrical flowerheads resulting in a downy seed head. Groundsel is especially a problem in forage crops because it is toxic to livestock.

**Influence:** Health, Healing

**Gender**: Feminine, **Element**: Water, **Planet**: Venus

Carried as an amulet against toothache, as well as to stop the pain if it starts. Also carried to keep the teeth in general good health.

**Cultivation**: Not a desirable plant to grow in the garden, Cultivation kills groundsel plants, and if done prior to seed formation is an effective control method. New plants, however, coming either from the reservoir of seeds in the soil or from seeds blown in from adjacent areas, will establish readily in newly-cultivated soil.

**Gulfwrack,** See Bladderwrack

**Gum Arabic** (*Acacia vera*)

**Description:** A small, undersized tree or shrub, which occasionally, however, attains a height of about 12 metres, with a trunk from 1 metre to 1.5 metres in circumference. The thorns are stipulary, sometimes long, sometimes short, or almost wanting. The flowers are small, yellow, and in globose heads. Each flower has a five-cleft corolla and numerous, distinct stamens. The bark is used to make a gum, most commonly known as Gum Arabic. Australian Acacias (Wattles) produce similar Gum.

**Influence:** Purify negativity and evil

**Gender**: Masculine, **Element**: Air, **Planet**: Sun

Add to incense's for good vibrations, or smoulder alone. Purifies the area of negativity and evil.

> **Cultivation**: The usual way of growing acacias from seed is by first soaking the seed in near boiling water and leaving it overnight. Alternatively, if only a few seeds are to be sown, the seed case can be "nicked" with a long sharp needle or blade (taking care not to damage the inner part of the seed) and then sow in the normal way. The phyllodinous acacias are quite successfully grown from cuttings and, if you want to grow more of a favourite plant, this is the only way to go. Unfortunately, hybridisation takes place in our gardens so you can't rely on the seed coming true to type from that source. The ferny leaved species appear to be much more difficult to strike as the tiny leaflets tend to fall off quickly and the cutting soon dies.

**Gum Plant,** See Comfrey

**Hagthorn,** See Hawthorn

**Hag's Tapers,** See Mullein

**Hawaiian Good-luck-plant,** See Ti

**Hawthorn** (*Crataegus oxacantha*)

> **Description:** Hawthorn is a deciduous tree or shrub, that can reach 12 metres tall. It grows throughout North America. It is tolerant of most soils, but prefers alkaline, rich, moist loam. Consult a nursery for the best species to use in your area.
>
> **Influence:** Fertility, Chastity, Fishing Magick, Happiness, Protection, Success in working matters, Purity.
>
> **Gender**: Masculine, **Element**: Fire, **Planet**: Mars

The wood is used in making magickal wands and other tools. A tea is made and drank during incantations of the wishes. Used to increase fertility; it is often used in weddings (especially those in spring) due to this power. Interestingly, the leaves are used to enforce or maintain chastity; place beneath the mattress or around the bedroom. Protects against lightning and evil ghosts. Protects against storm damage. The hawthorn is sacred to fairies and is part of the tree fairy triad of Britain ("Oak, Ash, and Thorn"). Where all three grow together, you can see fairies. Carry in a sachet on a fishing trip to ensure a good catch, and wear or carry to promote happiness in troubled, sad, or depressed people.

**Cultivation**: Best planted as a small tree obtained from a commercial nursery, Hawthorn is tolerant of most soils, but prefers alkaline, rich, moist loam. Consult a nursery for the best species to use in your area. The fruit is the part used in healing.

**Hazel** (*Corylus* spp.)

**Description:** This deciduous shrub or small tree which grows to 10 metres is a native of Europe, Asia and North Africa.

**Influence:** Wisdom, Luck, Fertility, Anti-Lightning, Protection, Wishes

**Gender**: Masculine, **Element**: Air, **Planet**: Sun

The Wood is used for all magickal tools, Especially good in all luck wishes. A sachet of the fruit of the tree is given to new brides for luck in marriage and fertility. Place the sprigs up high in the room for a powerful magickal protection and luck. Eat the nuts to give wisdom and increase fertility. Weave hazel twigs into a crown and wear when wishing. Twigs of hazel are placed in window frames to protect from lightning, and three pins of hazel wood driven into the house will protect it from fire.

**Cultivation**: Hazelnut trees do best when planted in a well-drained, fertile, slightly acid soil. Commercial varieties are available from nurseries. They do best where the winter temps are above -10.

**Hearts Ease,** See Pansy

**Heath see** Heather

**Heather** (*Calluna Vulgaris*)

**Description:** Heather (Calluna vulgaris) is an evergreen branching shrub. Heather flowers bloom in late summer. Wild species of Heather flowers are usually in purple or mauve shades. The flower's variuos cultivars come in colors ranging from white, through pink, a wide range of purples, and reds. Different varieties of Heather Flowers bloom from late July to November in the northern hemisphere. The flowers may turn brown but still remain on the plants over winter, and this can lead to interesting effects. The Heather plant is one of the primary plant species grown on the poor, acid, sandy soils typical of heaths.

**Influence:** Protection, Rain Making, Luck.

**Gender**: Feminine. **Planet**: Venus. **Element**: Water. **Deity**: Isis, Osiris, Venus

Robert Graves said heather is "a suitable tree for the inititation of Scottish witches." Brings one in touch with divinity and increases physical beauty. Wearing an amulet of the wood will bring a long physical life and put one in touch with the truly immortal soul. A valuable herb for those who pursue initiatory paths. Unfolds the inner self. Carried, it will guard against rape or other violent crimes or just to bring good luck. (White heather is best here.) Also promotes peace in the home when hung or used in decorations for the home, hang in the bedroom for peaceful sleep, place on the altar for boosting other herbs and items to enhance psychic awareness. When burned with fern will attract rain.

**Cultivation**: Heather prefers rocky or sandy soils and full sun. It is an evergreen shrub that grows 1 metre tall.

**Heliotrope** (*Heliotropium europaeum* or *H. arborescens*)

**Description:** Now common to Australia this plant is cultivated for it's attractive appearance. It is a half hardy perennial growing to around 70cm.

**Influence:** Exorcism, Prophetic Dreams, Healing, Wealth, Invisibility

**Gender**: Masculine, **Element**: Fire, **Planet**: Sun

Burn or carry for banishing or repelling negative influences around you, and for increasing courage and will power. Also used fresh under the pillow for psychic dreams. Place beneath the pillow to induce prophetic dreams; if you've been robbed, the thief will appear in your dream. Used in exorcism incenses and mixtures, as well as in healing sachets. Place in the pocket or purse to attract wealth and money, or ring green candles with this herb and burn completely for this purpose. Fill a small horn with heliotrope and wear or carry it; your movements and actions will not draw attention.

**Cultivation**: It is easily grown from seed sown 2 mm deep in light, sandy soil. It may be propagated by division of the rootstock in spring. It spreads itself rapidly by suckers rising from the roots. Fertile well drained soil, even loamy sand is ideal. Happy in Full sun or part shade.

## Hellebore, Black (*Helleborus niger*)  POISONOUS

**Description**: Helleborus niger (often known as "Christmas Rose") is a perennial plant which produces large white flowers that sometimes turn pink or deep red-pink as they age. H. Niger is one of the few species where double flowers have been found and disseminated commercially.

**Influence:** Protection. Provides an aura or mantle of invisibility.

**Gender**: Feminine. **Planet**: Saturn. **Element**: Water.

The safest use of this herb is to place pieces of the root or dried berries in an amulet or magick pouch. Used to bless farm animals and pets. Good for working with familiars. Scatter powdered hellebore before you as you walk and you shall be invisible. Once used in exorcism rituals and for inducing astral projection. This herb is very dangerous don't breathe the fumes or ingest!

**Cultivation**: Hellebore seed may take 6-18 months (or more) to germinate; however, if you start with fresh seed and sow it soon after harvest, then your chances of achieving high germination percentages are quite good. When sowing in pots, place seed about 5 mm below the surface and firm lightly. Top dress the pots with grit and water occasionally, just enough to keep the soil mixture slightly moist. Hellebores have extensive root systems, often deeper than the height of the plant. Though it is possible to divide at almost any time of the year in some climates, late spring and early fall generally provide the most opportune times for many gardeners. Dividing hellebores is the only simple way to produce more of a special plant. Though hellebores will grow in a great variety of soil conditions, a well-drained base containing plenty of organic matter suits them. Preparing deep beds will provide the extensive root systems plenty of growing room and potentially many decades of healthy growth. Ideally, the soil should receive regular moisture without being waterlogged. However, the plants are surprisingly drought-tolerant once established and can survive in less than optimum conditions.

## Helmet Flower, See Skullcap

## Hemlock (*Conium maculatum*) POISONOUS

**Description:** Hemlock is a tall biennial many branched graceful plant with elegantly cut foliage and white flowers. It has perfectly smooth hollow stems marked with irregular red spots or splotches. It grows to a height of 60cm to 120cm in height. It has a long forked yellow root, similar to parsnip, (to which it is related). It has numerous leaves, with first season leaves becoming very large, up to 60cm. The flowers are small and white.

**Influence:** Destroy Sexual Drive, Flying Purification

**Gender**: Feminine. **Planet**: Saturn. **Element**: Water. **Deity**: Hecate

A very dangerous herb. Destroys sexual drive. Induces astral projection. Juice rubbed on magickal blades empower and purify them. Used in medievel flying ointments.

**Cultivation**: Hemlock reproduces from seeds which usually germinate in autumn. Annual plants flower in the first spring, produce seeds and die in summer. Biennial plants remain in a vegetative state until their second spring, flower, then set seed and die in their second summer. It prefers moist, neglected situations. Hemlock grows rapidly after autumn rains, and on disturbed soils can exclude most other vegetation. It does not readily invade well managed established pastures.

**Hemp** (*Cannibus sativa*)

**Description:** Hemp is the common name for plants of the entire family of *Cannabis*, although the term is often used to refer only to *Cannabis* strains cultivated for industrial (non-drug) use. Millennia of selective breeding have resulted in varieties that look quite different. Also, breeding since circa 1930 has focused quite specifically on producing strains which would perform very poorly as sources of drug material. Hemp grown for fibre is planted closely, resulting in tall, slender plants with long fibres. Ideally the herb should be harvested before it flowers.

**Influence:** Healing, Love, Vision, Meditation

**Gender**: Feminine, **Element**: Water, **Planet**: Saturn

This herb is also known as marijuana, and is an illegal substance and so it isn't recommend trying any of these rituals, though non drug varieties are available. To see a vision of a future spouse, people would take a handful of hempseeds to a church at midnight. Once there, they walked around the church nine times and sprinkled the seeds as they went and repeated "Hempseed I sow, hempseed I sow, who will come after me and mow?". Was also once part of many vision, meditation, and scrying incenses. Mugwort and hemp were prescribed to be burned before a magick mirror to gain visions. Scourges made of hemp were used in China as imitation snakes to drive out illness-causing demons from a sick person. This was done by beating the hemp against the sickbed.

**Cultivation**: Hemp prefers deep, moist, humus rich soil. Best success comes from planting fresh seed, after danger of frost has passed.

**Henbane** (*Hyosycamus niger*)  **POISONOUS**

**Description:** Famous as the poison that killed Hamlet's father, this HIGHLY POISONOUS biennial which grows up to 90cm. The leaf is deeply divided, pale and covered in hair, grows up to 30cm, in lenghth. It had creamy white bell shaped flowers with purplish flowers which appear from spring through autumn.

**Gender**: Feminine. **Planet**: Saturn. **Element**: Water.

**Influence:** Love, Consecration, attracts Hares

A love-bringing herb when worn. Traditionally used in ointments and brews. Induces delirium. Used with wisdom, it could be an excellent herb for consecrating ceremonial vessels. Attracts hares, therefore would be an excellent herb for those who raise rabbits.

**Cultivation**: Henbane does well in most soils, as it is found wild in dry waste places. It is propagated easily by seed. Henbane seed is very viable. The seed should be planted in May or when the weather is in the 70's. It should be sown very thinly in rows 60 cm – 100 cm apart. The bed should be kept moist until sprouting, and the seedlings should be thinned to 45 cm to 60 cm apart in the row. They may also be sown in flats at room temperature and transplanted out on a cool day.

**Henbells see** Henbane

**Henna** (*Lawsonia inermis*)

**Description:** Henna is a tall shrub or small tree, 2–6 m high. It is glabrous, multibranched with spine tipped branchlets. Leaves are opposite, elliptical, and broadly lanceolate (1.5–5.0 cm x 0.5–2 cm), having depressed veins on the dorsal surface. During the onset of rainy intervals, the plant grows rapidly; putting out new shoots, then growth slows. The leaves gradually yellow and fall during prolonged dry or cool intervals. Henna flowers have four sepals and a 2 mm calyx tube with 3 mm spread lobes. Petals are obvate, white or red stamens inserted in pairs on the rim of the calyx tube. Fruits are small, brownish capsules, 4–8 mm in diameter, with 32–49 seeds per fruit, and open irregularly into four splits.

**Influence:** Healing. Love, Virility

**Gender**_____, **Element**_____, **Planet**: Jupiter.

Place on forehead to relieve headache. Attracts love if worn near the heart. Protects from illness and from evil eye. A body adornment originating in the Mediterranean. Modern witches use as a ritual adornment, especially for the Great Rite and other important ritual occasions. Henna mixed with olive oil, massaged on the penis at the rising and setting suns promotes virility. Henna body art is made by applying henna paste to the skin: the lawsone in the paste migrates into the outermost layer of the skin and makes a red-brown stain.

Whole, unbroken henna leaves will not stain the skin. Henna will not stain skin until the lawsone molecules are made available (released) from the henna leaf. Fresh henna leaves will stain the skin if they are smashed with a mildly acidic liquid. This will stain skin within moments, but it is difficult to form intricate patterns from coarse crushed leaves. Dried ground, sifted henna leaves are easily worked into a paste that can used to make intricate body art. Commercially available henna powder is made by drying the henna leaves and milling them to powder, then the powder is sifted. This powder is mixed with lemon juice, strong tea, or other mildly acidic liquids. Essential oils with high levels of "terps", monoterpene alcohols such as tea tree, eucalyptus, cajeput, or lavender will improve skin stain characteristics. The henna mix must rest for 6 to 12 hours so the leaf cellulose is dissolved, making the lawsone available to stain the skin.

**Cultivation:** Henna can be grown from seed or semi-hardwood cuttings. Henna in needs a high rainfall as well as a fairly good soil. Sow seeds in spring cover lightly with compost and be patient: germination can be slow, sometimes several months. The process may be speeded by sealing the pot inside a plastic bag and putting it in a warm place, such as an airing cupboard. Once germinated, pot seedlings up on into individual pots and keep in a sunny position. Water well during the growing season and repot annually every spring until the plant is in a 45cm pot. Flowering will not take place until the plants are at least 5 or 6 years old, and usually needs high winter temperatures to stimulate the plants to start, although once a pattern of flowering is begun, it usually repeats reliably in following years. Surplus leaves can be clipped form the plant as soon as it is large enough.

**Herb Bennet see** Hemlock

**Herb of Circe see** Mandrake

**Herb of Grace,** See Rue

**Hibiscus** (*Hibiscus* spp.)

> **Description:** *Hibiscus* is a large genus of about 200–220 species of flowering plants in the family <u>Malvaceae</u>, native to warm temperate, subtropical and tropical regions throughout the world. The genus includes both annual and perennial herbaceous plants, and woody shrubs and small trees. The leaves are alternate, simple, ovate to lanceolate, often with a toothed or lobed margin. The flowers are large, conspicuous, trumpet-shaped, with five or more petals, ranging from white to pink, red, purple or yellow, and from 4-15 cm broad. The fruit is a dry five-lobed capsule, containing several seeds in each lobe, which are released when the capsule splits open at maturity.
>
> **Gender**: Feminine, **Element**: Water, **Planet**: Venus
>
> **Influence:** Lust, Love, Divination
>
> The blossoms are used in love incenses and sachets. The flowers of a red hibiscus are brewed into a lust-inducing tea.
>
> **Cultivation**: In order to obtain the best results from your hibiscus, the selection of the planting position is most important. Make sure you choose an open sunny situation, preferably sheltered from cold prevailing winds. Full sun is essential, although hibiscus will grow and survive in shaded positions, they will not bloom as prolifically as if planted in full sun. Hibiscus do well on northern walls, and will grow with other shrubs, but they prefer to be planted on their own. Half a day's sun is the minimum requirement Hibiscus prefer a sandy soil which has been enriched by the addition of compost with good drainage being essential . If the drainage appears doubtful at all, it is a good idea to raise the level of the beds intended for planting about 25-35 cm. Hibiscus cannot tolerate "wet feet".

**Hickory** (*Carya* spp.)

> **Description:** Hickory nut is a nut from a tree in the Carya genus, which encompasses almost 20 species, most of which are native to North America. The nuts have long been used as a source of food, and the trees have also been bred to produce specific economically viable hybrids. It can be difficult to find true hickory nuts for sale, as the trees are not ideally suited to widespread commercial cultivation. When they are available, the nuts vary in quality, shape, and size, depending on the species. The hickory tree is in the walnut family, and the trees do look like walnuts at a glance. They are densely branched, with pinnately compound leaves. The leaves are very mildly serrated, and trees produce catkins in the spring. Some of these catkins will mature into hickory nuts if they are properly fertilized. Like other nuts in the walnut family, the hickory nut is hard shelled and covered in a woody outer layer. The trees are also cultivated for their highly commercially useful wood, which is often used in smoking and furniture making.

**Influence:** Legal Matters

Burn a piece of hickory root to ashes, mix with cinquefoil and place the mixture in a box. Hang over the door to make sure you won't have trouble with the law.

**Gender**_____, **Element**_____, **Planet:** _____

**Cultivation**: Plant young trees in a well drained site with the root collar just below the surface. The graft should be above the ground. Trees planted too deeply die. Use good topsoil and tamp it firmly but gently around the roots. Protect the roots from drying sun and wind while preparing the hole. Water well after planting. Prune the top about one fifth to promote vigor. Control of weeds and other competition in a two meter (yard) circle is very important for at least the first five years. A mulch is beneficial Generally two or more different cultivars are needed for cross pollination.

**High John the Conqueror** (*Ipomoea Purga* or *I. jalapa*)  **POISONOUS**

**Description:** High John the Conqueror is Jalap Root. This climbing vine has many names, both common and botanical. Some common names are Jalap Bindweed, Conqueror Root, High John Root, Ipomoea, and Turpeth. The plant is native to South America and Mexico. It has been grown in gardens in Europe as an ornamental. Jalap is a climbing, evergreen vine, reaching about 4 metres, with heart-shaped leaves and trumpet-like purple flowers. It is cultivated in Central America, parts of Peru, the West Indies, and Southeast Asia. Resin is derived from alcoholic extraction of the root powder. The tuberous, thickened, secondary roots, called black rhubarb tubers, are harvested from mid summer to autumn and dried in the sun, on hot ash, or over an open fire.

**Influence:** Money, Love, Success, Happiness

**Gender**: Masculine, **Element**: Fire, **Planet**: Mars

An excellent herb for increase in all areas of prosperity! Add to other money herbs and oils to enhance their effect. High John is useful in spells for winning and success, psychic powers, protection, love, and "making things happen". Annoint a root with Peppermint Oil and tie up in a green sachet. Carry this with you to attract prosperity, wealth, and success. You can also carry a yellow sachet to stop depression, or pink to draw love. To make a simple, all-purpose anointing oil, take three roots from this plant, make small cuts in them with a sharp knife, and place them in a bottle of carrier oil. Let them soak for several weeks. Leave the roots in the oil and use.

**Cultivation**: Requires a well-drained humus-rich soil in a sunny position. This species is not very frost tolerant, though it might be possible to grow it outdoors in a very sheltered position in mild areas. Either cut the plant back or thin out the shoots in the spring. Propagation is by seed, sown in spring in a greenhouse or by semi-ripe cuttings in the summer.

**Hog Apple see** May Apple

**Hogsbean see** Henbane

**Holy Ghost Herb,** See Holy Thistle

**Holly** (*Ilex aquifolium* or *I. opaca*)

**Description:** Hollies are shrubs and trees from 2–25 m tall, with a wide distribution. The leaves are simple, and can be either deciduous or evergreen depending on the species, and may be entire, finely toothed, or with widely-spaced, spine-tipped serrations. They are mostly <u>dioecious</u>, with male and female flowers on different plants, with some exceptions. Pollination is mainly by bees and other insects. The fruit is a small berry, usually red when mature, with one to ten seeds. Holly berries are mildly toxic and will cause vomiting and/or diarrhea when ingested by people; however they are extremely important food for numerous species of birds, and also are eaten by other wild animals. In the autumn and early winter the berries are hard and apparently unpalatable but after being frozen or frosted several times, the berries soften, and become milder in taste. During winter storms, birds often take refuge in hollies, which provide shelter, protection from predators (by the spiny leaves), and food.

**Influence:** Protection, Anti-Lightning, Luck, Dream Magick. One of the best protective herbs.

**Gender**: Masculine. **Planet**: Mars. **Element**: Fire. **Deity**: Holly King

The wood of the holly is very well suited for the handle of the ritual knife as it both attracts and repels energies. It is powerful when defense is needed in circle while preserving the gentleness within it. Holly water is sprinkled on newborn babies to protect them. Carried by men, it promotes luck. (Ivy is the corresponding plant of luck for women). Decorate the house with it at Yule for good luck. If you throw a holly plant at a wild animal, it will leave you alone.

**Cultivation**: Next to selecting varieties that are appropriate to your climate and landscaping needs, the most important concern is supplying the plants with an adequate growing medium. All hollies develop best in well-drained (but not dry), fertile, light loamy soil that has a neutral or slightly acid pH. Be sure to allow sufficient room for the full-grown plant, too (unless you're planning to trim the trees into a hedge), as many hollies require a good deal of space to develop. The best time to plant hollies is during the dormant season, which in most areas is in the early spring, before any new growth appears. However, in regions that have mild winters, such as the South, transplanting can also be done successfully in the late Autumn.

It's generally recommended that you buy your plants from a nursery, as transplanting hollies is often unsuccessful and it's impossible to be certain of the sex of small wild trees. And, of course, if you're seeking a specific cultivar, you'll *have* to purchase it from a nursery. Holly plants grow in male and female sexes. The female holly needs a <u>male</u> holly for pollination in order to grow berries and whilst male holly plants never grow berries, as long as there is a male holly bush within 30 metres of the female, the female plant will grow berries. Sometimes it can take up to 6 years for the holly bush to develop the full fruit and colour that it should. Once the holly grows fruit it will last 2-3 months and become an enjoyable source of food for the birds during winter..

**Holy grass,** See Sweetgrass

**Holy Wood see** Mistletoe

**Honesty** (*Lunaria* spp.)

**Description:** Lunaria or Honesty flowers are commonly called "Money Plants" because their prolific seed pods resemble coins. They are popular in home gardens and flowerbeds. The visual display of seed pods turn from green to golden brown. After the seed pods and stems have turned golden and dried, they can be used in dried floral arrangements and last for extended periods of time. Lunaria have large green leaves and is a biennial. Plant them year one and they will bloom the following year. If you want a low maintenance flower, you have come to the right plant. They are very easy to grow and experience few problems

**Influence:** Money, Repelling Monsters

**Gender**: Feminine, **Element**: Earth, **Planet**: Moon

Carry this plant to repel monsters. Used in money spells. Carry in a purse or pocket to draw wealth.

**Cultivation**: Lunaria are grown from seeds. Sow seeds early in the season and cover lightly with soil. They germinate easily and will grow large green leaves in the first year. Select a location in your garden where they can grow undisturbed for years and years. After blooming, they will drop seeds and regenerate year after year. Because Lunaria are biennials, if you want flowers every year, you have to plant them two years in a row. Lunaria are easy to grow and require little to no attention. They can be grown in almost any soils and thrive in partial and shady areas. They should have at least four to six hours of sunshine.

**Honeysuckle** (Lonicera caprifolium)

**Description:** This group consists of about 180, evergreen and deciduous, woody climbers and shrubs, commonly known as Honeysuckle. They are valued for their pretty flowers, which are sweetly scented, and their decorative fruits, which birds find delectable. The climbing Honeysuckles are suitable for growing over a trellis, arch, or pergola, while the shrubby kind are great for growing in borders and rock gardens, and as hedges. Their trumpet-shaped flowers are borne from late winter or early spring to late summer and range in color from cream and light yellow to vivid scarlet and purplish-rose. They are followed by pretty fruits that may be white, yellow, orange, red, blue, and black.

**Influence:** Money, Psychic Powers, Protection.

**Gender:** Masculine. **Planet**: Jupiter. **Element**: Earth

Ring green candles with honeysuckle flowers to attract money or place them in a vase in the house for the same purpose. Lightly crush flowers and rub on forehead to heighten psychic powers. The extracted oil is best for increasing spiritual sight. It enhances understanding of images and impressions collected in the astral. Connects one with the mysteries of the Cauldron of Cerridwen. In ritual, dried, powdered bark may be used as incense.

**Cultivation**: Seeds or cuttings may be used to increase these plants. Seeds should be sown in early spring in two parts sandy loam and one part leaf mulch. The young plants should be potted singly in small pots as soon as they are large enough to handle, and eventually out in a nursery bed. Cuttings of short side shoots about 10 cm long can be taken in autumn and inserted in a bed of sand in a closed propagating case. Roots should form in a few weeks. The new plants can be planted in a nursery bed in the spring. It prefers partial shade to full sun and moist soil. Prune back hard in winter to prevent the build-up of woody growth, provide a trellis. Climbing Vine, Shrub, it has a dense root system that may extend laterally for a distance of 2 to 3 metres, and attain depths of 1 to 1.5 metres.

**Hooded Skullcap** see Skullcap

**Hoodwort,** See Skullcap

**Hops** (*Humulus lupulus*)

**Description:** Hops is a perennial climber growing to 6 metres, dying back each autumn leaving fleshy root stock. The stems bear pairs of maple like leaves. Male and Female f lowers are found on separate stems with the male flowers carried in clusters.

**Influence:** Healing, Sleep

**Gender**: Masculine, **Element**: Water, **Planet**: Mars

A tea drank before bedtime helps with a restful sleep, also drank after magick acts to help balance and refocus oneself back to the everyday world. Use in healing sachets and amulets and the dried herb is also burned during healing prayers.

**Cultivation**: Propagation is usually from seed, own in a frame or trellis in spring. Moist fertile soil is best though not essential. Hops prefer full sun, though the base of the plant san be in shade once grown, making a trellis or arbour a suitable frame. Apply organic matter at the base at least every other spring.

**Horehound** (*Marrubium vulgare*)

**Description:** Horehound is an evergreen woody perennial, growing to 30 cm – 60 cm in height. Forming clumps as it grows, it has fine white hairs which give it a grey appearance. The leaves are somewhat rounded and have a corrugated texture.

**Influence:** Protection, Mental Powers, Exorcism, Healing

**Gender**: Masculine, **Element**: Air, **Planet**: Mercury, **Deity**: Horace

Burn as a sacrifice to Horus. As a tea, used for increased energy and strength when needed in situations and to clear your mind, promote quick thinking, and strengthen mental powers. Increases the power of strength and mental clarity wishes. Carried or burned for protection wishes. Used in protective sachets, and is carried to guard against sorcery and fascination. Scattered as an exorcism herb. Mix with ash leaves and place in a bowl of water to release healing vibrations. Place in a sickroom.

**Cultivation**: Sow seed in the final site in spring, or divide mature plants at this time. Horehound likes dry sandy soils and full sun. It is a perennial (except in very cold climates) that reaches to 1 metre tall. It is a vigorous grower and can become a pest if not carefully controlled. It needs little water, tolerates poor soils, and does best in full sun. It blooms during its second year. Cut back the tops to about 7 cm above ground level in early spring to maintain a neat plant and promote new growth.

**Horse Chestnut** (*Aesculus* spp.) ☠ **POISONOUS**

**Description:** This hardy deciduous tree grows to 40 metres, producing "conkers", the mahogany coloured fruit. Unlike sweet chestnuts these are unsuitable for human consumption, but fine as stock fodder, or for little boys as a plaything.

**Influence:** Money, Healing

**Gender**: Masculine, **Element**: Fire, **Planet**: Jupiter

Carry to ward off rheumatism, backaches, arthritis, and chills. Carry three to guard against giddiness. Wrap a dollar bill around a horse chestnut, place into a sachet, and carry to attract money. Also carry for success in all things.

**Cultivation**: As a tree, it can be sown from seed in autumn or purchased from nurseries. It does best in fertile soil with good drainage. Happy with full sun or part shade, it should be remembered this tree is quite large, growing to 40 metres.

## Horseradish (*Cochlearia armoracia*)

**Description:** Horseradish is a hardy perennial with large 50cm long basal leaves with thick petioles, forming a rosette near the ground. Leaves are unusual in that, two, quite different; leaf forms can appear on the same plant. Some are scalloped, wavy, lanceolate leaves, while others can be very deeply cut. Midribs beneath leaves are very raised. Flower stems rise higher than the leaves. Clusters of small, four-petalled, white flowers set at the stem terminals. Rarely, are seed viable.

**Influence:** Purification, Exorcism

**Gender**: Masculine, **Element**: Fire, **Planet**: Mars

The root, when dried and ground can be sprinkled around the house, in corners, on the front steps, and on doorsills to make all evil powers leave. This will also diffuse any spells that may have been sent against you.

**Cultivation**: Propagation from root cuttings of about 23cm is the usual method. These should be around the same size as a pencil with a horizontal cut on the upper side and a diagonal spike on the bottom. Planted vertically at 40 - 45 cm spacing in a sunny position. Soil needs to be well draining but moisture retaining, so plenty of organic matter and composted manure is important. Water in dry spells and keep the bed well weeded. The crop is ready in late autumn and roots for replanting should be stored in a frost free environment.

## Horse's Hoof, See Ginger

## Horsetail (*Equisetum* spp.)

**Description:** Surviving almost unchanged since prehistoric times, this hardy perennial grows to around 80cm. It is a particularly tenacious plant and should be well contained in a garden to prevent it becoming a nuisance.

**Influence:** Snake Charming, Fertility

**Gender**: Feminine, **Element**: Earth, **Planet**: Saturn

Whistles made of horsetail stems will call snakes to the musicians when played. Use in fertility mixtures, or place in the bedroom for this purpose.

**Cultivation**: Horsetail needs swamps and damp places to grow, in full sun to partial shade. It grows to 30cm to 60 cm tall. Propagate by division in spring. This plant becomes a problem easily and should be well contained in the garden.

## Houndstongue (*Cynoglossum officinale*)

**Description:** Houndstongue is a biennial, poisonous herb that is native to Eurasia. The plant is a member of the Borage family, which includes more commonly known plants such as Virginia bluebells, forget-me-nots and the fiddlenecks. It reproduces by seeds and appears as a leafy rosette in its first year. The stem is erect, stout, heavy, 30 cm to 1 metre high, usually branched above. The leaves are alternate, the basal and lower ones are broad, and are oblong to lance-shaped. The upper leaves are narrower and pointed, almost clasping. The flowers are terminal and reddish-purple in color. The fruit consists of four nutlets (seeds), each about 5 mm long, with the outer surface covered with short, barbed prickles. Nutlets break apart at maturity and are rapidly scattered by animals.Houndstongue commonly is found in disturbed areas, including roadsides and trails, and in pasture and woodlands following soil disturbance or overgrazing.

**Influence:** Stop Dogs Barking

**Gender**: Masculine, **Element**: Fire, **Planet**: Mars

Place this herb in your shoe to prevent dogs from barking at you. This herb ties their tongues.

**Cultivation**: Hounds tongue propagates easily from seed and in the wild prefers areas with more than 10% bare ground, and is common on gravelly, alkaline soils.

**Houseleek** (*Sempervivum tectorum*)

**Description:** This ornamental succulent grows it's tongue shaped leaves in a rosette shape making it an attractive container plant.

**Influence:** Luck, Protection, Love

**Gender**: Masculine, **Element**: Air, **Planet**: Jupiter

Grow on the roof for good luck and to prevent the building from lightning strikes. If worn fresh and replaced every few days, houseleek is a love-inducing herb.

**Cultivation**: As a succulent, this plant is happy in dry thin soil or gravel, but it must be well drained. Grown from seed planted in spring, or from leaf cutting, or from the small plantletes which it throws. It does best in full sun, growing to around 30 cm.

**Huckleberry** (*Gaylussacia* spp.)

**Description:** Very small, slender, multi-stemmed shrub up to 1.2 metres tall. Stems arise from numerous underground rhizomes. The leaves are alternate, simple, some species evergreen, elliptical to obovate, margins ciliate, 1 cm – 2 cm long, bright green above, underside with yellow resin dots (use lens) that will cause them to be sticky. The small flowers around 6mm are white to pink bell-shaped with 5 lobes in small axillary clusters and appear in spring before developing into small, round, blue-black, shiny berry-like drupe, edible but not very sweet, which ripen in late summer; easily distinguished from blueberries by its ten large seeds. The fruit of the various species of plant called huckleberry is generally edible. The berries are small and round, usually less than 5 mm in diameter, and contain 10 relatively large seeds. Berries range in color according to species from bright red, through dark purple, and into the blues. In taste the berries range from tart to sweet, with a flavor similar to that of a blueberry, especially in blue/purple colored varieties. Huckleberries are a favorite of many mammals such as bears and humans.

**Influence:** Luck, Protection, Dream Magick, Hex Breaking

**Gender**: Feminine, **Element**: Water, **Planet**: Venus

Carry the leaves for luck and to break/prevent hexes and curses.

**Cultivation**: The plant grows best in damp, acidic soil. Under optimal conditions, huckleberries can be as much as 1.5-2 m high, and usually ripen in mid-to-late summer; later at higher elevations.

**Hyacinth** (*Hyacinthus orientalis*)

**Description**: Grown for their dense spikes of highly fragrant, tubular flowers, hyacinths have been popular spring-flowering bulbs for centuries. These powerfully scented flowers are some of the first to bloom after winter. They're most effective planted in blocks of a single colour along a path or in containers near the house, where their fragrance can be fully appreciated.

Specially-treated, winter-flowering bulbs are also available for indoor Christmas displays. After flowering, these forced bulbs can be planted outdoors in a sheltered spot

**Influence**: Love, Protection, Happiness

**Gender**: Feminine, **Element**: Water, **Planet**: Venus

Carried in sachets and amulets to ease grief, childbirth pains. Used in dream pillows to ward off nightmares. Used as a protective charm in negative influences. Sniff the fresh flowers to relieve grief and depression, and the dried flowers are used in love mixtures. The oil is best to use and you can also anoint a candle for protection with this herb and oil.

**Cultivation**: Hyacinths can be propagated by planting up bulb offsets in late summer or early autumn however when selecting bulbs, make sure they're not damaged or drying out. Plant bulbs in the autumn before the ground freezes, in order to ensure proper root development. Place them 15cm to 20cm (6in to 8in) deep and 15cm (6in) apart. To encourage bigger blooms, spread a small amount of bulb fertiliser in the hole during planting. Hyacinths perform best in an open, sunny or partially shaded position with fertile, well-draining soil

**Hydrangea** (*Hydrangea arborescens*)

**Description:** The basics species of this large bushy North American shrub has flowers that are a mixture of tiny fertile florets and the larger more showy sterile ones, which in fact have coloured bracts in place of petals. The variety 'Annabelle' has only sterile florets, which makes the flower heads much larger, like spectacular white balls up to 30cm (12in) across. Plants are nominally very hardy but late frosts can damage the buds, so grow them in a sheltered corner or against a warm wall in cold gardens. Regular pruning keeps the naturally open plants dense and compact.

**Influence:** Hex Breaking

Use the bark of this plant to unhex; carry, scatter around the home, or burn.

**Gender**_____, **Element**_____, **Planet:** _____

**Cultivation**: Hydrangeas bloom best in full sun, but will do well in partial shade. They are best propagated by cuttings of green growth in Summer. The cuttings should be the ends of nonflowering shoots and should have two to three pairs of leaves. The bottom pair of leaves should be removed and the stem cut just below a joint. They should be placed in moist sand in a shady place. Seeds are uncommon but when available should be sown in a sandy, peaty soil in spring in a greenhouse or sheltered place.

**Cultivation**: The soil type determines the flower colour - acid, for example, produces blue flowers. To create blue on a limey soil, use a blueing compound composed of aluminium sulphate. However, the results won't compare with plants growing in acid soil. Hydrangeas are true survivors and can often be seen flowering in overgrown or neglected gardens. Mopheads and lacecaps prefer dappled shade against a north- or west-facing wall. If it's too bright they're likely to scorch. Their leafy shoots need plenty of moisture during the summer. Apply a mulch to drier soils to lock in moisture and promote decent-size flowers. Plants also need to be sheltered from cold winds, which can frazzle new foliage during the spring. Pruning isn't essential but can be done each spring as new shoots appear. With established plants, just remove one-third of the older, less productive stems and cut back old flowering stems to a strong pair of buds. Leave old flower-heads on over winter to provide frost protection to new growth. The brown papery domes look fantastic when covered with frost. Left unpruned, hydrangeas will continue to bloom but the size of the flower-heads will be reduced by the overcrowded stems.

**Hyssop** (*Hyssopus officinalis*)

**Description:** Hysop is a perennial shrubby plant growing to 90 cm tall with abundant aromatic leaves and tall spikes of purple flowers. It is a member of the mint family.

**Influence:** Purification, Protection, Healing

**Gender**: Masculine, **Element**: Fire, **Planet**: Jupiter

Used as a tea for protection of all types, physical and mental. Use as a healing bath and hung in the home to drive out evil and negativity.

**Cultivation**: Hyssop prefers light, friable, well-drained soil. It will grow in either a sunny or semi-shaded position. Seed can be planted in spring and cuttings can be taken in late spring or early summer. In autumn, new plants can be created by root division. This perennial is often used as a border plant in herb gardens as it lends itself well to hedging. Pruning after flowering will create a more compact plant and better flowering in the following year.

**Indian Bay,** See Bay

**Indian Paint,** See Bloodroot

**Indian Paint Brush** (*Castilleja* spp.)

**Description:** *Castilleja* comes in many colors and often these colors represent distinct species. But Paintbrush hybridizes often and therefore precise species identification on the basis of colour can be difficult. The attractive "flowers" that we admire, are actually leaf-like parts, the bracts and sepals. The flower petals themselves are fused in a long, narrow tube that is often greenish-yellow and tipped in the same colour as the showy bracts and sepals. The reproductive parts protrude from the tube. Some species of Paintbrush grow singly, others scattered, others in large, very attractive patches, and others in all three manners. Paintbrush is (partially parasitic), i.e., if its roots encounter roots of other plants they will penetrate these roots for nourishment. This at least partially explains why several species of *Castilleja*, especially *Castilleja chromosa*, commonly begin growing under taller plants such as Sagebrush.

**Influence:** Love

**Gender**: Feminine, **Element**: Water, **Planet**: Venus

The flowers of this plant have strong love attracting powers. Carry in sachets to find a love.

**Cultivation**: Loosened soil with plenty of organic matter at planting time will give the roots a better chance to get established. Liquid feed during establishment can be beneficieal, and don't let the soil get too dried out. Keep it moist. After the first growing season, Indian Paintbrush is adaptable to poor soils and doesn't need to be fertilized regularly, and don't continue to mulch. Indian Paintbrush is it has a parasitic relationship with Grama Grass, their roots need to mingleas the grass provides nutrients that the Indian Paintbrush needs throughout its lifespan.

**Inkberry** see Poke

**Iris** (*Iris* spp.)

**Description:** They are perennial herbs, growing from creeping rhizomes (rhizomatous irises), or, in drier climates, from bulbs (bulbous irises). They have long, erect, flowering stems, which may be simple or branched, solid or hollow, and flattened or have a circular cross-section. The rhizomatous species usually have 3-10 basal, sword-shaped leaves growing in dense clumps. The bulbous species have cylindrical basal leaves. The inflorescences are fan-shaped and contain one or more symmetrical, six-lobed flowers.

**Influence:** Purification, Wisdom

**Gender**: Feminine, **Element**: Water, **Planet**: Venus

Used for purification; place the fresh flowers in the area to be cleansed. The three points of the flower symbolize faith, wisdom, and valor, and so the flower can be used to induce these qualities.

**Cultivation**: The iris has a thick fleshy root called a "rhizome" about like a tough potato in texture. When you buy a new iris, you will probably receive a rhizome with clipped roots and leaves. It can remain out of the ground for a week or two without serious harm, but the sooner it is planted, the better. Iris can also be grown from seed, just put them in seed raising mix and keep them just barely moist, in semi shade, so it doesn't dry out. If it is fresh seed they should start to germinate after 6 weeks, if it is old seed it is better to soak it for a few days, changing the water daily. Plant them out into the garden, or larger pots in early Spring, and you will get some bloom on them the following Spring. Expect a wide variety of offspring if they are bearded irises, even if they look exactly like the parent plant, the will be genetically different.

**Irish Moss** (*Chondrus crispus*)

**Description:** Irish Moss is a seaweed or red alga, purple to green when fresh but dried to yellow-brown translucent forked fronds or thalli, 5-25cm long. It is found on the Atlantic coasts of Ireland, Europe and the United States

**Influence:** Money, Luck, Protection

**Gender**: Feminine, **Element**: Water, **Planet**: Moon

This herb is great to use in spells for money, luck, and protection. You can carry some with you or place some in your home to increase your luck and to ensure a steady flow of money into your house or pocket. Some place it under the rugs in their house for these purposes. Carry a little amulet filled with Irish Moss with you while travelling, for protection.

**Cultivation**: Gathered from the wild.

## Ivy (*Hedera* spp.)

**Description:** Ivy is a reliable, adaptable evergreen favourite with a host of uses in the garden. Easily maintained it grows happily indoors or out, it will quickly cover a shed or trellis. It can damage buildings with the roots growing into cracks between the brickwork.

**Influence:** Protection, Healing, Fertility and Love.

**Gender**: Feminine, **Element**: Water, **Planet**: Saturn

Use this plant by hanging in front of the door to the home to repel negative influences and unwanted guests. Place inside the home at open windows and arches Mixed with Holly it is a great wedding sachet to protect the bride and groom. Magickal love wands are made from this wood. Carried by women for good luck (this is the corresponding plant to holly). Where ivy is grown or placed, that place is guarded against negativity and disaster.

**Cultivation**: Ivy has many different varieties, and most will adapt to many different soil and growing conditions. It is happy with most soil types, though disliking waterlogged conditions. Happy with part shade though variegated varieties may require more sun. It grows from 10 – 30 metres but as a creeper requires supporting structures or becomes a ground cover.

## Jasmine (*Jasminum officinale* or *J. odoratissimum*)

**Description:** This hardy deciduous vine is a garden favourite, with its small white highly fragrant flowers. Growing to 10 meters this makes an ideal fence or trellis climber or over a garden arbour.

**Influence:** Love, Money, Prophetic Dreams

**Gender**: Feminine, **Element**: Earth, **Planet**: Jupiter

Used in dream pillows and sachets for sweet dreams during troubled times. The fresh flowers and oils are used for attracting and maintaining a spiritual love. Very powerful, only a little will do! Will cause prophetic dreams if burned in the bedroom, and the flowers are smelled to induce sleep.

**Cultivation**: Jasmine is best grown indoors in pots in cooler climates or as a trailing vine along a trellis or fence in warmer climates. It is an evergreen vine which likes bright light, but no direct sun, some support such as a trellis, lots of water, and occasional fertilizing. Varieties are readily available from nurseries or can be grown from seed planted in spring, or from semi ripe cuttings taken in summer. Requiring full sun, the plant should be cut back after flowering, whilst spring pruning will result in loss of blooms.

## Jobs Tears (*Coix lachryma*)

**Description:** One of 6 perennial grasses in the Croix genus, has been cultivated as an ornamental plant. It grows to about 1.5 meters.

**Influence:** Healing, Wishes, Luck

String the seeds onto a necklace and place around a child's neck to aid in teething. Adults wear this necklace for sore throats and colds. The seeds absorb pain and illness. Carry the seeds for good luck. For wishing magick, make a wish holding seven seeds and then throw into running water. Or, count out seven seeds, concentrating on your wish, then carry the seeds for a week and your wish should come true.

**Gender**_____, **Element**_____, **Planet:** _____

**Cultivation**: Grown from seed planted in spring Jobs tears requires damp soil in a sunny position. Fruit is harvested in autumn.

## Joe Pye Weed (*Eupatorium* spp.)

**Description:** A tall hardy perennial growing infertile marshy conditions. Enjoying sunny or partial shaded positions, it grows to between 90cm and 3 metres.

**Influence:** Love, Respect

Place a few leaves in the mouth when making love advances and you won't fail. Carry a few leaves so that you will be respected and favored by everyone you meet.

**Gender**_____, **Element**_____, **Planet:** _____

**Cultivation**: Grown from seed planted in spring, or by division when plant is dormant. Prefers damp fertile alkaline soils, in a sunny or part shaded position.

## Juniper (*Juniperus communis*)

**Description:** Juniper is an evergreen coniferous shrub or small tree occurring throughout the northern hemisphere from Europe to Siberia and grows up to 10m in height; it can be either prostrate or erect. Its preferred habitat is heath, moorland and chalk downs, but is also found as undergrowth in mixed open forests. It is particularly common in pastures where sheep graze as they eat the berries and distribute the seeds in their faeces.

**Influence:** Protection, Anti-Theft, Love, Exorcism, Health

**Gender**: Masculine, **Element**: Fire, **Planet**: Sun

Used as an oil to add to the other herbs for increasing money status, light a juniper scented candle for prosperity. Use in a string of the fruit for attracting love, burn leaves and fruit for magickal protection. Added to love mixtures. Place a sprig at the door to the home for protection against theft and unwanted visitors. Place a twig or leaves with valuables to safeguard.

**Cultivation**: Juniper is one of the few conifers that prefer alkaline soil. The plant requires a sunny position and good drainage. Trees can be propagated quite easily from cuttings. If you want berries, you must plant a male and a female juniper.

## Jupiter's Staff, See Mullein

## Kava-Kava (*Piper methysticum*)

**Description:** A member of the pepper family (Piperaceae), it is a large leafed swamp-loving shrub that can grow to an average height of 2 metres and rarely from 3 metres to 4 metres. The greatest concentration of the active psychotropic constituents called kava lactones is found in the fresh roots and rhizomes.

**Influence:** Visions, Protection, Luck

**Gender**: Feminine, **Element**: Water, **Planet**: Saturn

Used to treat insomnia and nervousness. Relieves stress after injury. Used as a tea for pains associated with nerve and skin diseases. **Large doses can cause a build up of toxic substances in the liver.** A tea of kava kava is drunk to offer protection against evil and to invite good luck. Sprinkle the tea around the home and property for the same uses. Infused and left to steep overnight in the refrigerator, drink to enhance psychic powers and to induce visions.

**Cultivation**: In the Pacific Islands kava does best in the cool, moist highlands up to 300 metres above sea level where the daytime summer temperatures are between 26 and 30 degrees Celciust. It prefers a loose, rich soil with good drainage and frequent watering. It does well on stony ground. The best crops are grown on virgin soil. If two consecutive crops are raised on the same soil the second crop will be poor. The plant rarely produces seeds and is generally propagated by cuttings of the firm wood. These are susceptible to fungus diseases because of the high humidity the plant requires. Plants should be spaced about 2 metres apart either way. This furnishes about 1200 plants per acre. Kava makes a good house plant.

**Kelp,** See Bladderwrack

**Kidneywort** see Liverwort

**Knitback,** See Comfrey

**Knit Bone** See Comfrey

**Knotweed** (*Polygonum aviculare*)

**Description:** Knotweed is an annual herb that usually grows prostrate, sending out straggly stems, 15 cm to 30 cm long, that form a thick mat. Narrow elliptical to oval leaves, 1 cm long, issue alternately from joints, or "knots, " on the stems. Tiny flower clusters (June-November), produced in the leaf axils, are pale green or pink to purple

**Influence:** Binding, Health

**Gender**: Feminine, **Element**: Earth, **Planet**: Saturn

Hold some knotweed in your hand, pour your problems into the herb and see it absorbing them. Burn it, and your miseries and troubles will be bound. Carry to strengthen and protect the eyes.

**Cultivation**: Knotweed is found in temperate regions throughout the world. Knotweed thrives in open areas and along shorelines. Knotweed is gathered throughout the summer. Succeeds in an ordinary garden soil but prefers a moisture retentive not too fertile soil in sun or part shade, and if grown in good soils the plant will cover an area up to a metre in diameter. Prefers an acid soil. Dislikes full shade. Knotweed is a common and invasive weed of cultivated ground. It also produces an abundance of seeds and these are a favourite food for many species of birds. The flowers have little or no scent or honey and are rarely visited by pollinating insects. Self-fertilization is the usual method of reproduction, though cross-fertilization by insects does sometimes occur. The plant also produces cleistogomous flowers - these never open and therefore are always self-fertilized

**Lad's Love** See Southernwood

**Lady Elder,** See Elder

**Lady's Mantle** (*Alchemilla vulgaris*)

**Description:** Alchemilla has lime green leaves and dainty star shaped flowers, and has been in gardens since before the 16th century and I'm sure in the wild much before then. The entire plant is covered in very fine hairs that cause dew or soft rain to gather in it's leaves. This liquid was known as "celestial water" and used in alchemy. These tiny jeweled drops inspired poetry and Magickover the years. The herb became known as Our Lady's Mantle because the scalloped shape of the leaves, were thought to resemble the mantle (cloak) of the Virgin Mary. Later, politics intervened, and the "Our" was taken from the name.

**Influence:** Love

**Gender**: Feminine, **Element**: Water, **Planet**: Venus

Use this herb in love spells and sachets.

**Cultivation**: Lady's Mantle can be planted from seeds or by purchasing plants. The seed will germinate in the garden, but will take up to 2 years to flower. The plants can be divided in the spring or fall and are hardy in Zones 4-8 and possibly Zone 3. It will grow from 15 cm for the alpine variety to about 30cm to 45 cm on the others. Space about 30 cm between plants. Lady's Mantle needs a fertile soil and some moisture-more than the standard herbs. It can be in full sun in northern climates, but can tolerate some shade and in the warm climates prefers it. Lady's Mantle can be invasive if left to seed.

**Lady's Slipper** (*Cypripedium pubescens*)

**Description:** Lady's Slipper is a perennial plant that is native to the woods and meadows of North America. The fleshy rootstock produces several round, hairy stems with alternate leaves and characteristic golden yellow flowers, lined with purple, blooming from May to July. This beautiful member of the orchid family has a characteristic lower lip that forms an inflated sac, which suggests the shape of a moccasin, thereby giving the plant one of its common names, Moccasin Flower. Lady's Slipper is a pungent, bittersweet herb with an unpleasant odor and thrives in moist, humus-rich soil in an open or shady situation, growing to about 60 cm in height. Like many other native orchids, Lady's Slipper is becoming increasingly rare, and its history as an ornamental is as rich as its distinguished medicinal past.

**Influence:** Protection

**Gender**: Feminine, **Element**: Water, **Planet**: Saturn

Used in protective sachets because it guards against all hexes, curses, and the evil eye.

**Cultivation**: Lady's slipper is native to eastern North America. Its natural habitat is woods and pastures, but due to overharvesting, lady's slipper is rarely found in the wild. Lady's slipper is cultivated to a limited degree.

**Lady's Sorrel,** See Sorrel, Wood

**Larch** (*Larix europaea*)

**Description:** The Larch is essentially are deciduous mountain tree, growing from 15-50 m tall. The shoots are dimorphic, with growth divided into long shoots typically 10-50 cm long and bearing several buds, and short shoots only 1-2 mm long with only a single bud. The leaves are needle-like, 2-5 cm long, slender (under 1 mm wide). They are borne singly, spirally arranged on the long shoots, and in dense clusters of 20-50 needles on the short shoots. It abounds on the Alps up to an altitude of 1000 metres, and occurs on the Apennines and Carpathians, but is unknown in a wild state on the Pyrenees, or in the Spanish or Scandinavian peninsulas. It forms large woods in Russia. The regularly-tapering stem, with its scaly, reddish-grey bark, so prone to become covered with the shaggy tufts of hoary lichen, then loses its stiff, erect posture, curving in a direction slightly sinuous, as well as oblique.

**Influence:** Protection, Anti-Theft

**Gender**: Masculine

Larch wood supposedly cannot be penetrated by fire, and so it is used in sachets designed to prevent them. Carry or wear to prevent enchantment and to protect against the evil eye.

**Cultivation**: Prefers an open airy position in a light or gravelly well-drained soil. It tolerates acid and infertile soils, though it dislikes very peaty or very chalky soils. Succeeds on rocky hill or mountain sides and slopes. The larch dislikes atmospheric pollution and so does not grow well in towns. It dislikes growing in wet ground or frost pockets, and grows best in areas with abundant rainfall. The larch is a very ornamental tree that is widely grown for forestry as it is very fast growing with new annual growth of 1.5 metres often found and trees can average 60cm or more growth for many years. The dormant trees are very cold hardy, but they can be excited into premature growth by mild spells during the winter, the plants are then subject to damage by late frosts and cold winds. The young shoots have a delicate mossy fragrance as the leaves unfold. Hybridizes freely with other members of this genus. Open ground plants, 1 year x 1 year are the best for planting out, do not use container grown plants with spiralled roots. Plants transplant well, even when coming into growth in the spring. Plants in this genus are notably resistant to honey fungus. Propagation is by Seed sown in late winter. It is best to give the seedlings light shade for the first year. As soon as they are large enough to handle, prick out the seedlings into individual pots. Although only a few centimetres tall, they can be planted out into their permanent positions in the summer providing you give them an effective weed-excluding mulch and preferably some winter protection for their first year. Otherwise grow them on in the cold frame for their first winter and plant them out in early summer of the following year. The seed remains viable for 3 years.

**Larkspur** (*Delphinium* spp.) **POISONOUS**

**Description:** *Delphinium* is a genus of about 250 species of annual, biennial or perennial flowering plants in the buttercup family Ranunculaceae, native throughout the Northern Hemisphere and also on the high mountains of tropical Africa. The leaves are deeply lobed with 3-7 toothed, pointed lobes. The main flowering stem is erect, and varies greatly in size between the species, from 10 cm in some alpine species, up to 2 m tall in the larger meadowland species; it is topped by many flowers, varying between purple, blue, red, yellow or white.

Many species are cultivated as garden plants, with numerous cultivars having been selected for their denser, more prominent flowers. All parts of the plant contain an alkaloid delphinine and are very poisonous, causing vomiting when eaten, and death in larger amounts.

**Influence:** Health, Protection

**Gender:** Feminine, **Element**: Water, **Planet**: Venus

Keeps away ghosts. Looks through a bunch of larkspur at a Midsummer fire and your eyes will be preserved until next Midsummer. The flowers frighten scorpions and other venomous creatures.

**Cultivation**: Sow seeds directly in garden in the spring. Sow them in the location you want them to grow as Larkspurs do not like to be transplanted. Plants should be spaced about 15 cm to 20 cm apart. Water deeply to encourage root development, but be sure the roots do not stand in water or they will be at risk for root rot. To use as cut flowers, scald ends in hot water before soaking in cool water.

## Lavender (*Lavendula offcinale* or *L. vera*)

**Description:** The Lavenders *Lavandula* are a genus of about 25-30 species of flowering plants in the mint family, Lamiaceae, native from the Mediterranean region south to tropical Africa and to the southeast regions of India. The genus includes annuals, herbaceous plants, subshrubs, and small shrubs. Lavenders are widely grown in gardens. Flower spikes are used for dried flower arrangements. The fragrant, pale purple flowers and flower buds are used in potpourris. Dried and sealed in pouches, they are placed among stored items of clothing to give a fresh fragrance and as a deterrent to moths. The plant is also grown commercially for extraction of lavender oil from the flowers. This oil is used as an antiseptic and for aromatherapy. Lavender flowers yield abundant nectar which yields a high quality honey for beekeepers.

**Influence:** Love, Protection, Sleep, Chastity (with rosemary), Longevity, Purification, Happiness, Peace

**Gender**: Masculine, **Element**: Air, **Planet**: Mercury

Burn to induce a restful sleep, place on the pillow or temples or burned as an incense for a restful sleep, use as a bath to purify and cleanse, or burn for the same reason. Long ago, it was believed if you carried this, you would see ghosts. Wonderful for use in love spells. Lavender has long been known to be a particularly attractive scent to men. Lavender Flowers can be sprinkled around the house to bring peacefulness, . Lavender has also been used for protection, chastity, longevity, purification, and happiness.

**Cultivation**: Plant lavender in a very well-drained position in full sun. Once established, the plants are very durable and require little water or fertiliser. Plants may be raised from seed or from tip cuttings taken in late spring. After several years, plants tend to become woody and can be replaced with new plants propagated from cuttings. The long flower stems should be harvested by cutting them close to the woody part of the plant. A light pruning of the foliage after flowering is also recommended. The plants do not take kindly to being pruned back into old wood. A hedge of English Lavender is a joy to walk beside as brushing past releases the magnificent perfume.

## Leek (*Allium* spp.)

**Description:** The **leek** is a vegetable belonging, along with the onion and garlic, to the *Alliaceae* family. Rather than forming a tight bulb like the onion, the leek produces a long cylinder of bundled leaf sheaths which are generally blanched by pushing soil around them (trenching). They are often sold as small seedlings in flats which are started off early in greenhouses, to be planted out as weather permits. Once established in the garden, leeks are hardy; many varieties can be left in the ground during the winter to be harvested as needed.

**Influence:** Love, Protection, Exorcism

**Gender**: Masculine, **Element**: Fire, **Planet**: Mars

When two people eat leeks, they will fall in love with each other. They are carried as protective amulets and are bitten to break hexes and drive away evil.

**Cultivation**: Leeks are easy to grow from seed and tolerate standing in the field for an extended harvest. Leeks usually reach maturity in the autumn months, and they have few pest or disease problems. Leeks can be bunched and harvested early when they are about the size of a finger or pencil, or they can be thinned and allowed to grow to a much larger mature size.

## Lemon (*Citrus limon*)

**Description:** Probably one of the best known citrus trees, Lemon is an evergreen Shrub growing to 3m by 1m at a medium rate. It is in leaf all year, in flower all year. The flowers are hermaphrodite (have both male and female organs) and are pollinated by Apomictic (reproduce by seeds formed without sexual fusion), insects. The plant is self-fertile. The plant prefers medium (loamy) and heavy (clay) soils and requires well-drained soil. The plant prefers acid, neutral and basic (alkaline) soils and can grow in very alkaline soil. It cannot grow in the shade. It requires moist soil.

**Influence:** Longevity, Purification, Love, Friendship

**Gender**: Feminine, **Element**: Water, **Planet**: Moon

Lemon juice mixed with water is used to wash second-hand magickal objects. It cleanses negative vibrations. Lemon juice is added to bath water at the Full Moon for purification. Add the dried flowers and peel to love sachets and mixtures, and use leaves in lust teas. Serve lemon pie to a spouse to promote fidelity. Place a slice of lemon under a visitor's chair to promote lasting friendship. Use a lemon as a poppet. Get an unripe lemon, no bigger than 3 cm in diameter, and a lot of color-headed pins (except black). Stick the pins one at a time into the lemon until it's full of them. Attach a piece of yarn or ribbon to the lemon and hang in the home to bring blessings and luck, or give to a friend.

**Cultivation**: The seed is best sown in a greenhouse as soon as it ripe after thoroughly rinsing it. Sow stored seed in March in a greenhouse. Germination usually takes place within 2 - 3 weeks at 13°c. Seedlings are liable to damp off so they must be watered with care and kept well ventilated. The seed is usually polyembrionic, two or more seedlings arise from each seed and they are genetically identical to the parent but they do not usually carry any virus that might be present in the parent plant. When large enough to handle, prick the seedlings out into individual pots and grow them on in the greenhouse for at least three growing seasons before trying them outdoors. Plant them out in the summer and give them some protection from the cold for their first few winters outdoors.

## Lemongrass (*Cymbopogon citratus*)

**Description:** A semi hardy clump forming grass which grows to 1.8metres in warm climates. Needs protection from the cold in temperate climates

**Influence:** Repel Snakes, Lust, Psychic Powers

**Gender**: Masculine, **Element**: Air, **Planet**: Mercury

Plant around the home and in the garden to repel snakes. Used in some lust potions and as an infusion to aid in developing psychic powers.

**Cultivation**: This plant needs a sunny but sheltered spot with protection from afternoon sun. Propagates easily by division of the clumps. Good drainage is important and soil rich in organic matter will achieve the best results. Ample water is needed. This is a tropical plant and it will not survive frost, but it can be grown in a container if you wish.

**Lemon Verbena** (*Lippia citriodora*)

**Description:** A deciduous frost tender shrub in temperate climates it grows to around 1.5 metres or more. Doesn't like extreme cold or heat.

**Influence:** Purification, Dream Protection, Love

**Gender**; Masculine, **Element**: Air, **Planet**: Mercury

Wear a sprig or a piece of it or drink some of its juice to protect you from dreaming. Carry the leaves or an amulet of the herb and use it in love spells and mixtures to attract the opposite sex. Also added to other wishes to enhance the power. Sometimes used to purify an area or added to bathwater for purification.

**Cultivation**: Needs a sunny position, protected from strong winds. Soil should be friable and well-drained. Mulch well. Prune in winter to prevent shrub becoming straggly. Hardwood cuttings can be struck in late winter, and softwood cuttings taken in late spring and summer. Will need protection from the winter elements in all but temperate climates.

**Lettuce** (*Lactuca sativa*)

**Description:** Annual/Biennial growing to 0.9m by 0.25m. Well known to most, it formes a tight "head" with it's leaves, which are eaten in salads.

**Influence:** Chastity, Protection, Love, Divination, Sleep

**Gender**: Feminine, **Element**: Water, **Planet**: Moon

Rub lettuce juice on your forehead or eat the leaves to help you fall asleep. Grow in the garden for protection, but too many will result in sterility. Eat lettuce to promote chastity, and also to prevent seasickness. Plant lettuce seeds in the form of a name of someone you love. If they sprout well, so will the love between you.

**Cultivation**: Sow a small quantity of seed in situ every 2 or 3 weeks from March (with protection in cooler areas) to June and make another sowing in August/September. Only just cover the seed. Germination is usually rapid and good, thin the plants if necessary, these thinnings can be transplanted to produce a slightly later crop (but they will need to be well watered in dry weather). More certain winter crops can be obtained by sowing in a seed frame in September/October and again in January/February

**Licorice** (*Glycyrrhiza glabra)*

**Description:** A very hardy, deciduous perennial growing to 1 metre or taller, growing from a strong root system made up of a taproot and many horizontal-spreading roots, spanning out 1 metre or more. Roots are 1-5cm thick, have a brown woody appearance, a yellow colour internally with fibre that can be pulled apart like long string. Above ground foliage forms on upright thin stems, pinnate leaves with 4-8 pairs of dark green elliptic leaflets 2-3cm long of fern-like appearance. Young leaves feel slightly sticky to touch. Lavender/blue pea flowers 1cm long form as axil clusters, followed by 2-3cm long smooth, brown pods containing 1-7 brown kidney shaped, pinhead-sized seeds.

**Influence:** Love, Lust, Fidelity

**Gender**: Feminine, **Element**: Water, **Planet**: Venus

Licorice root was buried in tombs and caskets to help the soul pass easily into the Summerland. Chewing on a piece of the root will make you passionate. It is added to love sachets, and an ingredient in spells to ensure fidelity.

**Cultivation**: Plant licorice in well-limed, well-drained, loose, deep soil; preferably in a sunny position. If soil tends to be clayey, plant on raised beds or hills. Enriching the soil with compost and well-rotted animal manure is beneficial. Licorice should be given room to spread, at least 1-3 square meters. It is a good sign when the plant starts to sucker and send up new shoots, as it signifies roots are growing, with potential for future harvesting. Low growing annual herbs or vegetables can be grown around it for 1-2 years.

**Life Everlasting** (*Anaphalis* spp.; *Gnaphalium uliginosum*)

**Description:** Perennial growing to 0.9m by 1m It is hardy and is not frost tender. It is in flower in summer, and the seeds ripen in about 4 weeks. The flowers are dioecious (individual flowers are either male or female, but only one sex is to be found on any one plant so both male and female plants must be grown if seed is required) and are pollinated by Insects. The plant is not self-fertile.

**Influence:** Longevity, Health, Healing

Use in spells aimed at longevity or restoring youth. Keep in the home or carry to prevent sickness and ill-health. Drink an infusion of life-everlasting every morning, before eating or drinking anything else, while saying "Chills and ills, pains and banes, do your fasting with life everlasting". This will ensure a long life with little illness.

**Gender**_____, **Element**_____, **Planet:** _____

**Cultivation**: Seed - sow spring in a cold frame. The seed is best sown when it is ripe in the autumn. It usually germinates in 4 - 8 weeks at 15°c. When large enough to handle, prick the seedlings out into individual pots and grow them on in a cold frame for their first winter. Plant them out into their permanent positions in late spring or early summer, after the last expected frosts. Division is very easy at almost any time of the year, the divisions can be planted straight into their permanent positions if required. The plant prefers light (sandy) and medium (loamy) soils, requires well-drained soil and can grow in nutritionally poor soil. It can grow in semi-shade (light woodland) or no shade. It requires dry or moist soil.

**Lignum Aloes see** Aloes, Wood

**Lilac** (*Syringa vulgaris*)

**Description:** They are deciduous shrubs or small trees, ranging in size from 2–10 m tall, with stems up to 20–30 cm diameter. The leaves are opposite (occasionally in whorls of three), and in most species simple and heart-shaped to broad lanceolate, but pinnate in a few species (e.g. *S. protolaciniata, S. pinnatifolia*). The flowers are produced in spring, each flower being 5–10 mm in diameter with a four-lobed corolla, the corolla tube narrow, 5–20 mm long; they are bisexual, with fertile stamens and stigma in each flower. The usual flower colour is a shade of purple (often a light purple or lilac), but white and pale pink are also found. The flowers grow in large panicles, and in several species have a strong fragrance. Flowering varies between mid spring to early summer, depending on the species. The fruit is a dry, brown capsule, splitting in two at maturity to release the two winged seeds.

**Influence:** Exorcism, Protection

**Gender**: Feminine, **Element**: Water, **Planet**: Venus

Drives away evil where it is planted or strewn, as was done in New England. Fresh lilac flowers can be placed in a haunted house to help clear it.

**Cultivation**: Succeeds in most soils, including chalk, but dislikes acid soils. It prefers a deep stiff well-drained loam in a warm sunny position. A very ornamental plant, it does tend to sucker quite freely though. There are many named varieties, developed for their ornamental value. The flowers attract butterflies and moths. Plants in this genus are notably susceptible to honey fungus. Propagation by seed sown Spring Prick the seedlings out into individual pots once they are large enough to handle. Plant them out in the summer if sufficient growth has been made, otherwise grow them on in a cold frame for their first winter and plant out in late spring of the following year. Cuttings of young shoots, 7cm with a heel in mid to late summer, or half-ripe wood, 7cm with a heel in Autumn. Layering in spring before new growth begins. Division of suckers in late winter, planted straight out into their permanent positions.

## Lily (*Lilium* spp.)

**Description:** The genus *Lilium* are herbaceous flowering plants normally growing from bulbs, comprising a genus of about 110 species in the lily family, Liliaceae. They are important as large showy flowering garden plants, and in literature. Some of the bulbs have been consumed by people. The species in this genus are the true lilies, while other plants with lily in the common name are related to other groups of plants.

**Influence:** Protection, Breaking Love Spells

**Gender**: Feminine, **Element**: Water, **Planet**: Moon

Plant lilies in the garden to keep away ghosts and evil, protect against the evil eye, and to keep away unwanted visitors. Good antidotes for love spells. Carry a fresh lily to break a love spell cast on a specific person. Bury an old piece of leather in a bed of lilies to gain clues in solving a crime committed within the past year. The first white lily of the season brings strength to whoever finds it.

**Cultivation**: Liliums can be propagated by division of the bulbs, by growing-on *bulbils* which are adventitious bulbs formed on the stem, by scaling, for which whole scales are detached from the bulb and planted to form a new bulb, or from seed; though seed germination patterns are variable and can be complex.

## Lily of the Valley (*Convallaria magalis*) **POISONOUS**

**Description:** It is a herbaceous perennial plant that forms extensive colonies by spreading underground stems called rhizomes that send out stolons. These send up numerous stems each spring. The stems grow to 15-30 cm tall, with one or two leaves 10-25 cm long, flowering stems have two leaves and a raceme of 5-15 flowers on the stem apex. The flowers are white tepals (rarely pink), bell-shaped, 5-10 mm diameter, and sweetly scented; flowering is in late spring. The fruit is a small orange-red berry 5-7 mm diameter that contains a few large whitish to brownish colored seeds that dry to a clear translucent round bead 1 to 3 mm wide. Plants are self-sterile, and colonies of one clone do not set seed.

**Influence:** Mental Powers, Happiness

**Gender**: Masculine, **Element**: Air, **Planet**: Mercury

Use to improve the memory and mind. Place in a room to cheer the heart and lift the spirits of all those in it.

**Cultivation**: Seed - best sown as soon as it is ripe, otherwise in late winter, in a cold frame. Germination, particularly of stored seed can be very slow, taking 2 - 12 months or more at 15°c. Sow the seed thinly so that the seedlings can be allowed to grow on undisturbed in the pot for their first year. Apply a liquid feed during the growing season to ensure that the seedlings are well fed. Divide the young plants into individual pots when they die down in late summer and grow them on in pots in a shady position in a cold frame for at least another year before planting them out into their permanent positions when they are dormant. Division in September. Very easy, larger clumps can be replanted direct into their permanent positions, though it is best to pot up smaller clumps and grow them on in a cold frame until they are rooting well. Plant them out in the spring.

## Lime (*Citrus aurantifolia* or *L. Limetta*)

**Description: Lime** is a term referring to a number of different fruits (generally citruses), both species and hybrids, which are typically round, green to yellow in color, 3-6 cm in diameter, generally containing sour pulp, and frequently associated with the lemon. Limes are often used to accent the flavors of foods and beverages.

**Influence:** Healing, Love, Protection

**Gender**: Masculine, **Element**: Fire, **Planet**: Sun

Pierce a fresh lime with old iron nails, spikes, pins, and needles and throw into a deep hole in the ground to rid yourself of all ills, hexes, etc. Wear a necklace of limes to cure a sore throat. Use lime peel in love mixtures and incenses. To cure a toothache, drive a nail into the trunk of a lime tree (but thank it first). Carry lime twigs to protect against the evil eye.

**Cultivation**: Whilst it can be grown from seed, It is easiest to obtain a small tree from your local nursery.

## Linden *(Viburnum dilatatum)*

**Description:** Growing to 2.5 metres tall and 4 metres wide this deciduous, bushy, multi-stemmed shrub has medium green leaves which are variable in size and shape. Autumn coloration is yellow, orange and red. It produces 400-600 creamy white flowers in early summer which completely cover the plant. Prolific production of fruit ripening in late summer / autumn, at first orange-red, then turning coral with first frost. Coral coloration is most intense after a few heavy frosts. Pendulous fruit clusters persist until late winter, becoming more conspicuous after the leaves have fallen.

**Influence:** Protection, Immortality, Luck, Love, Sleep

**Gender**: Masculine, **Element**: Air, **Planet**: Jupiter

Hang linden branches over a door or grow the tree in the garden for protection. Carry linden bark to prevent intoxication, and use the leaves and flowers in love spells. Use its leaves also in spells involving immortality. Mix equal parts lavender and linden into a pillow to cure insomnia. Good luck charms are carved from linden wood and carried.

**Cultivation**: An easily grown plant, it succeeds in most soils but it prefers a deep rich loamy soil in sun or semi-shade. Plants are self-incompatible and need to grow close to a genetically distinct plant in the same species in order to produce fruit and fertile seed. A very ornamental and polymorphic species, there are some named varieties developed for the ornamental value of the fruit. Seed is best sown as soon as it is ripe. Germination can be slow, sometimes taking more than 18 months, however; if the seed is harvested 'green' (when it has fully developed but before it has fully ripened) and sown immediately in a cold frame, it should germinate in the spring. Stored seed will require 2 months warm then 3 months cold stratification and can still take 18 months to germinate. Prick out the seedlings into individual pots when they are large enough to handle. Plant out into their permanent positions in late spring or early summer of the following year. Cuttings of soft-wood taken early summer, in individual pots, plant them out in late spring or early summer of the following year.

**Linseed,** See Flax

**Lion's Mouth,** See Foxglove

**Lion's Teeth/Tooth,** See Dandelion

**Liquidamber** (*Liquidambar* spp.)

**Description:** Sweetgum (*Liquidambar*) is a genus of four species of flowering plants in the family Altingiaceae, though formerly often treated in the Hamamelidaceae. They are all large, deciduous trees, 25-40 metres tall, with palmately lobed leaves arranged spirally on the stems. The flowers are small, produced in a dense globular inflorescence 1-2 cm diameter, pendulous on a 3-7 cm stem. The fruit is a woody multiple capsule 2-4 cm diameter (popularly called a "gumball"), containing numerous seeds.

**Influence:** Protect from Evil

**Gender**: Masculine, **Element**: Fire, **Planet**: Sun

Hold or place the seed pods on the altar during magickal rites to protect against evil forces. Substitute the bark of this plant for storax bark.

**Cultivation**: Seed is best sown as soon as it is ripe in the autumn in a cold frame. Harvest the seed capsules at the end of Autumn, dry in a warm place and extract the seed by shaking the capsule. Stored seed requires 1 - 3 months stratification and sometimes takes 2 years to germinate. Sow it as early in the year as possible. Germination rates are often poor. Prick out the seedlings into individual pots when they are large enough to handle and grow them on in a cold frame or greenhouse for their first winter. Since they resent root disturbance, it is best to plant them out into their permanent positions in early summer of their second year and give them some protection from cold for their first winter outdoors. Prefers a moist but not swampy loam in a sunny sheltered position

**Liverwort** (*Anemone hepatica*; *Peltigera canina*)

**Description:** Anemone hepatica is an herbaceous member of the Ranunculaceae or buttercup family that is native to the forest floors of temperate regions of the Northern Hemisphere. It has been called *Hepatica nobilis* also, [1] although at least one recent study of the phylogeny calls for all of *Hepatica* to be included in *Anemone*.[2] It grows on stone walls, rocks and in woodlands. The variety *H. nobilis* var. *nobilis* is native to Europe.

**Influence:** Protection, Love

**Gender**: Masculine, **Element**: Fire, **Planet**: Jupiter

To gain the love of a man, a woman can carry a liverwort sachet with her at all times.

**Cultivation**: Prefers a deep light alkaline soil with leafmould. Another report says that it grows best in a deep loam or clay soil. Grows well on limey woodland soils in half shade, though it also succeeds in deep shade and in full sun. A very ornamental plant. It grows well in the rock garden and in the woodland. Plants resent root disturbance and should be placed in their permanent positions as soon as possible. A greedy plant, inhibiting the growth of nearby plants, especially legumes. Propagation by seed sow in a moist soil in a shady position. The stored seed requires stratification for about 3 weeks at 0 - 5°c. Germination takes 1 - 12 months at 10°c. It is probably worthwhile sowing the seed as soon as it is ripe in a shady position in a cold frame. When they are large enough to handle, prick the seedlings out into individual pots and grow them on in the greenhouse for at least their first winter. Plant them out into their permanent positions in late spring or early summer, after the last expected frosts. Division just as the leafless plant comes into flower in late winter. Replant immediately into their permanent positions.

## Lobelia (*Lobelia inflata*)

**Description:** A native from Canada and eastern USA, growing with a rosette of soft, green, elliptic leaves to 10cm long. Leaves are covered with very fine hairs, and have soft, wavy margins. Upright flower stems 30-60cm high, with tiny, two-lipped, pale-blue flowers 4-6mm long. The plant is an annual, but if flowers are nipped out, it will extend over more than one season. Seed capsules look like round pouches, and this is reflected in the species name 'inflata'. As soon as the seed capsule is mature and dry, it releases brown seed, which is as fine as dust.

**Influence:** Weather, Attract Love

**Gender**: Feminine, **Element**: Water, **Planet**: Saturn

Throw some powdered lobelia at an oncoming storm to stop it. Also used to attract a love.

**Cultivation**: Succeeds in full sun or light shade. Grows well in heavy clay soils, prefers a slightly acid soil. Plants are usually annual, but are sometimes biennial.
This species is occasionally cultivated commercially as a medicinal plant

## Loosestrife (*Lythrum salicaria*)

**Description:** It is a herbaceous perennial plant, growing 1-1.5 m tall, forming colonies 1.5 m or more in width with numerous erect stems growing from a single woody root mass. The stems are reddish-purple or red to purple and square in cross-section. The leaves are, 3-10 cm long and 5-15 mm broad, downy and sessile, and arranged opposite or in whorls of three. The flowers are reddish purple, 10-20 mm diameter, with six petals (occasionally five) and 12 stamens, and are clustered tightly in the axils of bracts or leaves; there are three different flower types, with the stamens and style of different lengths, short, medium or long; each flower type can only be pollinated by one of the other types, not the same type, thus ensuring cross-pollination between different plants. The fruit is a small 3-4 mm capsule containing numerous minute seeds. Flowering lasts throughout the summer. When the seeds are mature, the leaves often turn bright red through dehydration in early autumn; the red colour may last for almost two weeks. The dead stalks from previous growing seasons are brown. The species is very variable in leaf shape and degree of hariness, and a number of subspecies and varieties have been described, but it is now generally regarded as monotypic with none of these variants being considered of botanical significance

**Influence:** Peace, Protection

**Gender**: Feminine, **Element**: Earth, **Planet**: Moon

Give some of this herb to a friend you are fighting with to settle the argument. Scatter about the home to bring peaceful vibrations and to keep evil forces away.

**Cultivation**: Succeeds in ordinary garden soil, especially if it is damp. Grows well in heavy clay and marshy soils and succeeds in shallow water at the edges of ponds. A very hardy plant, tolerating temperatures down to at least -25°c. This species can be very invasive and has been declared a noxious weed in some countries. Since being introduced in N. America it has invaded native marshlands, forming large areas of dense stands and crowding out many native species. A very ornamental plant. A good bee and butterfly plant. Plants usually self-sow when well sited. Propagation by seed sow in situ in the autumn or the spring. Division in Spring or Autumn. Larger clumps can be replanted direct into their permanent positions. Basal cuttings in the spring. Harvest the shoots with plenty of underground stem when they are about 8 - 10cm above the ground and plant them out in the summer.

**Lotus** (*Nymphaea lotus*)

**Description:** Nymphaea lotus, the Tiger Lotus or Egyptian White Water-lily, is a flowering plant of the family Nymphaeaceae that grows in various parts of East Africa and Southeast Asia. It is known to flower at night and close in the morning and remains of the flower have been found in the burial tomb of Ramesses II. This species of water lily has lily pads which float on the water, and blossoms which rise above the water. Lotus is often used as an aquarium plant. Sometimes it is grown for its flowers, while other aquarists prefer to trim the lily pads, and just have the underwater foliage. It is a perennial, grows to 45 cm in height, and prefers clear, warm, still and slightly acidic waters. The color of the flower is white and sometimes tinged with pink.

**Influence:** Protection, Lock-Opening

**Gender**: Feminine, **Element**: Water, **Planet**: Moon

Breathe the scent of lotus to receive its protection. Place a lotus root under your tongue and say "SIGN, ARGGIS" towards a locked door to open it. Lotus seeds and pods are used as love spells antidotes. Any part of the lotus carried or worn ensures good luck and blessings from the Gods.

**Cultivation**: A water plant requiring a rich soil and a sunny position. Succeeds in light shade. It is best grown in still water up to 250cm deep but it also tolerates slow moving water. Prefers shallow water. Plants are hardy to about -20°c. The flowers have a sickly scent. The flowers have a brandy-like scent. This unique smell is due to a combination of acetic acid and ethyl alcohol to form ethylacetate. Propagation by seed sow as soon as it is ripe in a greenhouse in pots submerged under 25mm of water. Prick out into individual pots as soon as the first true leaf appears and grow them on in water in a greenhouse for at least two years before planting them out in late spring. The seed is collected by wrapping the developing seed head in a muslin bag to avoid the seed being lost. Harvest it 10 days after it sinks below the soil surface or as soon as it reappears. Division in early summer. Each portion must have at least one eye. Submerge in pots in shallow water until established.

**Lovage** (*Levisticum officinale*)  **POISONOUS**

**Description:** The Garden Lovage is one of the old English herbs that was formerly very generally cultivated. It is sometimes grown in gardens for its ornamental foliage, as well as for its pleasant odour. It is a perennial that grows 1 metre to 2 metres tall. It is adaptable to many conditions, and does best in full sun.

**Influence:** Love, Psychic Sleep, Energy and Purification

**Gender**: Masculine, **Element**: Fire, **Planet**: Sun

Used as a tea for psychic dreams before bedtime or as an energy booster before exams or when clear thinking is needed. Use in a bath for cleansing. Added to other love herbs, enhances the attraction.

**Cultivation**: Divide mature plants or sow seed in spring. Lovage is one of the few herbs that will cope with a semi-shaded position though it prefers full sun (though not particularly fond of hot drying sun found in Australia). The plant does best in a well-drained, sheltered position where it gets morning sun. It needs fertile soil that has been enriched with organic material. The plant becomes dormant in winter.

**Love Lies Bleeding,** See Pansy

**Love Seed** (*Lomatium foeniculaceum*)

**Description**: Prostrate plant, leaves finely dissected, leaflets measured to 3 mm in length. Stems and leaves covered in hairs. Its foliage often has a grayish look to it. Flowers yellow in an umbel on a long flowering stem. Very early flowering. Could be mistaken for Musineon divaricatum, both are yellow-flowered, low growing plants in the Parsley family, share the same habitat, and bloom at the same time.

**Influence:** Friendship, Love

**Gender**: Feminine, **Element**: Water, **Planet**: Venus

Carry the seeds to attract love and new friendships. Pawnee Indians used this plant in magick.

**Cultivation**: A native of Kansas it prefers dry, open, prairie hilltops and slopes, most abundant on rocky limestone or chalk soils.

**Lucky Hand** (*Orchis* spp.)

**Description:** Lucky Hand is the root of the orchid plant.

**Influence:** Employment, Luck, Protection, Money, Travel

**Gender**: Feminine, **Element**: Earth, **Planet**: Moon

This is the root of the orchid plant which looks like a hand. It is used for protection, luck, success, and to obtain and maintain employment. Fill a jar with rose oil. Place several lucky hands in it and let them soak. When you need something, take one out and wear it (i.e., wear near your heart for love, in your shoe for travel, in your wallet for money, etc. )

**Cultivation**: See Orchid

**Mace** (*Myristica fragrans*)

**Description:** Mace and nutmeg both come from the fruit of *Myristica fragrans*, an aromatic evergreen that grows to 22 metres, with dark green leaves, aromatic flowers, and large, brownish/yellow fruit. The female trees produce the fleshy fruit that splits in half once mature. Nutmeg is the dried seed of this fruit, while the bright red, lacy covering (the aril) is the mace. Nutmegs can be harvested when the trees are 7 to 9 years old, and the tree reaches full harvest maturity after about 20 years. Native to Asia and Australasia, today nutmeg is commercially cultivated in Indonesia, Malaysia, Grenada, and Sri Lanka.

**Influence:** Psychic Powers, Mental Powers

**Gender**: Masculine, **Element**: Air, **Planet**: Mercury

Burn to increase psychic powers. Carry to improve the intellect.

**Cultivation**: Nutmegs are usually propagated by fresh seeds with their testa still attached. Seeds where the kernel rattle in the shell and old seeds will not germinate. In shaded nurseries the selected seeds are sown 2.5 - 5 cm deep and 30 cm apart in boxes or well prepared moistened nursery beds. Germination takes about one month or more. After two to three months the plants average about 15 cm in height. They are then transferred to baskets or plastic perforated bags. At six months they may be transplanted to the field but usually they are left for up to twelve or twenty four months Nutmeg is seen as a crop just to be harvested and traditionally and continuing into the present, not many farmers carry out any routine good cultivation practices. The plants are given some care when young but are basically neglected on maturity.

**Mad Dogweed,** See Skullcap

**MagickMushroom see** Agaric

**Maguey** (*Agave* spp.)

**Description:** **Agave** is the name of a succulent plant, Chiefly Mexican, they occur also in the southern and western United States and in central and tropical South America. The plants have a large rosette of thick fleshy leaves generally ending in a sharp point and with a spiny margin; the stout stem is usually short, the leaves apparently springing from the root. Various *Agave* species are popular ornamental plants. Each rosette is monocarpic and grows slowly to flower only once. During flowering a tall stem or "mast" grows from the center of the leaf rosette and bears a large number of shortly tubular flowers. After development of fruit the original plant dies, but suckers are frequently produced from the base of the stem which become new plants. It is a common misconception that Agaves are a cactus in fact they are closely related to the lily and amaryllis families, and are not related to cacti.

**Influence:** Lust

**Gender**: Masculine, **Element**: Fire, **Planet**: Mars

Use the juice of this herb in lust potions.

**Cultivation**: Requires a very well-drained soil and a sunny position. A monocarpic species, the plant lives for a number of years without flowering but dies once it does flower. However, it normally produces plenty of suckers during its life and these continue growing, taking about 10 - 15 years in a warm climate, considerably longer in colder ones, before flowering. In a warm climate suckers take 10 - 15 years to come into flower. Propagation by seed sown in a surface sow in a light positioning spring. The seed usually germinates in 1 - 3 months at 20°c. Prick out the seedlings into individual pots of well-drained soil when they are large enough to handle and grow them on in a sunny position until they are at least 20cm tall. Plant out in late spring or early summer, after the last expected frosts, and give some protection from the cold for at least their first few winters.

**Magnolia** (*Magnolia grandiflora*)

**Description:** It is a medium to large tree 20-30 m tall with a striking appearance, both in leaf and in bloom. The leaves are evergreen, simple and broadly ovate, 12-20 cm long and 6-12 cm broad, with smooth margins. They are dark green, stiff and leathery, and often scurfy underneath with yellow-brown pubescence. They will bronze, blotch, and burn in severe winters at the northern limits of cultivation, but most still cling until they are replaced by new foliage in the spring. In climates where the ground freezes, winter sun appears to do more damage than the cold itself. In the northern hemisphere the south side of the tree will experience more leaf damage than the north side of the tree. Two extremes are known, with leaves white underneath and with leaves brown underneath. The brown varieties are claimed to be more cold-hardy than the white varieties, but this does not appear to be proven as yet. The large, showy, citronella-scented flowers are white, up to 30 cm across and fragrant, with 6-12 petals with a waxy texture, emerging from the tips of twigs on mature trees in late spring

**Influence:** Fidelity

**Gender**: Feminine, **Element**: Earth, **Planet**: Venus

Place some magnolia near or beneath the bed to maintain a faithful relationship.

**Cultivation**: Stored seed must be kept cold over the winter and should be sown in late winter. The seed usually germinates in the spring but it can take 18 months. Prick out the seedlings into individual pots when they are large enough to handle and grow them on in light shade. They can be planted out into their permanent positions when they are more than 15cm tall, though should be well mulched and given some protection from winter cold for their first winter or two outdoors. Layering in early spring they are best grown in a warm position in a moderately rich free soil of an open texture. Tolerates moderately limey soils so long as they are deep and rich in humus. The branches are brittle so a sheltered position is required. Succeeds in full sun or semi-shade. Plants are hardy to about -10°c. The fleshy roots are easily damaged and any transplanting is best done during a spell of mild moist weather in late spring.

**Maidenhair** (*Adiantum pedatim*)

**Description:** Adiantum (maidenhair fern) is a genus of about 200 species of ferns in the family Pteridaceae, though some researchers place it in its own family, Adiantaceae. They are distinctive in appearance, with dark, often black stipes and rachises, and bright green, often delicately-cut leaf tissue. The sori are borne submarginally, and are covered by reflexed flaps of leaf tissue which resemble indusia. Dimorphism between sterile and fertile fronds is generally subtle. They generally prefer humus-rich, moist, well-drained sites, ranging from bottomland soils to vertical rock walls. Many species are especially known for growing on rock walls around waterfalls and water seepage areas

**Influence:** Beauty, Love

**Gender**: Feminine, **Element**: Water, **Planet**: Venus

Immerse some of this herb in water, then remove and wear it for grace, beauty, and love.

**Cultivation**: Ferns grow from rhizomes that are flat, horizontal, slightly woody masses usually just beneath the surface of the soil. In some species, the rhizome may be vertical and will produce a crown from which the stems of the ferns emerge. In either case, the rhizome is the foundation from which the roots will grow downward from underneath, while the stems will grow upward from the top. By cutting this rhizome, and separating the clump of ferns, it is possible to obtain double or triple the fern mass and in just a few weeks they should all be healthy adult ferns. This can be done with ferns growing outdoors or with potted ferns. Plant the new clump of ferns in the same kind of soil and light/shade conditions in which it was previously growing with the rhizome just below the surface of the soil. As this new fern grows, it may be divided again in one or two years. The advantage of propagating ferns in this manner is that, with ease, you can get larger ferns in a shorter period of time. The disadvantage is that you are limited by the number of new ferns that can be propagated at one time

**Male Fern** (*Dryopteris felix-mas*)

**Description:** Probably the best known of our native ferns with its tall upright leathery, tough looking fronds. Maybe a bit large for the small garden, many of the cultivars are smaller, see below. Although semi-evergreen it will benefit from being cut down in early spring to tidy up the older fronds. Fronds: 60-150cm. Soil preference: Neutral to Acid. Foliage: Semi-Evergreen.

**Influence:** Luck, Love

**Gender**: Masculine, **Element**: Air, **Planet**: Mercury

Carry as a luck attractant, and to attract women as well.

**Cultivation**: Ferns grow from rhizomes that are flat, horizontal, slightly woody masses usually just beneath the surface of the soil. In some species, the rhizome may be vertical and will produce a crown from which the stems of the ferns emerge. In either case, the rhizome is the foundation from which the roots will grow downward from underneath, while the stems will grow upward from the top. By cutting this rhizome, and separating the clump of ferns, it is possible to obtain double or triple the fern mass and in just a few weeks they should all be healthy adult ferns. This can be done with ferns growing outdoors or with potted ferns. Plant the new clump of ferns in the same kind of soil and light/shade conditions in which it was previously growing with the rhizome just below the surface of the soil. As this new fern grows, it may be divided again in one or two years. The advantage of propagating ferns in this manner is that, with ease, you can get larger ferns in a shorter period of time. The disadvantage is that you are limited by the number of new ferns that can be propagated at one time

**Mallow** (*Malva* spp.)

**Description:** Very easily grown, short-lived perennials often grown as ornamental plants. Mild tasting young mallow leaves make a very good substitute for lettuce, whereas older leaves are better cooked as a leafy green vegetable. The flowers can be used in salads.

**Influence:** Love, Protection, Exorcism, Peace and Happiness, Femininity

**Gender**: Feminine, **Element**: Water, **Planet**: Moon

Use as a tea to soften the character for a woman, or appreciate the small things and beauty in life. Use also in a bath to be able to do these things. Carried to attract love. Steep mallow leaves and stems in vegetable shortening, then strain it. This ointment, rubbed on the skin, casts out devils and protects against black magick.

**Cultivation**: Cultivation is by sowing the seeds directly outdoors in early spring. The seed is very easy to collect, and they will often spread themselves by seed.

**Mandrake** (*Mandragora officinale* or *Atropa Mandragora*)  **POISONOUS**

**Description:** A stemless herbaceous perennial with ovate 30 cm long leaves rising directly from the root. The flowers are 2 cm long, purple or greenish yellow, followed by an oblong greenish berry. Native of southern Europe.

**Influence:** Protection, Love, Money, Fertility, Health.

**Gender**: Masculine. **Planet**: Mercury. **Element**: Fire. **Deities**: Circe, Diana, Hecate, Hathor, Saturn

Few herbs are as steeped in magickal lore as mandrake. It is associated with the most intense practices of magick and especially well suited for love magick. It has great power as a visionary herb. It empower visions, providing the impetus to bring them into manifestation. It intensifies the magick of any situation. A whole mandrake root placed in the home will bring protection and prosperity. Carried, it will attract love. The human shape of the root makes it well suited for use as poppet. (Substitute ash roots, apples, root of the briony, or the American may apple if the cost is prohibitive). To activate a dried mandrake, place it on the altar undisturbed for three days. Then place it in warm water overnight. The root will then be activated and ready for any magickal purpose. Ash roots, briony roots, and May Apple can substitute for mandrake.

**Cultivation**: It likes a light, deep soil, as the roots run far down. They will do poorly in a soil that is chalky or excessively gravelly. If the soil is too wet in winter, the roots will rot. It is propagated from seeds which should be sown in deep flats or, better, singly in pots. These should be kept well-watered and when they reach a good size they should be carefully set out at least 60 cm apart.

**Manna grass,** See Sweetgrass

**Maple** (*Acer* spp.)

**Description:** Maples are mostly trees growing to 10-40 meters (30-130 ft) in height. Others are shrubs less than 10 meters tall with a number of small trunks originating at ground level. Most species are deciduous, but a few in southern Asia and the Mediterranean region are evergreen. Most are shade-tolerant when young, and are often late-successional in ecology; many of the smaller species are usually understory trees growing under the canopies of other larger trees, while the larger species eventually become dominant canopy trees.

**Influence:** Love, Longevity, Money

**Gender**: Masculine, **Element**: Air, **Planet**: Jupiter

Maple leaves are used in love and money spells, and maple branches serve as magick wands. A child passed through the branches of a maple tree will have a long life.

**Cultivation**: Maple Trees are not easy to propagate. Commercially they are normally grafted on to a strong growing rootstock and there are a couple of reasons for this. Firstly, many varieties are not strong growing trees and would produce weak trees if grown on their own rootstock. Secondly, growing trees from seed produces variable results in vigour and form. The best solution for the amateur is to grow Maple Trees from seed. Sow several seeds and select only the most vigorous seedlings. The best time to sow is when the seed is ripe, normally around the middle of autumn. The seed pod will have begun to go slightly crispy. Sow the seeds on the same day as they collected because acer seeds do not keep well. Remove the seed from the seed pod and place in a pot of normal potting compost. Cover with about 2cm of compost and water well. Over winter the pots in a cold frame or in a position that will not suffer from hard frosts. The seedlings should emerge in mid spring the next year. When the roots start to appear at the bottom of the pot, transfer to a larger pot. When the trees are about 30cm high they can be transplanted to their final positions.

**Marcory,** See Stillengia

**Marigold** (*Calendula officinalis*)

**Description:** Marigold is a flowering annual plant that comes in many sizes and colors. It is adaptable to many soils.

**Influence:** Protection, Prophetic Dreams, Legal Matters, Psychic Powers

**Gender**: Masculine. **Planet**: Sun. **Element**: Fire.

Aids visionary sight and helps find stolen property by producing a vision of the thief in the mind and the location of the stolen property. Dried petals may be used alone or mixed with dried incense to consecrate divination tools. Petals may be macerated in sunflower oil to make an oil of consecration. Adds a special, loving magick to rituals of death and dying. Added to other herbs in sachets, amulets and even incense for attracting a new love or adding new life to a present relationship. Place above the bed for psychic dreams, or use in dream pillows. Carry marigold petals with a bay leaf to quiet gossip. If a girl touches the petals of the marigold with her bare feet, she will understand the language of the birds.

**Cultivation**: Marigold is an annual plant that comes in many sizes and colors. It is adaptable to many soils. Propogation is from seed only, sown in it's final place in early spring, or in mild areas late summer or early autumn. Give plenty of water and full sun. Remove spent flower heads to promote further flowering.

**Marjoram** (*Origanum majorana* or *O. vulgare*)

**Description:** Marjoram is a highly perfumed herb with thick trusses of dainty white or purple flowers, which make it a highly decorative herb that is suitable for the flower garden. In warmer climates it is a perennial, but it is treated as a half-hardy annual in colder areas since it will not survive a severe winter. Plants grow to 30 cm to 60 cm with a spread of about 20 cm. Flowers are tiny but plentiful and grow in clusters around the stem.

**Influence:** Protection, Love, Happiness, Health, Money, Helps to accept deep changes in life, Prediction, Balancing.

**Gender:** Masculine, **Element:** Air, **Planet:** Mercury

Burn over burner when someone or something dies, either figuratively or physically or place herb under pillow and ask for a revealing dream. Place a pinch of the herb in the corners of the home for protection, Added as a booster for all love wishes. Use in love spells, and add to food to strengthen love. Carry for protection. Shields against evil when grown in the garden. Mix with violets and wear during winter to prevent colds. Give marjoram to a depressed person to bring happiness. Use in money mixtures and sachets.

**Cultivation:** Marjoram grows naturally in poor soils. Too much water and fertiliser will make the plants sappy and lacking in flavour. Marjoram can be grown from seed planted in spring. Sow seed in punnets and transplant later. New plants can also easily be propagated from cuttings taken in late spring. Marjoram likes a lightly textured soil in a bright, open, sunny location. It's quite drought tolerant and survives hot summer weather very well. Cut back in late winter to promote a fresh flush of spring foliage.

**Marrubium,** See Horehound

**Marsh Skullcap** see Skullcap

**Marshmallow see** Althea

**Marybud see** Marigold

**Marygold see** Marigold

**Mary's grass,** See Sweetgrass

**Masterwort** (*Imperatoria ostruthium*)

**Description:** It is a smooth, perennial plant, the stout, furrowed stem growing 2 to 1 metre high. The dark-green leaves, which somewhat resemble those of Angelica, are on very long foot-stalks and are divided into `three leaflets, each of which is often again sub-divided into three. The umbels of flowers are large and many-rayed, the corollas white; the fruit has very broad wings.

**Influence:** Strength, Calming, Manifestations

**Gender:** Masculine, **Element:** Fire, **Planet:** Mars

Wear to gain physical strength and reinforce the body. Carry to aid the will and calm emotions, and also as an amulet against evil. Scatter it about to make spirits appear.

**Cultivation:** The seed requires cold stratification to germinate. Wet a paper towel (with kelp solution is especially helpful) and wring out, put seeds in the towel and fold into a square, gently pressing the towel against the seeds. Place in a baggie and refrigerate for 3 months and then take out and sow the seeds as usual. Or just plant outside in fall to germinate in the spring. Transplant to full sun and moist soil. The sweet-scented flowers appear on heavy stalks up to 4 ft/1.2m tall in late summer. Harvest the root in spring or autumn and dry. This plant is hardy to zone 5 (temperate), where winter temperatures don't go below -20F/-28C.

**Mastic** (*Pistacia lentiscus*)

**Description:** Mastic is an evergreen shrub or small tree of the Pistacio family growing up to 4 m (13 ft) tall, which is cultivated for its aromatic resin on the Greek island of Chios, [1]. It is native throughout the Mediterranean region, from Morocco and Iberia in the west through southern France and Turkey to Syria and Israel in the east; it is also native on the Canary Islands.[ Mastic has a sweet, aromatic, licorice like flavour that's highly prized throughout the Middle East as a flavouring for a variety of edibles including desserts, breads, chewing gum, and some savoury dishes like couscous and tagines. It's also used to flavour liqueurs

**Influence:** Psychic Powers, Manifestations, Lust

**Gender**: Masculine, **Element**: Air, **Planet**: Sun

Add to incenses where a manifestation is desired. Burn to gain the Sight. Has been used in lust potions in the Middle East. Lends potency and power to any incense it is added to.

**Cultivation**: Pre-soak the seed for 16 hours in alkalized water, or for 3 - 4 days in warm water, and sow late winter. Two months cold stratification may speed up germination, so it might be better to sow the seed in early winter. The germination is variable and can be slow. Plant out into their permanent positions in early summer and consider giving some protection from winter cold for their first year or two outdoors. Prefers a well-drained to dry sandy or stony alkaline soil

**May Apple** (*Podophyllum peltaltum*)  **POISONOUS**

**Description:** These plants reach 15 cm – 45 cm in height and grow in patches. Each plant has a single stalk topped with one or two broad, deeply divided leaves that vaguely resemble umbrellas. The two-leaved plants normally produce a single, small white flower (usually in the northern hemisphere in May, thus the name) from the fork in the stem. The flower develops into a pulpy, lemon-yellow berry which ripens in late summer and is the only part of the plant that isn't poisonous (however, the berries should only be eaten in moderation, if at all).

**Influence:** Money.

**Gender**: Masculine. **Planet**: Mercury. **Element**: Fire.

Generally used as a substitution for European (true) mandrake. Its uses are practically identical. The May Apple is not related to the true mandrake.

**Cultivation**: Prefers a moist peaty soil and filtered light or shade. Grows well in a moist open woodland. Hardy to about -20°c, it takes some years to become established but is very long lived in a suitable habitat. Young leaves may be damaged by late frosts but otherwise the plants are quite hardy. Over collection of the plant from the wild is becomimg a cause for concern as local populations are being endangered. Young plants only produce one leaf each year, older plants have 2 or 3 leaves each year. The sub-species P. hexandrum chinense. Wall. has larger flowers and more deeply divided leaves. Seed is best sown as soon as it is ripe. The seed germinates in 1 - 4 months at 15°c. Prick out the seedlings into individual pots when they are large enough to handle and grow on in a shady part of the greenhouse for at least 2 growing seasons. Plant them out into their permanent positions in the winter when the plants are dormant.

**Meadow Rue** (*Thalictrum* spp.)

**Description:** The plants' compound leaves consist of three stalked leaflets. The small fuzzy flowers, which grow in clusters, are often greenish, yellow, or purple, with four or five sepals; petals are absent.

**Influence:** Divination, Protection, Love

Worn around the neck by Native Americans as a protective amulet, and carried to attract love.

**Gender**_____, **Element**_____, **Planet:** _____

**Cultivation**: Succeeds in most fairly good soils in sun or semi-shade. A greedy plant, inhibiting the growth of nearby plants, especially legumes. Seed is best sown as soon as it is ripe in the. When they are large enough to handle, prick the seedlings out into individual pots and plant them out in the summer. The seed can also be sown in an outdoor seedbed in spring. Plant them into their permanent positions the following spring. Division in spring as new growth commences or in the autumn. Larger divisions can be planted out direct into their permanent positions.

## Meadowsweet (*Spiraea filipendula*)

**Description:** A medium sized perennial with square reddish stems and serrated leaves, dark green on the top of the leaf and white on the under side. The flowers are creamy white, small and highly perfumed, appearing in spring and summer.

**Influence:** Love, Divination, Peace, Happiness

**Gender**: Masculine, **Element**: Water, **Planet**: Jupiter

A subtle but beautifully aromatic herb this is used for the symbol of love when mixing up your potions. Add a fresh pinch to boost. Burn the dried herb to relieve disharmony in the home or to relieve tensions when the in-laws are coming. continue to burn in a scented candle, no one will know! Keeps peace when strewn about the house.

**Gender**_____, **Element**_____, **Planet:** _____

**Cultivation**: Meadowsweet prefers moist conditions in an open to semi shaded position and humus-rich soil. Succeeds in full sun only if the soil is reliably moist throughout the growing season. Dislikes dry or acid soils but does well in marshy soils and in heavy clay soils..

## Medicine Plant see Aloe

## Melampode see Hellebore, Black

## Melilot (*Melilotus officinalis*) **POISONOUS**

**Description:** The dried leaves can be toxic, though the fresh leaves are quite safe to use. The dried plant has a sweet aromatic fragrance like newly mown hay. Melilot (Melilotus), also known as Sweet Clover, is a genus in the family Fabaceae. Members are known as common grassland plants and as weeds of cultivated ground. Originally from Europe and Asia, it is now found worldwide.

**Influence:** Memory enhancing, Healing

**Gender**_____, **Element**: Air , **Planet:** _____

Use as a decoction, it is rinsed over the head to increase the power of memory when needed, good for the student to do before studying or an exam! As a bath, heals and soothes.

**Cultivation**: Seed - sow spring to mid-summer in situ. Pre-soaking the seed for 12 hours in warm water will speed up the germination process, particularly in dry weather. Germination will usually take place within 2 weeks. Prefers a well-drained to dry neutral to alkaline soil in a sunny position. Dislikes shade. Established plants are drought tolerant. The flowers are rich in pollen making this a good bee plant. If they are cut back before flowering, the plants will grow on for at least another year before dying.. This species has a symbiotic relationship with certain soil bacteria, these bacteria form nodules on the roots and fix atmospheric nitrogen. Some of this nitrogen is utilized by the growing plant but some can also be used by other plants growing nearby

**Melissa,** See Balm, Lemon

**Mesquite** (*Prosopis juliflora*)

**Description:** These deciduous trees generally reach a height of 6 to 9 meters (20 to 30 ft), although in most of their range they are shrub size. They have narrow, bipinnately compound leaves 50 to 75 mm long, of which the pinnules are sharply pointed. Twigs have a characteristic zig-zag form. Mesquite is an extremely hardy, drought-tolerant plant because it can draw water from the water table through its long taproot. However, it can also use water in the upper part of the ground, depending upon availability. The tree can easily and rapidly switch from utilizing one water source to the other.

**Influence:** Healing

**Gender**: Feminine, **Element**: Water, **Planet**: Moon

Add to healing incenses and mixtures. Used to fuel magickal fires.

**Cultivation**: Mesquite should be grown in full sun on well-drained soil. The tree is very drought tolerate. Young plants can be successfully transplanted while small, but they need irrigation until established. Fire used to limit its invasive habit. It has become an unimaginable weed in Texas due to fire control. Prior to fire control, heat from flames killed many trees and this kept the tree from spreading throughout the region. Propagation is by seed.

**Millefoil,** See Yarrow

**Mimosa** (*Acacia dealbata*)

**Description:** The Sensitive plant (Mimosa pudica L.) is a creeping annual or perennial herb often grown for its curiosity value: the compound leaves fold inward and droop when touched, re-opening within minutes. The stem is erect in young plants, but becomes creeping or trailing with age. The stem is slender, branching, and sparsely to densely prickly, growing to a length of 1.5 m (5 ft). The leaves are bipinnately compound, with one or two pinnae pairs, and 10-26 leaflets per pinna. The petioles are also prickly. Pedunculate (stalked) pale pink or purple flower heads arise from the leaf axils. The globose to ovoid heads are 8-10 mm in diameter (excluding the stamens). On close examination, it is seen that the floret petals are red in their upper part and the filaments are pink to lavender. The fruit consists of clusters of 2-8 pods from 1-2 cm long each, these prickly on the margins. The pods break into 2-5 segments and contain pale brown seeds some 2.5 mm long.

**Influence:** Protection, Love, Prophetic Dreams, Purification

**Gender**: Feminine, **Element**: Water, **Planet**: Saturn

Used in spells involving purification (scatter around the area), love, healing, and prophetic dreaming (place beneath the pillow). A bath of mimosa destroys hexes and curses, and guards against them.

**Cultivation**: Growing best in full sun locations, Mimosa is not particular as to soil type but has low salt-tolerance. Grows well in acid or alkaline soil. Mimosa tolerates drought conditions well but has a deeper green color and more lush appearance when given adequate moisture. The litter problem of the blooms, leaves, and especially the long seed pods requires consideration when planting this tree. Also the wood is brittle and has a tendency to break during storms though usually the wood is not heavy enough to cause damage. Typically, most of the root system grows from only two or three large-diameter roots originating at the base of the trunk. These can raise walks and patios as they grow in diameter and makes for poor transplanting success as the tree grows larger.

**Mint** (*Mentha* spp.)

**Description:** Mint is a perennial herb that is propagated by root division or rooting cuttings in water. The common types of mint are peppermint, pennyroyal, crinkle-leafed spearmint, spearmint, and applemint.

**Influence:** Money, Love, Lust, Healing, Exorcism, Travel, Protection, Clear thinking.

**Gender**; Masculine, **Element**: Fire, **Planet**: Venus

Use as tea for clearing the head before meditation or performing magick. Can also be used to calm when situations in a relationship are explosive. Used in healing potions and mixtures. Mint worn on the wrist ensures good health. Used in travel spells, to induce lust, money and prosperity spells, and to rid a place of evil. Fresh mint on the altar will call good spirits.

**Cultivation**: Mint generally likes semi-shaded positions where the soil is moist but not waterlogged. It can become invasive as it spreads aggressively via underground stems. Propagation can be achieved by division or by cuttings struck in spring. Seed can also be sown in spring.

**Mistletoe** (*Viscum Album*)  **POISONOUS**

**Description:** Mistletoes are aerial parasitic plants that use other plants to obtain their water and mineral nutrients. However, they usually undertake their own photosynthesis through their leaves.

**Influence:** Protection, Love, Hunting, Fertility, Health, Exorcism.

**Gender**: Masculine. **Planet**: Sun. **Element**: Air. **Deities**: Balder, Apollo, Freya, Frigga, Venus, Odin

Harvested on a Waning Moon, used to repel negative influences and protect against unwanted advances. Used in sachets and amulets, or hung in the home, it is a general all-purpose protector. Use in a bath for healing wishes or the herb added to a prayer bowl enhances the healing. Worn, it is said to help conceive and to hold on to your current love. Hunters were said to carry some of this for luck and protection. Wear when astral traveling for protection.

**Cultivation**: As a parasitic plant cultivation is unlikely, however in the wild the following applies: Many of the mistletoes are very host specific, and as such have often developed leaf foliage that mimics the foliage of the host plant. They reproduce from single seeds contained within small, sweet, sticky fruits, which when attached to the branches of the host plant develop into new mistletoe plants. When the seeds germinate, a modified root penetrates the bark of the host's stem and forms a connection through which water and nutrients pass from the host to the mistletoe. They do this by melding their root structure into the woody structure of the host's stem, and thereafter it becomes a living part of the stem receiving all the nutrients that the foliage of the host plant receives.

**Monkshood,** See Aconite

**Monument Plant,** See Deerstongue

**Moonwort** (*Botrychium* spp.)

**Description:** Western Moonwort is a small perennial fern with a single erect frond, 3-13 cm high. It is divided into a sterile segment and a fertile segment. The sterile segment has a stalk 0-4 mm long, and a broadly lance-shaped to triangular blade that is pinnately divided with 1-6 pairs of closely adjacent leaflets (pinnae). The basal pinnae are usually partly to wholly pinnately divided and are larger than the lobed or entire-margined upper pinnae. The fertile segment is 2-3 times as long as the sterile segment and 1-3 times pinnately divided into linear segments that bear the spores.

**Influence:** Money, Love

**Gender**: Feminine, **Element**: Water, **Planet**: Moon

Supposedly, this herb produces silver when placed in boxes or bags. Used in money spells. Used in opening locks (placing it in the keyhole) and breaking chains (touching them with the herb). Horses and humans who accidentally step on moonwort lose their shoes. Used in love spells.

**Cultivation**: Ferns grow from rhizomes that are flat, horizontal, slightly woody masses usually just beneath the surface of the soil. In some species, the rhizome may be vertical and will produce a crown from which the stems of the ferns emerge. In either case, the rhizome is the foundation from which the roots will grow downward from underneath, while the stems will grow upward from the top. By cutting this rhizome, and separating the clump of ferns, it is possible to obtain double or triple the fern mass and in just a few weeks they should all be healthy adult ferns. This can be done with ferns growing outdoors or with potted ferns. Plant the new clump of ferns in the same kind of soil and light/shade conditions in which it was previously growing with the rhizome just below the surface of the soil. As this new fern grows, it may be divided again in one or two years. The advantage of propagating ferns in this manner is that, with ease, you can get larger ferns in a shorter period of time. The disadvantage is that you are limited by the number of new ferns that can be propagated at one time.

**Morning Glory** (*Ipomoea* spp.)  **POISONOUS**

**Description:** The ornamental sweet potatoes (*Ipomoea batatas*) are fast growing, twining vines with palmately lobed leaves. These showy forms produce a tuberous root identical in appearance to the common (green leaved) sweet potato but probably not tasty. Late in the season tubular, fairly large flowers appear which are similar to morning glories. Usually they are not particularly noticeable, though, because the foliage claims most of the attention. Three types are of ornamental sweet potato are cultivated for annual, summer vines: 'Blackie' with dark purple, nearly black foliage; 'Margarita' with chartreuse leaves; and 'Tricolor' with pale green, white and pink margined leaves. 'Blackie' and 'Margarita' come back with the same colour foliage as the mother plant, but 'Tricolor' may revert to green.

**Influence:** Stop Nightmares, Peace and Tranquility

**Gender**: Masculine, **Element**: Water, **Planet**: Saturn

Place the seeds beneath the pillow to stop nightmares. Grow in the garden, the blue variety bring peace and happiness. The root of this plant substitute for High John the Conqueror.

**Cultivation**: Morning glories thrive in a strong, well-drained soil in a sunny site with plenty of water, but they will do well almost anywhere. The seeds have a hard seedcoat and should be nicked or soaked two hours in warm water before sowing. If the seeds are nicked and soaked, the vines will generally flower 6 weeks after sowing. The seeds should be planted 5 mm to 15 mm deep and not less than 15 cm apart. This species tends to run to vine unless the roots are cramped. This may be done by standing the vines in pots and allowing them to become slightly potbound before setting them out. Although morning glories like a lot of water, if the roots are kept damp constantly, the vines will produce few flowers and they will set very little seed.

**Mortal,** See Bittersweet

**Moss**

**Description:** Mosses are small, soft plants that are typically 1–10 cm tall, though some species are much larger. They commonly grow close together in clumps or mats in damp or shady locations. They do not have flowers or seeds, and their simple leaves cover the thin wiry stems. At certain times mosses produce spore capsules which may appear as beak-like capsules borne aloft on thin stalks.

**Influence:** Luck, Money

**Gender**: Masculine, **Element**: Earth, **Planet**: Jupiter

Carry moss taken from a gravestone in your pocket to ensure good luck, especially with finances. Used to stuff general-purpose poppets.

**Cultivation**: Rules of cultivation are not widely established. Moss collections are quite often begun using samples transplanted from the wild in a water-retaining bag. However, specific species of moss can be extremely difficult to maintain away from their natural sites with their unique combinations of light, humidity, shelter from wind, etc. Growing moss from spores is even less controlled. Moss spores fall in a constant rain on exposed surfaces; those surfaces which are hospitable to a certain species of moss will typically be colonised by that moss within a few years of exposure to wind and rain. Materials which are porous and moisture retentive, such as brick, wood, and certain coarse concrete mixtures are hospitable to moss.

**Mountain Ash,** See Rowan

**Mountain Tea**, see Wintergreen

**Muggons see** Mugwort

**Mugwort** (*Artemisia vulgaris*

**Description:** Seldom used now, this wayside weed was used as a tonic and before hops in the production of malt beer as a clearing agent. Widely distributed in Northern Hemisphere temperate zones it readily populates waste places and in some areas is considered a weed. Clump forming it grows to 60 – 120 cm in height. It has deeply lobed leaves with a greywhite down on the undersides.

**Influence:** Strength, Psychic Powers, Protection, Prophetic Dreams, Healing, Astral Projection.

**Gender**: Feminine, **Planet**: Venus, **Element**: Earth, **Deities**: Artemis, Diana

Use a wash or the oil to consecrate or anoint crystal balls or any tool of divination. Produces visionary dreams and is a prime ingredient in dream pillows. Keeps one safe from dark forces. Protects children. Incense brings protection. Carried, it brings loved ones safely home from journeys. A tonic for the soul, it keeps us aware of our spiritual direction. Burn with sandalwood or wormwood during scrying sessions. A mugwort infusion sweetened with honey will enhance divination. Carried, it also increases lust and fertility. Harvested at the Full Moon, this is carried for protection when travelling long journeys. Used as a tea to enhance psychic powers or rub the leaves on the forehead and on the divination tool to increase clairvoyance. Mugwort can also be placed next to the bed to aid in achieving astral projection. Its other magickal uses include strength, protection, prophetic dreams, and healing When carrying it, you are protected from poison, wild beasts, or sunstroke. In a building, it prevents evil things from entering.

**Cultivation**: Propagation is easiest by plant division of established clumps in autumn or spring, though it can be grown from seed. Mugwort likes dry areas in full sun, though partial shade is tolerated. It is a perennial shrubby plant that grows 60cm – 120cm tall, depending upon growing conditions. Soil type is not particularly important as Mugwort is quite tolerant. The plant should be trimmed with secateurs in Autumn back to near ground level.

**Mulberry** (*Morus rubra*)

**Description:** All three mulberry species are deciduous trees of varying sizes. White mulberries can grow to 80 ft. and are the most variable in form, including drooping and pyramidal shapes. In the South on rich soils the red mulberry can reach 70 ft. in height. The black mulberry is the smallest of the three, sometimes growing to 30 ft. in height, but it tends to be a bush if not trained when it is young. The species vary greatly in longevity. Red mulberry trees rarely live more than 75 years, while black mulberries have been known to bear fruit for hundreds of years. The mulberry makes an attractive tree which will bear fruit while still small and young.

**Influence:** Protection, Strength

**Gender**: Masculine, **Element**: Air, **Planet**: Mercury

Protects the garden from lightning. A good aid when working on the will, and the wood is protective against evil.

**Cultivation**: Mulberries can be grown from seed, although the plants can take 10 years or more to bear. Seed should be sown as soon as extracted from the fruit, although white mulberry seeds germinate better after stratifying one to three months before planting. Sprig budding is the most common method for grafting mulberries. Mulberries need full sun and also adequate space. The distance between trees should be at least 5 metres. The trees should not be planted near a pathways as the fallen fruit will not only stain the walkway, but are likely to be tracked indoors. The trees are quite wind-resistant with some cultivars used as windbreaks. Mulberries like a warm, well-drained soil, preferably a deep loam. Shallow soils such as those frequently found on chalk or gravel are not recommended. Although somewhat drought-resistant, mulberries need to be watered in dry seasons. If the roots become too dry during drought, the fruit is likely to drop before it has fully ripened.

**Mullein** (*Verbascum thapus*)

**Description:** Mellein is a furry leafed plant which grows to around 2 metres in height and the same in diameter

**Influence:** Courage, Protection, Health, Love, Divination, Exorcism

**Gender**: Feminine, **Element**: Fire, **Planet**: Saturn

Used usually in an amulet to protect against any unwanted influences. Also, carry with you to guard against any wild animals when in the wilderness. Burn the leaves when banishing heavy bad influences and an immediate halt to bad habits. Instils courage, attracts love, and prevents colds when worn in the shoe. Hung over doors to protect against evil spirits and black magick. Banishes demons and negativity. Powdered mullein leaves can substitute for graveyard dust.

**Cultivation**: Mullein is adaptable to many soils, however prefers well drained fertile soils. It prefers full sun. It is a biennial plant growing to 2 metres tall. It is a prolific self-sower.

**Mustard** (*Brassica* spp.)

**Description:** Mustard (also known as mustard greens, spinach, leaf mustard and white mustard), is a quick-to-mature, easy-to-grow, cool-season vegetable for greens or salads. Although mustard is often associated with the Deep South, it is also suitable for gardens in the central and northern United States in the cool parts of the growing season. Mustard greens are high in vitamins A and C.

**Influence:** Fertility, Protection, Mental Powers

**Gender**: Masculine, **Element**: Fire, **Planet**: Mars

Sprinkle mustard seed on the doorsill to protect the home, and bury it under the doorstep will keep supernatural beings out of your house. Eat it if you are a woman looking for greater fertility.

**Cultivation**: Black Mustard grows very readily from seed sprinkled where the plants are to grow. The plants need a sunny, well-drained location. As a member of the Brassica genus, the plant attracts cabbage white butterflies and their caterpillars. The plant has the capacity to become a weed as it has done elsewhere. To prevent self-seeding and to ensure that the mustard seeds are not lost, pods should be harvested as soon as they start to colour and kept in paper or cloth bags until they dry out and split open.

**Myrrh** (*Commiphora myrrha*)

**Description:** Myrrh is a large shrub or small tree that grows in the Middle East and Ethiopia and Somalia. A pale yellow oil drips from the cuts in its dull gray bark and hardens to form teardrop-shaped nuggets of myrrh, which are powdered for use as a healing herb.

**Influence:** Protection, Exorcism, Healing, Spirituality, Used extensively in magickal scents High Psychic Vibrations, Purification

**Gender**: Feminine, **Element**: Water, **Planet**: Sun

Burn the herb and walk through the area you wish to cleanse, use the smoke from the incense to purify and bless charms, amulets, talismans, magickal jewellery, tools, etc. Useful in meditation. Burn during healing wishes. Mixed with other magickal herbs, a standard in magick enhancement. Its other magickal uses include protection, healing, and exorcism. It is often combined with Frankincense to increase its power.

**Cultivation:** ~~~~

**Myrtle** (*Myrtus communis*)

**Description:** Myrtle is an evergreen plant that prefers warm climates. It has small pointed leaves, and grows to about 4 metres high. Its blossoms are small, white, and in clusters. The leaves are gathered and dried for use in August.

**Influence:** Love, Fertility, Youth, Peace, Money

**Gender**: Feminine, **Element**: Water, **Planet**: Venus

The wood is used to make magickal charms and other tools, especially those involving love. Wear a caplet of the leaves while preparing other love potions, burn with any love wish. Add also to friendship wishes for true friends. Added to love sachets and spells, especially to keep love alive and exciting. Carry myrtle wood to preserve youthfulness. Drink a cup of myrtle tea every three days has the same effect, but must be done every three days without fail. Carry to preserve love. Grown on each side of the house to bring love and peace, and is lucky to grow in window-boxes if planted by a woman. Used in money spells.

**Cultivation**: Easily grown from heeled semi hardwood cuttings, taken in late summer. Myrtle demands a well drained soil with moderate fertility. In pots a good potting mix is ideal. Sunny place protected from all but the mildest winters.

**Myrtle Grass,** See Calamus

**Narcissus,** See Daffodil

**Naughty Man see** Mugwort

**Neem** *(Melia Azadirachta)*

**Description:** Neem is an extraordinarily hardy tree that thrives in ecosystems ranging from the Sahara Desert to the wet salty environment of the Florida Keys

**Influence:** Purifying

Neem leaves were traditionally strewn on the floor of temples at weddings, to purify and bless the area and the couple, and the air was fanned with neem branches during the ceremony. The bark was burned to make a red ash for religious decoration of the body in adulthood. Neem branches were used to cover the body at death, and the wood used to burn the funeral pyre. Neem is considered to be the Goddess Neemari Devi.

**Gender**_____, **Element**_____, **Planet:** _____

**Cultivation**: For best results, plant your neem tree in the largest pot you can move, since they're happiest spending winter months in a sunny window and summers outdoor. They're also like goldfish and they'll only grow as large as their pots allow. If you don't have a compost pile or favorite potting soil, ask your local nursery to recommend their best soil for houseplants. For optimum growth, fertilize weekly with fish emulsion at half the recommended rate and use a balanced organic fertilizer monthly while the tree is growing. Neem trees, like many tropical plants, are day-length sensitive and will stop growing in the winter unless supplemental light is provided. If you expect to harvest neem year-round, make sure your tree receives as much natural light as possible during the day, then several hours of artificial light at night during the short days of winter.

## Nettle (*Urtica diocia*)

**Description:** Over 500 species of nettle grow worldwide, some more obnoxious than others for their powerful sting. Greater Nettle (Urtica dioica) is a very hardy, perennial, 1-1.8 metres high, with sprawling or erect, quadrangular stems, covered with fine stinging hairs. Ovate shaped leaves, to 10cm long, with deeply serrated margins, covered in fine hairs. The species name, 'dioica', indicates that the male and female flowers usually form on different plants. The white/green flowers form in tiny clusters. Propagation is by seed, cuttings or root division. Roots spread underground, similar in habit to mint. For this reason, it is wise to plant within a barrier, or give it a spot on its own where it will not grow into other plants. Nettle is adaptable to any soil or climate. This is the species I prefer to grow, as it is a perennial, which means I have leaves to pick all year around. In very cold climates, this nettle may die down for winter. Nettle will grow well in a bucket-sized pot, or a styrofoam box, which gives people living in flats with limited space, an opportunity to use the herb.

**Influence:** Exorcism, Protection, Healing, Lust

**Gender**: Masculine, **Element**: Fire, **Planet**: Mars

Sprinkle nettle around the room to protect it. It is also burned during ceremonies for exorcism. Stuffed in a poppet and sent back to the sender of a curse or bad spell, it will end the negativity. Nettles gathered before sunrise and fed to cattle is said to drive evil spirits from them. Throw on a fire to avert danger, hold in the hand to ward off ghosts, carry with yarrow to allay fear. Infuse the flowers as a tea, sprinkle on self and other people, (with their permission of course!) or in a room to remove petty jealousies, gossip, envy and uncomfortable situations. Use with a poppet to send bad vibes back to the person sending to you then bury it. Burn during banishing wishes. Used as a lust-inducing herb, and is also used in purification baths.

**Cultivation**: Propagation is by seed, cuttings or root division. Roots spread underground, similar in habit to mint. For this reason, it is wise to plant within a barrier, or give it a spot on its own where it will not grow into other plants. Nettle is adaptable to any soil or climate. In very cold climates, this nettle may die down for winter. Nettle will grow well in a bucket-sized pot, or a styrofoam box, which gives people living in flats with limited space, an opportunity to use the herb.

## Norfolk Island Pine (*Auricaria excelsa*)

**Description:** Resembles a true pine tree. Branches are horizontal to main stem, in tiers of bright green, with soft, awl-shaped needles and although they may reach a height of 24 metres in their natural habitat, they will maintain a reasonable size when grown in a container, in the home. The beauty and symmetry of the plant, as well as the soft texture of the foliage will make you want to decorate it, and use it for your living Christmas tree.

**Influence:** Protection, Anti-Hunger

**Gender:** Masculine, **Element:** Fire, **Planet:** Mars

Protects against hunger and evil spirits when grown in or near the home.

**Cultivation:** Propagation of Norfolk Island Pine is by seed which germinates fairly rapidly (10-15 days). Seed should be placed flat on the germination medium without covering and lightly misted or fogged until the tap root emerges and top growth is initiated. At that time, seedlings can be irrigated as needed to keep the medium moist. Suggested light level for propagation is 50% shade. Often about 5% albino seedlings will germinate and these will die or can be discarded when potting seedlings. Potting media used for Norfolk Island Pine must be supportive of trunks and help make up for the limited root systems of these trees. A mixture such as 3: 1 peat: sand will help keep trunks straight, yet provide good water and fertilizer retention. Mixes with slightly more aeration should be used for seedling trees, but care must be taken not to transplant them before they start leaning because of weak root systems. Norfolk Island Pine will tolerate a wide temperature range. Trees grown in full sun will be compact, have a strong trunk and a light to medium green color, whereas shade grown plants have a more open appearance, a weaker trunk and dark green foliage.

**Nosebleed,** See Yarrow

**Nuts**

**Description:** A nut in botany is a simple dry fruit with one seed (rarely two) in which the ovary wall becomes very hard (stony or woody) at maturity, and where the seed remains unattached or unfused with the ovary wall. Most nuts come from pistils with inferior ovaries and all are not open at maturity.

**Influence:** Fertility, Prosperity, Love, Luck

Potent fertility inducers; carried for this purpose. Included in many prosperity and money mixtures. Heart shaped nuts are carried to promote love, and double nuts are powerful lucky charms.

**Gender**_____, **Element**_____, **Planet:** _____

**Cultivation:** Dependant on specific species.

**Nutmeg** (*Myristica fragrans*)

**Description:** Myristica fragrans is a large evergreen tree that's fruit contains a large central seed (the nutmeg). It is used as a spice as well as acting as a deliriant if consumed in large quantities. Its effects are long-lasting and are considered unpleasant by most who experience them.

**Influence:** Clairvoyance

**Gender:** Masculine, **Element:** Air, **Planet:** Jupiter

Used to strengthen your psychic powers. Carry the seed or anoint candles with this herb, used also with other appropriate herbs to enhance psychic dreams and wishes. Carried to ward off rheumatism, cold sores, boils, and sties. Hang it around a baby's neck to aid in its teething. Included in many money and prosperity spells.

**Cultivation**: The nutmeg tree thrives in a hot, moist climate, in a well-drained soil with partial shade. It requires a moist soil, but should not be kept wet, as the roots will rot. To obtain nutmegs both sexes should be planted. One male is sufficient to pollinate ten to twelve females. When grown from seed, they should be planted singly in pots, and transplanted when 20cm to 15 cm high. The trees will begin to bear in 7 to 9 years.

## Oak *(Quercus alba)*

**Description:** Oaks have spirally arranged leaves, with a lobed margin in many species; some have serrated leaves or entire leaves with a smooth margin. The flowers are catkins, produced in spring. The fruit is a nut called an acorn, borne in a cup-like structure known as a cupule; each acorn contains one seed (rarely two or three) and takes 6-18 months to mature, depending on species.

**Influence:** Protection, Health, Money, Healing, Potency, Fertility, Luck

**Gender**: Masculine, **Element**: Fire, **Planet**: Sun

The most sacred of all trees, its wood is often used for many magickal tools. Many things are buried under an Oak Tree for the manifestation of wishes. Burn the leaves to purify the area. The fruit is used for most fertility wishes and is used in sachets and amulets or just alone. A sprig hung in the home wards off negativity and strengthens the family unit. Carried also for wisdom and strength in any given situation. Carry an acorn to prevent illness and pain, for longevity, to preserve youthfulness, to increase fertility, and to strengthen sexual potency.. Men carry to increase their attractiveness. Never cut an Oak for magickal purposes unless it is during the Waning Moon.

**Cultivation**: Collect fresh acorns that have no weevil holes and sow them immediately, as once the acorns dry out they cannot absorb water again and will not germinate. The seedlings have long tap roots, so the acorns should be planted individually into 4cm deep pots into any free-draining, mildly acid potting mix. Cover the acorn to its own depth. The seedlings should be potted up once or twice before being planted out into the ground. Oaks self-seed readily, so you might be able to find a few seedlings already growing around the parent tree.

## Oats (*Avena sativa*)

**Description:** Oats are an annual grass that grows up to 1.2 metres tall. Easiest to purchase from a health food store, as much is needed to be beneficial, and takes up more room than the average gardener has available. It does make a pretty ornamental grass in the garden and around foundations.

**Influence:** Money

**Gender**: Feminine, **Element**: Earth, **Planet**: Venus

Oats are a traditional food for those recovering from an illness. Oats made into packs and pastes clear up many skin disorders, such as acne. Oats are used in prosperity and money spells, and in rituals to the harvest.

**Cultivation**: Grows from seed as a grass.

**Old-Man** See Southernwood

**Old Woman,** See Wormwood

**Oleander** (*Nerium oleander*)  **POISONOUS**

**Description:** Oleander is a large fast growing evergreen shrub, native to Asia and the Mediterranean region. This plant with glossy, 10cm to 25cm long narrow dark green leaves and funnel-shaped flower clusters, single or double can reach 1 metre to 8 metres tall. There are different varieties with varying heights and flowers in some varieties are delightfully fragrant. This dense plant which flowers abcan be used as borders, hedges, backgrounds and tall screens. Dwarf varieties are suitable for container gardens.

**Influence:** Brings sickness, disgrace and misfortune.

Italian magicians say that keeping any part of this plant in the house brings sickness, disgrace, and misfortune of all kinds to its inhabitants. Occasionally used in love spells.

**Gender**: female, **Element**: Earth, **Planet**: Saturn

**Cultivation**: Propagation is through vegetative cuttings. This species commonly produces many side shoots which can be replanted in their own pots in a standard mix of well drained sand and peat. In the ground, the plant can be spaced 2 – 3 metres apart depending on its variety. When in growth water often and allow plants to remain moist. When not actively growing, water plants sparingly and allow them to dry out between watering. Yellowing of new leaves indicates over watering. Fertilize regularly during the growing period.

**Olive** (*Olea europaea*)

**Description:** The Olive is an evergreen tree or shrub native to the Mediterranean, Asia and parts of Africa. It is short and squat, and rarely exceeds 8–15 meters in height. The silvery green leaves are oblong in shape, measuring 4–10 cm long and 1–3 cm wide. The trunk is typically gnarled and twisted. The small white flowers, with four-cleft calyx and corolla, two stamens and bifid stigma, are borne generally on the last year's wood, in racemes springing from the axils of the leaves. The fruit is a small drupe 1–2.5 cm long, thinner-fleshed and smaller in wild plants than in orchard cultivars. Olives are harvested at the green stage or left to ripen to a rich purple color (black olive).

**Influence:** Healing, Peace, Fertility, Potency, Prote ction, Lust

**Gender**: Masculine, **Element**: Fire, **Planet**: Sun

Olive is the universal symbol of peace, and is associated in spiritual workings with bringing happiness, purity, and harmony. Olive was considered sacred to Athena, as she caused olive to spring from the ground at the foundation of her city, Athens, in Greece. Olive oil has been used for centuries to light lanterns in temples and churches of many different religions, and is used for anointing as well. It is also what the dove brought back to Noah to indicate that the flood waters recorded in the Bible were receding. Moses referred to it as "the Tree of Life". Italians have been known to hang an olive branch over the doors of their homes to ward off evil. The oil is used for anointing and healing. Brings luck when worn.

**Cultivation**: Climate: Olives prefer long warm summers and cold winters. The tree will tolerate harsh conditions, including steep stony soils, where few other plants will survive.

They do not like heavy soils that hold water for long periods of time., preferring free draining neutral to alkaline soils (optimal pH of 7.0-8.0).

When planting one or many olives in your backyard / orchard, plant it right to begin with and the tree will go about its way for many years to come with little attention required. Planting instructions specific to Olives are simple. Prepare the site (3x3m) with one wheelbarrow load of manure and one barrow load of crusher dust. Lime may be applied at this point if necessary depending on the pH of the soil. Keep the root ball intact when planting, they don't like being teased.

## Onion (*Allium cepa*)

**Description:** Onion is a perennial herb that grows from a bulb. It prefers rich garden soils and plenty of water. The greens above ground can be used alone, and the bulb harvested by pulling from the ground, and allowing the tops to dry before storing in a dry location,

**Influence:** Protection, Exorcism, Healing, Money, Prophetic Dreams, Lust, Banishing, Purifying, and some Healing.

**Gender**: Masculine, **Element**: Fire, **Planet**: Mars

An onion cut in half and placed in the corners of the room will absorb illnesses, and bury or burn in the morning. Rubbing a magickal tool on the half of the bulb, will cleanse it. Also sacred to the Moon so it should be used in any wish involving energies of the Moon itself. Place onion bulbs and flowers around the house for protection. Burn the flowers for banishing any bad habits and negative influences. A large red onion tied to the bedpost protects against sickness and aids in recovery. Burn in a fireplace stove to attract riches.

**Cultivation**: Onion is a perennial herb that grows from a bulb. It prefers rich garden soils and plenty of water. Division in spring is the preferred method of propogation, though seed can be used and commercial varieties are available.

## Orange (*Citrus sinesis*)

**Description:** The plants are large shrubs or small trees, reaching 5–15 m tall, with spiny shoots and alternately arranged evergreen leaves with an entire margin. The flowers are solitary or in small corymbs, each flower 2–4 cm diameter, with five (rarely four) white petals and numerous stamens; they are often very strongly scented. The fruit is a hesperidium, a specialised berry, globose to elongated, 4–30 cm long and 4–20 cm diameter, with a leathery rind surrounding segments or "liths" filled with pulp vesicles.

**Influence:** Love, Divination, Luck, Money, Mental Agility, Business, Balancing Thought and Emotion

**Gender**: Masculine, **Element**: Water: **Planet**: Sun

Use the flowers for a herbal bath to not only refresh and stimulate but also to make one attractive for a special event, add the rinds to a love sachet to help someone make up their mind, wear the oil when dealing in business negotiations that need an extra "uumph"! Carry as a sachet or amulet or hang a sprig up in the home to aid in the "heart says one thing, the head the other" situation. When you eat an orange, think of a yes/no question you want answered. Count the seeds; an even number means no, an odd, yes. Orange peel is added to prosperity powders, and the orange is a symbol of good luck and fortune.

**Cultivation**: Available as tree stock, Oranges prefer a rich, sandy soil, and warm year-round temperatures and can be planted all year round. Planting is quite simple. Dig a large hole, 2x3 times the size of the pot. Incorporate 20 L of organic matter / composted poultry manure and 200 g of blood and bone. Blood and bone should be set into the bottom of the hole with a layer of soil over the top, NOT in direct contact with the roots. When removing the tree from the pot, see that there is minimal disturbance around the root ball. Set the tree into the hole at the same level as the surrounding soil and fill in, firming as you go. When hole is half filled with soil add a bucket of water to settle the soil in the bottom of the hole. Water well and keep moist while settling in. Mulch heavily. This initial application of fertilizer is sufficient for the first few months.

**Orchid** (*Orchis* spp.)

**Description:** It is any flower which consists of three petals and three sepals. Sepals protect a flower bud before the petals emerge. In orchids the sepals are usually the same colour as the petals. The third petal is modified in that it is usually highly coloured or intricately patterned in order to attract the plant's natural pollinator to the reproductive portion of the bloom.

**Influence:** Love

**Gender**: Feminine, **Element**: Water, **Planet**: venus

Used in love spells. This flower is popularly exchanged among lovers. Some types are used in creating visions, trance-states, and inducing psychic powers.

**Cultivation**: Orchids enjoy good filtered light, application of water as often as they become dry, occasional encouragement with liquid fertiliser and an airy environment where the atmosphere is never stagnant. Growing from a bulb, propagation is easiest by division of bulbs.

**Oregon Grape** (*Berberis aquifolium*)

**Description:** Berberis aquifolium is a shrug having stems about 2 metres high, erect, and of rapid growth. The leaves are alternate and consist of 3 or 4 pairs of leaflets, and an odd one. They are evergreen, coriaceous, bright and shining upon the upper surface, and very ornamental; hence, the shrub is frequent in cultivation, often under the improper name "holly." The leaflets are smooth, ovate, from 5cm to 8cm long, and one-half as wide. The root of Berberis aquifolium is from 1 cm to 3 cm in diameter, often increasing to 5cm to 8cm at the base of the stem. It is woody, yellow throughout, very hard. The bark is deep-yellow beneath and brown upon the surface. It is without odour and very bitter.

**Influence:** Money, Popularity

Carry the root to draw money and financial security, and also to gain popularity.

**Gender**_____, **Element**_____, **Planet:** _____

**Cultivation**: A very easy plant to grow, thriving in any good garden soil and tolerating dense shade under trees. It grows well in heavy clay soils and also succeeds in dry soils if it is given a good mulch annually. It dislikes exposure to strong winds. It is very tolerant of pruning and plants can be cut back into old wood if they grow too large and straggly. Spring is the best time to do this. Suckers are fairly freely produced, with established plants forming dense thickets

**Oregano** *(Origanum vulgare)*

**Description:** Oregano originates from the Mediterranean and is closely related to marjoram. Its pungency is in direct proportion to the amount of sun it receives. It grows to a height of about 20 cm with woody stems and dark green leaves around 2 cm long. Small, white flowers are borne on long spikes.

**Influence:** Forget lost love, Letting go

Oregano is used to promote perspiration as a treatment for colds, flu, and fevers. A tea of oregano is often used to bring on menses and relieve associated menstrual discomfort. It is also used in baths and inhalations, as well drinking the infusion, to clear lungs and bronchial passages. Internally and externally it can help alleviate dry itching skin. The essential oil is used to treat viral infections, respiratory ailments, and muscle aches. Pregnant women should not ingest large amounts of oregano. Oregano is used to help forget and let go of a former loved one, such as a former spouse, boyfriend, girlfriend, etc. Burn in incenses or drink the infusion to aid in spells for letting go.

**Cultivation:** Oregano is a wild form of marjoram and grows naturally in poor soils. It can be grown from seed planted in spring. Sow seed in punnets and transplant later. Oregano likes a lightly textured soil in a bright, open, sunny location. It's quite drought tolerant and survives hot summer weather very well. Cut back in late winter to promote a fresh flush of spring foliage. The rooted stems are easily separated from the main plant and planted elsewhere. It is rarely attacked by pests.

**Orris** (*Iris florentina* or *Phizoma Iridis*)

**Description:** Orris is a hardy iris, native to temperate climates.

**Influence:** Love, Protection, Divination.

**Gender:** Feminine. **Planet:** Venus. **Element:** Water. **Deities:** Aphrodite, Isis, Osiris, Hera, Iris

The root is used to find and hold love. The root powder is known as "Love Drawing Powder." Protects from evil spirits. The roots and leaves hung in the house and added to the bath are good for personal protection. Make a pendulum with a small piece of the wood. Carry an amulet or sachet for drawing a new love. Add to other love herbs to create a loving environment and stimulate the thoughts of love with someone. Place small pinch's in the corners of the room to open a new love or burn during a new love wish. Bathe for attraction of the opposite sex.

**Cultivation:** Easily propagated by division of the clump over winter. It prefers moist well drained fertile soil.

**Our Lady's Candle,** See Mullein

**Paddocstol,** See Toadstool

**Paddockstool,** See Toadstool

**Puddockstool,** See Toadstool

**Palm, Date** (*Phoenix dactylifera*)

**Description:** The Date Palm is a palm in the genus Phoenix, extensively cultivated for its edible fruit. It is a medium-sized tree, 15–25 m tall, often clumped with several trunks from a single root system, but also often growing singly. The leaves are pinnate, 3–5 m long, with spines on the petiole and about 150 leaflets; the leaflets are 30 cm long and 2 cm broad. The full span of the crown ranges from 6–10 m.

**Influence:** Fertility, Potency

**Gender**: Masculine, **Element**: Air, **Planet**: Sun

A fertility tree whose leaves and dates are eaten for this purpose. the pits are carried by impotent men to cure their ailment. Protects from bad weather where it is grown. Palm leaves kept near the entrance of the home prevent evil creatures from entering.

**Cultivation**: Available as young trees from commercial nurseries. Date palm is a dioecious species and consequently half of the progeny will be males and half will be females, with no certain way to determine at an early stage the sex of the progeny, nor fruit or pollen quality prior to flowering (often only seven years later); so whilst seed propagation is by far the easiest and quickest method of propagation. However, it is not a true to type propagation technique and no two seedlings will be alike. Alternately offshoots are produced by a palm with only three or four offshoots being suitable for planting out in one year. They mustl go into the nursery for 1 to 2 years before field planting. Zahidi, Berim and Hayani varieties are known to produce large numbers of offshoots, while Mektoum and Barhee varieties produce relatively low numbers of offshoots.

Offshoots are recognised by their curved form while seedlings have a straight form. Another way to differentiate between the two is that seedlings have roots all around their base with no connecting point to the palm, while an offshoot does not have any roots on the side where it was connected to the mother plant. Furthermore, an offshoot always has a mark on one side which is a result of detachment from its parent palm.

**Pansy** (*Viola tricolor*)

**Description:** Pansy, a member of the violet family, is a cool-season crop that may be grown in borders, edging and window boxes. It can even be used for cut flowers. Pansies are considered a perennial plant, which means they live longer than one growing season. This makes them ideal for planting in the spring and fall. Pansies may be used as understory plantings for spring bulb gardens. They also make perfect massed plantings.

**Influence:** Love, Rain Magick, Divination

**Gender**: Feminine, **Element**: Water, **Planet**: Saturn

Attracts love when worn or carried. If pansies are picked with the dew still on them, it will soon rain.

**Cultivation**: You can start pansies from seed, but most gardeners purchase them in packs. When planting them outdoors, make sure they are hardened off. Growing compact, free-blooming pansies is easy. Just be sure to choose a site that receives some sun during the day. Pansies do best in loamy soil that is rich in organic matter, but they also do well in the heavier clay. Increase the organic matter in clay soils to improve drainage and aeration for the plants. Canadian sphagnum peat moss and well-rotted compost are good sources of organic matter. Water plants thoroughly after transplanting and mulch lightly with leaf mold or bark mulch.

**Papaya** (*Carica papaya*)

**Description:** The papaya is a short-lived, fast-growing, woody, large herb to 3 to 4 metres in height. It generally branches only when injured. All parts contain latex. The hollow green or deep purple trunk is straight and cylindrical with prominent leaf scars. Its diameter may be from 5 cm to over a 30 cm at the base.

Foliage: The leaves emerge directly from the upper part of the stem in a spiral on nearly horizontal petioles 30 cm – 1, 5 metres long. The blade, deeply divided into 5 to 9 main segments, varies from 30 – 60 cm in width, and has prominent yellowish ribs and veins. The life of a leaf is 4 to 6 months.

**Influence:** Love, Protection

**Gender**: Feminine, **Element**: Water, **Planet**: Moon

Tie a rag around a limb of a papaya tree while visualizing your need. Hang several twigs of papaya wood over the door to keep away evil. Eat the fruit and serve to a loved one to intensify feelings of love.

**Cultivation**: Papayas need a light, well-drained soil. They are easily killed by excess moisture. The soil needs to be moist in hot weather and dry in cold weather. They also like to be as free from wind as possible, although this is not as critical as their need for sun. Papayas can be grown successfully in shade, but the fruit is rarely sweet. They are best planted in mounds or against the foundation of a building where water can be controlled. Papayas are normally propagated by seed. To start a plant, extract the seeds from ripe papayas and wash them to remove the gelatinous covering. They are then dried, dusted with a fungicide and planted as soon as possible. Plant the seeds in warm sterile potting mix. Seeds should be planted in sterile soil as young papaya seedlings have a high mortality rate from damping off. Under ideal conditions the seeds may germinate in about two weeks, but may take three to five weeks. Seedlings usually begin flowering 9 - 12 months after they germinate. Seedling papayas do not transplant well. Plant them in large containers so the seedlings will have to be transplanted only once, when they go into the ground. Transplant carefully, making sure not to damage the root ball. Set the plants a little high to allow for settling. A plastic mulch will help keep the soil warm and dry in wet winter areas, but remove it as soon as the weather becomes warm. Plant at least three or four plants to ensure yourself of having females or plant hermaphroditic plants. Papaya plants can also be grown from cuttings, which should be hardened off for a few days and then propped up with the tip touching moist, fertile soil until roots form. Semihardwood cuttings planted during the summer root rapidly and should fruit the following year.

## **Papyrus** (*Cyperus papyrus*)

**Description:** *Cyperus papyrus* is a stately aquatic member of the sedge family. The plants are easily cultivated and suitable for medium to large water features, especially in warmer climates. The most conspicuous feature of the plants are the bright green, smooth, rounded culms (flowering stems) which are up to 40 mm thick at the base and may be up to 5 m tall in ideal conditions. Each is topped by a dense cluster of thin, bright green, shiny stalks, which resemble a feather duster when young. The stalks elongate later and bend gracefully downward under their own weight so that the cluster becomes almost spherical in shape. During summer these stalks bear small brown spikelets (groups of flowers) and eventually numerous tiny dark brown fruits are borne in the axils of glumes (tiny scales). The culms are connected by stout horizontal rhizomes which creep along the substrate under water and are anchored by numerous roots. The younger parts of the rhizome are covered by red-brown, papery, triangular scales, which also cover the base of the culms and represent reduced leaves. It is therefore incorrect to describe the plants as leafless. Similar brown papery structures (termed bracts) occur at the tops of the culms below the clusters of thin stalks.

**Influence:** Crocodiles

**Gender**: Masculine, **Element**: Air, **Planet**: Mercury

Place in a boat to prevent crocodile attacks.

**Cultivation**: Ideally, the plants need a muddy or sandy substrate in water at least half a metre deep so that the tall culms will not topple. They need full sun but also need to be sheltered from strong winds, and for best effect should be allowed to form a large colony. In winter the oldest culms dry off and can be removed with a sharp implement. New culms will be formed in spring from the growing point of the rhizome. Propagation is by division of the rhizome in spring. Germination from seed is not recommended. The time period from seed to flowering is not known but it is undoubtedly several years.

**Parsley** (*Petroselinum sativum*)

**Description:** Parsley is one of the best known and most widely used herbs. It is actually a biennial, but is usually cultivated as an annual because the first year leaves have the best flavour. The crisp, tight foliage of the curly parsley is the most attractive variety to use fresh as a garnish, but the flat-leaved Italian parsley has a superior flavor when cooked. The curly variety grows 20 cm to 30 cm tall and the Italian about 45 cm, although a dwarf variety is available. In the second year, 60 cm tall flower stalks appear, and their blossoms ripen into seeds. Seeds collected from second year plants and dried thoroughly will keep for two or three years.

**Influence:** Love, Protection, Purification, Healing and Vitality

**Gender:** Male, **Element**: Air, **Planet**: Mercury

Provokes lust and promotes fertility when eaten. If you're in love and you cut parsley, you cut your love too. Romans tucked parsley into their togas every morning for protection. Placed on plates of food to guard against contamination. Used in purification baths, and to stop misfortune. A wreath of parsley worn on the head prevents (or delays) intoxication. Has associations with death and is often regarded as evil. Call the power of the Element of Earth and drink as an infusion. Restores a sense of well-being. Used for increasing strength and vitality after surgery or sickness, adds new life to "in-a-rut" situations. Can be added to other healing herbs to quicken the wish.

**Cultivation**: Parsley prefers an open, sunny, well-drained position and rich soil. If it is to be grown in a pot, it needs a tall container as it has a long tap root. The seed is not easy to germinate, though if left to run to seed, self-seeding is possible. Soaking seed before sowing can assist germination. The addition of side dressings of blood and bone throughout the growing season will keep the plants lush and healthy. It is not generally bothered by pests.

**Parsley Fern,** See Tansy

**Partridge Berry**, see Wintergreen

**Passion Flower** (*Passiflora incarnata*)

**Description:** There are over 400 hundred species in the genus *Passiflora*. Most are tender evergreen tropical vines and most are commonly called passion flowers. *Passiflora incarnata* is an exception in that it is deciduous, can survive winter freezes and is commonly called maypop as well as passion flower. It is a fast growing perennial vine that employs tendrils to grab hold of adjacent shrubs, structure and other supports to lift itself to heights of 2.4-3.7 m. The large serrated leaves grow 13-15 cm wide by 15-20 cm long. They typically have three to five lobes and are arranged alternately on the stem with flowers and branches emerging from the base of the leaf stem.

**Influence:** Peace, Sleep, Friendship

**Gender**: Feminine, **Element**: Water, **Planet**: Venus

Passionflower will calm a troubled household when placed inside the home. Spanish missionaries believed the flowers were a symbol of Christ's crucifixion, and the crown of thorns of Christ's passion, giving this plant its name. Carried, it attracts friends and popularity. Place below your pillow if you have trouble sleeping.

**Cultivation**: It prefers a light, rich soil, and does well in dry areas. Passiflora grows readily from the seed, but takes several weeks to sprout. It is best sown on the surface of light soil or peat moss with bottom heat. The young plants may be planted in the open after 6 months. It may be propagated easily by cuttings of half-ripened growth. These should be about 15 cm long; they will root easily in sand and do not require bottom heat. The vines may eventually overgrow and tangle themselves. Thin them out by cutting branches back to their beginnings. Passionflower dies back at the first frost.

**Patchouli** (*Pogostemon cablin* or *P. patchouli*)

**Description:** Of West Indies, Indian, and oriental origin, patchouli is a delightfully aromatic, perennial herb to 1 metre high. An evergreen bush, with new stems forming square, which mature into round, woody, brown branches. Ovate-eliptic shaped leaves 5-15cm long, have small soft toothed margins. Flower spikes of clusters of very tiny, pink lip flowers form on axillary and terminal stems. As the flowers fade, the fine, brown seeds form in small capsules, that look like tiny knots on the spike. Leaves, flowers and seeds freely give off their aroma, but even more so if crushed between the fingers. When the stems are cut, their aroma will permeate the room as they dry, which is quite delightful.

**Influence:** Money, Fertility, Lust, Business Growth

**Gender**: Feminine, **Element**: Earth, **Planet**: Saturn

Used primarily in attracting a powerful passionate love. Burned for new business growth and also placed in the garden to help it grow healthy. Worn in a sachet or an oil for fertility. Also used with other Earth element herbs for divination and increasing psychic awareness. Used in money and prosperity mixtures and spells. Used in fertility talismans, and substitutes for graveyard dust. Used also to promote lust and attract people.

**Cultivation**: Patchouli is a tender perennial grown from seed, a native of Malaysia, that grows approximately 1 metre to 1.3 metres tall with a bushy habit. The leaves are large and furry. Cold will kill it, so try growing it as a houseplant if you enjoy its fragrance, giving you the added benefit of helping to repel insect predators from your houseplants. Patchouli prefers average to rich soil and partial shade with high humidity. In tropical areas where the plant is cultivated commercially, they are spaced 60 cm to 100 cm apart. They reach heights of 40 to 80 cm. In areas with hot, dry summers, patchouli will benefit from frequent watering. Use a sprinkler or misting nozzle to increase the humidity as much as possible. If you grow it outdoors in summer, a dressing of well-rotted manure or application of liquid fish fertilizer will be helpful. When the temperatures begin to drop in fall patchouli will shed its leaves. It is necessary to move it indoors in a bright sunny window. Or, you can take stem cuttings and start new plants.

**Pavil,** See Stillengia

**Pea** (*Pisum sativum*)

> **Description:** Peas are one of the oldest cultivated vegetables. Originally the tender tops of the plants were cooked along with the pea pods. Today we have shelling, snap, snow and sugar pod peas. They are a rather brief, cool season vegetable that are well worth the easy effort to enjoy them fresh from the garden.
>
> **Influence:** Money, Love
>
> **Gender**: Feminine, **Element**: Earth, **Planet**: Venus
>
> Shelling peas brings fortune and profits in business. Dried peas are used in money mixtures. If a woman finds a pea pod with nine peas, she should hang it over the door. The first eligible man who walks under it will be her husband.
>
> **Cultivation**: Full sun in cooler temperatures or partial shade. Varieties can be tall between 30 cm and 2 metres. Harvest when the peas have enlarged in the pods. To judge this you will need to gently squeeze the pods. The exception is snow peas, which are grown for their edible pods and are harvested when the pods reach about 8cm in length, but are still flat. Peas will grow on most soils, although they prefer a medium well-dug soil with plenty of organic material. Do not add nitrogen to the soil before planting (or after) - peas extract nitrogen from the air sufficient for the needs. An over-rich soil will cause lots of leafy growth, but a reduced cop of peas. Peas like moisture, so do not plant too near walls or fences. Sow after the danger of frost has passed.

**Peach** (*Prunus persica*)

> **Description:** It is a deciduous tree growing to 5–10 m tall, belonging to the subfamily Prunoideae of the family Rosaceae. It is classified with the almond in the subgenus Amygdalus within the genus Prunus, distinguished from the other subgenera by the corrugated seed shell. The leaves are lanceolate, 7–15 cm long and 2–3 cm broad. The flowers are produced in early spring before the leaves; they are solitary or paired, 2.5–3 cm diameter, pink, with five petals. The fruit is a drupe, with a single large seed encased in hard wood (called the "stone" or "pit"), yellow or whitish flesh, a delicate aroma, and a skin that is either velvety (peaches) or smooth (nectarines) in different cultivars. The flesh is very delicate and easily bruised in some cultivars, but is fairly firm in some commercial cultivars, especially when green. The seed is red-brown, oval shaped and 1.5-2 cm long. Peaches, along with cherries, plums and apricots, are stone fruits (drupes).
>
> **Influence:** Love, Exorcism, Longevity, Fertility, Wishes
>
> **Gender**: Feminine, **Element**: Water, **Planet**: Venus
>
> The fruit induces love when eaten, and also gives wisdom. Peach pits are worn to keep demons away.
>
> **Cultivation**: Commercially available grafted varieties are preferred, however can be grown from seed. Peaches require full sunlight and should not receive shade from buildings or tall trees. If possible, select a site with a high elevation so that cold air can drain away from the tree on a cold night during bloom. The best site will have well drained sandy loam type soil. Peach or nectarine tree roots or rootstocks will not tolerate

soils where water remains on or near the surface for more than one hour after a heavy rain. Prepare the soil one to two years before planting so that soil pH, organic matter, and nutrient status can be modified for the production of high quality peaches and/or nectarines. Prepare a bed at least 2 metres in diameter by cultivating (spading) 30 cm deep and adding organic matter such as manure, leaves, grass clippings, and compost. Plant your tree in the spring in the center of your prepared area. Keep the bud union 2 cm above the soil. Planting a peach or nectarine tree too deep in the soil can cause poor growth or death.

## Pear (*Pyrus communis*)

**Description:** They are medium sized trees, reaching 10–17 m tall, often with a tall, narrow crown; a few species are shrubby. The leaves are alternately arranged, simple, 2–12 cm long, glossy green on some species, densely silvery-hairy in some others; leaf shape varies from broad oval to narrow lanceolate. Most pears are deciduous, but one or two species in southeast Asia are evergreen. Most are cold-hardy, withstanding temperatures between −25 °C and −40 °C in winter, except for the evergreen species, which only tolerate temperatures down to about −15 °C. The flowers are white, rarely tinted yellow or pink, 2–4 cm diameter, and have five petals. Like that of the related apple, the pear fruit is a pome, in most wild species 1–4 cm diameter, but in some cultivated forms up to 18 cm long and 8 cm broad; the shape varies in most species from oblate or globose, to the classic pyriform 'pear-shape' of the European Pear with an elongated basal portion and a bulbous end.

**Influence:** Lust, Love

**Gender**: Feminine, **Element**: Water, **Planet**: Venus

Pear fruit is used in love spells, and eaten as a aphrodisiac. Pear wood is good to use for magick wands, and it's said that Witches once danced beneath pear trees.

**Cultivation**: Commercially available grafted varieties are preferred, however can be grown from seed. Pears need a location with good circulation where the ground is slightly elevated and sloping. This is because the trees bloom early and the flowers may be damaged in the spring by frosty air, which settles in low-lying areas. Pears should be grown in heavier soil types such as clayey loam with porous subsoil, or medium or sandy loam. Pear trees will not survive on ground that is saturated with water. Pear trees may be planted in the autumn in mild climates or the spring in cooler ones. They should be set 7 metres apart, except the more vigorous varieties, which need to be spaced 8 metres apart. Soak the roots in water for 30 to 60 minutes before setting in the ground. The hole for the tree should be large enough to spread the roots about naturally. The soil should be worked in and around the roots to eliminate air pockets. There shouldn't be a depression around the tree when you have finished planting and the tree should be set at the same level as it was previously growing. Water the tree thoroughly and check for air pockets, carefully lifting the tree to the correct level if it settles.

## Pearl Moss, See Irish Moss

## Pecan (*Carya illinoensis*)

**Description:** It is a large deciduous tree, growing to 20–40 m in height (rarely to 44 m; taller trees to 50–55 m have been claimed but not verified), with a trunk up to 2 m diameter. The leaves are alternate, 40–70 cm long, and pinnate with 9–17 leaflets, each leaflet 2–1 cm long and 2–7 cm broad. The flowers are wind-pollinated, and monoecious, with staminate and pistillate catkins on the same tree; the male catkins are pendulous, up to 18 cm long; the female catkins are small, with three to six flowers clustered together. The fruit is an oval to oblong nut, 2.6–6 cm long and 1.5–3 cm broad, dark brown with a rough husk 3–4 mm thick, which splits off in four sections at maturity to release the thin-shelled nut.

**Influence:** Money, Employment

**Gender**: Masculine, **Element**: Air, **Planet**: Mercury

Added to money and prosperity spells. Obtain a small amount of pecans, shell them, eat them slowly while visualizing yourself working and enjoying your job. Take the shells, wrap them in a bag, and place them somewhere at work where they won't be found or removed. This prevents you from losing your job.

**Cultivation**: Generally available as nursery saplings, Pecan can be grown from fresh seed. Collect well-filled seed nuts in Autumn, and dry to about 5 percent moisture, or until the kernel snaps when bent. Store the seed nuts in refrigeration in poly bags, with or without slightly moist packing material. Do not let the temperature drop to freezing point. One week before planting, remove the seed from refrigeration and warm to room temperature. One day before planting, soak the seed in running water. After at least 24 hours, remove nuts, which have swelled, showing a split in the suture. Some may need longer soaking to split. Plant the seed sideways 7 – 8 cms deep in either a nursery row, a raised bed, or a large barrel with both ends cut out. After one year, the seedlings should be 15 – 20 cm tall. The pecan-nut tree is deciduous and can therefore only be transplanted during the winter. The average monthly maximum temperature should be higher than 28 °C during summer and lower than 23 °C in winter. The average monthly minimum temperature during the summer must rise above 16 °C, but drop below 8 °C in winter. The most suitable production areas are therefore those with short, cold winters and long, hot summers, with no early or late frost and a humidity below 55 % during the greater part of the growing season. The pecan-nut tree performs best in a fertile, well-drained, deep soil with a loose to medium texture.

**Pee in the Bed,** See Dandelion

**Pennyroyal** (*Mentha pulegium*)

**Description:** Pennyroyal is a perennial that grows to 45 cm high. It tolerates most soils, and prefers direct sun.

**Influence:** Strength, Protection, Peace, Banishment

**Gender**: Masculine, **Element**: Earth, **Planet**: Venus

Burn for protection in meditation and astral travel. Used also for ridding oneself or the home of negative thoughts against you. Carry in a sachet or amulet when dealing with negative vibrations of all kinds. Place a little on a candle before or during uncomfortable meetings. Place this in the shoe to prevent weariness during travel. Aids in business deals when worn. Considered to be an herb of peace.

**Cultivation**: Pennyroyal is a perennial that grows to 45 cm high. It tolerates most soils, and prefers direct sun. Grow as you would any member of the mint family.

**Pennywort** see Liverwort

**Peony** (*Paeonia officinalis*)

**Description:** Peonies are a perennial shrub-like plant, growing 60 cm to 1.2 metres high. They prefer rich, humousy, well-drained soils, and full sun.

**Influence:** Protection, Exorcism, Luck

**Gender**: Masculine, **Element**: Fire, **Planet**: Sun

A great all-purpose protection herb. Use the dried root for all types of protective charms, including dream pillows. Hang in the home or car, burn for ridding of negative influences of any type. Used with other herbs to attract luck. Wear to protect the body, spirit and soul. Wards off evil spirits when placed in the home, and protects against evil and storms when planted in the garden. Hang the seeds or roots around a child's neck to protect against fairies and imps. Peony roots worn with coral and flint guards against incubi. Used in exorcisms and carried to cure lunacy. It should only be gathered at night. Substitutes for mandrake.

**Cultivation**: Peonies are a perennial shrub-like plant, growing 60 cm to 1.2 metres high. They prefer rich, humousy, well-drained soils, and full sun. Seedlings and seed are available through nurseries..

## Pepper (*Piper nigrum*)

**Description:** An evergreen vine, it climbs to a height of 3m. The stem is slender, twining and rounded; the leaves are oval-acuminate, green and smooth; the flowers are green, occurring in spikes; the fruit are fleshy, red berries.

**Influence:** Protection, Exorcism

**Gender**: Masculine, **Element**: Fire, **Planet**: Mars

Another wonderful and cupboard ready herb for banishing negativity. Burn to rid the home or office of bad vibrations or before you move into a new place (make sure you then use Sage.) Carry with you to ward off petty jealousy against you. Aids in summoning up your courage to face things or do things you just don't want to do but have to. Protects against the evil eye and frees the mind of envious thoughts. Mixed with salt and scattered around the property, it dispels evil.

**Cultivation**: Pepper vines will only thrive in tropical or sub-tropical locations. They need soil that is enriched with organic matter and do best in dappled shade eg under trees. They need a stout support. Pepper vines can take 4 years to begin fruiting and they will generally fruit generously for more than a decade.

## Peppermint (*Mentha piperita*)

**Description:** Peppermint is a perennial herb with a woody stem and fragrant leaves.

**Influence:** Purification, Sleep, Love, Healing, Psychic Powers

**Gender**: Masculine, **Element**: Fire, **Planet**: Mercury

Peppermint makes a wonderful tea to increase your psychic ability (drink some before reading the Tarot, consulting runes, scrying, dowsing, etc. ). Drinking Peppermint tea is also useful for healing (especially stomach aches and to help ease tensions), producing visions, and helping with sleep. Smell to help you sleep, and place beneath the pillow for prophetic dreams. The herb can also be sprinkled around your home for purification. Burn the herb in a new home to clear out all negative sickness energies. Carry with other herbs for boosting love and abundance. Place on person or their picture for haste in healing. Also used when changes are needed in ones life, gives the added push needed. Excites love.

**Cultivation**: Peppermint is a perennial grown in full sun, is tolerant of most soil types, and grows to 1 metre tall.

## Pepper Tree (*Schinus molle*)

**Description:** Pepper tree is a large spreading tree growing to a height of 12m. It has drooping fern-like leaves with many leaflets which are aromatic when crushed. Flowers hang in clusters with male and female flowers on separate plants. Flowers on the female trees develop into bright red berries with a hard stone. The seed is very hard and germinates best when passed through the guts of birds. A large number of seeds are stored in the soil. Mature trees are resistant to fire and drought and are able to sprout from the rootstock if damaged.

**Influence:** Healing, Purification, Protection

**Gender**: Masculine, **Element**: Fire, **Planet**: Mars

A sick person can be brushed with pepper tree branches to absorb disease, then the branches are buried to destroy the illness. Rue can be used with this herb. The leaves are added to purification baths, and the berries are carried for protection.

**Cultivation**: Prefers a well-drained soil in full sun. It likes growing in sandy soils and succeeds in a hot dry position. A fast-growing tree in its native habitat, though it is likely to be much slower in areas where it is marginally hardy. The oily leaves smell and taste of pepper when they are crushed. Dioecious, male and female plants must be grown if seed is required. Available from nurseries commercially.

## Periwinkle (*Vinca minor*)  **POISONOUS**

**Description:** Periwinkle is a perennial plant that spreads by putting out runners, mostly used for a ground cover in partial to full shade. It prefers moist, well-drained soils.

**Influence:** Patron herb of Wiccans. Love, Lust, Mental Powers, Money, Protection.

**Gender**: Feminine, **Planet**: Venus, **Element**: Water.

Best when gathered when the moon is one night old, nine nights old, 11 nights old, 13 nights old, or 30 nights old. The dried flowers may be added to any magickal mixture to enhance the working. Banishes negative energy. Makes one feel desirable. Add dried flowers or root to amulets to bring necessary changes to one's life to attract a loving partner. Plant on graves of children. Helps grieving parents heal from their loss. Keeps memory of lost child alive without unhealthy attachments. Carry to obtain grace, attract money, and to protect against snakes, poison, wild beasts, terror, the evil eye, and evil spirits. Place over the door to protect the home. Used in love spells; thought to increase one's passions when carried or sprinkled under the bed. Gaze upon it to restore lost memories.

**Cultivation**: Periwinkle is a perennial plant that spreads by putting out runners, mostly used for a ground cover in partial to full shade. It prefers moist, well-drained soils.

## Persimmon (*Diospyros virginiana*)

**Description:** The persimmon is a multitrunked or single-stemmed deciduous tree to 7.5 metres high and at least as wide. It is a handsome ornamental with drooping leaves and branches that give it a languid, rather tropical appearance. The branches are somewhat brittle and can be damaged in high winds. Persimmon leaves are alternate, simple, ovate and up to 18 cm long and 10 cm wide. They are often pale, slightly yellowish green in youth, turning a dark, glossy green as they age. Under mild autumn conditions the leaves often turn dramatic shades of yellow, orange and red. The inconspicuous flowers surrounded by a green calyx tube are borne in the leaf axils of new growth from one-year old wood. Female flowers are single and cream-colored while the pink-tinged male flowers are typically borne in threes. Commonly, 1 to 5 flowers per twig emerge as the new growth extends (typically March). Persimmon trees are usually either male or female, but some trees have both male and female flowers.

**Influence:** Healing, Lust

**Gender**: Feminine, **Element**: Water, **Planet**: Venus

To stop chills, tie a knot in a piece of string (one for every chill you've had) and tie it to a persimmon tree. To have good luck, bury green persimmons.

**Cultivation**: The flowers are dioecious (individual flowers are either male or female, but only one sex is to be found on any one plant so both male and female plants must be grown if seed is required) The plant is not self-fertile. The plant prefers light (sandy), medium (loamy) and heavy (clay) soils and requires well-drained soil. The plant prefers acid, neutral and basic (alkaline) soils. It can grow in semi-shade (light woodland) or no shade. It requires moist soil. Many cultivars are parthenocarpic (setting seedless fruit without pollination), although some climates require pollination for adequate production. When plants not needing pollination are pollinated, they will produce fruits with seeds and may be larger and have a different flavour and texture than do their seedless counterparts. Fruit: Persimmons can be classified into two general categories: those that bear astringent fruit until they are soft ripe and those that bear non-astringent fruits. An astringent cultivar must be jelly soft before it is fit to eat, and such cultivars are best adapted to cooler regions where persimmons can be grown. A non-astringent persimmon can be eaten when it is crisp as an apple. These cultivars need hot summers, and the fruit might retain some astringency when grown in cooler regions. The shape of the fruit varies by cultivar from spherical to acorn to flattened or squarish. The colour of the fruit varies from light yellow-orange to dark orange-red.. The entire fruit is edible except for the seed and calyx. Alternate bearing is common. This can be partially overcome by thinning the fruit or moderately pruning after a light-crop year.

**Pigeon Berry** see Poke

**Pimento** (*Pimenta dioica*)

**Description:** Medium sized tree producing small purple berries that contain one or two large seeds that are the allspice of commerce. Leaves and bark also contain the allspice scent.

**Influence:** Love

**Gender**: Masculine, **Element**: Fire, **Planet**: Mars

Used in love spells and sachets, especially among Gypsies. Eat it for the same effect.

**Cultivation:** A small to medium sized tree to 40ft, needing near-tropical conditions to survive. Mature trees will stand only short periods of light frost, to 26F. Allspice makes an excellent container plant for indoor or greenhouse culture. Propagation: is often by seeds which loose viability quickly.

**Pimpernel** (*Pimpinella* spp.)

**Description:** Its creeping, square stems, 30 cm in length at most, have their eggshaped, stalkless leaves arranged in pairs. The edges of the leaves are entire and quite free from indentations of any sort, and in whatever direction the stem may run, either along the ground, or at an angle to it, the leaves always keep their faces turned to the light. The flowers appear singly, each on longish, thin stalks, springing from the junction of each leaf with the stem. The little flower-stalks are erect during flowering, but curved backward when the seed is ripening. The corolla is made up of five petals, joined together at their base into a ring. A purple spot often appears in the centre of the flower. The petals are very sensitive, the flowers closing at once if the sky becomes overcast and threatens rain. Even in bright weather, the flowers are only open for a comparatively short time - never opening until between eight and nine in the morning and shutting up before three o'clock in the afternoon. As the petals are only brilliantly coloured on their upper faces, the flowers when closed disappear from view among the greenness of the leaves.

**Influence:** Protection, Prevent Deception

**Gender**: Masculine, **Element**: Air, **Planet**: Mercury

Carried for protection and to prevent deception. Placed in the home to prevent illness and accidents.

**Cultivation**: Propagation is entirely by seeds, as the plant is an annual, completely dying at the end of each season, both above and below ground. ~

**Pine** (*Pinus* spp.)

**Description:** A pine is a coniferous tree in the genus Pinus, in the family Pinaceae. They make up the monotypic subfamily Pinoideae. There are about 115 species of pine.

**Influence:** Healing, Fertility, Protection, Exorcism, Money

**Gender**: Masculine, **Element**: Air, **Planet**: Mars

Pinecones are carried to increase fertility and to have vigorous old age and the nuts eaten for the same reason. . A pinecone gathered on Midsummer that still has its seeds protects against gunshots, so long as the person eats one pine nut from it every day. Pine needles are burned in winter to purify and cleanse the house, and to exorcise the area of negativity. This is good when mixed with equal parts juniper and cedar. Scatter on the floor to drive away evil. Also burn them to reverse and send back spells. It was customary to place a pine branch over the door of the house to ensure continual joy due to the evergreen leaves. Make a cross of pine needles and place it before the fireplace to keep evil from entering. Use in money spells. Sawdust from pine is used an an incense base. Pine branches are often used for sweeping the forest floor before performing Magickoutside. Add the crushed needles to the bath sachet for a good winter cleansing bath.

**Cultivation**: Cultivation and location are species specific however as an overview, Pines are mostly monoecious, having the male and female cones on the same tree, though a few species are sub-dioecious with individuals predominantly, but not wholly, single-sex. The male cones are small, typically 1-5 cm long, and only present for a short period (usually in spring, though autumn in a few pines), falling as soon as they have shed their pollen. The female cones take 1.5-3 years (depending on species) to mature after pollination, with actual fertilization delayed one year. At maturity the cones are 3-60 cm long. Each cone has numerous spirally arranged scales, with two seeds on each fertile scale; the scales at the base and tip of the cone are small and sterile, without seeds. The seeds are mostly small and winged, and are anemophilous (wind-dispersed), but some are larger and have only a vestigial wing, and are bird-dispersed (see below). At maturity, the cones usually open to release the seeds, but in some of the bird-dispersed species (e.g. Whitebark Pine), the seeds are only released by the bird breaking the cones open. In others, the fire climax pines (e.g. Monterey Pine, Pond Pine), the seeds are stored in closed ("serotinous") cones for many years until a forest fire kills the parent tree; the cones are also opened by the heat and the stored seeds are then released in huge numbers to re-populate the burnt ground.

## Pineapple (*Ananas comusus*)

**Description:** It is a medium tall (1–1.5 m) herbaceous perennial plant with 30 or more trough-shaped and pointed leaves 30–100 cm long, surrounding a thick stem. The pineapple is an example of a multiple fruit: multiple, spirally-arranged flowers along the axis each produce a fleshy fruit that becomes pressed against the fruits of adjacent flowers, forming what appears to be a single fleshy fruit. The leaves of the cultivar 'Smooth Cayenne' mostly lack spines except at the leaf tip, but the cultivars 'Spanish' and 'Queen' have large spines along the leaf margins. Pineapples are the only bromeliad fruit in widespread cultivation.

**Influence:** Luck, Money, Chastity

**Gender**: Masculine, **Element**: Fire, **Planet**: Sun

Place dried pineapple in bags and add to baths to draw good luck. Add the juice too. Drink pineapple juice to hinder lust, and add the dried peel or flesh to money mixtures.

**Cultivation**: Once removed during cleaning, the top of the pineapple can be planted in soil and a new fruit bearing plant will grow in a similar manner that a potato or onion will re-sprout from a cutting.

## Pistachio (*Pistachia vera*)

**Description:** The pistachio is a small tree up to 10 m tall. It has deciduous pinnate leaves 10–20 cm long. The plants are dioecious, with separate male and female trees. The flowers are apetalous and unisexual, and borne in panicles. The fruit is a drupe, containing an elongated seed (a nut in the culinary sense, but not a true botanical nut) with a hard, whitish shell and a striking kernel which has a mauveish skin and light green flesh, with a definitive flavour. When the fruit ripens, the husk changes from green to an autumnal yellow/red and the shells split partially open

**Influence:** Breaking Love Spells

**Gender**: Masculine, **Element**: Air, **Planet**: Mercury

Eat as an antidote to love spells. The nuts are given to zombies to bring them out of their trances and bring them the rest of death. Pistachios which have been dyed red are best for this purpose.

**Cultivation**: Pistachio trees are fairly hardy in the right conditions, and can survive temperature ranges between −10°C in winter to 40°C in summer. They need a sunny position and well-drained soil. Pistachio trees do poorly in conditions of high humidity, and are susceptible to root rot in winter if they get too much water and the soil is not sufficiently free draining. Long hot summers are required for proper ripening of the fruit. The trees are planted in orchards, and take approximately seven to ten years to reach significant production. Production is alternate bearing or biennial bearing, meaning the harvest is heavier in alternate years. Peak production is reached at approximately 20 years. Trees are usually pruned to size to make the harvest easier. One male tree produces enough pollen for eight to twelve nut-bearing females.

**Plantain** (*Plantago* spp.)

**Description:** Plantago is a genus of about 200 species of small, inconspicuous plants commonly called plantains. They share this name with the very dissimilar plantain, a kind of banana. Most are herbaceous plants, though a few are sub-shrubs growing to 60 cm tall. The leaves are sessile, but have a narrow part near the stem which is a pseudo-petiole. They have three or five parallel veins that diverge in the wider part of the leaf. Leaves are broad or narrow, depending on the species. The inflorescences are borne on stalks typically 5-40 cm tall, and can be a short cone or a long spike, with numerous tiny wind-pollinated flowers.

**Influence:** Healing

**Gender**: Feminine, **Element**: Earth, **Planet**: Venus

Hang in the car to guard against the intrusion of evil spirits. Put a piece of its root in your pocket to protect from snakebites Use the dried leaves and roots in a healing bath. Place a few pinch's in the flame of the candle or throw to the East wind in all healing wishes.

**Cultivation**: Plantains are common weeds, some varieties being annual and some perennial. They are found in all soil types, and prefer full sun.

**Plum** (*Prunus domestica*)

**Description:** A plum or gage is a stone fruit tree in the genus Prunus, subgenus Prunus. The subgenus is distinguished from other subgenera (peaches, cherries, bird cherries, etc) in the shoots having a terminal bud and the side buds solitary (not clustered), the flowers being grouped 1-5 together on short stems, and the fruit having a groove running down one side, and a smooth stone.

**Influence:** Healing

**Gender**: Feminine, **Element**: Water, **Planet**: Venus

Plum branches are placed over doors and windows to guard against evil intrusions. Eat the fruit to inspire or maintain love.

**Cultivation**: Generally obtained as saplings from commercial nurseries, though can be grown from seed. Plums need a well-drained soil and one containing plenty of humus to hold moisture during the growing season. A very acid soil should be limed, but an alkaline soil should not be planted with plums. Plums (and other stone fruits) do need calcium but they will not prosper in an alkaline soil. Plum trees planted in thin soils overlaying chalk often suffer seriously from lime-induced iron deficiency. When it flowers in the early spring, a plum tree will be covered in blossom, and in a good year approximately 50% of the flowers will be pollinated and become plums. Flowering starts after 80 growing degree days. If the weather is too dry the plums will not develop past a certain stage, but will fall from the tree while still tiny green buds, and if it is unseasonably wet or if the plums are not harvested as soon as they are ripe, the fruit may develop a fungal condition called brown rot.

**Pocan Bush** see Poke

**Poison Parsley see** Hemlock

**Poison Tobacco see** Henbane

**Poke** (*Phytolacca americana*)  **POISONOUS**

**Description:** Also known as American nightshade, cancer jalap, coakum, garget, inkberry, pigeon berry, pocan bush, poke root, pokeweed, redweed, scoke, red ink plant. American Pokeweed is a large, shrubby perennial growing up to 3 metres in height, native to eastern North America. Pparts of this plant are highly toxic to livestock and humans, and is considered a major pest plant by farmers. Nonetheless parts of the plant in different stages, can be used as food, medicine or poison. The plant has a large white taproot, green or red stems, and large, simple leaves. White flowers are followed by purple to almost black berries, which are a good food source for songbirds such as Northern Cardinal, Brown Thrasher, and Northern Mockingbird.

**Influence:** Courage, Hex Breaking

**Gender**: Masculine, **Element**: Fire, **Planet**: Mercury

Used at the new Moon to break hexes and curses; make an infusion and sprinkle around the home. Add some to the bath water (don't drink!). Carry to gain courage. Mix poke with hydrangea, violet, and galangal and sprinkle around the area where an object was lost to find it. The crushed berries are used as magickal ink.

**Cultivation**: This seed germinates slowly over a period of 2 months at room temperature. Sow 2-3 times as much as you need. You can also try soaking the seed in the fridge for 2 weeks. Change cold water for fresh daily - some say distilled works better. It likes rich soil and full sun or partial shade, and is good in open woodland. It thrives on hot summers. This perennial can grow 3 metres high, and the stems turn a striking red as the plant matures

**Poke Root** see Poke

**Pokeweed** see Poke

**Polar Plant,** See Rosemary

**Pomegranate** (*Punica granatum*)

**Description:** The pomegranate is a fantastically versatile tree that produces large fruits used to produce delicious juices and preserves growing to 5–8 m tall. The plant itself is very hardy and highly ornamental, it has large showy flowers and is suitable for use as a feature plant, for hedges and container growing. The leaves are opposite or sub-opposite, glossy, narrow oblong, entire, 3–7 cm long and 2 cm broad. The flowers are bright red, 3 cm in diameter, with four to five petals (often more on cultivated plants). The fruit is between a lemon and a grapefruit in size, 5–12 cm in diameter with a rounded hexagonal shape, and has thick reddish skin and around 600 seeds.[5] The seeds and surrounding pulp, ranging in colour from white to deep red, called arils, are edible; indeed, the fruit of the pomegranate is a berry.

**Influence:** Divination, Luck, Wishes, Wealth, Fertility

**Gender**: Masculine, **Element**: Fire, **Planet**: Mercury

Eat the seeds or carry the skin for fertility. Make a wish before eating a pomegranate and it may come true. A pomegranate branch finds hidden wealth or will attract money. The dried skin is added to money and wealth incenses. To determine the number of children she will have, a woman can throw a pomegranate hard on the ground. The number of seeds that fall out equal the number of children. Hang pomegranate branches over doorways to guard against evil. Use the juice as a blood substitute or magickal ink.

**Cultivation**: Pomegranate is not fussy about soil condition, preferring a moderately fertile, well-drained soil enriched with organic material and is best suited to mild temperate and subtropical climates as it favours cool winters and hot summers although it will settle for less and still fruit. Pomegranates like a position in full sun. It is extremely drought hardy and will tolerate some frost as it is deciduous. In dry periods young tree may need deep watering every 3-4 weeks..

**Poor Man's Treacle,** See Garlic

**Poplar** (*Populus tremuloides*)

**Description:** Populus is a genus of between 25–35 species of flowering plants in the family Salicaceae, native to most of the Northern Hemisphere. English names variously applied to different species include poplar, aspen, and cottonwood. They are medium-sized to large or very large deciduous trees growing to 15–50 m tall, with trunks up to 2.5 m diameter. Many poplars are grown as ornamental trees, with numerous cultivars selected. Trees with fastigiate (erect, columnar) branching are particularly popular, and very widely grown across Europe and southwest Asia in particular. However, like willows, poplars have very vigorous and invasive root systems stretching up to 40 m from the trees; planting close to houses or ceramic water pipes may result in cracked walls and pipes due to their search for moisture. **Influence:** Money, Flying

**Gender**: Feminine, **Element**: Water, **Planet**: Saturn

Popular buds and leaves are carried to attract money or are added to money incenses. Was an ingredient in flying ointments which are used to facilitate astral projection. Place on the body for this purpose also.

**Cultivation**: In the coldest part of winter, take cuttings at least the thickness of a thumb. Cut to about 15 cm lengths. Place upside down in a bucket filled with sand. Fill with water to the top of the sand. Keep in cool place, but frost-free. In spring, you will find little knobs on the sticks where roots will set. That's the right time to set each one right side up in a pot of soil. Do not plant willow or poplar within 40 metres of a building. The roots go wandering, looking for water. They end up plugging sewer lines. You have to have really wet springs to satisfy their thirst.

**Poppy** (*Papaver* spp.)

**Description:** A poppy is any of a number of showy flowers, typically with one per stem, belonging to the poppy family. They include a number of attractive wildflower species with showy flowers found growing singularly or in large groups; many species are also grown in gardens. Those that are grown in gardens include large plants used in a mixed herbaceous boarder and small plants that are grown in rock or alpine gardens. The flower colour of poppy species include: white, pink, yellow, orange, red and blue; some have dark center markings. The species that have been cultivated for many years also include many other colours ranging from dark solid colours to soft pastel shades. The center of the flower has a whorl of stamens surrounded by a cup- or bowl-shaped collection of four to six petals. Prior to blooming, the petals are crumpled in bud, and as blooming finishes, the petals often lie flat before falling away.

The poppy of wartime remembrance is the red corn poppy, Papaver rhoeas. This poppy is a common weed in Europe and is found in many locations, including Flanders Fields. This is because the corn poppy was one of the only plants that grew on the battlefield. It thrives in disturbed soil, which was abundant on the battlefield due to intensive shelling. During the few weeks the plant blossomed, the battlefield was coloured blood red.

**Influence:** Fertility, Love, Sleep, Money, Luck, Invisibility

**Gender**: Feminine, **Element**: Water, **Planet**: Moon

Eat or carry to promote fertility and to draw luck and money. Get a dried seed pod, cut a small hole in it to remove the seeds, and write a question on a small piece of yellow paper. Stuff the paper inside the pod and lay it beside your bed. Prophetic dreams may answer the question by morning. Carry the dried seed pod as a prosperity amulet, or use the seeds in prosperity amulets. Soak poppy seeds in wine for fifteen days, then drink the wine each day for five days while fasting to make yourself invisible at will. The seed heads were once gilded and worn as wealth talismans.

**Cultivation**: Poppies are perennials that like poor to average soils that tend toward dryness. There are varieties that will grow most anywhere. Their foliage tends to die off by Autumn, after a spectacular showing of flowers in the spring, but the foliage begins rejuvenation in late winter, and waits until spring to begin growing again.

**Potato** (*Solanum tuberosum*)

**Description:** Potato is the term which applies either to the starchy tuberous crop from the perennial plant Solanum tuberosum of the Solanaceae, or nightshade, family, or to the plant itself. Potato is the world's most widely grown tuber crop, and the fourth largest food crop in terms of fresh produce.

**Influence:** Image Magick, Healing

**Gender**: Feminine, **Element**: Earth, **Planet**: Saturn

Often used as poppets. Carry in the pocket to cure toothaches and guard against rheumatism, warts, and gout.

**Cultivation**: Any potato variety can also be propagated vegetatively by planting tubers, pieces of tubers, cut to include at least one or two eyes. Potatoes like a fertile, deeply dug, moist, acidic soil with a pH of less than 6. They do not grow well in heavy clay or a limed soil, which promotes potato scab. To avoid this, always rotate your potato patch each year. Many potatoes have lost favour commercially because of either deep eyes or an irregular shape but these varieties may have many advantages to the home grower in hardiness, disease resistance and prolific production. For early potatoes, plant shortly before the last expected frost, planting can continue into summer. Plant the seed potatoes

13 cm deep and then cover with a mulch 25-30 cm deep. Choose seed potatoes with at least 2 eyes per piece, if cutting into smaller pieces leave plenty of flesh with each eye and allow the cuts to dry for 24 hours before planting. Space the tubers 30-35 cm apart. Potatoes are ready for harvesting when the majority of the tops have withered. Early potatoes may be dug for table use at any time but for storage the potatoes should be fully mature. After they are dug, dry as quickly as possible, and then store immediately in a cool, dark, dry place. Exposure to light will turn the potatoes green; green potatoes are poisonous and should not be eaten.

**Potentilla see** Cinquefoil

**Prickly Ash** (*Zanthoxylum americanum*)

**Description:** Prickly ash is an aromatic, spiny, thicket-forming deciduous shrub or small tree that, as the common name suggests, resembles (particularly in leaf) an ash with prickles. It is not an ash, however, but a member of the citrus family and is closely related to the also spiny hardy orange, Poncirus trifoliata. Prickly ash typically occurs on bluffs, upland rocky hillsides, open woods, moist ravines and thickets in most of the State except for the Ozark region. It is most often seen in the wild as an 3 -4 metre tall multi-stemmed shrub. However, it will grow larger and is occasionally seen as a small tree up to 8 metres tall.

**Influence:** Love

**Gender**: Masculine, **Element**: Fire, **Planet**: Mars

Use the fruit as a perfume to attract love.

**Cultivation**: Preferring moist, shady sites, such as woodlands. Prickly ash is propagated from seed in autumn. The bark is harvested in spring, and the berries are collected in summer.

**Primrose** (*Primula vulgaris*)

**Description:** It is a herbaceous perennial plant, low growing, to 10-30 cm tall, with a basal rosette of leaves. The leaves are 5-25 cm long and 2-6 cm broad with an irregularly crenate to dentate margin, and a usually short leaf stem. The flowers are 2-4 cm diameter, borne singly on a slender stem, pale yellow, white, red, or purple with a superior ovary which later forms a capsule which opens by valves to release the small black seeds. The flowers are hermaphrodite however individual plants bear either pin flowers (with the capita of the style prominent) or thrum flowers (with the stamens prominent). Fertilisation can only take place between pin and thrum flowers. Pin to pin and thrum to thrum pollination is ineffective. It flowers in early spring, one of the earliest spring flowers in much of Europe, and in appropriate conditions, can cover the ground in open woods.

**Influence:** Protection, Love

**Gender**: Feminine, **Element**: Earth, **Planet**: Venus

Plant Primrose in garden for protection, especially red and blue it and to attract fairies. It is especially powerful planted in pots sitting on the front and back porches. Women carry them to attract love. Worn to cure madness and sewn into children's pillows to gain their undying respect and loyalty.

**Cultivation**: The seeds of Primroses are very tiny. They should be sown in a tray in early spring on a seedbed of moist peat moss which is layered over sterile potting soil. The tray must then be chilled in the refrigerator for 3-4 weeks, after which it must be kept at 20C for germination, which takes from 3-6 weeks. The seeds need light to germinate, so do not cover them with soil, but a sheet of clear plastic or glass placed over the tray will help to retain the moisture until the seeds sprout at which time the cover sheet should be removed. Transplant the seedlings to individual pots when they are 5 cm tall. They will be ready to bloom the following spring.

## Purslane (*Portulaca sativa*)

**Description:** Purslane is a pleasant salad herb, and excellent for scorbutic troubles. The succulent leaves and young shoots are cooling in spring salads, the older shoots are used as a pot-herb and the thick stems of plants that have run to seed are pickled in salt and vinegar to form winter salads. Purslane is largely cultivated in Holland and other countries for these purposes. It is used in equal proportion with Sorrel to make the well-known French soup *bonne femme*.

**Influence:** Sleep, Love, Luck, Protection, Happiness

**Gender**: Feminine, **Element**: Water, **Planet**: Moon

Lay on the bed to prevent nightmares. Carry purslane to draw love and luck, and to keep away evil. Soldiers carried this plant to protect themselves in battle. Sprinkle around the home to spread happiness.

**Cultivation**: Sow the seeds in drills, on a bed of rich light earth, during any of the summer months. The Green Purslane is quite hardy, the Golden Purslane less so. Keep the plants clear from weeds, and in dry weather water them two or three times a week. The Purslanes need rather more watering than most herbs. In warm weather, they will be fit for use in six weeks. When the leaves are gathered, the plants must be cut low and then a fresh crop will appear.

## Quack Grass seeWitches Grass

## Quassia (*Picraena excelsa*)

**Description:** Two varieties of quassia are used commercially; a West Indian large tree, to over 30 metres, with thick upright trunk, and pinnate, oblong leaves, yellow/green, small flower spikes and pea size, shiny, black seed capsules. The second variety is a smaller tree grown in Surinam, Brazil, Columbia and the West Indies. It is said the 2 trees have identical properties. The wood of the tree is odorless but has a very bitter taste, and its resin, called quassin, is a natural insecticide, making the tree virtually impervious to insects.

**Influence:** Love

**Gender**: Feminine, **Element**: Earth, **Planet**: Saturn

Used in love mixtures to draw and maintain love. The powdered wood is used in incense bases.

**Cultivation**: Native to tropical America and the Caribbean, quassia grows in forests and near water. Quassia is cultivated mainly for medicinal use. The bark is harvested throughout the year. Raspings of the wood are collected after felling the tree. No details on domestic cultivation could be found.

**Queen's Delight,** See Stillengia

**Queen's Root,** See Stillengia

**Queen Elizabeth Root see** Orris

**Queen of the Meadow,** See Meadowsweet

**Quince** (*Cydonia oblonga.*)

> **Description:** The Quince (Cydonia oblonga) is the sole member of the genus Cydonia and native to warm-temperate southwest Asia in the Caucasus region. It is a small deciduous tree, growing 5-8 m tall and 4-6 m wide, related to apples and pears, and like them has a pome fruit, which is bright golden yellow when mature, pear-shaped, 7-12 cm long and 6-9 cm broad. The immature fruit is green, with dense grey-white pubescence which mostly (but not all) rubs off before maturity in late autumn when the fruit changes colour to yellow with hard flesh that is strongly perfumed. The leaves are alternately arranged, simple, 6-11 cm long, with an entire margin and densely pubescent with fine white hairs. The flowers, produced in spring after the leaves, are white or pink, 5 cm across, with five petals.
>
> **Influence:** Protection, Love, Happiness
>
> **Gender**: Feminine, **Element**: Earth, **Planet**: Saturn
>
> Quince seed is carried to protect against evil, physical harm, and accidents. In Roman times, was shared by a bridal couple to ensure happiness. Pregnant women eat quince cause their child to be ingenious. Serve quinces to loved ones to ensure fidelity.
>
> **Cultivation**: The Cydonia or Quince trees are self fertile however the Clhaenomeles or flowering quince bushes need two varieties to pollenate. Preferring a sunny position the plants should be spaced at 4 - 5 metres for Quince trees. And 3 – 4 metres for flowering quince bushes. The bushes have a very spreading habit. It should be noted that Cydonia is best grafted on Quince rootstocks and so commercial varieties are easiest. Quince can be grown in a wide variety of soils and tolerate wetter soils. Quince bear on new wood, often off small branches that come off of long new shoots, so prune to encourage vigorous new growth.

**Racoon Berry see** May Apple

**Radish** (*Raphanus sativus*)

> **Description:** The radish (Raphanus sativus) is an edible root vegetable of the Brassicaceae family that was domesticated in Europe in pre-Roman times. They are grown and consumed throughout the world, and in addition to their use as a food, radishes have uses as an alternative treatment for a variety of medical conditions, and the seeds can be used as a biofuel. Radishes have numerous varieties, varying in size, color and duration of required cultivation time.
>
> **Influence:** Protection, Lust
>
> **Gender**: Masculine, **Element**: Fire, **Planet**: Mars
>
> Carry to protect yourself from the evil eye. Increases lust when eaten. A type of German wild radish was carried to determine where sorcerers were.
>
> **Cultivation**: Summer radishes mature rapidly, with many varieties germinating in 3-7

days, and reaching maturity in three to four weeks. A common garden crop, the fast harvest cycle makes them a popular choice for children's gardens. Harvesting periods can be extended through repeated plantings, spaced a week or two apart. Radishes grow best in full sun and fertile, acidic to neutral soil. They are in season from April spring to autumn. As with other root crops, tilling the soil helps the roots grow. Most soil types will work, though sandy loams are particularly good for winter and spring crops, while soils that form a hard crust can impair growth. The depth at which seeds are planted affects the size of the root, from 1 cm deep recommended for small radishes to 4 cm for large radishes.

## Ragweed (*Ambrosia* spp.)

**Description:** Ragweed is best known for the fact that its pollen produces severe and widespread allergies and their tenaciousness, which makes it hard to rid an area of them if they occur as invasive weeds. Ragweeds occur in temperate regions of the northern hemisphere and South America. Ragweeds prefer dry, sunny grassy plains, sandy soils, and to grow along river banks, along roadsides, disturbed soils, vacant lots and ruderal sites. Ragweed was far less common in the Eastern United States before major land clearance by European settlers began in the late 18th century.

**Influence:** Courage

Chew on the root at night to drive away fear.

**Gender**_____, **Element**_____, **Planet:** _____

**Cultivation**: Cultivation is not advised due to high allergic effects.

## Ragwort (*Senecio* spp.) **POISONOUS (to stock)**

**Description:** The plant is biennial or perennial. The stems are erect, straight, have no or few hairs, and reach a height of 0.3-2.0 metres. The leaves are pinnately lobed and the end lobe is blunt. The many names that include the word "stinking" (and Mare's Fart) arise because of the unpleasant smell of the leaves. The hermaphrodite flower heads are 1.5-2.5 cm diameter, and are borne in dense, flat-topped clusters; the florets are bright yellow.

**Influence:** Protection

**Gender**: Feminine, **Element**: Water, **Planet**: Venus

Was once used an amulet against spells.

**Cultivation**: A prolific seed producer this plant self sows. Due to its weed status cultivation is not recommended.

## Raspberry (*Rubus idaeus*)

**Description:** The raspberry (plural, raspberries) is the edible fruit of a number of species of the genus Rubus. The name originally refers in particular to the European species Rubus idaeus, and is still used for that species as its standard English name in its native area. Raspberries are an important commercial fruit crop, widely grown in all temperate regions of the world.

**Influence:** Protection, Love

**Gender**: Feminine, **Element**: Water, **Planet**: Venus

Raspberry is served as a love-inducing food and the leaves are carried by pregnant women to ease the pains of pregnancy and childbirth.. The brambles are hung at the entrance to the home to prevent unwanted spirits from entering.

**Cultivation**: Red Raspberry is a biennial or perennial, depending on the variety, growing 1 to 2 metres tall. They need a cold winter and a long cool spring, They aren't too picky about soil, so long as they get plenty of water. Propagation is by planting dormant cane cuttings.

**Rattlesnake Root** (*Polygala senega*)

**Description:** Rattlesnakeroot is a perennial herb with many unbranched stems growing to about 30 cm, from one base. The leaves are small, lance-shaped, and the flowers are greenish-white, in terminal spike-like inflorescences. The roots are yellowish or greyish-brown and have a twisted snake-like appearance. The crown bears traces of old stems, and the root smells and tastes somewhat like wintergreen. The root is the part of the plant that is commercially important.

**Influence:** Protection, Money

Make an infusion of rattlesnake root and add to the bath or use in the rinse water for clothing to offer protection from people trying to harm you. The infusion, rubbed on the hands or feet, can lead you to money. The root was carried to guard from rattlesnake bites.

**Gender**_____, **Element**_____, **Planet:** _____

**Cultivation**: Rattlesnakeroot takes 4 years to produce a marketable root. The seed requires cold stratification for 60 days before planting, and shows a 60 - 80 percent germination rate. Young shoot cuttings can also be propagated. Harvesting is usually done in the late summer or early fall. The roots are dug, washed and dried in the sun or with low heat. The roots lose two-thirds of their weight with drying, and it may take 160 roots to yield one kg of dried material.

**Redcap see** Agaric

**Redweed** see Poke

**Red Eye Bright,** See Eyebright

**Red Pucoon,** See Bloodroot

**Red Ink Plant** see Poke

**Red Root,** See Tormentil

**Septfoil,** See Tormentil

**Shepherd's Knapperty,** See Tormentil

**Shepherd's Knot,** See Tormentil

**Thormantle,** See Tormentil

**Rhubarb** (*Rheum* spp.)

**Description:** Rhubarb are herbaceous perennials with hermaphrodite flowers, consisting of a colored perianth, composed of six to nine segments, arranged in two rows. The flowers have nine stamina inserted on the torus at the base of the peranthium, they are free or subconnatent at their base. The ovary is simple and triangular shaped with three styles. The fruits are a three-sided caryupsis with winged sides, the seeds are albuminous and have straight embryos.

**Influence:** Protection, Fidelity

**Gender**: Feminine, **Element**: Earth, **Planet**: Venus

Wear a piece of rhubarb root around the neck on a string to protect against stomach pain. Rhubarb pie served to a mate ensures his or her fidelity.

**Cultivation:** Plant rhubarb roots in early spring. Planting seeds is not recommended as it may take too long for the plants to become established, and the seedlings would not come true to colour and size. Space rhubarb roots 60cm to 1.2 metres apart in rows 1 metre wide. Much smaller than this will seriously crowd the plants and result in a diminished crop and increase the likelihood of spreading disease. A 2-3 year old plant, the Victoria variety can be 1.25 meters in diameter and 1 meter tall. Plant the roots with the crown bud 5 cm below the surface of the soil. The hole for the crown should be dug extra large and composted manure, peat moss or dairy organic should be mixed with the soil to be placed around the roots. Firm the soil around the roots but keep it loose over the buds. Water the crowns after planting. Good garden drainage is essential in growing rhubarb. For home gardeners, planting in raised beds helps ensure against rotting of the crowns. Crowns will have a longevity of many years, but because of diseases and insects, it is Normal to reset a bed after 4-5 years.

**Ribwort,** See Plantain

**Rice** (*Oryza sativa*)

**Description:** Rice is a monocarpic annual plant, growing to 1–1.8 m tall, occasionally more depending on the variety and soil fertility. The grass has long, slender leaves 50–100 cm long and 2–2.5 cm broad. The small wind-pollinated flowers are produced in a branched arching to pendulous inflorescence 30–50 cm long. The seed is a grain (caryopsis) 5–12 mm long and 2–3 mm thick.

**Influence:** Protection, Fidelity

**Gender**: Masculine, **Element**: Air, **Planet**: Sun

Place on the roof to guard against misfortune. A small jar of rice near the entrance of the house protects it. Throwing rice into the air can cause rain. Rice is added to money spells, and is thrown after wedded couples to increase their fertility.

**Cultivation**: Methods of growing differ greatly in different localities, but in most Asian countries the traditional hand methods of cultivating and harvesting rice are still practiced. The fields are prepared by plowing (typically with simple plows drawn by water buffalo), fertilizing (usually with dung or sewage), and smoothing (by dragging a log over them). The seedlings are started in seedling beds and, after 30 to 50 days, are transplanted by hand to the fields, which have been flooded by rain or river water. During the growing season, irrigation is maintained by dike-controlled canals or by hand watering. The fields are allowed to drain before cutting.

**Roots**

**Description:** A generic name for any herb that has a prominent root.

**Influence:** Protection, Power, Divination

Wear a root around your neck while sleeping outside to guard against wild animals. An old superstition says that roots dug from a churchyard or any other old sacred site will avert death as long as the person wears or carries them. A person planning to study magick should go into a field at night and pull up a weed, roots and all. The amount of dirt of the roots indicates how much power and skill the student will achieve.

**Gender**_____, **Element**_____, **Planet:** _____

**Cultivation** See specific plant

**Rose** (*Rosa* spp.)

**Description:** A rose is a flowering shrub of the genus Rosa, and the flower of this shrub. There are more than a hundred species of wild roses, all from the northern hemisphere and mostly from temperate regions. The species form a group of generally prickly shrubs or climbers, and sometimes trailing plants, reaching 2–5 metres tall, occasionally reaching as high as 20 metres by climbing over other plants.

**Influence:** Love, Psychic Powers, Healing, Divination, Luck, Protection

**Gender**; Feminine, **Element**: Water, **Planet**: Venus

The ultimate in love wishes, this will aid in bringing a true lasting love and help also to mend any spats between you in an already committed relationship. The petals can be bathed with while thinking a new love to you, the dried flowers are burned in love wishes. Sleeping with the flowers will protect your dreams. Drinking a tea of rosebuds before bed induces prophetic dreams. Carry a sachet or amulet for protection against bodily injury or when working healing wishes. Rose buds/petals can also be used for psychic powers (especially when used for a tea), healing, protection, and luck. Roses in the garden attract fairies and are said to grow best when stolen.

**Cultivation**: Roses of all varieties are adaptable to most soils as long as they have adequate water, and are occasionally fed through the growing season.

**Rosemary** (*Rosmarinus officinalis*)

**Description:** This decorative evergreen shrub grows to around 3 meteres, though it can grow as a low laying ground cover. In Summer it has blue and violet flowers which attract bees. It is not a hardy plant and dislikes cold climates or excess wet. It can be grown as a container plant in these environments.

**Influence:** Protection, Love, Lust, Mental Powers, Exorcism, Purification, Healing, Sleep, Youth

**Gender**: Masculine, **Element**: Fire, **Planet**: Mars

Rosemary can be used as a substitute for just about any herb. Its powers include love, lust, protection, exorcism, purification, healing, longevity, youth, mental powers, and sleep. This is a good all around herb to have and even better that you can find it in your cupboard. Used primarily for contentment and happiness to the home and to the person, a branch is hung, food is cooked with it or it can be worn to be a tension relieving and contented feeling. This also added to other appropriate herbs is a great boost for money, when you don't need your own money making press, just enough to say, cover those concert tickets you want. Carried in a sachet, talisman or amulet, this is a great guard against negative energies. Tea is drunk to improve mental clarity and aid in the memory. Good for students! Rosemary is a wonderful incense, .smoulder a bit of it to emit powerful cleansing and purifying vibrations and to rid negativity in the area in which it is burned (especially helpful to burn before performing any magick!) Place a bit of rosemary under your pillow to ensure a good night's sleep. Add an infusion of rosemary to your bathwater to perserve youthfulness and to purify you. Carry a bit of rosemary with you to remain healthy. Burn this herb for cleansing and purification. Hung on the porch to deter theives and carried to stay healthy. Used in love and lust mixtures, and healing poppets. Attracts elves.

**Cultivation**: Rosemary requires a sunny, well-drained spot and thrives in sandy, poor soil. Once established, the shrub is very durable and long-lived. It is often used to create a dense aromatic hedge. Cuttings strike easily.

**Rowan** (*Sorbus acuparia*)

**Description:** A native species seen at its best amongst the acid rocky uplands of the north and in Wales. Its display of golden leaves and bunches of radiant scarlet berries on a fine October day is a memorable sight. In woodlands it grows well in association with sessile oak.

**Influence:** Psychic Powers, Healing, Protection, Success

**Gender**: Masculine, **Element**: Fire, **Planet**: Sun

Tie two twigs together with red thread for a good all-purpose charm. Use the rowan branches in divining water. An excellent protection against lightning. Sometimes used to make Magickwands. Carry the wood with you as a good luckand to increase psychic powers. A necklace of the berries is very healing. Add the leaves and berries to divination and psychic incenses. The berries and bark are used in healing and health mixtures and sachets, as well as power, success, and luck sachets. Make a walking stick from rowan wood, especially if you walk in woods and fields at night. Carry on a ship to avert storms, and keep in the house to prevent lightning strikes. Plant on a grave to prevent the person from haunting the place. Also plant near the house to protect it and its inhabitants; those growing near stone circles are the most potent.

**Cultivation**: Available as a small tree from nurseries. Prefers cool to cold climates best. Likes well-drained, loamy acidic soils. Avoid high pH soils.

**Rue** (*Ruta graveolens*)

**Description:** Rue is a bushy perennial growing to 1 metre tall

**Influence:** Healing, Health, Mental Powers, Exorcism, Love, Repentance, Seeing mistakes. Banishment.

**Gender**: Masculine, **Element**: Fire, **Planet**: Saturn

Hang this dried herb indoors from the ceiling to the floor to help others and yourself see and understand their mistakes, preferably in an inconspicuous place. Burn for banishing any type of negativity or bad habits you may want to get rid of. Place rue leaves on the forehead to cure headaches, or wear around the neck to heal faster from illness; this also helps to prevent future sickness. Often used in healing incenses and poppets. Sniff fresh rue to clear your head in love matters. Carry to protect yourself from poison and werewolves.

**Cultivation**: Choose a sunny, well-drained position. Rue can be grown from seed sown in spring. Sow into punnets and transplant later. Cuttings can also be taken in spring, or established plants can be divided. Damp soils can cause root rot. Do not fertilise. The plant prefers slightly alkaline soil so add lime if your soil is acid. Prune back hard after flowering or it will become straggly.

**Rye** (*Secale* spp.)

**Description:** Rye (Secale cereale) is a grass grown extensively as a grain and forage crop. It is a member of the wheat tribe (Triticeae) and is closely related to barley and wheat.

**Influence:** Love, Fertility

**Gender**: Feminine, **Element**: Earth, **Planet**; Venus

Roman gypsies used rye in love spells. Serve rye bread to loved ones to ensure their love.

**Cultivation**: Planted from seed, cereal rye thrives on well-drained loamy soils but it's tolerant of both heavy clays and droughty, sandy soils. Rye can withstand drought better than other cereal grains, in part because of its prolific root system. It grows best with ample moisture, but excessive rainfall can suppresses subsequent vegetative growth and flooding can it. Rye can grow in low-fertility soils where other cereal grains may fail.

**Sacred Bark,** See Cascara Sagranda

**Saffron** (*Crocus sativa*)

**Description:** Saffron is a delicious and colorful seasoning that is used in breads, desserts, and main dishes in many parts of the world, from England to India, from the Middle East to Scandinavia, and all around the Mediterranean. Without it, an Indian curry or a Spanish paella just wouldn't be the same. The bright red-orange threads you get when you buy saffron are actually the stigmas, or female portion, of the Saffron Crocus flowers. For the home gardener, however, two dozen Saffron Crocus will supply enough of the precious spice in the first year for a few memorable dishes. Then, with each successive year, the corms (which look like bulbs) will multiply, the size of the planting will increase, and you'll be able to harvest more of the spicy stigmas. After 4 to 6 years, you should divide and replant the corms (do it right after the foliage has faded). Division prevents overcrowding, which can lead to a decrease in flowering.

**Influence:** Love, Healing, Happiness, Wind Raising, Lust, Strength, Psychic Powers

**Gender:** Masculine, **Element**: Fire, **Planet**: Sun

Another cupboard-ready herb, this herb whether burned, worn, carried or drank, helps to develop and strengthen your psychic awareness. Use liberally when working with the chakras. Use as a substitute for Orange. Also used with other herbs for healing. Added to love and lust sachets. Used in healing spells. Drink an infusion of this to forsee the future, and eases depression. Saffron in the home keeps lizards out.

**Cultivation**: Saffron grows from a bulb commonly known as a corm and you should plant the corms as soon as you receive them. Saffron Crocus do best in full sun and well-drained soil that is moderately rich in organic matter. Ideally, the site should be relatively dry in summer, when the corms are dormant. Plant the corms 10cm deep and 10 cm apart. Flowers will appear the first fall after planting and last for about 3 weeks. The grass-like leaves may emerge soon after the flowers or wait until the following spring. In either case, the leaves persist for 8-12 weeks, then wither and vanish, leaving no trace of the corms below until the flowers appear again in Autumn. It's not a bad idea to mark the area where you've planted your corms, so you don't inadvertently dig them up while planting something else.

**Sage** (*Salvia officinalis*)

**Description:** Sage is a spreading evergreen shrub, growing to around 60cm high. It has wrinkled grey-green leaves and tubular purple flours that sprout in summer.

**Influence:** Immortality, Longevity, Wisdom, Protection, Wishes, Healing, Purifying

**Gender**: Masculine, **Element**: Earth, **Planet**: Jupiter

Used in sachets and amulets for all healing wishes and also burned or placed near a personal object of the person for whom the healing wish is made. Burned and the smoke is walked to the four corners of the room to repel and rid negative energies and influences. Especially good when moving into a new home. Can be drunk as a tea to help promote a hasty healing. Also used when meditating. Add powdered Sage to homemade yellow candles. Burn on a Wednesday during the Waxing Moon to increase knowledge and wisdom Aids in longevity when eaten every day. Carried to promote wisdom, and the leaves are used in money and healing spells. It is bad luck to plant sage in your own garden. It is also bad luck to have a full bed of sage.

**Cultivation**: Sage requires a very well-drained position in full sun. It does best in light sandy soils. Sage is propagated in spring. Seeds can be sown, cuttings taken and established clumps may be layered or divided during spring. Avoid over-watering and over-fertilising. Planting into a raised bed is a good idea.

**Sagebrush** (*Artemisia* spp.)

**Description:** It is a coarse, hardy silvery-grey bush with yellow flowers and grows in arid sections of the western United States. It is the primary vegetation across vast areas of the Great Basin desert. Along rivers or in other relatively wet areas, sagebrush can grow as tall as 3 m, but is more typically 1-2 m tall. Sagebrush has a strong pungent fragrance, especially when wet, which is not unlike common sage. It is, however, unrelated to common sage and has a bitter taste. It is thought that this odour serves to discourage browsing. Sagebrush leaves are wedge-shaped 1-4 cm long and 0.3-1 cm broad, and are attached to the branch by the narrow end. The outer and wider end is generally divided into three lobes (although leaves with two or four lobes are not uncommon), hence the scientific name tridentata. The leaves are covered with fine silvery hairs, which are thought to keep the leaf cool and minimize water loss. Most of the leaves are carried year-round, as sagebrush tends to grow in areas where winter precipitation is greater than summer precipitation.

**Influence:** Purification, Exorcism

**Gender**: Feminine, **Element**: Earth, **Planet**: Venus

Bathe with this herb to purify yourself of all past evils and negative deeds. Burn to drive away evil forces. Useful in healing.

**Cultivation**: Easily grown in a well-drained circumneutral or slightly alkaline loamy soil, preferring a sunny position. Succeeds in most soils including those of low fertility. Plants are longer lived, more hardy and more aromatic when they are grown in a poor dry soil. Established plants are very drought tolerant

**St. John's Plant,** See Mugwort

**St. John's Wort** (*Hypericum perforatum*) **POISONOUS**

**Description:** St. John's Wort is an easy to grow herb, with over three hundred of varieties. It is used primarily for medicinal purposes. St. John's is a perennial herb that grows into a small shrub if allowed. With attractive leaves, it has clusters of bright yellow flowers that bloom through Summer.

**Influence:** Health, Power, Protection, Strength, Love, Divination, Happiness

**Gender:** Masculine, **Element**: Fire, **Planet**: Sun

Use the leaves in a necklace to ward off sickness and tensions. Carry to strengthen your courage and conviction, or when about to confront a nasty situation. Burn to repel and banish negative thoughts and energies from yourself or others. Hung in the home or carried, it will prevent spells of others from entering, and it is used in exorcisms. If you pick the plant on the night of St. John and hang it on your bedroom wall, you will dream of your future husband. Gathered on Midsummer or on a Friday and worn, it will keep away mental illness and cure melancholy. Place in a jar and hang by a window to protect against lightning bolts, fire, and evil spirits; use both the leaves and flowers. It's dried over Midsummer fires and hung near the window to keep ghosts, necromancers, and other evil doers from the house. Burn to banish spirits and demons. Use in rituals or carry to detect other magicians.

**Cultivation**: Almost any area of your garden or flower bed will be acceptable to St. John's Wort. They grow well in full to partial sun, tolerating shade. They prefer moist, and light soils. Sandy and coarse soils are fine. Being a perennial, St. John's Wort is hardy. But to assure a good start, it should be started outdoors after the last frost in your area.When seedlings are about 5 cm tall, thin or transplant them. Different varieties will require varying amounts of space. Once started, these plants will grow well with little or no attention. Fertilizer always helps, but is only necessary in the poorest of soils. Just make sure to provide water during extended period of dry weather.

**Sailor's Tobacco see** Mugwort

**Sambuccus,** See Elder

**Sandalwood** (*Santalum album*)

**Description:** Santalum album, a terrestrial plant species of the Santalaceae family, is commonly known as a source of sandalwood. It is a hemi-parasitic tree, occurring in semi-arid areas from India to the South Pacific and the northern coast of Australia. It is known as the source of a timber and essential oil, which command high prices for fine woodworking and as a fragrance respectively. For this reason, along with Santalum spicatum, it is has a high commmercial value. To preserve this vulnerable resource from over-exploitation, legislation protects the species, and cultivation is researched and developed.

**Influence:** Protection, Healing, Exorcism, Spirituality

**Gender**: Feminine, **Element**: Air, **Planet**: Moon

Burn to enhance your meditations and healing wishes. Use the wood also for a healing wand or tie a piece on a healing wand. Burn to cleanse and purify yourself or the home by passing the smoke over your body or through the house. Used with other herbs in developing your spirituality. Scatter sandalwood powder around your home to clear it of negativity. Use in healing and exorcism spells. Write a wish on a sandalwood chip and burn in your cauldron. As it burns it sets your magick flowing. Sandalwood mixed with Lavendar makes a wonderful incense which is intended to conjure spirits.

**Cultivation**: As a parasitic plant cultivation is not undertaken and it harvested from the wild. To preserve this vulnerable resource from over-exploitation, legislation protects the species, and cultivation is researched and developed.

**Sarsaparilla** (*Smilax aspera*)

**Description:** The Common Smilax is a variable, creeping or scrambling, extremely tough shrub. Its leaves are glossy, heart-shaped, very leathery and are accompanied by a pair of tendrils at the base of the petiole. Flowers are greenish-white to greenish-yellow, approximately 3 - 5 mm (1/10 - 1/5 in), borne in branched clusters, with male and female are on separate plants. Berries, which are between 2 - 4 mm (1/12 - 1/6 in), take on a red or black colour when ripe. It can be found growing in garrigue, shrub and bushy places, frequently forming hedgerows. The young asparagus-like shoots are edible when cooked

**Influence:** Love, Money

**Gender**: Masculine, **Element**: Fire, **Planet**: Jupiter

Mixed with cinnamon and sandalwood powder and sprinkled around the home to draw money. Also used in love spells.

**Cultivation**: Smilax is a very damage-tolerant plant capable of growing back from its rhizomes after being cut down or burned down by fire. This, coupled with the fact that birds and other small animals spread the seeds over large areas, makes the plants very hard to get rid of. It grows best in moist woodlands with a soil pH between 5 and 6. The seeds have the highest percent chance of germinating after being exposed to a freeze.

**Sassafras** (*Sassafras albidum*)

**Description:** It is a medium-sized deciduous tree growing to 15–35 m tall, with a trunk up to 60 cm diameter, and a crown with many slender branches. The bark on trunk of mature trees is thick, dark red-brown, and deeply furrowed. The branching is sympodial. The shoots are bright yellow green at first with mucilaginous bark, turning reddish brown, and in two or three years begin to show shallow fissures. The leaves are alternate, green to yellow-green, ovate or obovate, 10–16 cm long and 5–10 cm broad with a short, slender, slightly grooved petiole. They come in three different shapes, all of which can be on the same branch; three-lobed leaves, unlobed elliptical leaves, and two-lobed leaves; rarely, there can be more than three lobes. In fall, they turn to shades of yellow, tinged with red. The flowers are produced in loose, drooping, few-flowered racemes up to 5 cm long in early spring shortly before the leaves appear; they are yellow to greenish-yellow, with five or six tepals. It is usually dioecious, with male and female flowers on separate trees; male flowers have nine stamens, female flowers with six staminodes (aborted stamens) and a 2–3 mm style on a superior ovary. Pollination is by insects. The fruit is a dark blue-black drupe 1 cm long containing a single seed, borne on a red fleshy club-shaped pedicel 2 cm long; it is ripe in late summer, with the seeds dispersed by birds. The cotyledons thick and fleshy. All parts of the plant are aromatic and spicy. The roots are thick and fleshy, and frequently produce root sprouts which can develop into new trees.

**Influence:** Health, Money

**Gender**: Masculine, **Element**: Fire, **Planet**: Jupiter

Used to attract money by burning or placing in a wallet or purse. Aids healing.

**Cultivation**: This tree is a very cold-hardy ornamental tree which is well-worth growing in temperate areas. It requires light and slightly acidic soils, that remain slightly moist in summer. It can be propagated by seeds, cuttings or air-layers. As an established ornamental it is available through nurseries.

**Satyrion,** See Lucky Hand

**Savory, Summer** (*Satureja hortensis*)

**Description:** This slender erect annual herb became popular in Roman times and grows to around 30 cm. It has wiry stems and narrow lwaves with lavender or white flowers appearing in late summer.

**Influence:** Mental Powers

**Gender**: Masculine, **Element**: Air, **Planet**: Mercury

Strengthens the mind.

**Cultivation**: Seeds can be sown in spring and germinate quite easily. Choose a sunny position in a light, well-drained soil and water regularly. It will also grow happily in a pot.

**Scoke** see Poke

**Scotch Broom,** See Broom

**Sea Wrack,** See Bladderwrack

**Seneca grass,** See Sweetgrass

**Senna** (*Cassia marilandica* or *C. acutifolia*)

**Description:** This tall native American plant looks quite exotic as its large leaves give it a feathery appearance from a distance. Birds love this plant as it provides them shelter while the large seeds offer up a nutritious meal. Blooming with bright yellow flowers in summer, the golden tones are repeated in the fall as the foliage turns colour.

**Influence:** Love

**Gender**: Masculine, **Element**: Air, **Planet**: Mercury

Senna is used as a very effective laxative, often used as a cleanser during a fast. It is strong, so you should combine it with fennel or ginger. Do not use for prolonged periods to avoid the bowel becoming dependent, and do not use in cases of dehydration. Senna is used in love sachets.

**Cultivation**: Cold, moist stratification. Mix seed with moist but not wet, sterile growing medium. Place mixture in a labeled, sealed plastic bag and store in refrigerator for six to eight weeks. Another method is to sow seed outdoors in late autumn so that they may overwinter. Wild Senna grows best in a moist, sandy loam soil. Full sun or part shade are the preferred light conditions.

**Red Root,** See Tormentil

**Septfoil,** See Tormentil

**Sesame** (*Sesamum orientale*)

**Description:** Sesame is a tropical herb growing to around 60cm. It has erect stemms and lance like leaves with leafy spikes of plae white tubular flowers at the stem tips.

**Influence:** Money, Lust

**Gender**: Masculine, **Element**: Fire, **Planet**: Sun

Lust inducing when eaten. A jar of sesame seeds left open in the house draws cash to it. Change the seeds monthly. "Open sesame!" refers to the plant's ability to find hidden treasure, reveal secret passageways, and open locked doors.

**Cultivation**: Seed is the only method of propagation planted in spring, into fertile soil that is enriched with organic matter. It must be moist but well drained. Sunny sheltered position is best with protection from the wind. Once the seed pods ripen and begin to split they should be cut and dried in a warm place.

**Shallot** (*Allium* spp.)

**Description:** A bulbous plant growing in clumps to a height of 60 cm.

**Influence:** Purification

**Gender**: Masculine, **Element**: Fire, **Planet**: Mars

Add to the bath to cure misfortunes.

**Cultivation**: Prefers full sun and a well drained fertile soil. Propagation is by dividing clumps and planting bulblets in early spring. Can be grown from seed.

**Shamrock,** See Sorell, Wood

**Sheep Sorell,** See Sorell, Wood

**Shepherd's Knapperty,** See Tormentil

**Skunk Cabbage** (*Symplocarpus foetidus*)

**Description:** The leaves are large, 40-55 cm long and 30-40 cm broad. It flowers early in the year; the flowers are produced in a 5-10 cm long spadix contained within a spathe, 10-15 cm tall and mottled purple in colour. It flowers in the early spring, when only the flowers are visible above the mud, with the stems buried below and the leaves emerging later. The rhizome is often 30 cm thick. Breaking or tearing a leaf produces a pungent odor. This property lends itself to the 'skunk' in the common name. The foul odor attracts its pollinators, scavenging flies, stoneflies, and bees. The odor in the leaves may also serve to discourage large animals from disturbing or damaging this plant which grows in soft wetland soils. Skunk cabbage is notable for its ability to produce heat of up to 15-35° C above air temperature by cyanide resistant cellular respiration in order to melt its way through frozen ground, placing it among a small group of plants exhibiting thermogenesis. Although flowering whilst there is still snow and ice on the ground it is successfully pollinated by early insects that also emerge at this time.

**Influence:** Legal Matters

**Gender**: Feminine, **Element**: Water, **Planet**: Saturn

Wrap a small amount of skunk cabbage in a bay leaf on a Sunday to make a good fortune talisman. It also helps in court cases.

**Cultivation**: Skunk cabbage really, really likes wet feet and as they have a suprisingly extensive root system, they are almost impossible to successfully transplant. The hard, pea-size seeds ripen in late summer, and drop into the mud. Some are carried away by animals or floods, the rest either die or germinate in place.

**Silver Root,** See Stillengia

**Silver Leaf,** See Stillengia

**Silverweed see** Cinquefoil

**Skullcap** (*Scutellaria galericulata*)

**Description:** Common Skullcap, also known as Marsh Skullcap or Hooded Skullcap, is a hardy perennial herb native to Britain, Europe, and Asia. It is a member of the mint family Lamiaceae, which also includes many other herbs. The form is upright and is usually 0.2m to 0.45m in height . It is a wetland loving species and grows along fens and shorelines. The blue flowers appear in July to September and are 10-20mm long. The flowers are in pairs and are all on the same side of the stem. The flowers do not appear at the top of the stem.

**Influence:** Love, Fidelity, Peace

**Gender**: Feminine, **Element**: Water, **Planet**: Saturn

Used in spells of relaxation and peace. A woman who wears this protects her husband from committing adultery. Used as a tea, drank before meditation or to enhance the development of. As a bath, used for calming the aura of tensions and stress. Burned for relief of disharmony and disruptive situations.

**Cultivation**: Succeeds in a sunny position in any ordinary garden soil that does not dry out during the growing season. Seed can be sown in situ outdoors in late spring. If there is only a small quantity of seed it is better to sow it in a pot in a cold frame in early spring. When they are large enough to handle, prick the seedlings out into individual pots and plant them out in the spring.

**Slippery Elm** (*Ulmus fulva*)

**Description:** It is a deciduous tree that grows 15 to 25 metres tall.

**Influence:** Halts Gossip

**Gender**: Feminine, **Element**: Air, **Planet**: Saturn

Burn and use in charm bags to stop others from gossiping about you or your friends. A child who wears this will have a persuasive tongue when grown.

**Cultivation**: It is a deciduous tree that grows 15 to 25 metres tall. It needs full sun and good soils. It is native to areas from Canada to Florida, west to the Dakotas and Texas. Nurseries can supply young plants.

**Slippery Root see** Comfrey

**Sloe** (*Prunus spinosa*)

**Description:** Dwarf growing shrub found throughout Europe. Widely used at one time for jellies, syrups, conserves, olives and flavoring for gin and herbal teas. Eaten fresh the fruit is very bitter. Sloe plum is the plant that is found in Irish folklore said to create good effects. Dense branching with lots of fruit spurs.

**Influence:** Protection, Banishing, Divining

**Gender**: Masculine, **Element**: Fire, **Planet**: Mars

Carry or hang over doorways to ward off evil and calamity, banish demons, and release negative vibrations. The wood can be used to make divining rods and wishing rods. Wishing rods are all-purpose magick wands.

**Cultivation**: Collect the sloes from September onwards when they become soft. Separate the stones from the skin and flesh. The seeds require a period of warmth before a lengthy period of cold in order to grow. Mix the seed with compost, place in a container and keep warm for one month. Do not allow to dry out. Move them outside and sow in the spring. Protect from mice and birds. The seedlings are usually large enough to be planted out after one year. It occurs on a wide range of soils, avoiding only extremely acid conditions. It suckers freely, producing new shoots from the roots and can form dense thickets. As a plant it is completely hardy, but the flowers can be damaged by late frosts. It is not tolerant of heavy shade but withstands exposure to winds in lowland areas.

**Snakeroot** (*Aristolochia serpentaria*) also known as Virginia Snakeroot

**Description:** Snakeroot is a genus of about 290 annual herbs and rounded shrubs from the Sunflower family (Asteraceae). These plants grow mainly in the warmer regions of America. A few occur in the cooler regions of eastern United States. Two Mexican species have become a pest in parts of Australia. These plants used to belong to the genus Eupatorium, but have been split off. The inflorescence consists of many fluffy red or pinkish-white capitula in clusters. These lack the typical ray flowers of the composites. There are many, much-branched woody stems. The leaves are triangular, serrate and opposite. The petioles are rather long. The leaves are fragrant with a rather nasty musky scent.

**Influence:** Luck, Money

Carried as a good luck talisman and to break hexes and curses. Said to lead its bearer to money.

**Gender**_____, **Element**_____, **Planet:** _____

**Cultivation**: As a wild plant it is threatened. Virginia snakeroot grows in shady woods in rich, well-drained soil. Probably grown from seed.

**Snakeroot, Black** (*Sanicula marilandica*)

**Description:** Maryland black snakeroot (Sanicula marilandica) is a flowering plant widespread in North America but rare along the Pacific coast of the continent and Texas. It has leaves with deeply incised lobes radiating out from the same point. Every leaf has no set number of leaflets, but commonly will have 5–7. The plant is not tall but the fruiting stalk will rise up to 60 cm, bearing green diminuitive flowers in spring. In fall the fruiting stalk carries dehiscent fruit that splits, bearing small spines.

**Influence:** Love, Lust, Money

**Gender**: Masculine, **Element**: Fire, **Planet**: Mars

Worn to attract lovers; placed in the bedroom and added to baths for the same purpose. Carry to attract money.

**Cultivation**: This peculiar plant is common through woods and copses throughout the United States, and often annoys persons with woolen clothing by the tenacity with which the fruit (late in the autumn) will cling to their garments. Not known to be grown domestically.

**Snakeweed,** See Plantain

**Snapdragon** (*Antirrhinum majus*)

**Description:** The species is often planted in gardens for its flowers. Although perennial, it is often treated as an annual plant, particularly in colder areas where they may not survive the winter. Numerous cultivars are available, including plants with lavender, orange, pink, yellow, or white flowers. Growing snapdragon provides months of colour ranging from pale pastels to vibrant reds and oranges. They are a favourite flower for cutting and fragrance. Plants grow 30 cm to 90 cm tall. Self-seeding annual, it often escapes from cultivation.

**Influence:** Protection

**Gender**: Masculine, **Element**: Fire, **Planet**: Mars

Wear to prevent people from deceiving you. The seed worn around the neck ensures that you will never be hexed. If you are outside and feel evil nearby, step on a snapdragon or hold one of its flowers until it passes. Place a vase of fresh snapdragons on the altar while performing protective rituals. If someone has sent negative energy to you, place some snapdragons on the altar with a mirror behind them. This will send the curses back.

**Cultivation**: Snapdragons thrive in the cooler temperatures of late spring and do best in sunny locations with rich, well-drained soil. Plants will not flourish where temperatures are high for long periods of time. Blooms will tolerate some frost. Under favourable conditions, snapdragons will self-sow in the garden. May be grown from cuttings or from seed. If planting from seed, sow indoors on the surface of the soil for 8 weeks before last frost. Seeds will germinate in 10-20 days. For best results, sow in vermiculite and water from below. Plant outdoors after last frost. Pinch back young plants after 4-6 leaves have appeared to encourage a bushy habit and apply an all-purpose organic fertilizer for optimum plant health. Spent flowers should be picked often to encourage more blooms.

**Solomon's Seal** (*Polygonatum officinale* or *P. multiflorum*)

**Description:** Solomon's Seal is a perennial herb that grows from 30cm – 1 meter high. It prefers moist woods, thickets, and roadsides and full to partial sun.

**Influence:** Protection, Exorcism, Cleansing and Protection

**Gender**: Feminine, **Element**: Water, **Planet**: Saturn

Burn for cleansing rooms and yourself of negative influences. Carry in an amulet or sachet for protection in all sorts of situations. Use with other herbs in dream pillows. Used in exorcism and protection spells. Sprinkle an infusion of the root around to clear the area of evil. Used in offeratory incenses.

**Cultivation**: Solomon's Seal is a very hardy plant. It prefers a light soil and a shady situation, being a native of woods. If in a suitable soil and situation and not crowded by shrubs, it will thrive and multiply very rapidly by the creeping rootstocks. It will be better for occasional liberal dressings of leaf mould, or an annual top dressing of decayed manure in late winter. Seeds, sown as soon as gathered in the autumn, germinate in early spring, or the roots may be divided to any extent. The best time to transplant or part the roots is in autumn, after the stalks decay, but it may safely be done at any time, if taken up with plenty of soil, until they begin to shoot in the spring, when the ground should be dug about them and kept clean from weeds. They should also have room to spread and must not be removed more frequently than every third or fourth year. To give Solomon's Seal a good start when planting, the soil should be well broken up with a fork and have a little mild manure worked in.

**Sorcerer's Berry see** Belladonna

**Sorceror's Root see** Mandrake

**Sorcerer's Violet see** Periwinkle

**Sorrel Wood** (*Oxalis acetosella*)

**Description:** This clump forming plant can grow to 90cm if allowed to flower. It has dark green leaves shaped like a spear head. Reddish spikes of flowers grow in summer but if not required for seed are best removed once seen.

**Influence:** Healing, Health

**Gender**: Feminine, **Element**: Earth, **Planet**: Venus

The dried leaves are carried to protect the heart against disease. Aids in recovery from wounds and illness.

**Cultivation**: Grown from divisions or seedlings, set around 30 cm apart in spring in well drained fertile soil. Organic rich soil is best, and should be kept moist.

**Sour Grass,** See Sorell, Wood

**Southernwood** (*Artemisia abrotanum*)

**Description:** Also known as Old Man and Lad's love this herb is an oldtime favourite. It is a deciduous shrub, growing to 90cm or more, but takes well to clipping. The fine green-grey leaves are between 2.5 cm and 6.5 cm long. It is ideal as a small hedge in the herb garden and has sweetly aromatic smell.

**Influence:** Love, Lust, Protection

**Gender**: Masculine, **Element**: Air, **Planet**: Mercury

Used in love spells; carry or place in the bedroom. Sometimes placed beneath the bed to rouse lust. Burned as an incense, guards against trouble of all kinds and drives away snakes.

**Cultivation**: Plant semi hard wood cuttings in late summer and protect from frost, in milder areas hardwood cuttings can be planted from late autumn. Preferring a free draining fertile soil, it will grow in poor soil including chalky or sandy areas. Preferring a sunny position, up to half a day shade will be tolerated. Set out young plants in their permanent position in spring or autumn. Keep pruned for tidiness.

**Spanish Moss** (*Tillandsia usneoides*)

**Description:** Spanish moss is not biologically related to either mosses or lichens. Instead, it is a flowering plant in the family Bromeliaceae (the bromeliads) that grows hanging from tree branches in full sun or partial shade, growing wherever the climate is warm enough and has a relatively high average humidity. The plant consists of a slender stem bearing alternate thin, curved or curly, heavily scaled leaves 2-6 cm long and 1 mm broad, that grow vegetatively in chain-like fashion (pendant) to form hanging structures 1-2 m in length, occasionally more.

**Influence:** Protection

Grown on or in the home to protect it. Use to stuff protection poppets and add to protective sachets.

**Gender**_____, **Element**_____, **Planet:** _____

**Cultivation**: The plant lacks roots and its flowers are tiny and inconspicuous. It propagates both by seed and vegetatively by fragments that blow on the wind and stick to tree limbs, or are carried by birds as nesting material. Simply divide the plant.

**Spearmint** (*Mentha spicata*)

**Description:** Probably the most popular of the mint family, this evergreen woody shrub grows to around 60cm in height. It has lance shaped pointy leaves it bears white, lilac and pink flowers on woody stems in late summer.

**Influence:** Healing, Love, Mental Powers

**Gender**: Feminine, **Element**: Water, **Planet**: Venus

Burn for healing wishes especially respiratory. Carry the herb in sachet for healing, drink the tea for healing or take a bath for strength and vitality. Smell to sharpen and increase mental powers. For protection while asleep, stuff a pillow or mattress with spearmint.

**Cultivation**: Mint generally likes semi-shaded positions where the soil is moist but not waterlogged. It can become invasive as it spreads aggressively via underground stems. Propagation can be achieved by division or by cuttings struck in spring. Seed can also be sown in spring.

**Spiderwort** (*Tradescantia Virginia*)

**Description:** Spiderwort is any member of the genus Tradescantia (family Commelinaceae), which includes 20 or more erect to trailing, weak-stemmed herbs native to North and South America. Several species are grown as indoor plants in baskets and garden. Certain species resemble but should not be confused with Zebrina species.

**Influence:** Love

Dakota indians carried this herb to attract love.

**Gender**_____, **Element**_____, **Planet:** _____

**Cultivation**: The spiderworts are of extremely easy culture, taking root readily from cuttings, and thus are very popular indoor plants

## Spikenard (*Inula conyza*)

**Description:** Biennial/Perennial growing to 1.2m by 0.4m . It is in flower in summer, and the seeds ripen late summer to autumn. The scented flowers are hermaphrodite (have both male and female organs) and are pollinated by Bees and flies. The plant is self-fertile.

**Influence:** Love

**Gender**: Feminine, **Element**: Water, **Planet**: Venus

Wear around the neck to bring good luck and ward off disease. It is also used to remain faithful to a partner.

**Cultivation**: Seed - sow spring or autumn in a cold frame. When they are large enough to handle, prick the seedlings out into individual pots and plant them out in the summer. If you have sufficient seed, it is worthwhile trying a sowing in situ in the spring or the autumn.

## Spotted Hemlock see Hemlock

## Squill (*Urginea scilla*)

**Description:** Squill is a bulb which sends up large dull green leaves followed by inflorescences of small white flowers. The bulb can get quite large, reaching over five pounds in weight. It grows in coastal regions in sandy soil.

**Influence:** Protection, Money, Hex Breaking.

**Gender**: Masculine, **Element**: Fire, **Planet**: Mars

To protect your home, hang a squill over the window. Place one into a jar or box and add silver coins to draw money. To break a hex, carry a squill with you.

**Gender**_____, **Element**_____, **Planet:** _____

**Cultivation**: Seed - best sown as soon as it is ripe in a greenhouse. Sow the seed thinly so that the seedlings can be left in the pot for their first growing season. Give them regular liquid feeds when in active growth to ensure that they do not suffer nutrient deficiency. Divide the young bulbs once the plant becomes dormant, placing 2- 3 bulbs in each put. Grow them on for at least another year in pots and plant them out into their permanent positions when they are dormant. Division of offsets in late summer when the bulb is dormant. Larger bulbs can be replanted immediately into their permanent positions. It is probably best to pot up smaller bulbs and grow them on in a greenhouse for a year before planting them out when they are dormant in late summer.

## Star Anise (*Illicium verum*)

**Description:** Attractive slow growing tree to 20 metres from South China. Known for its ornamental value as an attractive Magnolia-like tree with ovate leaves, and for its star shaped fruits. The unripe fruits are the source of the culinary spice and a distilled oil used in medicine and in industry for flavoring which is recognized as Star Anise.

**Influence:** Psychic Powers, Luck

**Gender**: Masculine, **Element**: Air, **Planet**: Jupiter

Burn the seeds in incense to bring clairvoyance, or use in making herbal pendulums. They are sometimes strung on a string with nutmegs and tonka bean, etc. to make a magickally-charged (and very fragrant) necklace. Sometimes four seeds are placed on the altar, one in each direction, to bring power. Good luck bringer.

**Cultivation**: While the plant comes from sub-tropical areas it grows naturally in mild upland areas where the temperature rarely exceeds 20 degrees C. It requires well-drained, acid soil and filtered sunlight. It needs ample water. The tree may take more than 5 years to flower but is very long-lived.

**Stillengia** (*Stillingia sylvatica*) also known as Queen's Root, Queen's Delight, Yawroot, cockup hat, marcory, silver root, silver leaf, pavil.

**Description:** It is a perennial herb, with a glabrous somewhat angled stem, which, upon being broken, gives out a milky sap, and which attains the height of 60 cm to 1.2 metres. The leaves are sessile, lance-oblong, tapering at the base, serrulate, and somewhat leathery. The flowers are yellow, on a terminal spike; the male flowers with a hemispherical involucre, many-flowered or wanting, perianth tubular, erose, florets scarcely longer than the bracteal scales; stamens 2 or 3, and exserted. Female flowers with an inferior, 1-flowered calyx; style 3-cleft; capsule 3-grained

**Influence:** Psychic Powers, Finding lost items

Burn the root to develop psychic powers. If you've lost something, burn the plant and follow the smoke to its hiding place.

**Gender**_____, **Element**_____, **Planet:** _____

**Cultivation**: From seed; direct sow outdoors in autumn or direct sow after last frost. Prefers full sun to partial shaded position.

**Straw**

**Description:** Straw is an agricultural byproduct, the dry stalk of a cereal plant, after the nutrient grain or seed has been removed. Straw makes up about half of the yield of a cereal crop such as barley, oats, rice, rye or wheat.

**Influence:** Luck, Attracts Fairies

Straw is often carried in small bags because it is lucky. Take a used horseshoe and some straw, sew up into a small bag, and place it above or below the bed for a luck talisman. Images can be made from straw and used in image magick as poppets. Straw attracts fairies.

**Gender**_____, **Element**_____, **Planet:** _____

**Cultivation**: See details for the specific grain.

**Strawberry** (*Fragaria vesca*)

**Description:** The strawberry (Fragaria) (plural strawberries) is a genus of plants in the family Rosaceae and the fruit of these plants. There are more than 20 named species and many hybrids and cultivars. The strawberry is an accessory fruit; that is, the fleshy part is derived not from the ovaries which are the "seeds" (actually achenes) but from the peg at the bottom of the hypanthium that held the ovaries. So from a technical standpoint, the seeds are the actual fruits of the plant, and the flesh of the strawberry is modified receptacle tissue. It is whitish-green as it develops and in most species turns red when ripe.

**Influence:** Love, Luck

**Gender**: Feminine, **Element**: Water, **Planet**: Venus

Served as a love food, and the leaves are carried for luck. Pregnant women can carry a small packet of strawberry leaves to ease pregnancy pains.

**Cultivation**: Basic considerations when locating a strawberry patch include Full sun and well drained, sandy loam . Don't plant where tomatoes, potatoes, peppers or eggplant have been grown recently (Verticillium Rot) Plant in the spring as soon as the soil is dry enough to be worked. or in late Autumn, being sure you have certified disease free plants. Select plants with large crowns with healthy, light-colored roots Keep weeds from competing with your strawberry plants Make a hole large enough to spread the roots. Hill the center of the hole and place the crown at soil level. Spread the roots downward on the hill. Bury the plant so that the soil only goes half way up the crown.

**Sugar Cane** (*Saccharum officinarum*)

**Description:** Sugarcane is a tropical grass. Its stalk contains sweet juice from which sugar can be extracted. Most varieties are hybrids of the 4 cultivated species of sugarcane. Saccharum officinarum is the main "ingredient" of the cultivated hybrids.

**Influence:** Love, Lust

**Gender**: Feminine, **Element**: Water, **Planet**: Venus

Used in love and lust potions. Chew a piece of the cane while thinking of your loved one. Scatter to dispel evil and to cleanse and purify areas before rituals and spells.

**Cultivation**: It is grown by planting "seed cane, " pieces of sugarcane stalk that germinate and produce new sugarcane plants. The cutting needs to be put horizontaly on the ground and buried completely.

**Sumbul** (*Ferula sumbul*)

**Description:** The plant that produces the sumbul-root of commerce, is an herbaceous perennial, with an erect, milk-bearing stem, and is a native of central Asia. The leaves are mostly radical, large, and ternately decompound, with the ultimate segments narrow and toothed. The upper stem leaves are reduced merely to the sheathing bases of the petioles. The flowers are small, yellow, and disposed in compound umbels. The terminal umbels are perfect, the lateral, only staminate. They have 5 stamens, 5 petals, and a 2-carpeled pistil. The fruit consists of 2 dry, seed-like carpels, compressed laterally, and each carpel having 3 dorsal ribs, and 2 narrow lateral wings.

**Influence:** Love, Psychic Powers, Luck, Health

Burn as incense or add the infusion to the bath to attract love. Burn to increase psychic powers. Wear around the neck to gain good luck and keep away disease.

**Gender**_____, **Element**_____, **Planet:** _____

**Cultivation**: Succeeds in most soils prefering a deep fertile soil in a sunny position Plants are hardy to about -5°c and have a long taproot and are intolerant of root disturbance. They should be planted into their final positions as soon as possible. Seed is best sown as soon as the seed is ripe in autumn. Give the plants a protective mulch for at least their first winter outdoors. Division in autumn may be inadvisable due to the plants dislike of root disturbance.

**Sunflower** (*Helianthus annuus*)

**Description:** The sunflower is an annual plant native to the Americas in the family Asteraceae, with a large flowering head. The stem of the flower can grow as high as 3 metres tall, with the flower head reaching up to 30 cm in diameter with the "large" seeds. What is usually called the flower is actually a head (formally composite flower) of numerous flowers (florets) crowded together. The outer flowers are the ray florets and can be yellow, maroon, orange, or other colors, and are sterile. The florets inside the circular head are called disc florets. The disc florets mature into what are traditionally called "sunflower seeds", but are actually the fruit of the plant. The true seeds are encased in an inedible husk.

**Influence:** Fertility, Wishes, Health, Wisdom

**Gender**: Masculine, **Element**: Fire, **Planet**: Sun

Sunflower seeds are eaten by women who want to conceive. Wear sunflower seeds around the neck to protect against smallpox. Cut a sunflower at sunset while making a (realistic) wish, it will come true before another sunset. Sleep with a sunflower under the bed to know the truth in all manners. Anoint yourself with juice from the stem of the sunflower if you want to be virtuous. Grow in the garden to guard against pests and bring luck to the gardener.

**Cultivation**: To grow well, sunflowers need full sun. They grow best in fertile, moist, well-drained soil with a lot of mulch. In commercial planting, seeds are planted 45 cm apart and 2.5 cm deep.

**Sweetbalm,** See Balm, Lemon

**Sweet Bay,** See Bay

**Sweet Elder,** See Elder

**Sweet Flag,** See Calamus

**Sweetgrass** (*Hierochloe odorata*), also known as Sweetgrass, Holy grass, buffalo grass, Vanilla grass, Manna grass, Seneca grass, Mary's grass, Zebrovka, or Bison grass.

**Description:** is an aromatic, very hardy native perennial herb which grows in northern Eurasia and North America. It is used in herbal medicine and manufacture of alcoholic beverages. It owes its specific aroma to the presence of coumarin. Grows to about 60 cm in height, leaves grow 60 cm long by late summer. Base of leaves, just below soil surface is broad and white, without hairs, underside of leaves are shiny, no hairs

**Influence:** Attract spirits,

Burn to attract good spirits or beings before performing spells.

**Gender**_____, **Element**_____, **Planet:** _____

**Cultivation**: Most easily propagated by cutting out plugs from established plants. Grown in sun or partial shade, they do not like drought.

**Sweet Laurel,** See Bay**Sweetpea** (*Lathyrus odoratus*)  **POISONOUS (Seeds)**

**Description:** Annual climbers bearing clusters of flowers in a wide variety of colors including red, pink, blue, white and lavender. The stems appear folded and the flowers resemble fringed butterflies. The old-fashioned varieties were selected for their vibrant colors and intense fragrance. Many modern cultivars are on the market offering sweet peas in almost every color except yellow. Not all Sweet pea varieties are fragrant. They have a long season of bloom and make excellent cut flowers. Unlike most peas, the seeds of the sweet pea are poisonous as they contain a neurotoxin, and should not be eaten. Sweet pea vines have tendrils and will attach themselves to most any type of support with meshing or lines.

**Influence:** Friendship, Chastity, Courage, Strength

**Gender**: Feminine, **Element**: Water, **Planet**: Venus

Wear fresh sweetpea flowers to attract people and cause friendships to develop. Carry or hold to cause you to tell the truth. Preserves chastity if placed in the bedroom. Gives courage and strength when worn.

**Cultivation**: Sweet peas are usually direct seeded. To assist germination, seeds should be nicked or soaked in water for several hours, to soften the seed coating. Seed can be started outdoors, as soon as the ground has warmed to about 10 C. and is not too wet. At about 8 cm to 15 cm, pinch the seedlings to encourage strong side shoots. Seed can be started earlier indoors, in pots. Pinch off all flowers and buds when transplanting seedlings, to encourage root development. Regular deadheading or cutting for display, will keep them blooming longer. Sweet peas require regular watering, especially as the temperature increases. They prefer a somewhat rich soil and can be fed monthly with a fertilizer high in potassium, as used for tomatoes. Adding a bit of blood meal to the soil is thought to help keep the stems long and suitable for cutting.

**Sweet Sedge,** See Calamus

**Sweet Weed see** Althea

**Sweet Wood see** Cinnamon

**Tadstoles,** See Toadstool

**Tadstooles,** See Toadstool

**Tamarind** (*Tamarindus indica*)

**Description:** Tamarinds are slow-growing, long-lived, evergreen trees that under optimum conditions can grow 25 metres high with a spread of 7 – 8 metres, in its native eastern Africa and Asia. It is extensively cultivated in tropical areas of the world. The tamarind is well adapted to semiarid tropical conditions, although it does well in many humid tropical areas of the world with seasonally high rainfall. Young trees are very susceptible to frost, but mature trees will withstand brief periods of 0° C without serious injury Dry weather is important during the period of fruit development. The tree is too large to be grown in a container for any length of time.

**Influence:** Love

**Gender**: Feminine, **Element**: Water, **Planet**: Saturn

Carry to attract love.

**Cultivation**: The tamarind ultimately becomes a fairly large tree, so this should be kept in mind when planting out the tree. It should be planted in full sun and is highly wind-resistant with strong, supple branches. The tree generally forms a beautiful spreading crown that casts a light shade. Tamarinds tolerate a great diversity of soil types but do best in deep, well drained soils which are slightly acid. Trees will not tolerate cold, wet soils but are tolerant of salt spray and can be planted fairly near the seashore. The tamarind is adapted to semiarid regions of the tropics and can withstand drought conditions quite well. Young trees require adequate soil moisture until they become established, but mature trees do quite well without supplemental irrigation. Avoid over-watering which results in soggy soils. It is not very demanding in its nutritional requirements. Bearing trees can be fertilized with 8-3-9 NPK or similar analysis, at rates of about 1 kg. per application per year of tree age. Microelements, particularly iron may be required for trees in alkaline soils. Young trees are pruned to allow three to five well spaced branches to develop into the main scaffold structure of the tree. Maintenance pruning only is required after that to remove dead or damaged wood. Rootstocks are propagated from seed, which germinate within a week. Seeds retain their viability for several months if kept dry. Plant seeds 2 cm deep in containers filled with a UC soilless type potting media. They should be selected from trees of good production and quality. Even so, seedlings will be variable in quality and slow to bear. Veneer grafting, shield budding and air layering may be used to propagate desirable selections. Such trees will usually fruit within 3 - 4 years if provided optimum growing conditions. Seedlings should begin to produce fruit in 6 - 8 years, while vegetatively propagated trees will normally bear in half that time. Young trees should be planted in holes larger than necessary to accommodate the root system. They should be planted slightly higher than existing ground level to allow for subsequent settling of the soil and a water basin should be built around each tree to assure adequate moisture for young trees.

**Tamarisk** (*Tamarix* spp.) Drive out demons, snakes

**Description:** They are deciduous or evergreen shrubs or small trees growing to 1-15 m in height and forming dense thickets, The largest, Tamarix aphylla, is an evergreen tree that can grow to 15 m tall. They usually grow on saline soils, tolerating up to 15, 000 ppm soluble salt and can also tolerate alkali conditions. Tamarisks are characterized by slender branches and grey-green foliage. The bark of young branches is smooth and reddish-brown. As the plants age, the bark becomes brownish-purple, ridged and furrowed. The leaves are scale-like, 1-2 mm long, and overlap each other along the stem. They are often encrusted with salt secretions. The pink to white flowers appear in dense masses on 5-10 cm long spikes at branch tips. Seedlings require extended periods of soil saturation for establishment. Tamarix species are fire-adapted, and have long tap roots that allow them to intercept deep water tables and exploit natural water resources. They are able to limit competition from other plants by taking up salt from deep ground water, accumulating it in their foliage, and from there depositing it in the surface soil where it builds up concentrations temporarily detrimental to some plants. The salt is washed away during heavy rains.

**It is regarded as one of the worst weeds in Australia because of its invasiveness, potential for spread, and economic and environmental impacts. Tamarisk affects the pastoral industry by forming dense stands along inland rivers. It consumes**

**water more quickly than native plants, thereby reducing the number and quality of watering holes.**

**Influence:** Repel Demons, Snakes

**Gender**: Feminine, **Element**: Water, **Planet**: Saturn

Used in exorcism rites; a branch of the tree is held and the leaves are scattered around to drive out demons and evil. Cut with a gold axe and a silver pruning knife for best results. The smoke of burning tamarisk drives away snakes.

**Cultivation**: Tamarix can spread both vegetatively, by adventitious roots or submerged stems, and sexually, by seeds. Each flower can produce thousands of tiny (1 mm diameter) seeds that are contained in a small capsule usually adorned with a tuft of hair that aids in wind dispersal. Seeds can also be dispersed by water. Seedlings require extended periods of soil saturation for establishment. Tamarix species are fire-adapted, and have long tap roots that allow them to intercept deep water tables and exploit natural water resources.

**Tansy** (*Tanacetum vulgare*)

**Description:** A very hardy clump forming herb which grows to a height of around 1 metre. It dies back to the roots in winter from which it re-grows in spring. It can become invasive. Foliage makes an insect repellent.

**Influence:** Health, Longevity

**Gender**: Feminine, **Element**: Water, **Planet**: Venus

Helped to cure persistent fevers by being placed in the shoe. Ants don't like tansy.

**Cultivation**: This herb is not fussy about soil type, but needs a sunny, well-drained position. Cuttings can be taken now and the plant can also be propagated by seed and root division. Cut the stalks back to ground level in winter.

**Tea** (*Camellia sinensis.*)

**Description:** Camellia sinensis is the tea plant, the plant species whose leaves and leaf buds are used to produce tea. White tea, green tea, oolong and black tea are all harvested from this species, but are processed differently to attain different levels of oxidation. Kukicha (twig tea) is also harvested from camellia sinensis, but uses twigs and stems rather than leaves. Older names for the tea plant include Thea bohea, Thea sinensis and Thea viridis. Camellia sinensis is native to mainland South and Southeast Asia, but is today cultivated across the world, in tropical and subtropical regions. It is an evergreen shrub or small tree that is usually trimmed to below two metres when cultivated for its leaves. It has a strong taproot. The flowers are yellow-white, 2.5–4 cm in diameter, with 7 to 8 petals. The seeds of Camellia sinensis and Camellia oleifera can be pressed to yield tea oil, a sweetish seasoning and cooking oil that should not be confused with tea tree oil, an essential oil that is used for medical and cosmetical purposes and originates from the leaves of a different plant.

**Influence:** Riches, Courage, Strength

**Gender**: Masculine, **Element**: Fire, **Planet**: Mars

Burn the leaves to ensure future riches and add to money mixtures and sachets. Included in courage and strength talismans. The infusion is a base for mixing lust drinks.

Processing the "Tea leaves"

- Green tea
  Pluck the very youngest leaves and leaf buds and blot the leaves dry, and let dry in the shade for a few hours. Steam the leaves (like you would vegetables) on your stove for about a minute. For a different flavour, try roasting them in a skillet for 2 minutes instead of steaming. Spread the leaves on a baking sheet and dry in the oven at 250F for 20 minutes. Store the dried tea leaves in an air-tight container

- Oolong Tea
  Pluck the very youngest leaves and leaf buds. Spread them out on a towel under the sun and let them wilt for about 45 minutes. Bring your leaves inside and let them sit at room temperature for a few hours. Make sure to stir the leaves up every hour. The edges of the leaves will start to turn red as they begin to dry. Spread the leaves on a baking sheet and dry in the oven at 250F for 20 minutes. Store the dried tea leaves in an air-tight container.

- Black Tea
  Pluck the very youngest leaves and leaf buds. Roll the leaves between your hands, and crush them until the leaves start to darken and turn red. Spread them out on a tray, and leave them in a cool location for 2-3 days. Dry them in the oven at 250F for about 20 minutes. Store in an air-tight container.

**Cultivation**: The Camellia sinensis plant is a small shrub about 1-2 meters in height, though it will grow taller if you don't prune it. In the fall, your tea shrub will flower with small white blossoms that have a delightful scent. These plants are often grown as ornamentals. For planting, Camellia sinensis likes well-drained and sandy soil that is on the acidic side. If you are going to grow your tea in a container, add some sphagnum moss to the potting mix. You'll need some patience, too. Your plant should be around 3 years old before you start harvesting leaves. You might be able to get seeds at your local nursery.

**Teaberry,** See Periwinkle

**Tetterwort,** See Bloodroot

**Thea bohea,** See Tea

**Thea sinensis,** See Tea

**Thea viridis,** See Tea

**Thistle** (*Carduus* spp.)

**Description:** Carduus is a genus of about 90 species of thistles in the family Asteraceae, native to Europe, Asia and Africa. (Carduus is the Latin for a thistle. Cardonnacum, derived from carduus, is the Latin for a place with thistles. This is believed to be the origin of name of the Burgundy village of Chardonnay, Saône-et-Loire, which in turn is thought to be the home of the famous Chardonnay grape variety.)

**Influence:** Strength, Protection, Hex Breaking, Healing

**Gender**; Masculine, **Element**: Fire, **Planet**: Mars

A spray of thistles aids in the speedy recuperation after surgery or illness, Hang in the home or plant around the home to ward off unwanted visitors and thieves. Place a bowl of thistles in a room to strengthen people's spirits. Grow in the garden to ward off theives , and grown in a pot on the doorstep, guard against evil. Throw onto a fire to deflect lightning from the house. Wear a shirt made of thistle fibers to break hexes and curses. Stuff hex breaking poppets with thistle. Used in healing spells. Men carry it to be better lovers. To call spirits, place some thistle in boiling water. Remove from heat and sit or lie beside it. As the steam rises, call the spirits and listen; they may answer you.

**Cultivation**: Generally considered a weed and so not cultivated. Thistles favor grasslands, woodlands, and chaparral vegetation types. Frequently found in disturbed areas, often with basaltic soils, fertile soils, or soils with a relatively high pH.

**Thistle, Holy** (*Centaurea benedictus*) also known as Blessed Thistle.

**Description:** It is an annual plant growing to 60 cm tall, with leathery, hairy leaves up to 30 cm long and 8 cm broad, with small spines on the margins. The flowers are yellow, produced in a dense flowerhead (capitulum) 3-4 cm diameter, surrounded by numerous spiny basal bracts.

**Influence:** Purification, Hex Breaking

**Gender**; Masculine, **Element**: Fire, **Planet**: Mars

Wear to protect yourself from evil, and add to purification baths. Use in hex breaking spells.

**Cultivation**: Blessed thistle is grown from seed, which should be sown in the Spring. It is a very hardy plant, but it prefers well-drained soil and full sun. It should be harvested when it is flowering. Cut the whole plant at ground level and dry hanging upside down. The blessed thistle will regrow from the roots.

**Thistle, Milk** (*Carduus Marianus*)

**Description:** Erect, annual to biennial herb, with a thick, centre stem that can grow 1-2 metres tall. Leaves are very frilly, deeply-indented and armed on the margins with extremely prickly, yellow spines. Another eye catching feature of the leaves, is the variegated markings in dark-green with thick, white veins, which look mottled or even marbled. This quite stunning, colourful leaf display of large patches of blotchy-white on the green leaves, gave man in early AD, the reason for creating a colourful folk legend, about the plant. The legend says, that as the Virgin Mary was feeding baby Jesus, some of her milk dropped on the thistle near her feet, which produced the white 'spilt-milk' effect, which has distinguished this herb ever since and as a consequence it has been a revered herb, receiving the many common names, listed above. The crowning glory, of the herb is the multiple flower stems, a magnificent display in violet/purple fluffy centres that look like thick shaving brushes.

**Influence:** Snake enraging

**Gender**; Masculine, **Element**: Fire, **Planet**: Mars

According to the Anglo-Saxons, a man who wore a milk thistle around his neck would cause all snakes in his presence to begin fighting.

**Cultivation**: Generally considered a weed and so not cultivated. Thistles favor grasslands, woodlands, and chaparral vegetation types. Frequently found in disturbed areas, often with basaltic soils, fertile soils, or soils with a relatively high pH.

**Thousand Leaf,** See Yarrow

**Thunderbesom see** Mistletoe

**Thyme** (*Thymus vulgaris*)

> **Description:** Com mon thyme is an evergreen shrub with a wiry bushy appearance. It grows to 30cm and a spread of twice it's height. It has tiny greyish leaves which contrast the tiny pink flower heads.
>
> **Influence:** Health, Healing, Sleep, Psychic Powers, Love, Purification, Courage
>
> **Gender**: Feminine, **Element**: Water, **Planet**: Venus
>
> Use in dream pillows to ward off nightmares, burn to attract good health or use with other oils for aid in psychic awareness, wear a sprig to ward off severe grief, Burn and/or hang a sprig to banish and purify a home or room. Use with other herbs for healing and take a cleansing bath before working candle magick. Place beneath the pillow to deter nightmares. Carry for courage and energy, and to see fairies.
>
> **Cultivation**: Thyme requires a hot, sunny location and is at its aromatic best if grown in well-drained soils that are low in nutrients. It will thrive in stony soil and requires little watering once it is established. Plant seed in spring, preferably in punnets, to be transplanted later. New plants can easily be propagated by layering from an established clump or by dividing the plants and replanting rooted sections. The plant will also grow readily from cuttings taken in late spring. Garden Thyme can be used as an attractive drought tolerant ground cover. The plant should be sheared back after flowering is complete to encourage future bushy growth.

**Thormantle,** See Tormentil

**Ti** (*Cordyline terminalis*) also known as Green Ti and Hawaiian good-luck-plant

> **Description:** Cordylines are known to the tropical world by many names and are crowned as "King of tropical foliage". With a vast rampant range of colors and sizes, it is reaching high popularity among gardners, landscapers and collectors alike. Cordyline Terminalis (Green Ti) Lush large broad green leaves 60 cm to 90 cm long and 15 cm to 20 cm wide. Native Hawaiians foster a strong belief that growing Ti plants around the home protects and brings good luck to the home. Ti's can grow to a height of 3 metres but are slow growing. They prefer more shade than sun, which keeps the leaves a darker green. The leaves have many useful purposes where the leaves are used for cooking and fashioned into hula skirts for Polynesian dancers among other uses. Cut off sections of cane will sprout new plants if planted in well drained soil and moderate water. Very lush tropical!
>
> **Influence:** Wards off Storms, Protection
>
> **Gender**; Masculine, **Element**: Fire, **Planet**: Jupiter
>
> Carried on a ship, the leaves keep storms away and ensure that the bearer won't drown. Plant around the house to create a protective barrier. Don't plant the red variety, though, because it causes bad luck when planted. Place beneath the bed for protection. Rub on the red to relieve headaches.
>
> **Cultivation**: Propagation by rooting of cuttings, including cane. Seed from a few

selections of ti will germinate rather true to type and is sold by seedsmen accordingly. Seed are sown in ground beds, raised beds or in trays on benches. They are covered with about 5 mm of peat or peat-lite mix which is kept moist until germination and development when the seedlings are large enough to be easily transplanted to small pots, usually about 5 cm to 10 cm high. There is no reason why seeded flats cannot be placed in chambers for germination, thus utilizing production space more efficiently.

**Tiger Lotus** See Lotus

**Toadflax** (*Linaria vulgaris*)

**Description:** Toadflax grows upright and branches, with flowers covering the upper third of the stems. Leaves are long and narrow. The species has blue-violet flowers with white or yellow markings, but new selections include many other colors as well: blue, lilac, pink, yellow, red, and white. They're still marked with a contrasting lip. They grow up to 30 cm tall, but often stay shorter.

**Influence:** Protection, Hex Breaking

**Gender**; Masculine, **Element**: Fire, **Planet**: Mars

Used as an amulet to keep away evil and to break hexes.

**Cultivation**: Toadflax requires full sun and well-drained soil. Low fertility is preferred over a rich soil. Plant as early as the ground can be worked. Seeds can be sown indoors early or directly in the ground outside. They grow and bloom so quickly that an earlier start is not necessary, except in those areas where early heat would diminish their bloom time. Because they are small, plant or thin them to a spacing 8 -12 cm apart. Linaria self-sows readily. Start new toadflax from seed. Sow outdoors as early as ground can be worked. Indoors, seed 4 to 6 weeks earlier. They germinate in 10 to 15 days at 13 to 15 degrees Celcius.

**Toadstool**, also known as tadstoles, frogstooles, frogge stoles, tadstooles, tode stoles, toodys hatte, paddockstool, puddockstool, paddocstol, toadstoole, and paddockstooles

**Description:** A mushroom is the fleshy, spore-bearing fruiting body of a fungus, typically produced above ground on soil or on its food source. The terms "mushroom" and "toadstool" go back centuries and were never precisely defined, nor was there consensus on application. The term "toadstool" was often but not exclusively applied to poisonous mushrooms or to those that have the classic umbrella-like cap-and-stem form. There may have been a direct connection to toads (in reference to poisonous properties) for toadstools. However, there is no clear-cut delineation between edible and poisonous fungi, so that a "mushroom" may be edible, poisonous, or unpalatable. The term "toadstool" is nowadays used in storytelling when referring to poisonous or suspect mushrooms.

**Influence:** Rain Making

Accidentally breaking down toadstools causes rain.

**Gender**_____, **Element**_____, **Planet**: _____

**Cultivation**: Mushroom farms are commercially available for edible mushrooms. Toadstools can be generally collect from the wild if wanted though can be grown from spore as follows. Toadstools, like all mushrooms, grow from microscopic spores, not seeds. Plants growing from spores are called fungi. A mature mushroom will drop as many as 16 billion spores. Spores must be collected in the nearly sterile environment of a laboratory and then used to inoculate grains or seeds to produce a product called spawn (the mushroom farmer's equivalent of seed). Because mushrooms have no chlorophyll, they must get all their nutrients from organic matter in their growing medium. The medium-called compost is scientifically formulated of various materials such as straw, corn cobs, cotton seed and cocoa seed hulls, gypsum and nitrogen supplements. Preparing the compost takes one to two weeks. Then it's pasteurized and placed in large trays or beds. Next the spawn is worked into the compost and the growing takes place in specially constructed houses, where the farmers can regulate the crucial aspects of heat and humidity. In two to three weeks, the compost becomes filled with the root structure of the mushroom, a network of lacy white filaments called mycelium. At that point, a layer of pasteurized peat moss is spread over the compost. The temperature of the compost and the humidity of the room must be carefully controlled in order for the mycelium to develop fully. Eventually, tiny white protrusions form on the mycelium and push up through the peat moss. Farmers call this pinning. The pins continue to grow, becoming the mushroom caps, which are actually the fruit of the plant, just as a tomato is the fruit of a tomato plant. It takes 17 to 25 days to produce mature mushrooms after the peat moss is applied. Size is no indication of maturity in mushrooms. Perfectly ripe ones vary from small buttons to large caps. Each crop is harvested over a period of several weeks and then the house is emptied and steam-sterilized before the process begins again. The remaining compost is recycled for potting soil. The harvested mushrooms are set in carts, refrigerated and then packaged and shipped quickly to supermarkets, food processors and restaurants. The entire process from the time the farmer starts preparing the compost until the mushrooms are harvested and shipped to market takes about four months.

**Tode stoles,** See Toadstool

**Tobacco** (*Nicotiana* spp.) **POISONOUS**

**Description:** Tobacco is an agricultural product processed from the fresh leaves of plants in the genus Nicotiana. It is often smoked (see tobacco smoking) in the form of a cigar or cigarette, or in a stem pipe, water pipe, or hookah. Tobacco can also be chewed, "dipped" (placed between the cheek and gum), or sniffed into the nose as finely powdered snuff. Many countries set a minimum smoking age, regulating the purchase and use of tobacco products.

**Influence:** Healing, Purification

**Gender**; Masculine, **Element**: Fire, **Planet**: Mars

Burned on charcoal to remove negativity. Throw tobacco into a river on the start of a boat journey. Sometimes used to cure illnesses by blowing the smoke on the diseased part of the body. Nightmares which can cause sickness are prevented by washing in a running stream immediately upon waking and throwing tobacco into the water as an offering to the Water Spirit. A magickal substitute for sulfur, as well as for datura and belladonna, both related to tobacco. However they're all poisonous.

**Cultivation**: Tobacco seeds initially require temperatures of 21-16°C, so start growing them in a propogator. Alternatively, you can place a covered seed tray in a warm cupboard for 7 to 10 days. Once at the seedling stage, a recommended 13°F is required to bring them on. You may wish to transplant the seedlings into small pots and keep them indoors for this stage. For 10-12 weeks after this period, they are grown outside (in frost free conditions) as normal. Most soils will suit tobacco plants, with the exception of heavy clay which needs breaking up with peat. Tobacco even thrives on poor sandy soil where other plants often fail. Plenty of water must be available as tobacco plants are a thirsty crop. You will find that your second year's crop will adjust to your soil and conditions and often produce better tobacco. A soil area of approximately 1 metre by 8 metres will be able to sustain 50 plants, producing enough tobacco for well over 5, 000 cigarettes.

**Tomato** (*Lycopersicon* spp.)

**Description:** A tomato is the fruit of the tomato plant, a vine which in its wild state is a resilient perennial with an indefinite life span that can grow to 8 metres high. It is a member of the nightshade or Solanaceae family, a cousin of the eggplant, pepper, potato, ground cherry, tomatillo, and the highly toxic belladonna, or deadly nightshade.

**Influence:** Repel Evil, Protective, Love

**Gender**; Feminine, **Element**: Water, **Planet**: Venus

When a tomato is placed on the windowsill, it repels evil from entering. Grown in the garden, they are protective. They have the power of inspiring love when eaten.

**Cultivation**: The soil temperatures in late spring are usually warm enough to start planting tomatoes. As tomatoes are susceptible to disease and if you put your tomatoes in during showery weather there is a risk that fungal diseases in the soil are splashed up onto the plant. You should have already prepared your soil by digging a trench, putting in different manures and organic material, and then leaving it to settle for several weeks.Put your tomato seedlings in on either side of the trench and eventually the roots will make their way down to that rich source of material. You can protect your tomatoes from disease by using wettable sulphur. You can put on two or three sprays before mid summer or use tomato dust which has a fungicide and insecticide. Mulching will stop weeds from growing and hold moisture. Don't over water once a week or once a fortnight once the plants are established is sufficient

**Tonka Beans** (*Coumarouna odorata; Dipteryx odorata*)  **POISONOUS**

**Description:** The seed is black and wrinkled in appearance, with a smooth brown interior. It is known mostly for its fragrance, which is reminiscent of vanilla, almonds, cinnamon, and cloves: it has sometimes been used commercially as a substitute for vanilla. It is also sometimes used in perfume and was commonly used in tobacco before being banned. They have a high coumarin content, which provides a sweet, herblike fragrance. Coumarin is an anti-coagulant and can be lethal in large doses. Tonka beans were and may still be used as an adulterant to vanilla. The beans are used to flavor tobaccos and snuffs. The essential oil is widely used in the perfume industry. Tonka beans are often used in sachets and potpourri. They are said to lighten one's mood and be emotionally balancing.

**Influence:** Love

**Gender**; Feminine, **Element**: Water, **Planet**: Venus

Simply put, carry the bean in your pocket, as a sachet, amulet or even place next to the candle or stone in all love drawing wishes. Used in love sachets and mixtures, and carried to attract love. Worn or carried to attract money, bring luck, grant courage, and prevent illness. To make your wishes come true, hold a tonka bean in your hand, visualize your wish, then toss the bean into running water.

**Cultivation**: Tonka is suitable for planting both in full sun and in partial shade, making it both a good option for reforestation and for agroforestry systems. If couramin or oil uses find new markets, this fast-growing leguminous tree could make an interesting multipurpose component in regional agroforestry schemes.

**Toodys hatte,** See Toadstool

**Tormentil** (*Potentilla tormentilla*) also known as bloodroot, septfoil, thormantle, biscuits, shepherd's knapperty, shepherd's knot, English sarsaparilla, red root

**Description:** Tormentil (Potentilla erecta) is a perennial herb of the family Rosaceae native to Europe, western Siberia and the Azores. It has a stout, almost tubular rootstock which has astringent qualities and is used for tanning. the stems are long, slender and hairy. the leaves are divided into three or five oval, wedge-shaped leaflets, and the yellow flowers have four or five petals.

**Influence:** Protection, Love, Avoid Possession, Repel Evil

**Gender**; Masculine, **Element**: Fire, **Planet**: Sun

The infusion is drunk to give protection, or given to a loved one to keep their love. Mediums drink it to guard themselves against permanent possession by spirits. Hang the plant up in the home to drive away evil. Carry to attract love.

**Cultivation**: Grows in damp meadows, dry pastures, hills and marshes. open woods, moorlands. The tormentil's buttercup-like golden-yellow flowers secrete a nectar that attracts pollinating insects to pollinate it, however in wet weather or at night, when the petals close up, the tormentil flower has the ability to pollinate itself. It prefers light acid soils.

**Trefoil,** See Clover

**Trillium** (*Trillium* spp.)

**Description:** Perennial herb from the lillium family; stem unbranched with 3 leaves at the top; flower solitary, either erect above the leaves or pendant on a curved stalk, 3-parted, white, yellow, pink, or maroon-purple; fruit a berry. Trillium is one of many plants whose seeds are spread by ants and mice. Trillium seeds have a fleshy organ called an elaiosome that attracts ants. The ants take the seeds to their nest, where they eat the elaiosomes and put the seeds in their garbage, where they can be protected until they germinate. They also get the added bonus of growing in a medium made richer by the ant garbage.

**Influence:** Money, Love

**Gender**; Feminine, **Element**: Water, **Planet**: Venus

Carry to attract money and luck. The root of this plant is rubbed onto the body to attract love.

**Cultivation**: Liliums can be propagated by division of the bulbs, by growing-on *bulbils* which are adventitious bulbs formed on the stem, by scaling, for which whole scales are detached from the bulb and planted to form a new bulb, or from seed; though seed germination patterns are variable and can be complex.

**Tulip** (*Tulipa* spp.) also known as Beth Root

**Description:** Tulip (Tulipa) is a genus of about 100 species of flowering plants in the family Liliaceae. They are perennial bulbous plants growing to 10–70 centimetres tall, with a small number of strap-shaped, waxy-textured, usually glaucous green leaves and large flowers with six petals. The fruit is a dry capsule containing numerous flat disc-shaped seeds.

**Influence:** Money, Luck, Protection, Love

**Gender**; Feminine, **Element**: Earth, **Planet**: Moon

Worn to safeguard against poverty and bad luck. "Tulip" means "turban" and is often worn in turbans for protection. Placed on the altar during love spells.

**Cultivation**: Tulips cannot be grown in the open in tropical climates, as they require a cold winter season to grow successfully. Manipulation of the tulip's growing temperature can, however, allow growers to "force" tulips to flower earlier than they normally would. Tulips can be grown in either of two ways: through offsets or seed. Being genetic clones of the parent plant, offsets are the only way to enlarge the stock of a given tulip cultivar. By contrast, tulips do not come true from seed; the mixing of genes between parent tulips is very unpredictable. A tulip grown from seed will usually bear only a passing resemblance to the flower from which the seeds were taken. This makes for great potential in breeding new tulip flowers, and great variation in the wild. However, tulip growers must be patient: offsets often take at least a year to grow to sufficient size to flower, and a tulip grown from seed will not flower for anywhere between five and seven years after planting.

**Turmeric** (*Cucurma longa*)

**Description:** A perennial plant of the ginger family, native to India and parts of Asia. Propagated in spring from thick knobbly roots, called rhizomes, which have thick, side-shoots called 'fingers'. Leaf stalks rise to 1 metre or more high. Leaves are lanceshaped. Floral spikes 20cm long, with thick clusters of palegreen pockets with creamy/yellow foxglove-like flowers peeping out of each pocket, and a mild spicy aroma.

**Influence:** Purification

Salt water and turmeric are mixed together and sprinkled in the area to be purified, sometimes with a ti leaf. Sometimes scattered on the floor or about the magick circle for protection.

**Gender**_____, **Element**_____, **Planet:** _____

**Cultivation:** Turmeric needs rich moist soil, ample water and a warm, sunny location. In cooler climates it can be grown in a greenhouse or conservatory. It needs generous feeding, preferably with animal manure. Plant the rhizomes in spring and lift them around 7 months later or when the lower leaves begin to yellow. Choose pieces of rhizome with healthy buds to replant for next year's crop.

**Turnip** (*Brassica rapa*)

**Description:** The most common type of turnip is mostly white-skinned apart from the upper 1–6 centimeters, which protrude above the ground and are purple, red, or greenish wherever sunlight has fallen. This above-ground part develops from stem tissue, but is fused with the root. The interior flesh is entirely white. The entire root is roughly conical, but occasionally squircle in shape, about 5–20 centimeters in diameter, and lacks side roots. The taproot (the normal root below the swollen storage root) is thin and 10 centimeters or more in length; it is trimmed off before marketing. The leaves grow directly from the above-ground shoulder of the root, with little or no visible crown or neck. Turnip leaves are sometimes eaten, and resemble mustard greens; varieties specifically grown for the leaves resemble mustard greens more than those grown for the roots, with small or no storage roots. Varieties of B. rapa that have been developed only for use as leaves are called Chinese cabbage. Both leaves and root have a pungent flavor similar to raw cabbage or radishes that becomes mild after cooking. roots weigh up to about 1 kilogram, although they can be harvested when smaller. Size is partly a function of variety and partly a function of the length of time that the hot turnip has grown. Most very small turnips (also called baby turnips) are speciality varieties. These are only available when freshly harvested and do not keep well. Most baby turnips can be eaten whole, including their leaves. Baby turnips come in yellow-, orange-, and red-fleshed varieties as well as white-fleshed. Their flavor is mild, so they can be eaten raw in salads like radishes.

**Influence:** Protection, Ending Relationships

**Gender**; Feminine, **Element**: Earth, **Planet**: Moon

Large turnips were once hollowed out on Samhain and candles were lit in them. They were carried or placed in windows to scare off evil spirits. Place a dish of turnips in front of an unwanted admirer to send him or her away. Place in the home to ward off every form of negativity.

**Cultivation**: Grown from seed, turnips are easy to grow if sown in the proper season. They mature in two months and may be planted either in the spring, late summer or autumn for roots or greens. The spring crop is planted for early summer use. The Autumn crop, which is usually larger and of higher quality, is often stored for winter use.

**Uva Ursa** (*Arctostaphylos uva-ursi*)  **POISONOUS**

**Description:** Arctostaphylos uva-ursi is a species of Arctostaphylos, one of several related species referred to as bearberry. It is a small procumbent woody shrub 5-30 cm high. The leaves are evergreen, remaining green for 1-3 years before falling. The fruit is a red berry. The leaves are shiny, small, and feel thick and stiff. They are alternately arranged on the stems. Undersides of leaves are lighter green than on the tops. New stems can be red in areas with high sun, but are otherwise green. Older growth stems are brown. In spring, they have white or pink flowers.

**Influence:** Psychic Workings

Add to sachets to increase psychic powers.

**Gender**_____, **Element**_____, **Planet:** _____

**Cultivation**: Uva Ursi rarely grows more than a 10 cm to 15 cm tall. It is best propogated from cuttings. It takes an unusually long time to root, so consider instead buying small plants from nurseries. It does poorly in rich soil, as it prefers poor soils in full sun. Once established, it spreads and becomes an attractive, hardy ground cover, surviving temperatures of -45 C.

**Valerian** (*Valeriana officinalis*)

**Description:** Valerian (Valeriana officinalis, Valerianaceae) is a hardy perennial flowering plant, with heads of sweetly scented pink or white flowers. This "sweet" smell is quite overpowering when the flower is placed into a vase. The flowers are in bloom from June to September in the northern hemisphere. Valerian was used as a perfume in the sixteenth century.

**Influence:** Sleep, Purification, Protection, Dream Magick, Reconciliations, Love and Harmony wishes.

**Gender**; Feminine, **Element**: Water, **Planet**: Venus

Use fresh herbs in sachets for dream magick and sleep protection baths, burn for reconciliations in love relationships (make sure you have all parties permission first!), drink as a harmonizing tea infusion. Place in the home or grow in the garden to aid in keeping harmony. Add to other herbs for love wishes. A sprig of this plant pinned to a woman's clothing will cause men to 'follow her like children'. Sometimes used as graveyard dust.

**Cultivation**: Valerian is a perennial plant that grows to 1 metre tall. It prefers full sun, and average to rich well-drained soil. Root cuttings are best for propagation, and once the plants are established, they self-sow and spread by root runners. Valerian has a similar effect on cats as catnip, so you may need to protect your patch with chicken wire. Harvest roots for medicinal use in the autumn of their second year.

**Vanilla** (*Vaniila aromatica* or *V. planifolia*)

**Description:** The main species harvested for vanillin is Vanilla planifolia. Although it is native to Mexico, it is now widely grown throughout the tropics. Vanilla grows as a vine, climbing up an existing tree, pole, or other support. It can be grown in a wood (on trees), in a plantation (on trees or poles), or in a "shader", in increasing orders of productivity. Left alone, it will grow as high as possible on the support, with few flowers. Every year, growers fold the higher parts of the plant downwards so that the plant stays at heights accessible by a standing human. This also greatly stimulates flowering.

**Influence:** Love, Lust, Mental Powers

**Gender**: Feminine, **Element**: Water, **Planet**: Venus

Though most often used in oil form, the whole bean is sometimes added to love charms or carried on the body to make one attractive and ready for an evening of loving. Place in sugar, and the sugar can be used to sweeten love infusions. Carry a vanilla bean to restore lost energy and to improve the mind. A vitalising herb, used by some for get up and go.

**Cultivation**: While the vanilla orchid can be cultivated in areas where the climatic conditions are suitable, the likelihood of getting the orchid flowers to set fruit is quite remote. The vines grow naturally on the forest floor where they use trees as their support by anchoring the thick stems with roots into the bark of their hosts. A mature vanilla orchid can grow to more than 20m tall! The other major problem is that the flowers are naturally fertilised only by a tiny bee native to Mexico and commercial plantations have had to devise a method of hand pollination.

**Vanilla grass,** See Sweetgrass

**Velvet Dock,** See Vervain

**Venus Flytrap** (*Dionaea muscipula*)

**Description:** The Venus Flytrap (Dionaea muscipula) is a carnivorous plant that catches and digests animal prey (mostly insects and arachnids). The trapping structure is formed by the terminal portion of each of the plant's leaves. It is a small herb, forming a rosette of four to seven leaves, which arise from a short subterranean stem that is actually a bulb-like rhizome. Each leaf reaches a maximum size of about three to seven centimeters, depending on the time of year; longer leaves with robust traps are generally formed after flowering. Flytraps that appear to have more leaves are generally colonies, formed by rosettes that have divided beneath the ground.

**Influence:** Protection, Love

**Gender**; Masculine, **Element**: Fire, **Planet**: Mars

Grown as a love attractant. Also grown in the home for protection and in order to "trap" something.

**Cultivation**: Venus Flytraps are very popular as cultivated plants, although they have a large reputation for being difficult to grow. This reputation is almost exclusively due to inappropriate treatment of the plants by retailers and their consequent ill-health on purchase. However, Venus Flytraps are safely grown in pots under conditions that mimic those in their natural habitat. Venus flytraps can be kept in pots on a patio, deck, window sill, or position in the garden that receives at least 6-8 hours of sunlight per day. In areas of lower humidity, the plant can survive with frequent watering and a drainage system to prevent fungal growth. It is also beneficial to keep it in a tray with about an 2 cm of water to maintain higher humidity levels. Stagnant water is dangerous for the plant, so using pebbles to elevate the plant from the water is safer for the plant. Venus flytraps grow better still in a greenhouse which often leads to healthy, vigorous and colourful plants. The colour of the trap leaves may be used as an indicator of sufficient light; in appropriate conditions the inside of each trap should be bright red in colour for most varieties. Venus flytraps are best grown in mixtures of sphagnum peat moss and/or peat often with the addition of sand, perlite or other inert salt free material. Soil pH should be in the range of 3.9 to 4.8. Flytraps ideally should not be watered with tap water as accumulated salts in tap water may kill carnivorous plants, both distilled water or clean rain water are ideal.

**Verbena,** See Vervain

**Vervain** (*Verbena officinalis*)

**Description:** Verbena (verbenas or vervains) is a genus of annual and perennial herbaceous or semi-woody flowering plants with about 250 species in the family Verbenaceae. The majority of the species are native to the New World from Canada south to southern Chile, but some are also native in the Old World, mainly in Europe including Common Vervain (V. officinalis) and V. supina. Several species in this genus are of natural hybrid origin. The leaves are usually opposite, simple, and in many species hairy, often densely so. The flowers are small, with five petals, and borne in dense spikes. Typically some shade of blue, they may also be white, pink, or purple, especially in cultivars.

**Influence:** Love, Protection, Purification, Peace, Money, Youth, Chastity, Sleep, Healing.

**Gender**: Feminine. **Planet**: Venus. **Element**: Earth. **Deities**: Cerridwen, Mars, Venus, Aradia, Jupiter, Thor, Juno

The Witches Herb. Empowers any magick, especially love spells. Enhances the dreaming process and is recommended for dream quests. Used to consecrate and empower any ritual tools. Recommended for cleansing baths and incenses before working magick as it both cleanses and protects any negative influences. Protects from negative emotions and depression. Used in house and home blessings. Turns back negativity. In love spells: add to recipes to attract mates, find true love, achieve sexual fulfilment, work sexual magick, an for bringing extra bliss on the wedding night. The herb of poets, singers, and bards. Inspires artistry. Instills a love of learning. Best when gathered at Midsummer. A crown of this herb worn on the head protects you while invoking spirits. Also used in money and prosperity spells. To discover if an ill person will live or die, put it in your hand and press it against the patient so that it is undetected, and ask them how they feel. If they are hopeful, they will live, if not, they may die. If vervain is placed in a baby's cradle, the child will grow up with a happy disposition and a love of learning. Burn this to dispel unrequited love.

**Cultivation**: Grown from seed, Vervain is a perennial herb that grows 30cm to 60 cm tall. It prefers full sun, average to rich soils, and is grown throughout temperate climates. It is rather short-lived, but self-sows. Harvest leaves and flower tops as the plants bloom.

**Vetch, Giant** (*Vicia* spp.)

**Description:** This native perennial species of the Pea Family has 10 to 16 leaves consisting of 5 to 8 pairs of linear to oblong-linear leaflets, often toothed or lobed, on smooth stems with many tendrils. The numerous leaflets distinguish it from other pea-like climbers. The drooping flowers are red to lavender-purple and grow in clusters of 6 to 15.

**Influence:** Fidelity

**Gender**; Feminine, **Element**: Earth, **Planet**: Venus

If your loved one has gone astray, rub the root of this plant on your body, then wrap it in cloth and place under your pillow. This will remind him or her that you're still there, waiting.

**Gender**_____, **Element**_____, **Planet:** _____

**Cultivation**: It grows even on sterile dirt, though is at its exuberant best in rich soil, with plentiful sunshine. Shade stunts vetch horribly. Nitrogen-fixing root swellings are easily viewed when you yank-up a vetch from the ground. Given good conditions, a vetch plant luxuriates and sends forth numerous long stems in all directions, making a substantial mass of tangled vegetation. When you weed-out such a vigorous plant, its tendrils sometimes break off and other times defiantly bring shredded bits of other plants with them. In late summer it shrivels up, and after winter's frosts there is only a faded brown memory of its twining stems' former lushness. The seeds can sprout during any month, needing only the right amount of moisture to do so.

**Vetiver** (*Vertiveria zizanioides*)

**Description:** A dense, clumping, non-running, perennial grass to 1.5 metres tall, native to Asia; growing from a deep, thick, matting root system that can delve deep into the earth 1-3 metres. Leaves 8mm wide stand stiff and erect. Whorled flower stems, usually taller than the leaves, have fine grass-like flowers with a bronze tinge. Some forms of vetiver do not produce viable seed, but be aware that varieties have been available in Australia that do set viable seed, which could have the effect of establishing where not wanted.

**Influence:** Love, Hex Breaking, Luck, Money, Anti-Theft

**Gender**; Feminine, **Element**: Earth, **Planet**: Venus

Burned to overcome evil spells. Used in love powders, sachets, and incenses, and is added to the bathwater in a sachet to make yourself attractive to the opposite sex. Used in money spells and mixtures, placed in the cash register to increase business, carried to attract luck, and burned in anti-theft incenses.

**Cultivation**: Propagation is by division of roots. These slips, with leaf tops cut off to 15cm and the root base trimmed to 10cm, can be established in pots or planted direct into position

**Violet** (*Viola odorata*)

**Description:** A small perennial, clump forming plant growing to 29cm. Flowers are strongly perfumed blue/violet and appear in late winter. Viloets are favourite garden border flower.

**Influence:** Protection, Love, Lust, Luck, Wishes, Peace, Healing

**Gender**: Feminine, **Element**: Water, **Planet**: Venus

These are wonderful for using in amulets for good luck and fortune. Given also to newly married couples and babies. They also work well in spells for lust and passion they are powerful love stimulants and also arouse lust, .try mixing them with Lavender Flowers for a potent combination Added to other love herbs for all types of love wishes. Have a spray of violets on hand when working night magick and to aid in divination and spirituality. They are also useful in spells for protection, wishes, peace, and healing . A powerful lust inducer if burned with lavender.

**Cultivation**: Preferring filtered light or part shade it can tolerate full sun in cooler climates. Somewhat drought resistant, but prefers moist, well drained, humus rich soil. Propagation by division in the autumn or by seeds in winter.

**Virginia Snakeroot,** see Snakeroot

**Wallwort,** See Comfrey

**Walnut** (*Juglans regia*)

**Description:** Walnuts are trees that grow to 20 metres tall. They prefer full sun, deep and well-drained soil, and regular water.

**Influence:** Health, Mental Powers, Infertility, Wishes

**Gender**: Masculine, **Element**: Fire, **Planet**: Sun

Carry to strengthen the heart and to ward off the pain of rheumatism. Don't carry one in a lightning storm because they attract lightning. Your wishes will be fulfilled if someone gives you a bag of walnuts. Place in a hat or around the head to prevent headaches and sunstroke. If a bride-to-be wishes not to have children right away, she should place in her bodice as many roasted walnuts as years she wants to remain childless. This must be done on her wedding day.

**Cultivation**: Preferring full sun and deep, well drained soil, walnut trees can be purchased from nurseries.

**Water-lily** See Lotus

**Water Parsley** see Hemlock

**Waxberry,** See Myrtle

**Wax Plant** (*Hoya carnosa*)

**Description:** Fast growing hoya with a compact habit suited for baskets or trained on ladders. Flowers 1cm across come in bunches of 20 to 40 hanging from along the stems. Hardy and easily grown in any environment, free flowers with a very good scent.

**Influence:** Protection, Power

**Gender**; Masculine, **Element**: Air, **Planet**: Mercury

Grown in bedrooms and throughout the house for protection. The flowers are dried and kept as protective amulets, and are also placed on the altar to give spells extra power.

**Cultivation**: Hoya Carnos prefers Light Shade and produces Pale Pink waxy flowers all year round in mild climates. This plant is suitable for growing indoors, Water regularly; do not overwater. It can be propagated from herbaceous stem cuttings and woody stem cuttings with seed pods allowed to dry on plant before breakin open to collect seeds. Seed does not store well; sow as soon as possible Do not remove the spent flower stalks as they will bloom again later.

**Wheat** (*Triticum* spp.)

**Description:** Wheat is a domesticated grass from the Levant that is cultivated worldwide. Globally, wheat is an important human food, its production being second only to maize among the cereal crops; rice ranks third. Wheat grain is a staple food used to make flour for leavened, flat and steamed breads; cookies, cakes, pasta, noodles and couscous; and for fermentation . Wheat is planted to a limited extent as a forage crop for livestock, and the straw can be used as fodder for livestock or as a construction material for roofing thatch

**Influence:** Fertility, Money

**Gender**; Feminine, **Element**: Earth, **Planet**: Venus

Carried or eaten to induce fertility and conception. Sheaves of wheat are placed in the home to attract money, and grains are carried in sachets for the same reason.

**Cultivation**: Grown from seed. Varieties exist for all climates. wheat normally requires between 110 and 130 days between planting and harvest, depending upon climate, seed type, and soil conditions.

**Wild Lemon see** Mandrake

**Willow** (*Salix alba*)

**Description:** The willows all have abundant watery juice, furrowed scaly bark which is heavily charged with salicylic acid, soft, pliant, tough wood, slender branches and large fibrous often stoloniferous roots. These roots are remarkable for their toughness, size, and tenacity of life. The leaves are typically elongated but may also be round to oval, frequently with a serrated margin. All the buds are lateral; no absolutely terminal bud is ever formed. These are covered by a single scale, inclosing at its base two minute opposite buds, alternate with two, small, scale-like, fugacious, opposite leaves. The leaves are alternate except the first pair which fall when about 2 cm long. They are simple, feather-veined, and typically linear-lanceolate. Usually they are serrate, rounded at base, acute or acuminate. In color they show a great variety of greens, ranging from yellow to blue.

**Influence:** Love, Divination, Protection, Healing and Moon Magick.

**Gender**: Feminine, **Element**: Water, **Planet**: Moon

The wood is often used in the making of magickal wands and tools. It is also considered a sacred WISHING tree. Used when working with spirits and all healing wishes, wear a sprig when someone close to you passes. Place on the altar for all moon magick wishes and for all divination. All parts of the tree guard against evil. To conjure spirits, crush willow bark and burn it outside with sandalwood during the waning Moon.

**Cultivation**: Willows prefer damp, low spaces, as a long rivers and streams, or areas that receive regular water. Willow grows easily from cuttings but is available from nurseries. It grows to 65 metres or more depending on variety.

**Wintergreen** (*Gaultheria procumbens*) also known as Teaberry. Boxberry. Mountain Tea. Checkerberry. Aromatic Wintergreen. Partridge Berry. Deerberry.

**Description:** Wintergreen is an evergreen ground cover known for its red-tinted winter leaves and red winter berries. Wintergreen grows best in regions with cool summers

**Influence:** Protection, Good Fortune, Spiritual Protection

**Gender**; Feminine, **Element**: Water, **Planet**: Moon

Placed in children's pillows to protect them and give them good fortune throughout their lives. Placed on the altar to call good spirits to watch and aid in your magick.

**Cultivation**: Propagation by division, it grows from a creeping underground stem that lies just below the surface of the soil. From this "root" individual plants rise some 5 to 15 centimetres. Give Wintergreen good, organic, well drained, acidic soil and shade. The better the soil, the more quickly it will spread.

**Witchbane,** See Rowan

**Witchen,** See Rowan

**Witches Bells,** See Foxglove

**Witches Berry see** Belladonna

**Witches Broom see** Mistletoe

**Witches Thimbles see** Foxglove

**Witch Grass** (*Agropyron repens*) Also known as Quackgrass

**Description:** Witch Grass-Agropyron repens--is a perennial weed, and a troublesome weed to eliminate from the home landscape. Quackgrass grows from underground rhizomes to an unmowed height of 30 cm to 1.2 metres. It has thin, flat, bright ashy green leaf blades and the seed spike grows from 7cm to 20cm long. Each quackgrass plant produces about 25 seeds; they remain viable 3 to 5 years in the soil. It takes 2 to 3 months for a newly germinated plant to develop rhizomes. It is very important to eliminate the plants before they reach this stage

**Influence:** Love, Hex Breaking, Disperse Spirits and Depression

**Gender**; Masculine, **Planet**: Jupiter

Carried or sprinkled under the bed to attract new lovers. Used in unhexing and uncrossing rituals. The infusion is sprinkled around the premises to disperse spirits. Dispels depressions when worn.

**Cultivation**: As agrass it is grown from seed, or transplanted root cuttings. BEWARE it is an ivasive weed.

**Witch Hazel** (*Hamamelis virginica*)

**Description:** Witch Hazel is a shrub or small tree that grows 1.5 – 5 meters to in height. It prefers full sun, and average soils.

**Influence:** Protection, Chastity

**Gender**; Masculine, **Element**: Fire, **Planet**: Sun

The forked twigs of the Witch Hazel are used for divining. It will help heal a broken heart and cool passions when carried. The bark and twigs are used to protect against evil.

**Cultivation**: Witch hazel should be grown in moist soil in a semi-shaded location. It is unsuitable for sub-tropical and tropical areas.

**Witchwood,** see Rowan

**Woodbine,** see Honeysuckle

**Wolf's Bane** see Aconite

**Wonder of the World Root,** See GinSeng

**Wood Avens,** See Avens

**Wood Rose** (*Ipomoea tuberosa*)

**Description:** Aggressive tropical vine with its large leaves digitately parted into 5-7 lobes. May be grown indoors if sufficient bright light and warmth are provided. Flowers yellow with globular fruit in the form of a woody pod which when open looks like a wooden rose making it very desirable to florists for special arrangements. Seeds are nearly marble size and covered with a velvety black pubescence. It can climb on adjacent trees or shrubs & smother them. Dried pods resemble brown roses hence the common name.

**Influence:** Luck

Carry a wood rose to bring good luck and fortune. Place some in the home to draw luck there too.

**Gender**_____, **Element**_____, **Planet:** _____

**Cultivation**: Propagation from seeds or stem cuttings, Wood Rose likes full sun. Keep well watered.

**Woodruff** (*Asperula odorata*)

**Description:** Woodruff is an herbaceous perennial which formes wide colonies of slender stems about 15cm in height. The leaves look like spokes of a wheel, bright green in colour. Small white tubular flowers open in clusters at the end of the stems.

**Influence:** Victory, Protection, Money, Purification

Used to clear away the closeness and drabness of winter. Carry when wishing to turn over a new leaf, or to change your outlook in life, especially in the spring. Add to the May Wine. Brings victory to those who carry it.

**Gender**_____, **Element**_____, **Planet:** _____

**Cultivation**: Propagation is easiest by division though seed can be sown in spring. Preferring soil with a high organic content, Woodruff will grow in poorer soils. Part shade or dappled light is best but in cooler areas with moist soil it tolerates full sun. Woodruff makes good ground cover under trees and shrubs. Best contained by pavers or edging around the bed.

**Woody Nightshade,** See Bittersweet

**Wormwood** *(Artemisia absinthium)*

**Description:** Wormwood is a woody shrub growing to 2 metres tall and several meters wide with silver grey foliage. It is a very hardy plant, adapting to very hot and very cold conditions.

**Influence:** Psychic Powers, Protection, Love, Calling Spirits

**Gender**; Masculine, **Element**: Fire, **Planet**: Mars

Burned in incenses designed to aid in developing psychic powers, and is also worn for this purpose. Carried, it protects from bewitchment and sea-serpent bites, and it counteracts the effects of poisoning by hemlock and toadstools (that's stretching it a little though...). Hang from the rearview mirror to protect your car from accidents on dangerous roads. Sometimes used in love infusions. Was once made into an alcohlic beverage called absinthe. It's dangerous, highly addictive, and illegal. Place under the bed to draw a loved one. Burned to summon spirits; sometimes mixed with sandalwood for this purpose. If burned in a graveyard, the spirits will rise and speak.

**Cultivation**: Wormwood does best in a sunny, warm, well-drained position though it will tolerate partial shade. Add plenty of organic material and some blood and bone to the soil before planting. Propagate plants from seed sown in spring or by tip cuttings in late Autumn. Pinch out plants to encourage bushy growth and prune back after flowering. The plants release chemicals into the soil which inhibit the growth of competing plants.

**Wymote see** Althea

**Yarrow** *(Achillea millefolium)*

**Description:** Yarrow is an attractive fern like, finely divided green leaved plant growing up to 50cm in temperate climates. It can become invasive.

**Influence:** Courage, Love, Psychic Powers, Exorcism

**Gender**; Feminine, **Element**: Water, **Planet**: Venus

Carried as a sachet or amulet it repels or rids of negative influences, also works to draw courage and to purify (exorcism). Drink as a tea to increase your psychic powers. Wear a sprig of yarrow for protection. Hold some in your hands when you are afraid. This will stop all fear and give you courage. Carry some with you to draw love. Said to keep a newly married couple together and any upsetting influences out of the relationship and their love alive.

**Cultivation**: Yarrow needs a well-drained sunny position and is not fussy about soil type. Plants can be divided in autumn or spring, or seed can be sown in spring. Yarrow dies down over winter and should be cut back to ground level. It will regenerate when the weather warms up.

**Yawroot,** See Stillengia

**Yellow Evening Primrose** (*Oenothera biennis*)

**Description:** Evening primrose is a flowering plant originally native to North America that now grows throughout much of Europe and parts of Asia. It blooms every other year and its large, fragrant yellow flowers open at dusk and remain open through the night.

**Influence:** Hunting, Snakes

Native Americans rubbed this plant on their shoes and body to ensure a good hunt and to drive away snakes.

**Gender**_____, **Element**_____, **Planet:** _____

**Cultivation**: They grow well in any ordinary situation, in welldrained, moderately rich soil. They need moisture and the soil should be prepared as deeply as it is possible to get good moisture. The clumps need not be transplanted often. Many of the species increase by producing small tufted plants at the base of the old ones. When the plants are divided it should be done in early Spring. They are easily grown from seeds, and self seed, potentially taking over the garden.

**Yerba Mate** (*Ilex paraguariensis*)

**Description:** Hardy, attractive evergreen bush to small tree, up to 6 metres high, which is drought hardy and light frost tolerant. Dark green, glossy, elliptic-shaped leaves to 10cm with fine, serrated margins. Petite, white flowers are inconspicuous, as they set close in the leaf axils. Small round seeds form in a bright red 5mm berry which makes the bush most attractive, giving it a similar appearance to Holly (Ilex aquifolium) to which it is related.

**Influence:** Fidelity, Love, Lust

**Gender**; Masculine

Wear to attract the opposite sex. Use the infusion as a lust potion and share with a loved one to ensure that you stay together. Spill some on the ground to end the relationship.

**Gender**_____, **Element**_____, **Planet:** _____

**Cultivation**: The natural habitat, as well as the area of cultivation, is limited to the South America, more precisely to the zone between the Atlantic Ocean and Paraguay river. Seed is the most common reproduction technique. The advantage of sexual propagation (seed) lies in the fact that the variability in descendants may give rise to individuals better suited to different environments (which on other occasions may not be desired). When the seeds are harvested they must be stratified or sown immediately, otherwise they quickly lose their viability. The relatively short period of viability together with the low germination rate have undoubtedly been the cause of the difficulties in its cultivation spreading to other continents in the past. Grafting, propagation by cuttings and layering are not very widespread. It is relatively difficult to obtain rooted cuttings and this is generally achieved by using young branches from the stools, irrespective of whether plant hormone treatment is used.

## Yerba Santa (*Eriodictyon californicum*)

**Description:** A low shrubby evergreen plant that grows up to 1.2 metres. The smooth stem and thick yellow leaves are covered with a resin, and the plant has blue flowers that cluster together in groups of six to 10. The leaves are 5–12 cm long. The leaves should be gathered in the spring and early summer

**Influence:** Beauty, Healing, Psychic Powers, Protection

**Gender**; Feminine

Carry to improve or attain beauty, or add the infusion to the bath for the same reason. The leaves are added to healing incenses and are also worn around the neck to ward off illness and injury. Carry for spiritual strength, to increase psychic powers, and for protection.

**Gender**_____, **Element**_____, **Planet:** _____

**Cultivation**: Gather seeds as the fruit capsules ripen. Yerba Santa seeds can be planted in the autumn or early spring. The seeds will store indefinitely if kept in a dry, cool location. Prior to sowing, mix the seeds with several parts of moist sand. This helps to ensure even distribution. Seeds can be sown directly into a prepared bed or into flats filled with a mixture of equal amounts of soil, sand, and leafmold. The seed coat can be scarified in order to allow moisture and air to enter. This may be accomplished by rubbing the seeds between two pieces of sandpaper. Adding charate burned and ground plant stems to the soil may also increase germination success. When the seedlings are large enough to handle they should be transplanted into larger pots. The plants can be placed into the ground the following spring. The plants are sunloving and do not tolerate shade. Plants may be grown in any texture of soil but prefer it to be slightly acidic and moderately fertile. The shallow roots allow them to establish in thin as well as deep soils. When selecting a site keep in mind that after two years Yerba Santa can reproduce vegetably through rhizomes. These underground stems can spread as much as 2.5 m in one year under excellent conditions and may overrun other plants. This vegetative spread results in cloned patches with plants spaced from 20 to 25cm apart.

## Yew (*Taxus baccata*) 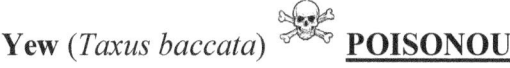 **POISONOUS**

**Description:** It is a small to medium-sized evergreen tree, growing 10-20 m tall, with a trunk up to 2 m diameter. The bark is thin, scaly brown, coming off in small flakes aligned with the stem. The leaves are lanceolate, flat, dark green, 1-4 cm long and 2-3 mm broad, arranged spirally on the stem, but with the leaf bases twisted to align the leaves in two flat rows either side of the stem, except on erect leading shoots where the spiral arrangement is more obvious. The leaves are highly poisonous. The seed cones are highly modified, each cone containing a single seed 4-7 mm long partly surrounded by a modified scale which develops into a soft, bright red berry-like structure called an aril

**Influence:** Raise Dead Spirits

**Gender**; Feminine, **Element**: Water, **Planet**: Saturn

Sometimes used in spells to raise the spirits of the dead. Used little today because of its high toxicity.

**Cultivation**: Most Yews bear either male or female flowers, although very occasionally a tree can be found which have flowers of both sexes born on different branches. In Nature the seeds lie on the ground for about 18 months in all weathers before they will germinate. If you want to grow Yews from seed, it is therefore best to imitate this lengthy process before planting them. Yews are more often grown from cutting or by layering the branches. It is also possible to graft Yew. If you live anywhere near Yew trees, you can also keep your eyes open to see if you can spot any seedlings, which may not have room to grow where they germinated and may be glad to find a new home. Young trees are well able to cope with shade.

**Yohimbe** (*Pausinystalia yohimbe*)  **POISONOUS**

**Description:** Yohimbe is the name of the bark of a tall evergreen tree in western Africa known as Pausinystalia yohimbe.

**Influence:** Lust, Love

The infusion is drunk as a lust potion, but only in small amounts. The powedered herb is added to love mixtures.

**Gender**: Male, **Element**: Fire, **Planet**: Mars

**Cultivation**: The bark is gathered at any time of year. An evergreen tree, it grows to a height of 30m with a spread of 8m. The stem is erect and branching, the leaves are oval, acuminate and about 10cm long; the seeds are small winged slivers, almost paper thin. A native of the rainforests of Nigeria, Cameroon and the Congo, it prefers rich soils in a protected part sun to shady position, and is drought and frost tender. Propagation is by seed or cuttings and can be difficult. Seed is sown in a free draining seed mix or sphagnum moss and will need temperatures above 25 deg C to germinate quickly. Seeds have a very short viability, which declines rapidly in dry and warm conditions.

**Yucca** (*Yucca* spp.)

**Description:** The yucca plant is native to the high deserts of the southwestern United States and Mexico. It is a wonderful, stately evergreen with huge, fragrant, ivory-white, flower panicles and marvelous, sword-like leaves that spread outwards from a basal rosette to give the whole plant a special sculptural or architectural quality.

**Influence:** Transmutation, Protection, Purification

**Gender**: Masculine, **Element**: Fire, **Planet**: Mars

Yucca is used to treat joint pain caused by arthritis, and to reduce inflammation in the joints. Shampoo made from the root is used to treat dandruff and other scalp conditions. Yucca protects your home from evil influences. It can be used to make a soap and/or shampoo that is used to cleanse the body prior to rituals. The Navajo use it to cleanse and purify, as do the Hopi. A hoop of twisted yucca fibers will transmute a person if he/she jumps through it, or you may wear a crown of it on your head. Soap made from the yucca plant is used to purify the body before magick

**Cultivation**: They thrive best in reasonably fertile soils that are well-drained and have the capacity to retain moisture in dry weather. They are reliable and very easy to grow on most sites, providing they have good drainage. Under no circumstances will they tolerate poor drainage or waterlogged conditions. The only maintenance that is required is to occasionally remove old leaves and the flowering stalk after flowering to prevent the formation of unwanted seeds. Choose the site carefully because once they become established the deep, tuberous taproots can be difficult to remove, with portions often persisting to sprout and re-emerge. Propagate from seed or cutting the side shoots.

**Zebrovka,** See Sweetgrass

# Section 7 - Index

Acacia, 38
Aconite, 38
African Violet, 39
Agaric, 39, 89, 141
Agrimony, 39
Alfalfa, 40
Allspice, 40
Almond, 40
Aloe, 41, 148
Aloes, Wood, 41
Althea, 42
Alyssum, 42
Amaranth, 42
American Mandrake. *See* May Apple
American Nightshade. *See* Poke
Anemone, 43
Angelica, 43
Anise, 43
Apple, 44
Apricot, 44
Arabic Gum. *See* Gum Arabic
Arbutus, 45
Aromatic Wintergreen. *See* Wintergreen
Artemis Herb. *See* Mugwort
Artemisia. *See* Mugwort
Asafoetida, 45
Ash, 45
Aspen, 46
Aster, 46
Avens, 47
Avocado, 47
Bachelor's Buttons, 47
Balm of Gilead, 48
Balm, Lemon, 48
Bamboo, 48
Banana, 49
Banewort. *See* Belladona
Banyan, 49
Barley, 50
Basil, 50
Bay, 51
Bayberry Tree. *See* Myrtle
Bean, 51
Bedstraw, 51
Beech, 52
Beet, 52
Belladonna, 53
Benzoin, 53
Bergamot, 53
Be-Still, 54
Beth Root. *See Trillium*

Betony, Wood, 54
Birch, 55
Biscuits. *See Tormentil*
Bison Grass. *See* Sweetgrass
Bistort, 55
Bittersweet, 55
Black Nightshade. *See* Henbane
Blackberry, 56
Bladderwrack, 56
Bleeding Heart, 56
Blessed Thistle. *See* Tea
Bloodroot, 57
Blue Buttons. *See* Periwinkle
Blue Flag, 58
Bluebell, 57
Blueberry, 58
Bodhi, 59
Boneset, 59
Borage, 59
Boxberry,. *See* Wintergreen
Bracken, 60
Brazil Nut, 60
Bromeliad, 61
Broom, 61
Bruisewort. *See* Comfrey
Bryony, 60
Buchu, 62
Buckeye. *See* Horse Chestnut
Buckthorn, 62
Buckwheat, 63
Buffalo grass. *See* Sweetgrass
Buglos. *See* Borage
Burdock, 63
Burn Plant. *See* Aloe
Buttons. *See* Tansy
Cabbage, 64
Cactus, 64
Calamus, 65
Calendula. *See* Marigold
Camellia, 65
Camphor, 66
Cancer Jalap. *See* Poke
Candleberry. *See* Myrtle
Caraway, 66
Cardamom, 67
Carnation, 67
Carob, 67
Carragheen. *See* Irish Moss
Carrot, 68
Cascara Sagrada, 68
Cashew, 68
Castor, 69

Catchweed. *See* Bedstraw
Catmint. *See* Catnip
Catnip, 70
Catsfoot. *See* Ground Ivy
Cattail, 70
Cedar, 71
Celandine, 71
Celery, 72
Centaury, 72
Chamomile, 72
Checkerberry. *See* Wintergreen
Cherry, 73
Chestnut, 73
Chickweed, 74
Chicory, 74
Chilli Pepper, 74
China Berry, 75
Chinese Parsley. *See* Coriander
Chrysanthemum, 75
Church Steeples. *See* Burdock
Cilantro. *See* Coriander
Cinnamon, 76, 202
Cinquefoil, 77
Citron, 77
Cleavers. *See* Bedstraw
Clover, 78
Cloves, 78
Club Moss, 79
Coakum. *See* Poke
Cocklebur. *See* Burdock
Cockup Hat. *See* Stillengia
Coconut, 79
Cohosh, Black, 80
Coltsfoot, 80
Columbine, 81
Comfrey, 81
Compas Weed. *See* Rosemary
Copal, 82
Coriander, 82
Corn, 83
Cotton, 83
Coughwort. *See* Ginger
Cowslip, 84
Crampweed. *See* Cinquefoil
Crocus, 84
Cucumber, 84
Cumin, 85
Curry, 85
Cyclamen, 86
Cypress, 86

Daffodil, 87
Daisy, 87
Damiana, 88
Dandelion, 88
Deadly Nightshade. *See* Belladonna
Deadmen's Bells. *See* Foxglove
Death Angel. *See* Agaric
Death Cap. *See* Agaric
Death's Herb. *See* Belladonna
Deerberry. *See* Wintergreen
Deerstongue, 89
Devil's Cherries. *See* Belladonna
Devil's Eye. *See* Henbane
Dill, 89
Dock, 90
Dogbane, 90
Dog's Finger. *See* Foxglove
Dogwood, 91
Donkey's Ear. *See* Mullein
Dragon's Blood, 91
Drunkard. *See* Marigold
Duck's Foot. *See* May Apple
Dulse, 92
Dutchman's Britches, 93
Dwale. *See* Belladonna
Ebony, 93
Echinacea, 94
Edelwiess, 94
Egyptian White Water Lily. *See* Lotus
Elder, 95
Elecampane, 95
Elf Leaf. *See* Rosemary
ElkWeed. *See* Deerstongue
Elm, 96
Endive, 96
English Sarsaparilla. *See* Tormentil
Eucalyptus, 97
Eye of the Star. *See* Horehound
Eyebright, 97
Fairy Clock. *See* Dandelion
Fairy Cup. *See* Cowslip
Fairy Fingers. *See* Foxglove
Fairy Thimbles. *See* Foxglove
Featherfew. *See* Feverfew
Febrifuge. *See* Feverfew
Felon Plant. *See* Mugwort
Felonwort. *See* Bittersweet
Fennel, 98
Fenugreek, 99
Fern, 99

© Copyright 2001 Robert Haigh

Fever Twig. *See* Bittersweet
Feverfew, 100
Fig, 100
Figwort, 101
Five Finger Blossom. *See* Cinquefoil
Five Finger Grass. *See* Cinquefoil
Flanel Leaf. *See* Mullein
Flax, 101
Fleabane, 102
Florentine Iris. *See* Orris
Fox Bells. *See* Foxglove
Foxglove, 102
Frankincense, 103
Frogge stoles. *See* Toadstool
Frogstooles. *See* Toadstool
Furze. *See* Broom
Galangal, 103
Gardenia, 103
Garget. *See* Poke
Garlic, 104
Gentian, 104
Geranium, 105
Gill-Over-the-Ground. *See* Ground Ivy
Ginger, 105
Ginseng, 106
Goats Leaves. *See* Honeysuckle
Goats Rue, 106
Golden Bough. *See* Mistletoe
Goldenrod, 106
Goldenseal, 107
Goosegrass. *See* Bedstraw
Gorse, 107
Gotu Kola, 107
Gourd, 108
Grain, 108
Grains of Paradise, 109
Grape, 109
Grass, 109
Gravel Root. *See* Meadowsweet
Green Ginger. *See* Wormwood
Ground Ivy, 110
Groundsel, 110
Gulfwrack. *See* Bladderwrack
Gum Arabic, 110
Gum Plant. *See* Comfrey
Hag's Tapers. *See* Mullein
Hagthorn. *See* Hawthorn
Hawaiian Good-luck-plant. *See* Ti
Hawthorn, 111
Hazel, 111
Hearts Ease. *See* Pansy

Heath. *See* Heather
Heather, 112
Heliotrope, 112
Hellebore, Black, 113
Helmet Flower. *See* Skullcap
Hemlock, 113, 116
Hemp, 114
Henbane, 114
Henbells. *See* Henbane
Henna, 115
Herb Bennet. *See* Hemlock
Herb of Circe. *See* Mandrake
Herb of Grace. *See* Rue
Hibiscus, 116
Hickory, 116
High John the Conqueror, 117
Hog Apple. *See* May Apple
Hogsbean. *See* Henbane
Holly, 117
Holy Ghost Herb. *See* Tea
Holy grass. *See* Sweetgrass
Holy Wood. *See* Mistletoe
Honesty, 118
Honeysuckle, 119
Hooded Skullcap. *See* Skullcap
Hoodwort. *See* Skullcap
Hops, 120
Horehound, 120
Horse Chestnut, 120
Horse's Hoof. *See* Ginger
Horseradish, 121
Horsetail, 121
Houndstongue, 121
Houseleek, 122
Huckleberry, 122
Hyacinth, 123
Hydrangea, 123
Hyssop, 124
Indian Bay. *See* Bay
Indian Paint. *See* Bloodroot
Indian Paint Brush, 124
Inkberry. *See* Poke
Iris, 125
Irish Moss, 125
Ivy, 126
Jasmine, 126
Jobs Tears, 126
Joe Pye Weed, 127
Juniper, 127
Jupiter's Staff. *See* Mullein
Kava-Kava, 127

Kelp. *See* Bladderwrack
Kidneywort. *See* Liverwort
Knit Bone. *See* Comfrey
Knitback. *See* Comfrey
Knotweed, 128
Lads Love. *See* Southernwood
Lady Elder. *See* Elder
Lady's Sorrel. *See* Sorrel, Wood
Lady's Mantle, 129
Lady's Slipper, 129
Larch, 129
Larkspur, 130
Lavender, 131
Leek, 131
Lemon, 132
Lemon Verbena, 133
Lemongrass, 132
Lettuce, 133
Licorice, 133
Life Everlasting, 134
Lignum Aloes. *See* Aloes, Wood
Lilac, 134
Lily, 135
Lily of the Valley, 135
Lime, 136
Linden, 136
Linseed. *See* Flax
Lion's Mouth. *See* Foxglove
Lion's Teeth/Tooth. *See* Dandelion
Liverwort, 137
Lobelia, 138
Loosestrife, 138
Lotus, 139
Lovage, 140
Love Lies Bleeding. *See* Pansy
Love Seed, 140
Lucky Hand, 140
Mace, 141
Mad Dogweed. *See* Skullcap
MagickMushroom. *See* Agaric
Magnolia, 142
Maidenhair, 142
Male Fern, 143
Mallow, 143
Mandrake, 144
Manna grass. *See* Sweetgrass
Maple, 144
Marcory. *See* Stillengia
Marigold, 145
Marjoram, 145

Marrubium. *See* Horehound
Marsh Skullcap. *See* Skullcap
Marshmallow. *See* Althea
Mary's grass. *See* Sweetgrass
Marybud. *See* Marigold
Marygold. *See* Marigold
Masterwort, 146
Mastic, 146
Meadow Rue, 147
Meadowsweet, 148
Medicine Plant. *See* Aloe
Melampode. *See* Hellebore, Black
Melilot, 148
Melissa. *See* Balm, Lemon
Mesquite, 149
Millefoil. *See* Yarrow
Mimosa, 149
Mint, 150
Mistletoe, 150
Monkshood. *See* Aconite
Monument Plant. *See* Deerstongue
Moonwort, 151
Morning Glory, 151
Mortal. *See* Bittersweet
Moss, 152
Mountain Ash. *See* Rowan
Mountain Tea. *See* Wintergreen
Muggons. *See* Mugwort
Mugwort, 153
Mulberry, 153
Mullein, 154
Mustard, 154
Myrrh, 154
Myrtle, 155
Myrtle Grass. *See* Calamus
Narcissus. *See* Daffodil
Naughty Man. *See* Mugwort
Neem, 155
Nettle, 156
Norfolk Island Pine, 156
Nosebleed. *See* Yarrow
Nutmeg, 157
Nuts, 157
Oak, 158
Oats, 158
Old Woman. *See* Wormwood
Old-Man. *See* Southernwood
Oleander, 159
Olive, 159
Onion, 160

Orange, 160
Orchid, 161
Oregano, 161
Oregon Grape, 161
Orris, 162
Our Lady's Candle. *See* Mullein
Paddockstool. *See* Toadstool
Paddocstol. *See* Toadstool
Palm, Date, 162
Pansy, 163
Papaya, 163
Papyrus, 164
Parsley, 165
Parsley Fern. *See* Tansy
Partridge Berry. *See Wintergreen*
Passion Flower, 165
Patchouly, 166
Pavil. *See* Stillengia
Pea, 167
Peach, 167
Pear, 168
Pearl Moss. *See* Irish Moss
Pecan, 168
Pee in the Bed. *See* Dandelion
Pennyroyal, 169
Pennywort. *See* Liverwort
Peony, 169
Pepper, 170
Pepper Tree, 171
Peppermint, 170
Periwinkle, 171
Persimmon, 171
Pigeon Berry. *See* Poke
Pimento, 172
Pimpernel, 173
Pine, 173
Pineapple, 174
Pistachio, 174
Plantain, 175
Plum, 175
Pocan Bush. *See* Poke
Poison Parsley. *See* Hemlock
Poison Tobacco. *See* Henbane
Poke, 176
Poke Root. *See* Poke
Pokeweed. *See* Poke
Polar Plant. *See* Rosemary
Pomegranate, 176
Poor Man's Treacle. *See* Garlic
Poplar, 177
Poppy, 177

Potato, 178
Potentilla. *See* Cinquefoil
Prickly Ash, 179
Primrose, 179
Puddockstool. *See* Toadstool
Purslane, 180
Quack Grass. *See* Witches Grass
Quassia, 180
Queen Elizabeth Root. *See* Orris
Queen of the Meadow. *See* Meadowsweet
Queen's Delight. *See* Stillengia
Queen's Root. *See* Stillengia
Quince, 181
Racoon Berry. *See* May Apple
Radish, 181
Ragweed, 182
Ragwort, 182
Raspberry, 182
Rattlesnake Root, 183
Red Eye Bright. *See* Eyebright
Red Ink Plant. *See* Poke
Red Pucoon. *See* Bloodroot
Red Root. *See Tormentil* , *See* Tormentil
Redcap. *See* Agaric
Redweed. *See* Poke
Rhubarb, 183
Ribwort. *See* Plantain
Rice, 184
Roots, 185
Rose, 185
Rosemary, 185
Rowan, 186
Rue, 186
Rye, 187
Sacred Bark. *See* Cascara Sagranda
Saffron, 187
Sage, 188
Sagebrush, 188
Sailor's Tobacco. *See* Mugwort
Sambuccus. *See* Elder
Sandalwood, 189
Sarsaparilla, 190
Sassafras, 190
Satyrion. *See* Satyrion
Savory, Summer, 191
Scoke. *See* Poke
Scotch Broom. *See* Broom
Sea Wrack. *See* Bladderwrack
Seneca grass. See Sweetgrass
Senna, 191
Septfoil \t, 183, 192

Sesame, 192
Shallot, 192
Shamrock. *See* Sorell, Wood
Sheep Sorell. *See* Sorell, Wood
Shepherd's Knapperty. *See* Tormentil , *See* Tormentil
Shepherd's Knot. *See Tormentil*
Silver Leaf. *See* Stillengia
Silver Root. *See* Stillengia
Silverweed. *See* Cinquefoil
Skullcap, 193
Skunk Cabbage, 192
Slippery Elm, 193
Slippery Root. *See* Comfrey
Sloe, 194
Snakeroot, 194
Snakeroot, Black, 194
Snakeweed. *See* Plantain
Snapdragon, 195
Solomon's Seal, 195
Sorcerer's Violet. *See* Perriwinkle
Sorceror's Root. *See* Mandrake
Sorrel Wood, 196
Sour Grass. *See* Sorell, Wood
Southernwood, 196
Spanish Moss, 197
Spearmint, 197
Spiderwort, 197
Spikenard, 198
Spotted Hemlock. *See* Hemlock
Squill, 198
St. John's Plant. *See* Mugwort
St. John's Wort, 189
Star Anise, 198
Stillengia, 199
Straw, 199
Strawberry, 199
Sugar Cane, 200
Sumbul, 200
Sunflower, 201
Sweet Bay. *See* Bay
Sweet Elder. *See* Elder
Sweet Flag. *See* Calamus
Sweet Laurel. *See* Bay
Sweet Sedge. *See* Calamus
Sweet Weed. *See* Althea
Sweet Wood. *See* Cinnamon
Sweetbalm. *See* Balm, Lemon
Sweetpea, 202
Tadstoles. *See* Toadstool

Tadstooles. *See* Toadstool
Tamarind, 202
Tamarisk, 203
Tansy, 204
Tea, 204
Teaberry. *See* Periwinkle
Tetterwort. *See* Bloodroot
Thea bohea. *See* Tea
Thea sinesis. *See* Tea
Thea viridis. *See* Tea
Thistle, 205
Thistle, Holy, 206
Thistle, Milk, 206
Thormantle, 183, 207
Thousand Leaf. *See* Yarrow
Thunderbesom. *See* Mistletoe
Thyme, 207
Ti, 207
Tiger Lotus. *See* Lotus
Toadflax, 208
Toadstool, 208
Tobacco, 209
Tode stoles. *See* Toadstool
Tomato, 210
Tonka Beans, 210
Toodys hatte. *See* Toadstool
Tormentil, 211
Trefoil. *See* Clover
Trillium, 211
Tulip, 212
Turmeric, 212
Turnip, 212
Uva Ursa, 213
Valerian, 213
Vanilla, 214
Vanilla grass. See Sweetgrass
Velvet Dock. *See* Vervain
Venus Flytrap, 214
Verbena. *See* Vervain
Vervain, 215
Vetch, Giant, 216
Vetiver, 216
Violet, 217
Virginia Snakeroot. *See* Snakeroot
Wallwort. *See* Comfrey
Walnut, 217
Water Lily. *See* Lotus
Water Parsley. *See* Hemlock
Wax Plant, 218
Waxberry. *See* Myrtle

Wheat, 218
Wild Lemon. *See* Mandrake
Willow, 218
Witch Grass, 219
Witch Hazel, 220
Witchbane. *See* Rowan
Witchen. *See* Rowan
Witches Bells. *See* Foxglove
Witches Berry. *See* Belladonna
Witches Broom. *See* Mistletoe
Witches Thimbles. *See* Foxglove
Witchwood. *See* Rowan
Wolf's Bane. *See* Aconite
Wonder of the World Root. *See* GinSeng
Wood Avens. *See* Avens

Wood Rose, 220
Woodbine. *See* Honeysuckle
Woodruff, 220
Woody Nightshade. *See* Bittersweet
Wormwood, 221
Wymote. *See* Althea
Yarrow, 221
Yawroot. *See* Stillengia
Yellow Evening Primrose, 222
Yerba Mate, 222
Yerba Santa, 223
Yew, 223
Yohimbe, 224
Yucca, 224
Zebrovka. See Sweetgrass

# Section 8 - Acknowledgements

This work was predominantly researched from the resources of the internet. This has presented a major problem in acknowledging the sources of much information, as many, many sites present identical information, in an identical format and it is impossible to identify the origin of the material.

The following sites and references provided a great deal of the information presented in this work.

http://www.herbs2000.com

http://www.botanical.com

http://www.global-garden.com.au

http://www.herbsarespecial.com.au

http://www.gardenguides.com

http://www.wicca-chat.com

http://en.wikipedia.org

http://www.pfaf.org

The Garden Library – Herbs, Kenneth A. Beckett, Doubleday 1984.